STRATEGIC MANAGEMENT IN THE THIRD SECTOR

STRATEGIC MANAGEMENT IN THE THIRD SECTOR

ROGER COURTNEY

palgrave
macmillan

First published 2013 by
PALGRAVE MACMILLAN

Palgrave Macmillan in the UK is an imprint of Macmillan Publishers Limited, registered in England, company number 785998, of Houndmills, Basingstoke, Hampshire RG21 6XS.

Palgrave Macmillan in the US is a division of St Martin's Press LLC, 175 Fifth Avenue, New York, NY 10010.

Palgrave Macmillan is the global academic imprint of the above companies and has companies and representatives throughout the world.

Palgrave® and Macmillan® are registered trademarks in the United States, the United Kingdom, Europe and other countries

ISBN 978–0–230–33693–3

This book is printed on paper suitable for recycling and made from fully managed and sustained forest sources. Logging, pulping and manufacturing processes are expected to conform to the environmental regulations of the country of origin.

A catalogue record for this book is available from the British Library.

A catalog record for this book is available from the Library of Congress.

CONTENTS

PART I   INTRODUCTION TO THE THIRD SECTOR AND STRATEGY

PART II STRATEGIC THINKING

PART III   STRATEGY CHOICES

PART IV   FORMULATING A STRATEGIC PLAN

PART V   IMPLEMENTATION

LIST OF BOXES

LIST OF FIGURES

LIST OF TABLES

ABOUT THE AUTHOR

The author is an organizational development lecturer and consultant working in the Third Sector in the UK and Ireland. He was born and brought up in Belfast. After obtaining a psychology degree and training as a community and youth worker, he set up and ran Crescent Youth & Community Resource Centre in South Belfast, which eventually became Crescent Arts Centre. He was appointed the Chief Officer of the Simon Community Northern Ireland in 1981, which by 1998 had expanded from two small rundown houses for people who are homeless, with three staff, to an organization with a turnover of over £2 million, more than 200 staff, which runs accommodation projects for people who are homeless all over Northern Ireland.

Over this period, in parallel with the practical experience of managing a rapidly expanding organization, he gained a Diploma in Management Studies, and Masters in Human Resource Development. He completed his doctoral research on strategic management in the Third Sector in 2005.

Since 1998, he has been working as a freelance lecturer, writer, trainer and organizational development consultant in the Third Sector in the UK and Ireland. He specializes in strategic planning, governance, research, fundraising strategy, evaluation, and mentoring.

Roger Courtney is the author of four previous books about management in the Third Sector, three books on fundraising, a guide to mentoring, a guide to research and a number of publications on homelessness.

He was awarded an MBE in 1996 for his work with people who are homeless.

ACKNOWLEDGEMENTS

I am very grateful to the various third organizations with which I have worked as an organizational development consultant over the last decade and a half for having the confidence in me to help guide their strategic management processes. I would also like to thank: my masters students at Queen's University Belfast who helped me to think through some of the issues; to Routledge for agreeing to the use of some material from a previous publication; to Caroline Copeman of Cass Business School for her comments on an earlier draft; to the staff at Palgrave Macmillan for their help and support; and, most of all, my wife, Christine for assistance with the proof-reading and tolerance in putting up with me while I worked on the book.

ROGER COURTNEY

The author and publishers would like to thank the following for permission to reproduce copyright material:

Action for Children for Box 1.2; Taylor & Francis for Figure 1.2 from Davis Smith, J. (1995) 'The Voluntary Tradition: Philanthropy and Self-help in Britain 1500–1945' in J. Davis Smith, C. Rochester and R. Hedley (eds) *An Introduction to the Voluntary Sector* (London: Routledge); Communities that Care for Box 7.4; Furniture Resource Centre for Box 8.2; TCC Group for Figure 8.1 from Connolly, P. and York, P. (2003) *Building the Capacity of Capacity Builders* (New York: TCC Group); *Harvard Business Review* for Figure 9.2 from Greiner, L. E. (1998) 'Evolution and Revolution as Organizations Grow', *Harvard Business Review*, 76(3) pp. 55–68; UK Vision Strategy for Box 10.8; Atlantic Philanthropies for Box 12.1; Action on Hearing Loss for Figure 12.4; Penguin Books for Figure 12.5 from Moore, J. I. (1992) *Writers on Strategy and Strategic Management* (London: Penguin); Pearson Education for Figures 12.6 and 12.7 from Neely, A., Adams, C. and Kennerley, M. (2002) *The Performance Prism: The Scorecard for Measuring and Managing Business Success* (Harlow: Financial Times/Prentice-Hall) and Figure 14.1 from Maslow, A. (1987) *Motivation and Personality,* 3rd edn (Englewood Cliffs, New Jersey: Pearson Education); Emerald Group Publishing Ltd for Figure 12.8 from Rouse, P. (2003) 'An Integral Framework for Performance Measurement', *Management Decision*, 41(8) pp. 791–805; John Wiley & Sons for Figure 12.9 from Kushner, R. and Poole, P. (1996) 'Exploring Structure Effectiveness Relationships in Nonprofit Arts Organizations', *Nonprofit Management and Leadership*, 7(2) pp. 119–36, Table 15.3 from Schmid, H. (2006) 'Leadership Styles and Leadership Change in Human and Community Service', *Nonprofit*

Management and Leadership, 17(2) pp.179–94, Figure 16.1 from Lewin, K. (1946) 'Action Research and Minority Problems', *Journal of Social Issues*, 2(4) pp. 34–46; Institute for Operations Research and the Management Sciences for Figure 12.10 from Quinn, R. and Rohrbaugh, J. (1983) 'A Spacial Model of Effectiveness Criteria: Towards a Competing Values Approach to Organizational Analysis', *Management Science*, 29(3) pp. 363–77; National Council for Voluntary Organisations for Figure 12.11 from 'Excellence in View: A Guide to the EFQM Excellence Model for the Voluntary Sector' (NCVO 2000); Cedar Foundation for Box 12.6; Table 12.2 is reproduced under terms of the Open Government Licence v1.0.

Every effort has been made to contact all copyright-holders, but if any have been inadvertently omitted the publishers will be pleased to make the necessary arrangements at the earliest opportunity.

PREFACE

The job of running a Third Sector organization, as a senior manager or a board member, is becoming increasingly complex. The external environment is changing rapidly and expectations are rising rapidly, yet resources have never been more challenging to find. There is some useful thinking going on in universities about strategic management, generally, and its application in the Third Sector in particular, but little of it finds its way onto the reading lists of busy Third Sector managers or board members. There is also a lot of learning from the real day-to-day experiences and struggles of Third Sector organizations trying to survive and develop, but which is often not captured or shared with others. Organizations, in particular, don't like sharing their mistakes or other negative experiences. There is very little material on strategic management in the Third Sector outside the USA that tries to bring together the practical, the theoretical and the empirical in a way that is useful.

When I was responsible for managing a rapidly expanding Third Sector organization, I became increasingly aware of the need to have in place planning and management systems that would help to ensure clear focus and direction for the organization. I therefore introduced a simple strategic planning process, more out of intuition than knowledge, and made some rudimentary mistakes. As the organization expanded I began to read more and more (much of it contradictory) about strategic management. As I continued to try and make sense of what I was reading and apply what seemed to be appropriate to my organization, I also began to try and put down in writing how I understood the relevance of the theory for the world of Third Sector organizations in which I had spent my whole career.

Moving to working freelance with a wide range of Third Sector organizations on their strategic development, and some further academic study and doctorate research, reinforced the need to help explain both the theory and practice of strategic management in a Third Sector context, both for the leaders of those organizations and for those studying the management of Third Sector organizations and who will hopefully become the leaders of the future.

The UK Voluntary Sector Skills survey (Clark 2007) has again highlighted the need to increase the skills and knowledge of 'strategic planning and forward thinking' in a quarter of voluntary organizations in England, regardless of size, despite the fact that three-quarters of organizations now have some form of 'formal business plan'.

This is not one of those 'one-best-way' practical guides to strategic management. I accept that there are many different perspectives and approaches, and readers should draw on what is useful. I hope, however, that like me, through sharing this journey, the reader will develop a better understanding of the various approaches to strategic management which will inform decisions about the models and approaches that may be most appropriate to help make your own organization more effective in changing the world.

ROGER COURTNEY

PART 1

INTRODUCTION TO THE THIRD SECTOR AND STRATEGY

1 WHAT IS THE THIRD SECTOR?

OVERVIEW

In considering the value of strategic management to the Third Sector, it is important to be clear about exactly what the sector is (if indeed it is a sector). The extent to which it is the same or different from the private sector will give an indication of whether the Third Sector requires different management approaches from the private sector, where much of the research and theoretical developments in relation to strategy have taken place. How homogeneous or diverse the sector is may also have implications for the extent to which it requires different management approaches for different parts of the sector. In this chapter therefore I attempt to define both the nature and scope of the Third Sector. In particular, the attributes that have been put forward to distinguish the Third Sector from both the public sector and, more particularly, the private sector will be investigated. How organizations within the Third Sector can be categorized will also be explored.

LEARNING OBJECTIVES

After studying this chapter, you should be able to:

- define the Third Sector;
- identify the difficulties in defining, and the different labels applied to, the Third Sector;
- highlight some ways the Third Sector is changing;
- describe the diversity of the Third Sector;
- identify various different ways of classifying the Third Sector;
- describe the way the boundaries of the Third Sector are defined for the purposes of this book;
- identify the perceived differences between the Third Sector and private sectors;
- understand the arguments for and against the nature and significance of the differences between the sectors;
- describe an alternative approach to framing organizations other than simply by sector.

DIFFICULTIES OF TERMINOLOGY

The Third Sector is a diffuse and varied one, ranging from tiny local neighbourhood groups to large regional or national organizations such as Comic Relief, the Co-operative Group, Action on Hearing Loss (Box 1.1) or Action for Children (Box 1.2) (see case studies in Part VI), to truly global organizations or movements, such as Emmaus and Habitat for Humanity (see also case studies in Part VI). The student of the Third Sector, therefore, faces serious difficulties in defining clearly the territory that is to be explored. Even finding agreement on an acceptable expression to describe the sector is problematic. The concept of 'sector', itself, is a contested one.

In the UK the expression 'the voluntary sector' is frequently used. A voluntary organization is defined by the sector's leading umbrella agency, the National Council for Voluntary Organisations (NCVO), as 'an independent, self-governing body of people who have joined together voluntarily to take action for the benefit of the community. This is similar to the French, *le secteur associatif*. A voluntary organisation may employ staff or volunteers, but must be established otherwise than for financial gain'. The increased role of professional paid staff has raised serious questions about how appropriate the word 'voluntary' is to define the sector. To try and deal with this issue, Osborne (1996) distinguishes between: 'voluntaryism', as the societal principle of voluntary action; 'volunteerism' which he views as individual action without personal benefit, i.e. by volunteers; and 'voluntarism', which he relates to organized voluntary action, which may or may not involve any significant number of volunteers. The breadth of the sector and the difference between community-based grassroots organizations and larger voluntary organizations has led to the increasing usage in the UK of the expression 'the voluntary and community sector' (Cairns *et al.* 2005).

BOX 1.1   ACTION ON HEARING LOSS

The National Bureau for Promoting the General Welfare of the Deaf in London was set up in 1911 by banker Leo Bonn. In 1919 it established the first residential home for elderly deaf women. Ten years later, renamed the National Institute for the Deaf (NID), it established the first hostel for deaf working boys in north London and began lip-reading classes for adults. In 1932 it acquired a home for deaf women in Bath, Somerset (which moved to Blackburn in 1948). In 1946, it set up a technical lab and two years later, after lobbying, the NHS provided free hearing aids and batteries UK-wide.

By 1958 the NID had five residential homes and opened a hostel for deaf boys in Wembley, north London. The NID Personal Advice Bureau was the forerunner of the information line opened in 1957. In 1960, the NID introduced the Picture Screening hearing test for children and, to mark Jubilee year, the Queen approved the addition of 'Royal' to the name.

In 1970, following lobbying by disability groups, the Chronically Sick and Disabled Persons Act was approved. Four years later, the NHS made behind-the-ear hearing aids available, following RNID research. In the 1980s, the RNID and the Royal Ear Hospital developed cochlear implants. The 1970s saw increasing attempts to respond to the issue of tinnitus, including research and

▶

the formation of the British Tinnitus Association, under the auspices of the RNID. A tinnitus helpline was launched in 1990.

Increased campaigning and awareness of the rights of disabled people in the 1980s and 1990s resulted in the Disability Rights Act of 1995. In the 1990s the RNID launched its telephone relay service, Typetalk, which it had trialled in 1980. It also launched the 'Breaking the Sound Barrier' campaign to encourage people to have a hearing test and began funding biomedical research into hearing loss.

In 2000, hearing screening for newborn babies began and the RNID began working with the NHS to deliver modern digital hearing aids across the UK as standard. In 2003, British Sign Language was formally recognized as a language and the RNID launched the 'Don't Lose the Music' campaign to encourage people to protect their hearing while listening to music. Two years later, the RNID introduced its telephone Hearing Check and the first hearing loss related gene was discovered.

In 2010 the Equality Act superseded the Disability Rights Act and the organization changed its name to Action on Hearing Loss and its overall brand image. It continued to manage 20 residential care homes, 16 supported housing schemes, and community and outreach services, as well as research, information, support and advice services and campaigning.
A strategy map of Action on Hearing Loss is shown in Figure 12.4.

(See 'Celebrating 100 years of Action on Hearing Loss',
www.actiononhearingloss.org.uk)

In the UK and Ireland, the expression 'the charitable sector' is also sometimes used. Those organizations which have charitable status within the definition of 'charitable' in charity law are a particular subset of the larger Third Sector. An organization can be accepted as a registered charity (Charities Act 2006) if it has charitable purposes and is for the public benefit (similar rules apply in Scotland, Northern Ireland and the Republic of Ireland). 'Charitable purposes' are defined as:

- the prevention or relief of poverty;
- the advancement of education;
- the advancement of religion;
- the advancement of health or the saving of lives;
- the advancement of citizenship or community development;
- the advancement of the arts, culture, heritage or science;
- the advancement of amateur sport;
- the advancement of human rights, conflict resolution or reconciliation, or the promotion of religious or racial harmony, or equality and diversity;
- the advancement of environmental protection or improvement;
- the relief of those in need, by reason of youth, age, ill-health, disability, financial hardship or other disadvantages;
- the advancement of animal welfare;

- the promotion of the efficiency of the armed forces of the Crown or of the police, fire and rescue services or ambulance services;
- other purposes recognized as charitable under the existing law and any new purposes which are similar to another prescribed purpose.

In terms of 'public benefit', two key principles must be met in order to show that an organization's aims are for the public benefit:

Principle 1: there must be an identifiable benefit or benefits:
- it must be clear what the benefits are;
- the benefits must be related to the aims;
- benefits must be balanced against any detriment or harm.

Principle 2: benefit must be to the public or a section of the public:
- the beneficiaries must be appropriate to the aims;
- where benefit is to a section of the public, the opportunity to benefit must not be unreasonably restricted – by geographical or other restrictions, or by ability to pay any fees charged;
- people in poverty must not be excluded from the opportunity to benefit;
- any private benefits must be incidental.

In general, aims are not charitable if they are mainly for the benefit of a named person or specific individuals. They will also not be charitable if the people who will benefit from them are defined by a personal or contractual relationship with each other. An exception to this general rule exists in the case of the prevention or relief of poverty, where the people to benefit can come from a more restricted group, such as people having the same employer.

No organization can be charitable if it is set up for the personal benefit of its trustees, employees or other specific individuals (other than in the case of relieving poverty), so it excludes mutuals, cooperatives, building societies, credit unions and trade unions. Nor can it be charitable if it is created for political aims (e.g. political parties), or if its aims are illegal. The following are examples of organizations or aims which are often assumed to be charitable, but in fact are not according to UK law:

- individual sports clubs set up to benefit their members or promote excellence (as distinct from sports facilities open for everyone or specifically provided for special groups of people, such as elderly people, or as a method of promoting healthy recreation);
- organizations which promote friendship or international friendship, for example, town twinning associations;
- the promotion of political or propagandist aims, or the promotion of a particular point of view;
- aims which include arrangements where people running the organization get significant personal benefit.

Fundraising is not a charitable object in itself: it is simply an activity which can be undertaken to help achieve a charitable purpose.

The main advantages which accrue to an organization that is registered as a charity are that they:

- do not normally have to pay income/corporation tax, capital gains tax or stamp duty, and gifts to charities are free of inheritance tax;
- pay only a proportion of normal business rates on the buildings which they use and occupy to further their charitable aims;
- can get special VAT treatment in some circumstances;
- are often able to raise funds from the public, grant-making trusts and local government more easily than non-charitable bodies;
- can formally represent and help to meet the needs of the community;
- are able to give the public the assurance that they are being monitored and advised by the Charity Commission.

There are restrictions, however, on what charities can do, both in terms of the types of work they do and the ways in which they can operate:

- there are strict rules applying to trading by charities and there are limits to the extent of political or campaigning activities which a charity can take on;
- trustees are not allowed to receive financial benefits from the charity which they manage unless this is specifically authorized by the governing document of the charity and by the Charity Commission, and they must avoid any conflicts of interest.

In terms of campaigning, organizations like Amnesty International, that are not-for-profit and would be accepted by the public as part of the voluntary sector, do not have charitable status for their main work. What is deemed to be charitable also changes as legislation and case law changes. For example, it was only relatively recently that promoting racial harmony, tackling unemployment or protecting the environment have been accepted as charitable by the Charity Commission for England and Wales. Box 1.2 highlights the development of a long-standing large UK charity, with faith based roots.

BOX 1.2 ACTION FOR CHILDREN

In 1868, a young Methodist minister, Thomas Bowman Stephenson, arrived in London to take up his new post at a chapel in Lambeth. Moved by the plight of children living on the streets, he came up with the idea of a home for young boys, where they would be safe from poverty and crime. Together with two Methodist friends, Alfred Mager and Francis Horner, Stephenson renovated a disused stable in Church Street, Waterloo. The first two boys, George and Fred, were admitted to the Children's Home on 9 July 1869.

The Children's Home reflected Stephenson's farsighted commitment to family-style childcare, which would be disciplined but loving. At a time when most orphaned or neglected children were sent to big institutions like the hated workhouse or even prison, Stephenson's establishing of small homes with a 'house mother' and 'house father' and supported by donations was pioneering. Within three years, girls were admitted to The Children's Home, and the Home had

►

moved to larger premises near Stephenson's new ministry in Bethnal Green, with a second home established at Edgworth Farm on the Lancashire moors in 1872.

In 1878, a group of young women originally taken in as orphans began a training course in childcare, and by 1892, 140 graduates, known as 'the Sisterhood' or 'the Sisters of the children', were working full time for The Children's Home. By 1908, the charity had grown to become the National Children's Home and Orphanage (later the National Children's Home, and then simply NCH), becoming an adoption agency in 1926.

The work of the charity has expanded and diversified to include: Children's Centres, Family Centres, family support including intensive support services, children's placements via fostering, adoption and schools, short breaks and other interventions for disabled children, supported apprenticeships and employment programmes, work with fathers, targeted youth support to prevent offending and youth arts.

In 2008, the organization changed its name to one that better reflects what it does and values – Action for Children – and is now one of the UK's leading children's charities. Its vision is a world where all children and young people have a sense of belonging and are loved and valued. A world where they can break through injustice, deprivation and inequality, so they can achieve their full potential. Its values are: passion, equality and hope.

Recognizing the increasing need for demonstrating the effectiveness of its work, Action for Children have developed an outcomes framework and produced an Impact Report in 2011, bringing together the findings from a range of processes for measuring the impact of its work on children, including social return on investment.

(Action for Children Impact Report 2011, www.actionforchildren.org.uk)

In Canada, the arrangements are very similar to those in the UK and Ireland. In Australia, attempts in 2003 to comprehensively reform charity law (based on the English Statute of Elizabeth and subsequent case law) floundered, although what is considered for the public benefit was clarified in 2004.

In the United States, a charitable organization is considered to be operated for purposes that are beneficial to the public interest. A distinction is made between types of charitable organizations:

■ *Private foundation*: every US and foreign charity that qualifies as tax-exempt under Section 501(c)(3) of the Internal Revenue Code is considered a 'private foundation' unless it demonstrates otherwise. A private foundation usually derives its principal fund from an individual, family, corporation or some other single source and is more often than not a grant-maker and does not solicit funds from the public. Foundations can be grant-making or operating, i.e. providing direct services for the benefit of the public.

■ *Public charity*: an organization that is not a private foundation is usually a public charity as described in Section 509(a) of the Internal Revenue Code. A public charity generally receives grants from individuals, government and private foundations and although some public charities engage in grant-making activities, most conduct direct service or other tax-exempt activities.

The precise requirements and procedures for forming charitable organizations vary from state to state, as do the registration and filing requirements.

In both the UK and the USA the expression 'Third Sector' is being increasingly used to describe the sector that exists for a social purpose and that is neither the private sector nor the public sector (Hudson 1995), although the term gives no indication at all as to any of the characteristics of the sector. The UK Department of Trade and Industry, in *Social Enterprise: A Strategy for Success*, defined a social enterprise as 'a business with primarily social objectives whose surpluses are principally reinvested for that purpose in the business or in the community, rather than driven by the need to maximise profit for shareholders and owners' (DTI 2002). Similar expressions are used in German (*dritter sector*) and French (*tiers secteur*).

In addition to charities and voluntary and community-based organizations, the Third Sector is considered to include social enterprises, i.e. 'non-governmental organisations which are value-driven and which principally reinvest their surpluses to further social, environmental or cultural objectives' (HM Treasury and Cabinet Office 2007; e.g. companies limited by guarantee which trade, community interest companies). Dees *et al.* (2001) argue that there are two key characteristics of a social enterprise:

- social enterprises have a social objective;
- social enterprises blend social and commercial methods.

Social enterprises fall into five main groups:

- *Mutuals*: businesses that are owned by their members. They can operate as employee owned, cooperative or wider social enterprises: (i) consumer-owned cooperatives, 'an autonomous association of persons united voluntarily to meet their common economic, social and cultural needs and aspirations through a jointly-owned and democratically-controlled enterprise' (International Co-operative Alliance Statement of Co-operative Identity 1995), e.g. the Co-operative Group (see case study in Part VI); (ii) employee-owned cooperatives, e.g. Poptel (see case study); (iii) producer-owned cooperatives, e.g. agricultural and fisheries cooperatives; (iv) housing cooperatives (see Part VI case study of Coin Street Community Builders); (v) employee-owned companies, e.g. John Lewis Partnership (see website case study); (vi) financial mutuals (credit unions, building societies, friendly societies).
- *Social enterprises (non-mutuals) with social aims which are subsidiaries of a charitable organization*: not-for-profit commercial enterprises with social aims developed by a charitable organization, e.g. Big Issue and Bryson Charitable Group (see Part VI case studies).
- *Income generating social enterprises which are subsidiaries of charitable organizations*: commercial enterprises developed to generate income for a charitable organization (e.g. charity shops).

- *Independent social enterprises*: not-for-profit commercial enterprises with social aims, e.g. Cosmic Ethical IT (Box 12.5), Furniture Resource Centre (Box 8.2), the Eden Project, Welsh Water and Fairtrade Foundation (see Part VI case studies).
- *Social firms*: not-for-profit enterprises established to provide work and/or work experience for particular disadvantaged groups, such as *The Big Issue* (see Part VI case study).

The European EMES research network attributes the following characteristics to social enterprises:

- continuous activity producing goods and/or selling services;
- a high degree of autonomy;
- an element of economic risk;
- involving some paid work;
- an initiative launched by a group of citizens;
- decision-making not based on capital ownership;
- a participatory nature;
- limited profit distribution;
- benefit to the community.

An example of a social enterprise, Cool2Care, is given in Box 1.3.

BOX 1.3 COOL2CARE

Cool2Care is a social enterprise, supporting families with disabled children or young adults, founded in 2007 by Phil Conway, the father of a disabled child, who worked for IBM for 20 years. He saw a need in the market for trained, flexible childcare for families with disabled children and young adults in order to enhance the lives of the children, both in their homes and out in the community, and to provide the parents with a break. Since then it has grown to over 60 staff and now covers many areas across the UK.

The care-workers or personal assistants (PAs) are young, trained, confident and skilled, who enjoy working with disabled children, acting as friends or buddies to the people they look after. They are from a variety of backgrounds. The organization recruits, selects, screens and Criminal Record Bureau (CRB) checks potential care-workers or buddies for families that need them, and provides support to the care-workers in their roles, both before and after placement, and offers in-depth training courses across the UK and further training on specific skills if required.
Cool2Care is a community interest company. Its vision is 'to be the leading provider of one-to-one matching services for disabled young people and their families in the UK, incorporating trained volunteers, care-workers, personal assistants, befrienders, buddies, and professionals'. As a social enterprise, Cool2Care aims to mix the power of business with the heart of charity – treating families with disabled children as highly valued customers – and to conduct itself as a sustainable venture.

The Cool2Care service is committed to growing the business. It is already available in a dozen areas of the UK, with workforce development training and volunteer befriending projects in

▶

specific locations, and anticipates more offices opening in the near future. It has also recently extended the service to include disabled adults in some locations.

In September 2010, Cool2Care launched a new social investment strategy to raise the capital necessary to fund future growth. As a community interest company (CIC), Cool2Care is eligible to raise funds from investors interested in supporting disabled children and in seeking moderate financial returns.

(See www.cool2care.co.uk)

In 2005, the UK government estimated that there were over 55,000 social enterprises in the UK, with a turnover of around £27 billion, contributing £8.4 billion to the economy. This includes large social enterprises like: the Nationwide Building Society, the largest such society in the world; The Co-operative Group (see Part VI case study); The John Lewis Partnership, including Waitrose (see website case study); Greenwich Leisure Limited (see website case study), the largest sports and leisure company in the UK; and the Welsh water company, Glas Cymru (see Part VI case study).

Some Third Sector organizations are wary of the term 'social enterprise' (Seanor and Meaton 2007; Leadbeater 2007), seeing it as a cover for the withdrawal of government grants and the expectation that voluntary and community organizations working with poor and marginalized groups should generate significant profits from trading, instead of receiving government support.

There are, however, private sector companies which see the brand advantages of the term 'social enterprise' and the opportunity to take advantage of the lack of any agreed legal definition. In August 2012, Social Enterprise UK warned global sales software company Salesforce about using the term to describe the benefits of the company to its customers and its attempt to have the term trademarked in the USA and Jamaica.

The UK (Labour) Government established an Office of the Third Sector in 2006, as part of the increase in government engagement with the sector, which included such initiatives as Futurebuilders, ChangeUp and Communitybuilders, though this was replaced by the incoming coalition government in 2010 with an Office for Civil Society, which focused on the concept of 'the big society'.

The concept of 'the independent sector' is also sometimes used in the USA, but it can also mean all organizations that aren't statutory, i.e. both the voluntary/community and private sectors. It can also be argued that these organizations are not independent financially and are often dependent on the state (Boris and Streurle 2006; Smith and Gronbjerg 2006). Also in the USA, the term 'the nonprofit sector' (sometimes 'not-for-profit') is most commonly used, highlighting the key negative characteristic that such organizations by definition may not distribute a profit to members or others with a beneficial interest. However, to define a sector by one characteristic alone, and in the negative, is not entirely satisfactory. Statutory bodies are also not permitted to distribute their profits, if any. Osborne (1996) favours the term 'voluntary' and 'non-profit organizations' (VNPOs). Peter Dobkin Hall (1994) prefers the 'private nonprofit sector'. The expression the 'social sector' or 'social sectors' is sometimes used in the USA to refer to organizations that are for the public benefit, including both statutory/public bodies and Third Sector non-profit bodies. Of course, many private companies provide social services.

In France, and increasingly in other parts of Europe and the USA, the concept of the 'social economy' is commonly used to define not only not-for-profit associations that we would traditionally think of as being in the voluntary or non-profit sector, but also other kinds of organizations such as cooperatives, where any profit is distributed to the members, which is closer to the concept of the Third Sector.

Internationally, particularly in Africa and South America, the concept of 'non-governmental organization' (NGO) is frequently used to define international and local organizations which are for the public benefit, but are not public bodies. This is another example of defining something by what it isn't, rather than by what it is.

Internationally, because of the differences of culture, legal structures and definitions amongst countries, the expressions 'civil society' and 'civil society organizations' (Edwards 2004) are sometimes used, and, like the concept of the Third Sector in the UK, *maatschappelijk middenveld* (Civil Society) in the Netherlands and *économie sociale* (social economy) in France, they tend to cover a very wide range of types of organizations, including churches, sports and recreation clubs, trade unions, political parties, mutuals and cooperatives. In Eastern Europe, stemming from the attempts to overthrow state socialism, these expressions also include spontaneous citizen action (Anheier and Salamon 2006). Civil society is normally considered to include the totality of voluntary social relationships, civic and social organizations, and institutions that form the basis of a functioning society, as distinct from the force-backed structures of a state and the commercial institutions of the market. There is no generally accepted definition of 'civil society'. The London School of Economic's Centre for Civil Society's working definition is:

> Civil society refers to the arena of uncoerced collective action around shared interests, purposes and values. In theory, its institutional forms are distinct from those of the state, and market, though in practice, the boundaries between state, civil society, and market are often complex, blurred and negotiated. Civil society commonly embraces a diversity of spaces, actors and institutional forms, varying in their degree of formality, autonomy and power. Civil societies are often populated by organizations such as registered charities, development non-governmental organizations, community groups, women's organizations, faith-based organizations, professional associations, trade unions, self-help groups, social movements, business associations, coalitions and advocacy groups. (Centre for Civil Society Report on Activities July 2005 – August 2006)

Definitions can be problematic when they are applied universally across social and cultural divides. As part of their research on the state of civil society in over 50 countries around the world, CIVICUS, the World Alliance for Citizen Participation, adopted the following definition of 'civil society' as a means of dealing with this issue: 'the arena, outside of the family, the state, and the market where people associate to advance common interests'. 'Civil society' is clearly a contested concept, with at least three dimensions (Carnegie 2007). It can refer to: associational life, or the 'space' of organized activity not undertaken by government or business organizations; the 'good' society, or the kind of democratic and fair society we want to live in; and arenas for public deliberation, or 'space' in which society's differences, problems and policy issues can be identified and debated.

The concept of 'value-led' (Hudson 1995) or 'value-based' (Edwards and Sen 2000) organizations to cover the sector is very attractive and accords with Jeavon's suggestion that the distinctive characteristic of a non-profit organization is that it gives 'expression to the social, philosophical, moral and religious values of their founders and supporters' (Jeavons 1992). DiMaggio and Anheier (1990) have suggested that Third Sector organizations have 'value rational' rather than 'means rational' ideological orientations. Gerard (1983), Waddock (2004) and Paton (1991) also argue that 'voluntary action is essentially value-based' (see Chapter 7 for a detailed discussion of values in Third Sector organizations). However, increasingly, organizations from all sectors may feel entitled, and have been encouraged, to consider themselves to be value-based organizations. Rosabeth Moss Kanter (2009) argues that it is private companies which are progressive, value-based and socially responsible and which will be the leaders of the future.

In the private sector, too, the concept of value has come to be used in the sense of economic value, i.e. increasing the value of a product or service. Westall (2009) highlights the ambiguities of the term 'value' and the limits of methodologies, such as social return on investment, which accept a concept of 'blended value' which can be monetarized (i.e. measured using a method that puts monetary values on outcomes). It, therefore, may not be helpful for defining the boundaries of this 'loose and baggy monster' (Davis Smith *et al.* 1995) in terms of the designation of 'value-based' or 'value-led'.

Kendall and Knapp's conclusion that 'there is no single "correct" definition which can or should be uniquely applied in all circumstances' (1995) would be very difficult to dispute. However, the substantial increase in organizations for social benefit engaging in trading, as part of the social economy, suggests that a broader term than 'voluntary and community sector' would be appropriate. For the purposes of this book, the terms 'Third Sector organizations' and 'Third Sector' are used throughout. Where this expression is deviated from it will be for a particular reason that will be explained in the text.

As indicated above, it is important to be clear about what is meant by Third Sector and in what ways the Third Sector can be considered to be different from other sectors. This differs amongst countries. For example, many of the US studies on strategic planning are concerned with museums, universities, libraries and/or hospitals, none of which would be generally considered to be part of the Third Sector in Britain. Because many of these institutions in the US are considered to be Third Sector organizations (e.g. half the hospitals and nearly half of the further education institutions), the basic texts on strategic planning and strategic planning for the Third Sector in the US are also often equally directed at the public sector (Nutt and Backoff 1992; Bryson 1995), whereas in Europe, for example, the two sectors tend to be considered very separately when writing on management issues.

Jochum and Pratten (2006) suggest that the Third Sector is united around a number of high level principles and values:

- independence: embodying people's right to associate and organize to help themselves and others, independently of the state;

- social justice: making a difference and promoting lasting social, environmental and economic change, for example through different ways of doing business, campaigning in the community or in the workplace, or in giving people a voice;
- diversity, dignity and respect: respecting and celebrating diversity and viewing this as a strength, both in relation to society and to the sector, promoting social inclusion and equality of opportunity by reaching out to and engaging with the most disadvantaged and excluded;
- participation and empowerment: enabling people to participate in their community and places of work, to give them a greater say in the decisions that affect their lives, collectively and individually, and greater control over the local economy;
- collective wealth creation and social entrepreneurship: using surpluses to further social objectives and investing in human and social capital;
- responsiveness: providing quality goods and services (including support and advocacy) in response to people's needs;
- accountability: achieving a mission, and being transparent and accountable to users, members and/or beneficiaries;
- sustainability: working towards sustainable economic and community development, for example through economic regeneration, developing people's skills and capacities, and building social capital within and between communities.

However, it would not be difficult to find Third Sector organizations that do not display many of these attributes and there are both public and private organizations that would argue that they do display many of them. Taylor and Warburton (2003) suggest that what government is looking for from Third Sector organizations is impact and quality of service, which are not included in the NCVO's list of characteristics.

CLASSIFICATION: BY FUNCTION

If it is difficult to find an agreed expression to describe the Third Sector, then it is also very difficult to define the boundaries that are covered by the sector. If it is difficult to define the boundaries, then it is equally difficult to define and categorize what is within the sector, and therefore to develop an appropriate taxonomy.

One frequent approach to defining what makes up the Third Sector is to categorize organizations by function (Brenton 1985; Handy 1988; Nathan 1990; Gutch *et al.* 1990). William Beveridge, for example, who was the architect of the Welfare State in the UK, distinguished between two forms of voluntary action: philanthropy and mutual aid.

Similarly, Hasenfield and Gidron (1993: 218) distinguish particularly between self-help groups and professional human service organizations:

A self-help group can be defined as a group of individuals who experience a common problem, who share their personal stories and knowledge to help one another cope with their situation, and who simultaneously help and are helped. In addition, the group emphasises face-to-face interactions and informal and interchangeable roles. In contrast, human service organisations are characterised by career-oriented staff members, who need not personally experience the problems they address, distinct staff and client roles, a professionally based body of knowledge, and formal division of labour.

This distinction between more professionalized human service organizations and smaller mutual aid groups based around volunteer members is viewed by some (usually within community-based organizations) to justify the two groups being seen to reflect two different sectors altogether, and therefore that the formal strategic management approaches that might be appropriate for the larger service bodies should not be considered suitable for the smaller community and other mutual aid groups (Klausen 1995; Harris 1997).

The service-providing philanthropic function is probably the one that most people think of when they think of the Third Sector. Organizations in this category may provide support, advice, accommodation, information and/or particular programmes or activities for people in need. Prior to the Second World War and the introduction of the NHS, these service-providing Third Sector organizations were often the only place that a person in need could turn for help. Kramer (1981) in his study of disability organizations in England, the USA, the Netherlands and Israel argues that, in fact, the provision of services is the least distinctive aspect of the Third Sector.

The mutual aid or mutual support (Handy 1988) function is one where a group of individuals who share a common need or interest get together to provide mutual support, advice and encouragement. This is what Brenton (1985) describes as 'self-help and exchange around a common need or interest'. This function has 'developed world-wide into a major social phenomenon' (Hasenfield and Gidron 1993). The most famous is probably Alcoholics Anonymous, but there are now a very large number of groups particularly in the medical and psychosocial field. Community development is also a process of engendering mutual support and self-help. This has been described as the social solidarity category of Third Sector organization (Gerard 1983; Knight 1993). Harris (1993) argues along with Billis (1993) and Davis Smith (1991) that such voluntary associations for mutual aid are 'conceptually and organizationally distinguishable from the bureaucratic service-delivering agencies of the broader nonprofit sector' although there is a strong pull on them to become more like the service-delivering agencies. For these associations, according to Harris, 'organization' is a matter of 'balancing competing interests, goals and values and of recognizing the motivations of volunteers' rather than formalizing or by 'adopting the management techniques' and 'rules of the game' of bureaucratic organizations.

Other writers have expanded on Beveridge's categories to include a number of additional functions. The pressure group function is one often identified with groups like Greenpeace, Amnesty International, the Howard League for Prison Reform, Liberty, etc. The Greenpeace case study, for example, highlights the range of important legislative changes that have come about, at least in part because of the lobbying and activities of Greenpeace and other Third Sector organizations. Box 1.4 provides a brief case study of a campaigning organization in the USA. This campaigning or policy advocacy role involves 'the production of pressure on decision-makers in any sector to change policy and practices usually on behalf of some identifiable groups' (Kendall and 6P 1994).

BOX 1.4   CAMPAIGN FOR COMMUNITY CHANGE (CCC) USA

'Real social change has to be built from the ground up through the participation of millions of people speaking in their own voices,' says Deepak Bhargava, Executive Director of the 40-year-old Center for Community Change (CCC).

In December 2007, CCC launched a coalition of 300 progressive community organizations, the Campaign for Community Values, which has advanced issues including poverty reduction and immigration reform. The Campaign and its allies successfully advocated for the State Children's Health Insurance Program (SCHIP), and CCC worked with other local and national organizations to win a provision in the legislation that ensures coverage for legal immigrant children.

To ensure that policymakers heard the voices of low-income families, CCC focused, in 2008, on strengthening and building relationships among community organizations nationwide, laying the groundwork for large-scale grassroots mobilization. It also engaged in targeted policy advocacy.

CCC also grew its profile in the media and saw a fivefold increase in applications for its Generation Change leadership development programme. One year after the Generation Change launch, CCC co-hosted 2,500 grassroots leaders at the first public event attended by high-level Obama Administration appointees. The event was the fruition of years of work to unite community organizations and develop a shared policy agenda.

CCC is a member of the Coalition for Comprehensive Immigration Reform and Health Care for America Now (HCAN) coalition, which harnessed incredible grassroots energy to a common purpose at a national level. The networks of families who were activated in support of SCHIP in 2008 were even more energized for the health reform campaign. Healthcare reform was finally introduced by the Obama Administration in 2010.

(See www.campaignforcommunities.org)

Campaigning is one of the areas where the law and practice on charitable status is controversial. Some campaigning organizations, like Amnesty International, have been refused charitable status. Others, like Oxfam and Christian Aid, have received warnings that they must desist from certain kinds of campaigning activities if they are not to lose their charitable status. The Charity Commission in England and Wales has issued detailed guidance to try and clarify this issue.

The individual 'citizen' advocacy function, such as advocating on behalf of, and/or with, for example, a child, or someone with a learning disability, to ensure that their individual voice is heard and they receive the services to which they are entitled, has been identified by Kendall and Knapp (1995) as a separate function. Others include it as a service-providing function or within a wider advocacy category, including public as well as individual advocacy.

Distinct resource and coordinating functions have been highlighted by Brenton (1985). Third Sector organizations particularly involved in resource and coordinating functions are often intermediary bodies whose role is to help coordinate and support other Third Sector organizations, usually within a particular field. Such bodies 'act as a central catalyst or repository of expertise, information, research, etc. on a specialist subject'. They frequently 'represent a membership of other voluntary bodies and seek to liaise between them and co-ordinate their activities, their public relations or their connections with Government' (Brenton 1985: 12).

Knight (1993) also includes two further categories in his classification: (i) mobilizing, where the purpose of the organization is to locate money or volunteers for causes; and (ii) creating, where the purpose is to express oneself through some form of creative arts in the company of others.

The substantial expansion in social enterprises which trade in order either directly to benefit a particular group of beneficiaries who are engaged in the delivery of the service or product(s), or indirectly to direct the profits from the social economy business towards charitable programmes or projects suggests that this is an increasingly important, and neglected, aspect of the Third Sector.

CLASSIFICATION: BY CONTROL/RESOURCING

An alternative way of categorizing Third Sector organizations is by methods of control and/or resourcing (Kendall and Knapp 1995). Gutch *et al.* (1990) distinguish between membership organizations which are essentially democratic in structure and those which are oligarchical (i.e. with a self-perpetuating group of trustees) or hierarchical (Anheier 2005; Reid and Griffith 2006). However, it is one thing to define an organization by its legal status as a trust, or an unincorporated association with a membership structure, and quite another to make assumptions about how these two different types of organizations work in practice. In particular, many organizations with a democratic membership structure, according to their constitution, operate in practice as a self-perpetuating oligarchy. Others which have a more top-down structure are very participative and consultative in their approach.

Gerard (1983), from two major surveys of the sector in Britain, also distinguishes between organizations on the basis of management style and structure:

- a hierarchical authoritarian approach;
- a consultative approach with considerable delegation of powers;
- a fully participative approach.

Hatch (1980) distinguishes between organizations that are primarily run by professional paid staff and those that are run mostly by volunteers. In the latter type of organization, he distinguishes between mutual aid organizations, highlighted above, which pursue members' interests, and those orientated towards non-members. In the professional staff organization category he distinguishes between those which are primarily statutory funded and those which are primarily funded from voluntary sources. While these are useful theoretical distinctions, they provide little useful practical guidance, because any organization may be at different points on any of the following three dimensions:

1. proportion of paid staff to volunteers;
2. proportion of statutory funding to voluntary or earned income;
3. proportion of services/resources directed to members against those directed to non-members.

A number of researchers (Hatch 1980; Ball 1989; Chanan 1991) have distinguished between three types of Third Sector organization:

1. Independent local organizations, more orientated to a community development process than providing services, e.g. Coin Street Community Builders or the Eden Project (see Part VI case studies). This make them 'notoriously difficult to classify in terms of an "industry" or market since, by their very nature, conventional distinctions – between demand and supply sides, user and volunteer or process and output, for example – often conflict with underlying ideologies and operating principles' Kendall and Knapp (1995: 69).
2. Organizations which are a federation of local groups with considerable local autonomy (e.g. Greenpeace – website case study, Habitat for Humanity, Emmaus – see Part VI case studies).
3. Professional national Third Sector organizations which directly run local services (e.g. Mencap, Cedar Foundation or Action for Children).

In the 1990s the British Red Cross moved from category 2 to category 3 by bringing all the local Red Cross groups under one legal structure and hierarchy. The merger of Age Concern and Help the Aged (see Part VI case study) has raised important questions about the relationship between Age UK as a national organization and local groups that were previously affiliated to Age Concern, some of which have refused to sign an agreement with the new national organization, preferring greater local autonomy.

Smith and Lipsky (1993), considering the implications of the contracting culture in the USA, distinguish between three main types of Third Sector service agencies:

1. the traditional philanthropic social services agency (see case studies of Action for Children (Box 1.2), Mencap (Part VI case study) and Médecins Sans Frontières (see website case study));
2. the more recent social service agencies established (or spun out of a public sector body) to take advantage of government funding/contracts especially in the fields of mental health and job training (Five Lamps – see Part VI case study, Greenwich Leisure Limited, My Time CIC – see website case studies);
3. agencies founded in response to unmet neighbourhood or other community needs and which often commence life on a very shaky financial basis, run by volunteers or poorly paid staff, sometimes called the 'people's sector' (see the Part VI case study of Coin Street Community Builders).

However, organizations may, over time, be in more than one of these categories. Traditional philanthropic social services agencies (like Bryson Charitable Group, Cedar Foundation, Mencap and Action for Children – Box 1.2), for example, have increasingly focused on being able to tender for government contracts. Local community groups also often develop a service delivery aspect to their activities.

All these categories of Third Sector organization, highlighted above, are less than exhaustive. As Kendall and Knapp (1995) point out, local fund raising groups, which are autonomous, but raise money for a particular cause, do not easily fit into these schemas. Organizations which are established to give grants to other organizations, either as a result of an endowment from a wealthy individual (see Box 12.1) or individuals, or as a result of ongoing support from a company or statutory body, also don't fit well into the categories suggested above. These categories were also developed before the huge increase in social economy initiatives, where organizations engage in trade for a social purpose.

CLASSIFICATION: BY BENEFICIARIES

Blau and Scott (1962) distinguish between organizations on the basis of who benefits. In mutual aid organizations, for example, it is the members. In a medical charity it will be individuals with a particular medical disorder. For an animal charity it will be particular species of animals. For an environmental charity it will be the natural environment. For an umbrella agency it will be other Third Sector organizations.

CLASSIFICATION: BY ACTIVITY

Finally, attempts have been made to try to categorize the sector in terms of the field of activity. Salamon and Anheier (1993) developed an International Classification of Non-profit Organisations (ICNPO) to help with international comparisons of the Third Sector, which identifies 12 groups of primary fields of activity. The revised classification (Salamon and Anheier 1996) is as follows:

- culture and recreation: culture and arts; sports; other recreation and social clubs;
- education and research: primary and secondary education; higher education; other education; research;
- health: hospitals and rehabilitation; nursing homes; mental health and crisis intervention; other health services;
- social services: social services; emergency and relief; income support and maintenance;
- environment: environment; animal protection;
- development and housing: economic, social and community development; housing; employment and training;
- law, advocacy and politics: civic and advocacy organizations; law and legal services; political organizations;
- philanthropic intermediaries and voluntarism promotion;
- international activities;
- religion;

19

- business, professional associations and unions;
- those not classified elsewhere.

Many of these are then further broken down into subcategories. For example, culture and arts is further broken down into:

- media and communications;
- visual arts, architecture, ceramic art;
- performing arts;
- historical, literary and humanistic societies;
- museums;
- zoos and aquariums.

In the UK, the Charity Commission for England and Wales had a classification system that was put in place in the 1960s, following the 1960 Charities Act, which they felt was very inadequate for present day purposes. They commissioned Aston Business School (ABS) to develop a new classification system. The ABS team considered various existing classification systems including the UK Standard Industrial Classification, the General Industrial Classification of Economic Activities,' The UN's International Standard Industrial Classification, the National Taxonomy of Exempt Entities, and the ICNPO mentioned above. The ABS team considered that, of these, the most useful was the ICNPO classification. However, they felt that only considering the field of activity limited the classification system and so they proposed a three-dimensional one:

- beneficiaries (i.e. individuals, institutions or the environment);
- function (i.e. provision of services, provision of facilities, finance/resourcing, intelligence and development, and representation);
- field of operation, using the ICNPO classification.

BOUNDARIES OF THE THIRD SECTOR

In order to understand the Third Sector, classifying organizations is both important and useful, particularly for international comparison. It is also crucial for research into the appropriateness of different types of strategy or forms of management or structure for different types of Third Sector organization. In Kendall and Knapp's (1995: 85) view, 'there appears to be a consensus that the identification of appropriate criteria is virtually obligatory if progress is to be made towards the description and analysis of a meaningful construct', or, to put it another way, to create 'islands of meaning' (Zerubavel 1991: 1), i.e. cognitive devices that group together objects to facilitate recognition and communication by developing a clear definition of the non-profit sector is crucial in trying to understand the sector. However, it does not help in establishing the boundaries of the sector or in clarifying the difference between the Third Sector and other sectors.

To address the question of boundaries, Hatch (1980), in *Outside the State*, identified three conditions for an entity to be in the voluntary sector: formal, independent of government, and not profit-distributing. Brenton (1985) included these three in his definition, but added two others: self-governing (private) and for the public benefit. Johnson (1981) adds the requirement that at least some of the income should come from voluntary sources. Kendall and Knapp (1995) considered that significant consensus has been achieved around four key criteria to define the non-profit sector which have been developed for international comparison purposes (Salamon and Anheier 1993). The four criteria are as follows:

- An entity must be formal, in the sense of having a structure, a constitution and a set of rules, registered with the Charity Commission, a government body or intermediate Third Sector umbrella body. This excludes informal family or friendship networks that exist and play a crucial role in supporting dependent relatives, etc.

- An entity must be constitutionally and institutionally independent of government and self-governing, with their own decision-making structures. The creation of bodies by public bodies, which are technically independent of government, but in which the trustees are all government appointees, and all, or nearly all, the funding comes from government, raises concerns about such bodies (Kendall and Knapp 1995).

- An entity must not be profit-distributing and must be primarily non-business. An organization may make a profit, but the profit must be ploughed back into the business and cannot be distributed to those who have an interest in the organization, such as trustees, members and officers. This excludes most cooperatives and mutual benefit institutions such as the John Lewis Partnership (see website case study) and The Co-operative Group (see Part VI case study) and building societies.

- Lastly, an entity must benefit to a meaningful degree from philanthropy or voluntary citizen involvement. This voluntary element may be income from voluntary sources, the commitment of voluntary labour to carry out aspects of the work, or the involvement of volunteers as trustees, the latter of which has been described by the then Chief Executive of NCVO as the single most defining characteristic of the sector (Prashar 1991).

Potentially, however, political parties and sacramental (as opposed to service providing) religious bodies could also be included under this definition, though they are often excluded for the purposes of discussing the Third Sector. Kendall (2003) describes the sector that includes political parties and religious congregations as 'the broad non-profit sector'. The exclusion of universities, schools, sports and social clubs, trade unions and business associations he describes as 'the narrow voluntary sector'.

The development of the social economy, in particular, challenges this consensus. The Third Sector is now often described in a way that includes both staff cooperatives (like John Lewis), which distribute dividends to staff, and member cooperatives (like The Co-operative Group – see Part VI case study), which do distribute profits to members.

COMPARISONS WITH THE PRIVATE SECTOR

Of particular interest to the discussion of the relevance of strategic choices and professional management models and techniques is the extent of the differences and similarities between the Third Sector and the private sector. It was in the private sector that many of the strategic management models and tools were first developed during the late 1960s and through the 1970s and which are now being used extensively in the Third Sector. An understanding of the differences between the two sectors may help us to understand to what extent the Third Sector requires a different approach from those used in the private sector.

There have been various attempts to define the features of the Third Sector which distinguish it from other sectors, the private sector in particular. Mason (1984) suggests the following as distinctive features of the Third Sector: motivation; economy; board effectiveness; staff departments; directing professionals; creative/innovation; commitment/loyalty; survivability; strategy; employee satisfaction; optimizing customer service; consumer concerns; service knowledge; and women workers. Kendall and Knapp (1998) suggest: consumer choice; specialization; cost-effectiveness; flexibility; innovation; advocacy; and participation.

There have, however, been very few studies to determine whether there is any empirical basis for these claims of difference between the Third Sector and private sectors. One notable exception to this is in relation to innovation. A Johns Hopkins University survey of 417 non-profit organizations found that 82 per cent had implemented an innovative programme or service within the previous five years. More than two-thirds of the organizations also reported having an innovation they wished to adopt in the previous two years, but were unable to, primarily because of lack of funding. Bolton (2003) identified 'innovative' as one of the 'reasonable' claims of where the Third Sector is different from other sectors. Despite the claims of Mason, Kendall and Knapp, and the Johns Hopkins survey, studies of innovation in the UK Third Sector (Osborne 1998; Osborne *et al.* 2008) have demonstrated that only one-third of such organizations show any true innovation, which is rather contingent on the organization's institutional and policy environment. It should, therefore, not be claimed as a distinctive characteristic of the sector.

Paton and Cornforth (1992) and Leat (1993) examined a number of characteristics that have been put forward to distinguish the Third Sector from the private sector and therefore have been used as a basis for arguing that the Third Sector needs to be managed differently from the private sector. These are as follows:

Profit-making versus non-profit-making

The most common characteristic which is put forward as distinguishing the Third Sector from the private sector is, as the name suggests, the fact that the Third Sector does not operate on the profit motive, while the private sector does. However, even this criterion is not quite as cut-and-dried as it might appear, because some Third Sector organizations do make a profit, intentionally or otherwise. In the UK, Guide Dogs for the Blind has, for example, made considerable profits and has built up a very substantial reserve. On the other hand there are many private sector companies who do not make any profit. How profitability is defined in the private sector is also often problematic, with a wide variety of different measures being used to define success, including market share, return on capital invested, return on sales and growth in sales revenue (Davis Smith 1992). Defining profit in the Third Sector is even more problematic.

Perhaps of more value is the concept of the non-distribution of any profits, discussed above. Most Third Sector organizations may make a profit, but may not distribute this profit to anyone with a beneficial interest in the organization, such as staff, trustees or members. In the private sector, profits may be distributed to shareholders. However, even in the Third Sector there may be bonuses paid to certain staff, e.g. fund-raising or charity shop staff, if the net income raised is over a certain amount. Social economy businesses, such as cooperatives and other mutuals, may distribute dividends to their members, who may include staff. CICs may develop investment vehicles that allow investors to receive a dividend.

Indicators of success

Of particular relevance to this current study, and linked to the issue of the lack of a profit motive, is the suggestion that a distinctive characteristic of Third Sector organizations is the lack of any clear indicators of success. As Drucker (1990: 107) says about Third Sector organizations, 'what is the bottom line when there is no bottom line?'. However, this view has been criticized (Anheier 2000), because, it is argued, the problem is not that Third Sector organizations do not have a bottom line, but that they have multiple bottom lines. Argenti (1965) has described this difficulty as 'the last unconquered peak in the study of management'. However, as mentioned above, it is not always entirely clear what the success indicators for a private company should be, and over what timescale performance indicators should be measured; and indeed many Third Sector organizations have put in place very well developed performance indicators and measurement systems (see, for example, the Social Audit PLAN in Box 8.3, the Furniture Resource Centre in Box 8.2, Cosmic Ethical in Box 12.5 and the Five Lamps Part VI case study).

Multiple stakeholders

For some commentators, the issue about lack of goal clarity in the Third Sector is caused by the multiple stakeholders that a Third Sector organization is expected to satisfy and be accountable to, compared with the equivalent private company. In Drucker's words (1985: 180) 'it has to satisfy everyone; certainly it cannot afford to alienate anyone'. The argument is that the private sector only has to satisfy the customer and the shareholder; the Third Sector organization, on the other hand, has usually to satisfy: multiple funders; individual, corporate and statutory as well as regulatory bodies; customers; trustees; volunteers; staff; the media; the local community; partners; etc.

It is the number and diverse nature of internal and external stakeholders and income sources that leads Anheier (2000) to suggest that the complexity of managing a Third Sector organization easily surpasses that of the equivalent sized for-profit firm. However, as Leat (1993) suggests, this argument is rather oversimplified, as, increasingly, private sector companies have had to become responsive to a wide range of different types of stakeholders, including: staff; trades unions; shareholders, individual and institutional; banks; directors; suppliers; statutory grant givers; regulatory bodies; and the local community. As a result stakeholder analysis has become an important aspect of strategy building in the private sector, despite its detractors (Argenti 1989), in order to satisfy its multiple constituencies. Although there are examples of Third Sector organizations which have a very wide range of stakeholders and private sector companies who appear to respond to a narrow range of stakeholders, there are also examples where this scenario can be reversed. It has also been argued (Teasdale 2010) that social enterprises, which are at the nexus of the voluntary and private sectors, have a larger number of stakeholders than traditional voluntary organizations, because they have customers as well as beneficiaries and funders to please and therefore engage in various forms of 'impression management' (presenting different faces to different stakeholders) to keep all the different stakeholders happy.

Resource acquisition/transactions

It has been suggested that the main difference between the private and Third Sectors is in relation to the resource acquisition activities in the two sectors (Moore 2000). Or to put it another way, the difference is between the forms of transactions that take place in a Third Sector organization compared with a private company (Hudson 1995). In the private sector there is a trading relationship where a customer purchases a product or service from the company and pays the price agreed – a simple two-way transaction. In the Third Sector, funding may come from government, businesses, charitable trusts or foundations, in the form of grants or contracts; and/or it may come from individuals in the form of private donations to pay for the product or, more usually, the service that the 'customer' receives. Instead of a two-way flow of resources as in the private sector, there is a one-way flow of resources from funder to Third Sector organization to client. However, the reality is more complex than indicated above. Many Third Sector organizations are increasingly involved in trading activities where there is clearly a two-way transaction between the organization and its customers, who may be purchasing a product or service (Morales 1997). Many beneficiaries of Third Sector organizations are required to pay for the service they receive, albeit at often less than the commercial rate. Commercial sponsors, too, are not only involved in a one-way transaction: they require a return on their investment in terms of branding, publicity, etc.

Culture and values

Others have concentrated on the issue of culture and values (Jeavons 1992). In particular it has been suggested that Third Sector organizations tend to be more participatory and egalitarian, with a greater commitment to equal opportunities. This is confirmed by research (Leat 1995) into the views of managers who have moved from the private to the Third Sector. The research found that these managers often experienced a significant culture shift, if not shock, in moving to organizations with an emphasis on participative decision-making. The practice, however, does not always match the rhetoric in Third Sector organizations. Others argue that it is the Third Sector's focus on fundamental social values that makes it distinctive (Moore 2000).

However, it may be that, over time, this difference in culture and values is reducing, because of an increased emphasis on participation and values in the private sector, as well as an increase in commercial activities within many Third Sector organizations. The message of Collins and Porras's (1994) successful book on corporate strategy, *Built to Last*, for example, is that for a commercial company to be both globally competitive and locally effective it must cultivate and embed a deep sense of practical ethics that are driven at all levels by sound human values. Ohmae (1982) and Pascale and Athos (1981) argue that espousing these fundamental values is precisely the reason that Japanese firms have been so successful over the last 30 years. This perspective has been encouraged by various management theorists for the last 25 years (Peters and Austin 1985; O'Toole 1986; Lawler 1986; Peters 1987; Kanter 1989; Collins 2001). This is an interesting example of where the private sector may be moving more in the direction of the Third Sector (Clutterbuck and Dearlove 1996).

The general argument that the Third Sector has a stronger link with moral values has also been criticized (Marshall 1996) on the grounds that there is no evidence that activity in self-help groups, community organizations or mutual societies is any less self-interested than the private sector (Richardson and Goodman 1983).

Cooperation versus competition

Another value that some argue is distinctive about the Third Sector is that of cooperation. Hudson (2005: 81), for example, argues that effective non-profit organizations develop various kinds of strategic alliances because 'they believe that they can achieve their missions more effectively through collaborations with other organisations'. The private sector, in contrast, is seen as being characterized by, almost defined by, competition (Porter 1980) and strategy as 'the art of war'. This makes some Third Sector organizations, who don't consider that they should be relating to other Third Sector agencies, as 'competitors to be beaten', and very suspicious of management theory.

However, the distinction between the two sectors is not as clear-cut as it might seem. Actual competition between Third Sector organizations for funds, volunteers and contracts is very common (Herman 1994) and has been increasing substantially, with the expansion of the social economy and the open tendering of government contracts. Many Third Sector organizations were set up to compensate for the perceived weaknesses in another Third Sector organization. Many private sector organizations have also realized that strategic alliances and cooperation (e.g. with major suppliers and customers, business support organizations, industry bodies) are as important as competition in being successful and have developed their own associations, strategic alliances, mergers and partnerships.

All these factors reduce the extent of the differences between the two sectors in relation to competition and cooperation. However, there probably does remain at least some difference in emphasis between Third Sector organizations – which have a commitment to ensuring the needs of a particular client group are met, which may often be best done through collaboration with other non-profit organizations and increasingly with organizations from other sectors (Butler and Wilson 1990) – and the private sector where competitive advantage over (even the destruction of) other companies is seen as the key to success (Porter 1980).

The nature of governance

The nature of governance in the private and Third Sectors has also been suggested as a key difference between the two sectors. In the private sector, the board will be made up, either partly or entirely, of the paid full-time directors. In the Third Sector, the paid staff are generally not permitted by charity law to be members of the governing body, which is therefore made up of unpaid volunteers. There is evidence, however, that in the Third Sector, the paid staff, and the chief executive in particular, often wield considerable influence on both the composition and decisions of the board (Cornforth and Edwards 1998). The development of CICs creates the potential for a wider range of governance structures than before, with some social enterprises, which do not have charitable status, having governance structures, with paid executive directors, closer to the private sector model than the traditional voluntary sector.

In relation to the private sector, the Cadbury report into governance in the private sector (Cadbury 1992) concluded that private companies in the UK needed to increase substantially the number of non-executive board members. In this respect, therefore, as well as some Third Sector organizations moving closer to the private sector, the private sector has been moving in the direction of the Third Sector in valuing the input and objectivity that non-executive board members can bring.

Bolton (2003) suggests that the role of Third Sector organizations in building social capital is a distinctive aspect of the Third Sector. Setting aside the extensive literature on the difficulty of even defining, let alone measuring, the concept of social capital, the location of social capital within the Third Sector has been criticized (Maloney *et al.* 2000) for ignoring the role of statutory organizations in social capital. The idea that there is a strong link between volunteering, as civil engagement, as a key builder of social capital, has also been criticized (Isham *et al.* 2006; Schneider 2007). In the investigation by Reed *et al.* (2005) of the differences between the private and Third sectors, the authors reached the conclusion that the differences are more difficult to identify than often supposed.

BECOMING MORE LIKE BUSINESS?

Jim Collins, in *Good to Great and the Social Sectors* (2006: 1) argues that, regardless of the similarities and differences between the sectors,

> we must reject the idea – well-intentioned, but dead wrong – that the primary path to greatness in the social sectors is to become 'more like a business'. Most businesses – like most of anything else in life – fall somewhere between mediocre and good. Few are great. When you compare great companies with good ones, many widely practiced business norms turn out to correlate with mediocrity, not greatness. So, then, why would we want to import the practices of mediocrity into the social

sectors?...The critical distinction is not between business and social, but between great and good. We need to reject the naïve imposition of the 'language of business' on the social sectors, and instead jointly embrace a *language of greatness*.

The above discussion indicates the complexity and diversity of the Third Sector and how difficult it is to create clear boundaries between sectors, particularly between the Third Sector and the private sector. It is possible to view the sectors as overlapping circles (see Figure 1.1). The Three-failures theory (Steinberg 2006) is a group of theories that is often used to explain the existence of each of the sectors, because of the failures inherent in each of the other sectors. The concept can be extended to four sectors, as it can be argued that the public and Third Sectors exist because of the failure of the informal sector and private sector to meet some of the needs and expectations of some of the population.

This raises the important question as to how many sectors there actually are. The general public and, until relatively recently, most of the modern social sciences, including economics, sociology and political science (Kendall and Knapp 1996), tended to think primarily about two sectors: the private and public. Writers about the Third Sector have, also until recently, tended to assume that there are three sectors: the public, private and Third Sector. This is however not an uncontentious view. Organizational theorists often make a clear distinction between sectors represented by formal organizations and the informal sector made up of family and friendship ties, which has been increasingly recognized as crucial to the provision of support to those in need, and in turn requiring support (e.g. carers' organizations), thus suggesting the existence of four sectors (see Figure 1.1).

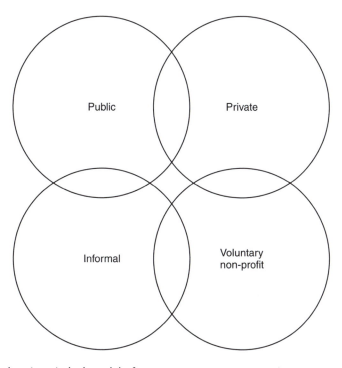

Fig 1.1 The 'four overlapping circles' model of sectors

Uphoff (1996), in exploring Third Sector organizations involved in world development, distinguishes between not-for-profit service organizations or NGOs and mutual benefit membership organizations. However, he goes further and argues that NGOs operate much more like private sector organizations and should be considered a subset of the private sector, whereas mutual benefit membership organizations, including cooperatives, occupy space between the private and public sectors and should be considered as a separate 'collective action' or 'membership' sector. Others have argued that religious or sacramental bodies should be defined as a separate sector (Kendall and Knapp 1995). The case has been made for political parties to be distinguished as a sector. There is also a case for including trade unions and business support organizations as a separate sector. A similar case can be made for recreational bodies, which don't easily fit in existing schemas.

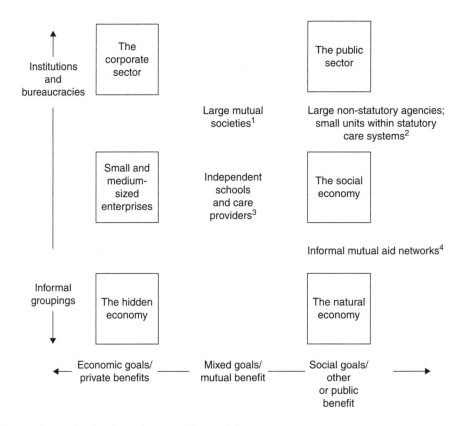

Fig 1.2   Types of organization in and around the social economy

> *Notes*: [1]For example, building societies, retail co-ops, the Automobile Association. [2] For example, large housing associations, Barnardo's, local authority centres, cottage hospitals. [3] For example, charitable public schools, nursing homes (private but professionally run). [4] For example, baby-sitting circles, mother and toddler clubs.
>
> *Source*: Davis Smith (1995).

The concept of 'sector' is clearly a problematic one, because as we have seen there is neither a consensus about what a sector is, nor how many sectors there are, nor how they should be defined. However, this is also true of many concepts that are social constructs (Berger and Luckmann 1967), such as race. It is impossible to separate the language that we choose to use from our own values and contexts. It does not mean that using such concepts does not have value, but it does mean that it is important to keep the contingent nature of the concept in mind when it is being used. Kramer (2004) has argued that because many public services are, or could be, provided by any type of organization, public, private or non-profit, and there is little research evidence to show any significant differences between their performance, the traditional concept of sector has lost much of its value as a theoretical and analytical concept.

The concept the 'Third Sector' will be used throughout the book in a descriptive sense. Following Osborne (1998), it does not assume any homogeneity in objectives, values or activities amongst Third Sector organizations. It is accepted that these are in fact extremely diverse. It also does not imply that the Third Sector is completely independent from the other sectors, because there is in fact considerable interdependence; and it does not assume that any particular organizational characteristics can be ascribed to an organization because it is in the Third Sector. It is accepted that these need to be addressed at subsectoral levels and on the basis of empirical evidence.

Table 1.1   Commercialism and mutuality matrix

		Degree of commercialism		
		Low	Medium	High
Degree of mutuality	High	Community associations Self-help groups Benevolent funds Churches	Community and self-help groups engaged in trading	Cooperatives (producer, consumer, housing)
	Medium	User- and member-led charities funded by grants/ donations Community associations engaged in service delivery	Community associations engaged in service delivery and trading User-led charities engaged in trading	Employee owned businesses Building societies Credit unions Football supporters' trusts Development trusts
	Low	Service delivery charities funded by grants/ donations Foundations Third Sector advocacy organizations	Charities with a trading arm or which compete for contracts	Non-mutual social enterprises trading in the open market Housing associations Leisure trusts

Organizations are also dynamic entities which may over time move from one category and legal status to another depending on the development of the organization and the legal, political, tax and financial framework in the country in which it operates at any particular time. In the UK, most schools, universities and hospitals that had previously been established by religious or philanthropic bodies became incorporated into the statutory sector during the twentieth century. In the twenty-first century this trend has been reversed with attempts to enable some public sector bodies, such as schools, to opt out of the statutory system and for hospitals to obtain trust or foundation status. It has already been mentioned that a different balance exists in the US, for example, where many hospitals, museums and universities are part of the Third Sector.

Davis Smith (1995), rather than trying to argue for a certain number of sectors, has developed a more complex and dynamic model of organizations in which to try to fit various aspects of the Third Sector, including the social economy. This model (see Figure 1.2) has two axes: the extent that the goals of the organization are social (i.e. for the public benefit) or private (i.e. for personal gain) and the size and degree of institutionalization and bureaucracy.

With the growth in social enterprises, only an alternative two-dimensional model of Third Sector organizations could reflect the degree of commercialism and the degree of mutuality (see Table 1.1).

SUMMARY

This chapter has explored the difficulties in trying to define the Third Sector, even in establishing an agreed and meaningful name for the sector (if indeed it is one). The boundaries between the Third Sector and other sectors, particularly the private sector, have been explored, and the fact that these change with time and geography is acknowledged. The incredible diversity of the sector has also been acknowledged and various ways of classifying the sector have been discussed. Three models that recognize the complexity of the issues involved have been presented.

QUESTIONS

1. How would you define a sector and how many sectors do you think there are and why?
2. What is the best term to define the Third Sector and why?
3. What are the defining characteristics of a Third Sector organization?
4. For what purposes might a third sector organization be registered as a charity?
5. What are the benefits of charitable status?
6. What different ways are there to categorize the Third Sector and which is most useful?
7. What are the key differences between private sector and Third Sector organizations?

8. Is a strategic management approach appropriate for any or all types of Third Sector organizations?

9. Why is the Third Sector important?

10. Is the Third Sector the same regardless of country? If not, what are the factors that makes it different?

11. Using the commercialism and mutuality matrix, allocate each of the organizations in the case studies (in Part VI) to a position in the matrix.

DISCUSSION TOPIC

Should mutual aid and member-led groups be in a separate sector from large service providing organizations?

SUGGESTED READING

Helmut Anheier and Lester M. Salaman (2006) 'The Nonprofit Sector in Comparative Perspective', in W.E. Powell and R. Steinberg (eds), *The Nonprofit Sector: A Research Handbook*, 2nd edition, Yale University Press.

Simon Bridge, Brendan Murtagh and Ken O' Neill (2008) *Understanding the Social Economy and the Third Sector*, Palgrave Macmillan.

Michael Edwards (2004) *Civil Society*, Polity.

Charles Handy (1988) *Understanding Voluntary Organizations*, Penguin.

Jeremy Kendall and Martin Knapp (1995) 'A Loose and Baggy Monster: Boundaries, Definitions and Typologies', in J.D. Smith, C. Rochester and R. Hedley (eds), *An Introduction to the Voluntary Sector*, Routledge.

Jeremy Kendall and Martin Knapp (1996) *The Voluntary Sector in the UK*, Johns Hopkins Nonprofit Sector Series, Manchester University Press.

Stephen P. Osborne (1996) 'What is "Voluntary" about the Voluntary and Non-profit Sector?', in S.P. Osborne (ed.), *Managing in the Voluntary Sector*, Thomson Business Press.

Rob Paton and Chris Cornforth (1992) 'What's Different about Managing in Voluntary and Non-profit Organisations' in J. Batsleer, C. Cornforth and R. Paton, *Issues in Voluntary and Non-profit Management*, Addison Wesley in association with the Open University Press.

2 WHAT IS 'STRATEGY'?

OVERVIEW

The words 'strategy' and 'strategic' are now a common part of discourse about, and within, Third Sector organizations. There is, however, probably little clarity about what they actually mean and little uniformity in how they are used. It has been argued that they are so frequently used that they have 'become a verbal tic: a word that can mean anything has lost its bite' (Rumelt 2011: 5). This chapter explores the concepts of strategy, strategic planning and strategic management, in general, and how it applies to the Third Sector, in particular.

LEARNING OBJECTIVES

After studying this chapter, you should be able to:

- define the concept of strategy;
- understand the relevance of some of the definitions of strategy for the Third Sector;
- understand the difference between strategy and planning;
- understand the difference between strategic planning and strategic management;
- explain why the Third Sector has begun adopting strategic management models and tools.

DEFINING 'STRATEGY'

One of the difficulties about the area of strategic management is the language, not to say jargon, that is often used, much of it inconsistently (see Box 2.1). There is not even clarity about the fundamental concept of 'strategy'. Many definitions of 'strategy' that have been developed for use in the private sector, or in the military, emphasize features that are alien to the culture and language, not to say purpose, of many Third Sector organizations. Some other definitions, however, would seem to be equally applicable to the Third Sector. To help create greater clarity, it may be useful to explore briefly the origins of the concept of strategy.

BOX 2.1 STRATEGY JARGON

Strategy: the overall direction and positioning of an organization, reflecting its distinctive capabilities and changing external environment.

Strategic plan: a written plan setting out the overall direction and positioning of an organization, reflecting its distinctive capabilities and changing external environment.

Corporate plan: the overarching strategy (strategic plan) of a diversified organization, which operates various different 'businesses'. The plan normally focuses on what businesses the organization should be in and how to create synergy amongst them.

Operational plan: usually a more detailed shorter-term plan (e.g. annual) with SMART objectives for how the strategic plan is going to be implemented.

Business plan: the expression 'business plan' is confusingly used in various different ways. In some contexts it is used in the same sense as a strategic plan, in others to mean an operational plan; in others it is used to mean a subsidiary plan of a 'business unit' within a diversified organization, with its overarching corporate plan. It is also commonly used to mean a plan for investors or lenders, to provide evidence of, and confidence in, how and when they should expect a return on their money.

Functional plans: the medium-term plans for a functional department within an organization, e.g. finance, human resources, communications, fundraising, towards achieving the overall strategic/corporate strategy.

Work plans: the, usually short-term, plans of an individual or team to guide their work towards achieving the higher level plans of the department, business or organization.

The word 'strategy' derives from the Greek *strategi*, 'office of general, command, generalship', which in turn comes from *strategos*, 'leader or commander of an army, general', a compound of *stratos*, 'army, host' and *agos*, 'leader, chief', which in its turn comes from *ago*, 'to lead'. In this sense, the word 'army' refers to an army encamped over a large area of ground. This concept of 'strategy' can be found in Byzantine documents from the sixth century onwards, and most notably in the work attributed to Emperor Leo VI the Wise of Byzantium. The word was first used in German as *Strategie* in a translation of Leo's work in 1777, and was first used in English in 1810.

The *Concise Oxford Dictionary* defines 'strategy' as 'the art of war' or 'a plan of action or policy in business or politics'. These two definitions probably give a good indication of where the concept of 'strategy' came from and what the lay understanding of the word currently means. 'Strategy' as 'the art of war', however, is perhaps not the best definition to use in considering the idea of strategic planning and management as it relates to the Third Sector, but it is useful to, at least, be aware of the roots of some of the concepts that have developed since the earliest historians and poets began to 'collect the accumulated lore of these successful and unsuccessful life-and-death strategies and convert them into wisdom and guidance for the future' (Quinn 1988: 11).

Box 2.2 gives a number of definitions given by key writers in the field which may be relevant to the Third Sector.

BOX 2.2 DEFINITIONS OF 'STRATEGY'

'Strategy is the determination of the basic long-term goals and objectives of an enterprise, and the adoption of courses of action and the allocation of resources necessary for carrying out these goals' (Chandler 1962:13).

'Strategy is defined by decisions an organization makes that: determine or reveal its objectives, purposes or goals; create the principal policies and plans for achieving its aims; define the range of businesses or services the organization is to pursue; identify the kind of economic and human organization it is or intends to be; and specify the nature of the economic and non-economic contribution to be made to the organization's shareholders or trustees, employees, customers and communities' (Andrews 1980:18–19).

'Strategy can be seen as a key link between what the organization wants to achieve – its objectives – and the policies adopted to guide its activities' (Bowman and Asch 1987: 4).

'Strategy is a disciplined effort to produce fundamental decisions and actions that shape and guide what an organization is, what it does, and why it does it' (Bryson 1988: 4–5).

'Strategy relates to the patterns/plans that integrate an organization's major goals/policies and action sequences into a cohesive whole' (Quinn 1988: 3).

[Strategy is] 'the fundamental pattern of present and planned resource deployments and environmental interactions that indicates how the organisation will achieve its objectives' (Hofer and Schendel 1978: 25).

'Strategy is the direction and scope of an organization over the long-term, ideally which matches its resources to its changing environment and in particular its markets, customers and clients so as to meet stakeholder expectations' (Johnson and Scholes 1993: 10).

The various definitions in Box 2.1 reflect a number of key concepts and themes. They suggest that strategy is concerned with:

- the long-term;
- mission, purpose, goals and objectives;
- direction, orientation and scope;
- decisions;
- plans;
- a course of action;
- allocation of resources;
- positioning the organization within its external environment;

- meeting stakeholder expectations;
- flexibility to changing circumstances;
- a pattern of organizational moves;
- patterns that integrate;
- shaping and guiding what an organization is, what it does and why it does it.

Some of the definitions assume that strategy is based on a formal planning process or deliberate decisions, others that the strategy of an organization can be determined from what it does, or has done, regardless of whether these actions were formally, or even informally, planned in advance. On that basis, every organization has a strategy whether it realizes it or not.

Some of the definitions also assume that an organization's strategy is a good thing, because it enables the organization to achieve its mission, goals or objectives. An examination of the actual strategy adopted by an organization, based on the strategic decisions it has made, or hasn't made, and therefore its actions, may, however, result in the conclusion that the strategy pursued did not, in fact, enable the organization to: achieve its mission, goals or objectives; respond to the external environment; meet its stakeholders' expectations; or integrate its goals and action sequences into a cohesive goal. There can, therefore, be bad as well as good strategies.

Richard Rumelt, in *Good Strategy/Bad Strategy* (2011), argues that there are four kinds of bad strategy:

- fluff: a form of nice-sounding gibberish masquerading as strategy concepts or arguments;
- failure to face the challenge: not defining the challenge to be overcome;
- mistaking goals for strategy: statements of desire, rather than plans to overcome obstacles;
- setting bad objectives because they don't address the real challenges, or are impractical.

Dawn Wood has suggested that there is a tendency for Third Sector organizations to default to producing a strategic plan which in the main simply describes what the organization already does: there is no sense of direction or ambition. Many organizational strategies are also not internally coherent: they do not articulate a clear unity of purpose or sense of direction. They are more like a group of mini-strategies, often, in the Third Sector, responding to the opportunities provided by particular funding sources. Or the relationship between one level of the strategy and the next level is not clear, so it is hard to understand how one set of actions helps to achieve the higher level aims. For example it may not be clear how the long-term aims help to achieve the mission and vision; or it is not clear how the priorities agreed contribute to the achievement of the aims. Sometimes, Third Sector strategies are created in written documents solely for the purpose of pleasing a funder, or a board member, but the organization has no intention of using it to guide the development of the organization.

If these are some of the aspects of bad strategy, what are the aspects of good strategy? The following may include some of the criteria used to describe a Third Sector strategy as 'good':

- provides clear direction;
- inspires people to commitment and action;
- honours the past as well as looking to the future;
- reflects the views, aspirations and expectations of beneficiaries;
- reflects the views, aspirations and expectations of other stakeholders;
- responds to the clearly assessed needs of beneficiaries;
- reflects the changing external environment and its uncertainties;
- contains an appropriate resource model to generate sufficient net income;
- is based on a clear logical model or theory of change;
- is evidence-based (McNeece and Thyer 2004), e.g. there is evidence from robust evaluations that certain actions will lead to certain outcomes;
- will be implemented by an organization with the distinctive skills and experience to implement it effectively;
- with clear outcomes that can be evaluated;
- enables the implementation of it to be effectively monitored.

For some Third Sector organizations which are funded by statutory sources it is also important to have a strategy that helps government to fulfil its priorities.

Some of the definitions in Box 2.1 focus on particular schools of strategy theory, which will be explored in Chapters 3 and 4, e.g. traditional planning, positioning, learning and stakeholder.

Henry Mintzberg (1994) has suggested that part of the problem in defining the concept of 'strategy' is that the word is used in a number of different ways. He argues that, in common language and dictionary definitions, 'strategy' is normally thought of as a *plan* of action to guide the future, although sometimes these are merely *ploys*, i.e. tactics or manoeuvres. The definition of 'strategy' as 'plan' suits the traditional strategic planning schools of the 1960s and 1970s well, which focus on intended strategies; but 'strategy' can also be used in a number of other senses. It can be viewed as a *pattern* of actions that have consistency and consequences, whether they were planned or intended or not. This perspective may perhaps be seen more clearly in hindsight or by an outsider. Here emergent strategies are crucial.

Strategy can also be seen as *position*, in the sense of the niche that the organization occupies – the fit of the organization to its environment, including other organizations, or its place in the product-market domain, i.e. what kinds of services or products should the organization provide, and to which target group(s)? Lastly, 'strategy' can be viewed as *perspective*. In this sense strategies are 'abstractions which exist only in the minds of interested parties'. 'Strategy' in this respect is to the organization as personality is to the individual. These different understandings of the concept are not necessarily conflicting but rather complementary, emphasizing different aspects of strategy that, individually, need to be considered. They do, however, represent different schools of thought – which will be explored further in Chapters 3 and 4.

This helpful taxonomy from Mintzberg makes it possible to separate the concept of 'strategy' from that of planning, which is important because an organization has a strategy, which can be perceived, whether or not it engages in any type of formal planning. The actual strategy might only be able to be perceived in hindsight. For example, a Third Sector organization without any clearly articulated strategy may, over time, apply to various funding sources that seem relevant to its work. Gradually the work of the organization may change to reflect more closely, for example, government priorities. Incrementally, the client group, kinds of services or geographical focus may have changed as a result of taking up the funding opportunities available. The organization's strategy, to be highly adaptable to the changing external environment (e.g. funding sources), within very broad parameters, may only be apparent over a period of time.

In practice, what is considered to be strategic and what is considered to be operational is also not always clear. Quite a lot of planning that takes place is not strategic: it is often more operational or action planning, in nature. Drawing on the definitions in Box 2.1, some of the criteria that might be applied to determine whether something is strategic or not might include:

- it concerns the medium to long-term (e.g. 3–10 years);
- it concerns the whole organization;
- it concerns the purpose, direction and scope of the organization;
- it concerns how the organization is positioned in relation to the external environment and other organizations;
- it concerns the allocation of significant resources;
- it involves making fundamental decisions (even by default) about which services to provide to which beneficiary groups.

Reflecting on some of the weaknesses of the classic early schools of strategy (see Chapters 3 and 4), where strategic plans are developed as a result of a formal process, say every five years, and a perceived lack of strategic thinking about the future, in the context of a changing external environment, Mintzberg *et al.* (1998: 77) suggest that 'strategic planning' should have been called 'strategic programming' and promoted as a process to 'formalise, where necessary, the consequences of strategies already developed by other means'.

There has been a change over the last two decades in the terminology used in practice in the strategy arena, from the traditional 'strategic *planning*', as 'a disciplined effort to produce fundamental decisions and actions that shape and guide what an organisation is, what it does, and why it does it' (Bryson 1995: 4–5) towards the idea of 'strategic *management*' as 'the process of strategic change' (Bowman and Asch 1987: 4), or as 'the process of making and implementing strategic decisions', 'strategic decisions' being those 'that determine the overall direction of an enterprise and its ultimate viability in light of the … changes that may occur in its … environments' (Quinn 1980: 4 as quoted in Mintzberg and Quinn 1996).

Using the term 'strategic *management*' as the whole process of innovation, strategic analysis, formulation, implementation and learning emphasizes the continuous nature of the process and makes it much more likely that any strategies which are decided on will actually be implemented. The term 'strategic management' will, therefore, be generally used throughout this book, unless specified otherwise.

SUMMARY

The potential benefits from the use of strategic management models and tools in the Third Sector have been summarized (Jackson and Irwin 2007) as follows:

- they help to clarify where the organization would like to be;
- they help the organization to understand risks;
- they help the organization to prioritize;
- they help to motive staff, volunteers, etc.;
- they help with fundraising;
- they help to coordinate different aspects of the work;
- they create opportunities for internal communication.

Courtney (2005) found that the benefits of engaging in strategic management were:

- creating a clearer organizational focus;
- increasing organizational unity;
- improved financial planning;
- improved programming and monitoring of performance;
- improved quality of services;
- improved organizational structure;
- improved sense of ownership by the staff;
- improved professionalism;
- improved funding/fundraising and the likelihood of long-term survival;
- assisting creative thinking and making the organization more business-like.

It has also been pointed out (Dart 2004; Reid and Griffith 2006) that strategic management processes have a legitimizing value, adopting what is seen as good practice, giving reassurance to stakeholders, including funders and board members.

Each of these potential benefits will be explored in Chapter 3 below. Some of the critiques of this approach will be examined in Chapter 4. The development of the use of strategic concepts and models in the Third Sector will be discussed in Chapter 5.

QUESTIONS

1. How would you define strategy, and why?
2. What defines something as 'strategic'?
3. What are the characteristics of a good strategy?

4. What is the difference between strategy and planning?
5. What is the difference between strategic planning and strategic management?
6. What are the potential benefits of strategic management?
7. Does a strategy have to be deliberate?

DISCUSSION TOPIC

Is strategy in the Third Sector different from in the private sector?

SUGGESTED READING

John M. Bryson (2011) *Strategic Planning for Public and Nonprofit Organizations*, Jossey-Bass.

Adrian Haberberg and Alison Rieple (2008) *Strategic Management Theory and Application*, Oxford University Press.

Sharon Oster (1995) *Strategic Management for Nonprofit Organizations*, Oxford.

3 THE DEVELOPMENT OF STRATEGIC MANAGEMENT

OVERVIEW

This chapter explores the development of the concept of strategy from its early origins in military and diplomatic contexts through the development of the various classic strategic planning schools in the 1960s and 1970s, which came to be adopted extensively by the private sector. Some of the limitations of each of the traditional strategic planning schools are explored.

LEARNING OBJECTIVES

After studying this chapter, you should be able to:

- describe the origins of the concept of 'strategy';
- explain the development of prescriptive military and diplomatic theories of effective strategies;
- describe the development of scientific 'one-best-way' approaches to management;
- describe the development of the concept of 'strategy' as applied to business;
- explain the ideas and critiques of the Design School;
- explain the ideas and critiques of the Planning School;
- explain the ideas and critiques of the Positioning School.

MILITARY AND DIPLOMATIC ORIGINS

In Athens around 508–7 BC, after leading a popular revolution against the Spartan supported oligarchy, Kleisthenes created ten political and military sub-units headed by an elected *strategos*. The Athenian war council was made up of these ten *strategoi*, who also, because of their roles, largely controlled non-military politics (Cummings 1993).

Strategos (as highlighted in the previous chapter) was a combination of the word *stratos*, which meant 'army', or more accurately an encamped army spread out over ground, and the word *agein*, which meant 'to lead'. The emergence of the term paralleled the development of the complexity of military decision-making.

The earliest known writings on strategy were by Sun Tzu, who lived 3,000 years ago and whose work, *The Art of War*, has been used to try to inform modern business leaders (Tzu 1963). Chanakya wrote the *Arthashastra* around 300 BC, in which he suggests various strategies, techniques and theories on the management of empires, the economy and the family. The work is often compared to the later works of Machiavelli. Aineias the Tactician wrote the earliest surviving Western volume on military strategy, *How to Survive under Siege*, in the mid-fourth century BC. He was primarily concerned with how to deploy the available human and other resources to best advantage. In the first century AD, Frontinus defined strategy as 'everything achieved by a commander, be it characterised by foresight, advantage, enterprise or resolution'.

Early Greek historians, poets and philosophers wrote extensively about the military and diplomatic exploits of key figures. Epaminondas of Thebes was said to have brought together the two divisions of the army, the infantry and the cavalry in a 'fruitful organisational blend'. His strategic principles included:

- economy of force coupled with overwhelming strength at the decisive point;
- close coordination between units and meticulous staff planning combined with speed of attack;
- the quickest and most economical way of winning a decision is defeat of the competition, not at its weakest point but at its strongest.

Epaminondas was advisor to Philip of Macedon, and under his guidance the Macedonian army was very successful, particularly under the control of Philip's son, Alexander the Great, famous for his contingency approach to strategy and whose battle strategies were said to have been replicated by Patton and Rommel in World War II (Quinn 1980).

Socrates, like von Clausewitz later (see p. 42), was aware of the analogy between warfare and business and the comparison between the duties of a general and a businessman, showing that both utilize plans to use resources to meet objectives.

In Europe, much was written about the mlitary campaigns of Napoleon, who even wrote his own military aphorisms published as *Maximes de Guerre* (Philips 1940; Chandler 2002), and Frederick the Great of Prussia, who introduced fundamental reforms to how an army should be organized. Machiavelli, considered by some to be the first real management thinker (Micklethwait and Wooldridge 1996), also wrote extensively about strategy in *The Prince*, applying many military concepts to the political and diplomatic arena. His writings too have been used to guide modern business leaders (Jay 1987). Amongst other things, Machiavelli (1950) was very conscious of the difficulties of bringing about organizational change:

> It should be borne in mind that there is nothing more difficult to arrange, more doubtful of success, and more dangerous to carry through than initiating changes...The innovator makes enemies of all those who prospered under the old order, and only lukewarm support is forthcoming from those who would prosper under the new. Their support is lukewarm partly from fear of their adversaries, who have the existing laws on their side, and partly because men are generally incredulous, never really trusting new things unless they have tested them by experience.

One of the greatest Western military thinkers was Karl von Clausewitz (1780–1831), famous for the saying that 'war is the continuation of politics by other means', who wrote in the aftermath of the Napoleonic Wars and drew on the experiences of Napoleon in defeating forces often much larger than his own. In the detailed *On War*, von Clausewitz (1976) proposed a number of principles of strategy to be used as building blocks in a particular situation. These included the following:

- have clearly defined, decisive and attainable objectives;
- offensive action is necessary to achieve decisive results;
- concentrate superior combat power at the critical time and place for decisive purpose;
- economic expenditure of resources;
- flexibility of manoeuvre to place the enemy at relative disadvantage;
- unity of command;
- security by measures to prevent surprise, preserve freedom of action and deny the enemy information;
- surprise the enemy;
- direct simple plans and clear concise orders to minimize misunderstanding.

The principles of von Clausewitz have been used to evaluate the military strategies of a range of different wars. They were used by Colonel Summers (1981) to demonstrate the shortcomings of the US military operation in Vietnam.

The two world wars in the twentieth century also provided enormous scope for military historians and strategists to analyse campaigns and try to draw out the lessons of success and failure. Communist leaders in the form of Lenin and Mao Zedong also wrote books about their own campaigns in order to educate others.

In more recent times many writers on business strategy have picked up on the spirit, and sometimes the letter, of these various military maxims. James (1985:56) describes 'the military experience (as) a veritable goldmine of competitive strategies all well tested under combat conditions'.

What, then, can be learnt from these exponents of military and diplomatic strategy? One of the most important lessons, perhaps, is, like von Clausewitz, to distinguish between strategy and tactics. Strategy is to do with achieving the overall political purpose; while tactics are to do with particular ploys or activities put in place to try to win advantage in a particular battle. How a particular battle is fought is a matter of tactics: the place, terms and conditions that it is fought on, and whether it should be fought at all, is a matter of strategy.

In the first book explicitly about strategy, as it relates to business, Chandler (1962) makes clear that tactical decisions must be made about day-to-day problems that might threaten the smooth functioning of the organization and its ongoing viability. However, strategic decisions are oriented to the future and are concerned with the long-term health of the organization. In his seminal work in 1954, *The Practice of Management*, Peter Drucker also highlighted the importance of this crucial distinction between strategic and tactical decisions for modern business.

Quinn (1980) argues that the analysis of military-diplomatic (and sporting) strategies provide some important insights into the nature of formal strategies of many kinds of organization. Firstly, he notes that the three main elements of successful military strategies are relevant to other sectors:

■ the development of clear goals to be achieved;

■ the setting of policies to guide or limit action;

■ the sequence of actions (within the limits set) to achieve the goals.

Secondly, he suggests that in a military context, effective strategies develop around 'a few key concepts and thrusts' which thereby provide cohesion and focus. Resources can then be allocated to ensure the success of these thrusts and that this is equally applicable in other non-military contexts.

Thirdly, he suggests that for all organizations, as well as the military, strategies need to be able to deal with the unpredictable and even unknowable, because it is never possible to be sure what will happen in future and what your opponent(s) may do. Therefore it is necessary to build a posture which is both flexible enough and strong enough to deal with all possible eventualities.

Lastly, for companies and other organizations, as well as the military, there needs to be a number of hierarchically integrated and supporting strategies, which are coherent in themselves with their own goals and thrusts and which are also integrated into the overall strategy.

Mintzberg *et al.* (1998) are particularly scathing of these kinds of maxims, which became popular following the publication of Peters and Waterman's (1982) *In Search of Excellence*. They produced four of their own maxims:

■ most maxims are obvious;

■ obvious maxims can be meaningless;

■ some obvious maxims are contradicted by other obvious maxims;

■ beware of maxims.

SCIENTIFIC MANAGEMENT

With its antecedents in military strategy it is perhaps no coincidence that the development of modern ideas of strategy and strategic planning for business began to develop shortly after World War II. However, a scientific approach to management had already been taking shape prior to this, starting with Adam Smith's *Wealth of Nations* in 1776 when he used the terms 'manage', 'manager' and even 'bad management' in referring to those persons responsible for running joint stock companies. Charles Babbage, who invented an early form of computer, published a treatise in 1832 advocating a scientific approach to the planning and organizing of work. However, it was two particular individuals in the early part of the twentieth century, who played a particularly important role in the development of the scientific approach to management, from their own experience in industry: Henri Fayol and Frederick W. Taylor.

Fayol, a Frenchman who became president director general of a mining company, in *General and Industrial Management* (1916) articulated five functions of management: planning, organizing, command, coordination and control. All of which would have made sense to the earlier military strategists discussed above, and which have become the classic descriptions of the role of a manager (see Chapter 15).

Taylor, an American and engineer by profession, published a ground-breaking book in 1911 entitled *The Principles of Scientific Management* which emphasized how better planning and organizing of work and training of staff could improve output. He advocated five basic principles:

1. shift all responsibility to the manager for the planning and design of the work;
2. use scientific methods to study each task and determine the most efficient and effective way that it can be carried out;
3. select the best person to carry out the specified task;
4. train the worker to do the job effectively and efficiently;
5. monitor the worker's performance to ensure the work is being carried out according to the specification.

Taylor advocated the use of detailed time and motion methods to observe, analyse and standardize work, so that even small tasks are broken down and performed in the prescribed and most efficient manner. Taylor's work focused very much on the operational aspects of the company at the level of operational workers.

Ralph C. Davis (1928, 1951) built on this early work on a scientific approach to management and introduced the rational-planning perspective, which has had enormous influence on both the theory and practice of strategy ever since. Davis viewed the primary purpose of a company as providing economic service. He thought that no firm could survive if it doesn't provide economic value. This economic value is created by the activities members engage in to create the organization's products or services. It is these activities that link the organization's objectives with its results. It is the responsibility of management to group these activities together in such a way as to form the structure of the organization – hence structure is contingent on objectives. This rational-planning perspective offered a simple model for designing an organization.

Lyndall Urwick, an English engineer, provided a biographical account of all the key figures in the development of the scientific approach to management in *The Golden Book of Management* (1956), having outlined his own views in *Elements of Administration* (as he described management). Interestingly he added 'forecasting' to the main elements of this fledgling science and acknowledged that flexibility is required in planning.

This 'scientific' rational closed-system approach to the planning and organizing of work has had a profound effect on management methods up to and including the present day (for example in the development of management by objectives and business process re-engineering initiatives). It describes well the approach of many current businesses, such as fast-food outlets. The approach has important strengths in the context of a stable environment, a simple product and where precision and standardization are paramount. However, the dehumanizing effect on human beings of being treated as a part of a machine has had major implications. The approach is also not appropriate when the environment is constantly changing, requiring the organization to adapt and change on a frequent basis; when the task is complex and requires the worker to use his or her brain to develop solutions; or when flexibility and cross-team working is required. It also sits uncomfortably in the Third Sector which often requires flexibility and a high level of participation in decision-making.

ECONOMIC GROWTH AND THE DEVELOPMENT OF THE STRATEGIC PLANNING CONCEPT

The 1950s saw a major expansion in Western industrial economies and the globalization of many large companies. Long-term financial and management planning and control became a key feature of the 1950s (Greenley 1989) as these large firms tried to control what was happening, perhaps thousands of miles away.

Peter Drucker's (1964) *Managing for Results*, where objectives are determined at the top of the organization and cascade down through the organization in a structured and systematic way, became very popular, creating strong alignment throughout organizations. This approach reflected the mechanistic paradigm articulated by Taylor, Fayol and others and the closed system paradigm of organizational theory at that time (Robbins 1990).

The 1960s represented a move towards a more open systems perspective on organizations (Katz and Kahn 1966) and the beginning of modern strategic planning theory and practice. The 1960s was also a period of substantial expansion of industrial economies and the growth of national and multinational companies into new markets and new products. This raised critical questions for expanding companies as to what products to produce and which markets to target. Strategic planning became the key tool to use to try and answer these questions. Indeed perhaps *the* seminal work on strategic planning, *Corporate Strategy* by H. Igor Ansoff (1965), professor at the Carnegie Institute of Technology, was subtitled 'an analytic approach to business policy for growth and expansion', which is an indication of how bullish American industry was during this period, prior to the oil crisis of the mid-1970s and the rise of the Japanese and other eastern economies.

The first use of the term 'strategy' to refer to business was by Chandler (1962) in his pioneering work *Strategy and Structure*, which studied the evolution of management in big corporations in the USA. It was used again, in 1964, in Drucker's seminal work mentioned above. Indeed Drucker has stated (1985) that he originally wanted 'strategy' in the title, but was dissuaded by the publishers because of the danger of misunderstanding.

The pioneers of strategy as applied to business in the 1960s and 1970s fall into three main overlapping schools, which remain extremely influential today despite their detractors. These are the Design School, the Planning School and the Positioning School.

DESIGN SCHOOL

The origins of the Design School can be traced back to two influential books written at the University of California (Berkeley) and at the Massachusetts Institute of

Technology: *Leadership in Administration*, by Philip Selznick (1957), and the already mentioned *Strategy and Structure*, by Alfred Chandler (1962). Selznick, in particular, introduced the idea of 'distinctive competence', highlighting the need to bring together an organization's 'internal state' with its 'external expectations' and arguing for building 'policy into the organisation's social structure', which later become known as 'implementation'. The Design School is represented primarily by Ken Andrews and others from the Harvard Business School, first of all in its basic textbook *Business Policy: Text and Cases* (Learned *et al.* 1965) and then in one of the seminal works of the Design School, *The Concept of Corporate Strategy*, by Andrews, first published in 1971. In it Andrews defined 'corporate strategy' as:

> the pattern of decisions in a company that determines and reveals its objectives, purposes or goals, and defines the range of business the company is to pursue, the kind of economic and human organisation it is or intends to be, and the nature of the economic and non-economic contribution it intends to make to its shareholders, employees, customers, and communities. (1987: 18–19)

Andrews stressed the crucial role of the CEO in corporate strategy, as the organization leader, personal leader and architect of the organization's purpose. He summarized the four responsibilities of the chief officer as:

1. securing the attainment of planned results in the present;
2. developing an organization capable of producing both technical achievement and human satisfaction;
3. making a distinctive personal contribution;
4. planning and executing policy decisions affecting future results.

Andrews distinguished clearly between the formulation of strategy, which involves matching external opportunity with corporate capability and attaching estimates of risk to each option, and its implementation. He summarized the four main components of strategy as:

1. market opportunity;
2. corporate competence and resources;
3. personal values and aspirations;
4. acknowledged obligations to people in society other than shareholders.

In 2, 3 and 4, Andrews was well ahead of his time, foreshadowing key themes which would play a key role in management thinking more than 30 years later on core competencies, business ethics, corporate responsibility and the importance of stakeholders. These concerns also reflect some of the particular values and interests of the Third Sector.

Andrews also recognized the importance of having the appropriate organizational structure in place, in order to: coordinate activities; appropriate organizational processes, which are directed towards the kind of behaviour required by the organizational purpose; and install suitable top management leadership. In relation to evaluating the various possible strategies, he suggested ten questions to help judge a strategy:

1. Is the strategy simple and identifiable, and has it been made clear either in words or in practice?
2. Is the strategy in some way unique/distinctive?
3. Does the strategy fully exploit domestic and international environmental opportunity?
4. Is the strategy consistent with corporate competence and resources, both present and projected?
5. Are the major provisions of the strategy and the programme of major policies of which it is comprised internally consistent?
6. Is the chosen level of risk feasible in economic and personal terms?
7. Is the strategy appropriate to the personal values and aspirations of the key managers?
8. Is the strategy appropriate to the desired level of contribution to society?
9. Does the strategy constitute a clear stimulus to organizational effort and commitment?
10. Are there early indications of the responsiveness of markets and market segments to the strategy?

In summary he suggested that, regardless of the size of the organization, the essential elements of the strategic management process are the same, namely:

- participation by key individuals in the identification of problems and strategic opportunities;
- inclusion of personal preferences, organization values and corporate capability in the analysis;
- the marshalling of accurate and relevant data on further market growth;
- the recognition of financial constraints with respect to capital sources and projected return.

Mintzberg (1994) summarized the main features of the Harvard-based Design School, which included Andrews, as follows:

- strategy formulation should be a controlled, conscious process of thought;
- responsibility for the process must rest with the CEO: that person is *the* strategist (i.e. the 'architect');
- the model of strategy formation must be kept simple and informal;
- strategies should be unique: the best ones result from a process of creative design, based on distinctive (now called 'core') competencies;
- strategies must come out of the design process fully developed;
- the strategies should be made explicit and, if possible, articulated, which means they have to be kept simple;
- once these unique, full-blown, explicit and simple strategies are fully formulated, they must then be implemented.

To the lay person however, the lasting overt legacy of the Design School is probably SWOT analysis which analyses the strengths and weaknesses of the firm and the threats and opportunities of the external environment and tries to produce an appropriate fit of the organization to its environment. SWOT analysis has become one of the most frequently used strategic planning tools (see Chapters 7 and 8).

Despite its enduring influence there have, however, been a number of important critiques of the Design School. These are summarized by Mintzberg *et al.* (1998) and include the following:

- it denies the importance of incremental or emergent strategies;
- by arguing that structure always follows strategy it denies the importance of existing competencies and therefore of structure on strategy;
- it ignores the importance of other players as well as the chief executive in formulating strategy;
- articulating strategy during periods of uncertainty can lead to blinkered thinking and 'premature closure';
- like other rational approaches the issue of creativity and innovation is not addressed. Great strategies, the authors argue, tend to be those that redefine the nature of the market and the business and do not just follow logically from the analysis.

Mintzberg *et al.* (1998) do, however, suggest that the approach of the Design School can be particularly valuable in particular circumstances where:

- one brain can, in principle, handle all of the information relevant for strategy formulation – and that brain is able to have full, detailed, intimate knowledge of the situation in question;
- the relevant knowledge must be established before a new intended strategy has to be implemented – in other words, the situation has to remain relatively stable or at least predictable;
- the organization must be able to cope with a centrally articulated strategy, i.e. defer to a central strategist.

PLANNING SCHOOL

At the same time as Harvard was publishing its original textbook on corporate strategy, Igor Ansoff at the Carnegie Institute of Technology was publishing his classic work, *Corporate Strategy* (Ansoff 1965). The Planning School, as those who become associated with Ansoff's ideas came to be known, had many similarities with the Design School. However, Ansoff did not believe that the process could be kept simple and informal and proposed a complex model of strategic planning. The Planning School also put much greater emphasis on setting formal objectives, rather than the Design School's stress on the concept of values.

Mintzberg in *The Rise and Fall of Strategic Planning* (1994) summarizes the three basic premises of the Planning School as follows:

1. strategy formation should be controlled and conscious as well as a formalized and elaborated process, decomposed into distinct steps, each delineated by checklists and supported by techniques;

2. responsibility for the overall process rests with the chief executive in principle – responsibility for its execution rests with the staff planners in practice;

3. strategies come out of this process fully developed, typically as generic positions, to be explicated so that they can then be implemented through detailed attention to objectives, budgets, programmes and operating plans of various kinds.

The particular model that Ansoff developed in the first edition of *Corporate Strategy* has a number of key features. Firstly, the strategic options for growth and expansion are potentially various combinations of new and existing products and new and existing markets. He developed a matrix of the various possibilities, to show that there are only four basic strategic options:

- sell existing products in existing markets;
- sell new products in existing markets;
- sell existing products in new markets; and/or
- sell new products in new markets.

The Ansoff matrix, as this became known, has also been adapted for use in the Third Sector (Courtney 1996).

Secondly, Ansoff stressed the importance of recognizing different levels of decisions: strategy, policy, programme, and standard operating procedure. The level of uncertainty and risk decreases as one moves down this list, which therefore can be delegated accordingly down the organization. All but the first (strategy) also reduce the requirement to make an original decision each time a decision is required. They thus create consistency of action, what Ansoff calls 'economies of management'. Ansoff also recognized the necessity of cascading decisions down through an organization from the aggregate to the specific.

Ansoff (1965: 25–26) proposed the importance of 'gap analysis', which he described as follows:

> The procedure within each step of the cascade is similar. (1) A set of objectives is established. (2) The difference (the 'gap') between the current position of the firm and the objectives is estimated. (3) One or more courses of action (strategy) are proposed. (4) These are tested for their 'gap-reducing properties'. A course is accepted if it substantially closes the gap; if it does not, new alternatives are tried.

Ansoff also argued for the importance of the concept of 'synergy' which has become of crucial importance in modern business thinking. He described it as the $2 + 2 = 5$ factor which helped to explain the basic notion of 'fit' in the design of organization strategy. He defined it as any 'effect which can produce a combined return on the firm's resources greater than the sum of its parts' (ibid.: 79).

The closely related Design and Planning Schools inspired the development of a large number of one-best-way strategic planning models and 'how to' publications which tended to have a number of common features. These features were:

- strategy as a rational decision-making process;
- a thorough analysis of the competitive environment;
- a thorough analysis of the organization's resources and distinctive/core competencies (i.e. what it does specifically well);
- the setting of clear goals/objectives;
- the evaluation of different strategic options;
- a hierarchy of objectives;
- effective implementation.

POSITIONING SCHOOL

Michael E. Porter, a professor at Harvard, in his seminal work in 1980, *Competitive Strategy*, used economic perspectives to analyse strategy and argued that the profit available in a particular industry was strongly affected by competition. This competition could be analysed using five key factors:

- the rivalry amongst existing firms in the industry;
- the threat of new entrants to the industry, depending on how easy or difficult it is to enter the industry;
- the bargaining power of buyers (are they few or many?);
- the bargaining power of suppliers, including labour (are there few or many?);
- the threat of substitute products.

To Porter (1980: 35), then, the purpose of formulating competitive strategy 'is to find a position...where the company can best defend itself against these...forces, or can influence them in its favour'.

Unlike the Design and Planning Schools which put no limitation on the type of strategies that an organization can adopt, Porter argued that there are basically only three generic strategies to deal with these five forces. These are:

- overall-cost leadership, i.e. producing more cheaply then your rivals;
- differentiation, i.e. producing a product or service that is seen as unique;
- focus on a very particular market segment or geographical area and meeting their specific requirements better than 'competitors who compete more broadly'.

From Porter's perspective, strategists do not so much design strategies but rather select them from the list of generic strategies.

Porter's (1985) second major work, *Competitive Advantage*, reinforced the message of his previous book but added a number of concepts that have played a crucial role in business thinking.

He stressed the importance, not only of gaining competitive advantage, but also of making this advantage sustainable over the long term, usually by continual improvement. In relation to Third Sector organizations, however, the lack of a profit bottom-line and identifiable competitors led to the suggestion that Porter's concept of 'competitive advantage' has little relevance for Third Sector organizations (Goold 1997). However, it has been adapted for use by non-profit organizations (see Oster 1995; Lindenberg 2001).

One of Porter's most important ideas, however, was, arguably, that of the value chain, i.e. the sequence of activities which are strategically relevant because they are what enables the firm to provide value for the buyer. These activities may fall into a number of different categories, which he separates into 'primary' and 'support'. Primary activities include:

- inbound logistics (inputs/supplies);
- operations (the transformation of these inputs into final products);
- outbound logistics (storage and distribution);
- marketing and sales;
- service (e.g. maintenance).

Support activities include:

- procurement;
- technology development;
- human resource management;
- firm infrastructure (e.g. planning, finance, legal, quality management).

Porter's concept of the value chain played an important role in the development of both total quality management and business process engineering. These initiatives were particularly influential in the 1980s and early 1990s.

Bruce Henderson (1979), founder of the Boston Consulting Group, was cynical about the traditional strategic planning that was prevalent in the late 1970s and early 1980s. He believed that sociobiology provided important clues to understanding the behaviour of firms. He viewed modern business as the product of selection brought about by natural competition and that it owes more to intuition, expediency and chance than it does to 'an integrated strategy' (1984). Whittington (1993) describes this as the 'evolutionary perspective', which asserts that the best businesses are selected by the competitive forces of the market. Such evolutionist theorists doubt the capacity of organizations to achieve deliberate adaptation *to* the environment, as opposed to the Darwinian selection *by* the environment. This perspective suggests that engaging in long-term planning is of little value: organizations should focus on trying to be as efficient as they can.

The Boston Consulting Group, however, developed a number of strategy models and tools that have been used by companies all over the world in the last 30 years. The most famous of the models and tools is the Boston Matrix for Portfolio Analysis. This is used to assess existing products, services or businesses and determine what the company's strategy should be in relation to each (i.e. invest, harvest or divest), depending on its relationship to market share and market growth.

Porter's approach has been criticized for focusing almost entirely on the environmental determinants of organizational performance and ignoring the unique characteristics and competencies of organizations, such as the ability to innovate (Barney 1991; Wright *et al.* 1994; Zack 2005). Lindenberg (2001), in a case study of US world development NGO, CARE, found Porter's framework useful for the organization in considering its position in the world development sector, although it only had medium adaptability to the Third Sector.

Mintzberg *et al.* (1998) criticize the Positioning School on a number of fronts, including the basic criticisms of the Design and Planning Schools, because it is based on similar predispositions (separating thinking and doing; the leader as the strategist; etc.). The other criticisms include:

- the focus is too narrow on economics, ignoring political, social and cultural factors;
- there is a bias towards the big stable established companies;
- what industry any particular company is in is not as clear in practice as it is in reality and the definition of an industry is constantly changing;
- the strategy process is a rational number-crunching one rather than a process of experimentation and learning;
- there is no place for engendering commitment and energy in the Positioning School;
- the focus on generic strategies tends to go against companies developing unique innovative strategies;
- the evidence is that there is more difference between companies in the same industry than between different industries (Rumelt 1991; McGahan and Porter 1997).

CHALLENGES TO THE RATIONAL STRATEGY SCHOOLS

The general consensus, in relation to the analytical rational approaches to strategy, began to be challenged in the mid-1970s. These challenges were (i) at the theoretical level, reflecting alternative perspectives on organizations that were being developed, including post-modernism, contingency theory, social constructionism, political and cultural perspectives; and (ii) at a practical level, as a result of the first oil crisis – when the failure of planners to predict the crisis and the resultant problems experienced by firms whose strategies were formulated with, as it turned out, an erroneous set of assumptions about fuel prices – and the relentless success of Japanese companies without the use of any apparent strategic planning methods.

The result was a shift of focus away from *planning* to the concept of *positioning to maximize profitability* (Craig and Grant 1993). Diversification was a common thrust in this period, whereby firms could limit the damage caused by incorrect assumptions about external factors in relation to one particular product or market by diversifying into various markets with a wider range of products.

SUMMARY

This chapter has explored the origins of the concepts of strategy and strategic planning, from its early military and diplomatic use, through the development of a 'scientific' approach to management, to the three classic, and still influential, approaches to strategic planning in the private sector, the Design, Planning, and Positioning Schools. The importance of each of these Schools and the critiques that have been made of each have been explored.

QUESTIONS

1. What are the origins of the concept of 'strategy'?
2. What military principles of strategy might be relevant to today's organizations?
3. In what ways are the scientific approaches of Taylor and Fayol still relevant today?
4. What assumptions underpin the Design and Planning strategy schools?
5. What are the weaknesses of the Design and Planning Schools?
6. Why did strategic planning expand from the 1950s onwards?
7. What are the strengths and weaknesses of Porter's five-factor industry analysis?
8. How relevant is Porter's five-factor industry analysis to the Third Sector?
9. What factors are most important for a Third Sector organization in assessing its existing portfolio of programmes?

DISCUSSION TOPIC

Do military and diplomatic strategies have any relevance for today's Third Sector?

SUGGESTED READING

Adrian Haberberg and Alison Rieple (2008) *Strategic Management Theory and Application*, Oxford University Press.

Henry Mintzberg (1994) *The Rise and Fall of Strategic Planning*, Prentice-Hall.

Henry Mintzberg, Bruce Ahlstrand and Joseph Lampel (1998) *Strategy Safari*, Prentice-Hall.

J. I. Moore (1992) *Writers on Strategy and Strategic Management*, Penguin.

4 CRITICISMS OF THE STRATEGIC MANAGEMENT APPROACH

OVERVIEW

The traditional schools of thought on strategy and strategic planning were discussed in Chapter 3 and have continued to dominate the practice of strategic management. Academia has developed various alternative ways of thinking about strategy. This chapter explores the criticisms of the traditional schools of strategic management and discusses a number of alternative perspectives, particularly the Learning and Political Schools. The more pragmatic 'new modernist' approaches to strategy in the 1990s, which are closer to the values and culture of many Third Sector organizations, are also explored.

LEARNING OBJECTIVES

After studying this chapter, you should be able to:

- explain the perceived weaknesses in the classic rational approaches to strategy;
- describe the importance of continuous learning and experimentation at all levels within an organization reflected in the Learning School;
- explain the bounded rationality of strategic decision-making and the importance of power and negotiation in the strategic choices that are made;
- outline the main characteristics of the pragmatic 'new modernist' approach to strategy being adopted in the 1990s.

LIMITS OF PLANNING

Mintzberg (1994) argues that, while planning is important, an over-emphasis on detailed formal long-range planning can push out other processes that are equally important. In particular, the creation and development of powerful visions can become ossified into rigid strategic positions, without the flexibility to respond to change. Quinn (quoted in Mintzberg 1994: 139) came to a similar conclusion, that

> a good deal of corporate planning I have observed is like a ritual rain dance; it has no effect on the weather that follows, but those who engage in it think it does.

Moreover, it seems to me that much of the advice and instruction related to corporate planning is directed at improving the dancing, not the weather.

In the traditional top-down rigid planning approaches, the process of continuous learning can also be lost, pushed out by long-range forecasts, one, three or five-year planning cycles, etc., which allow for little flexibility. Mintzberg, and Stacey (1993), argue for the crucial importance of learning (discovery, choice and action) in the continuous process of making strategic decisions. Mintzberg, indeed, argues that even the basic terminology surrounding strategy formulation is unhelpful. He sees it as much more of an art form, a craft like that of a potter. In crafting strategy,

> what springs to mind is not so much thinking and reason as involvement, a feeling of intimacy and harmony with the materials at hand developed through long experience and commitment. Formulation and implementation merge into a fluid process of learning, through which creative strategies evolve. (Mintzberg 1987: 66)

As well as various practical pitfalls to avoid in strategic planning, Mintzberg (1994) argues that traditional strategic planning is based on a number of fundamental and interrelated fallacies:

1. The assumption of detachment: that planners not involved in the operational aspects of the organization can successfully craft strategy. Mintzberg argues that they can't as they don't have a real intuitive feel for the business. Carr (1996) argues that strategic planning failed because companies tended to relegate it to its own separate department away from the realities and challenges companies faced, making it largely irrelevant.

2. The assumption of quantification: that strategy can be driven by hard facts about the organization and its environment, when strategy is actually about creating something new, which requires intuition based as much on 'soft' information.

3. The assumption of predeterminism: that it is in any way possible to predict the consequences of any particular action.

4. The assumption of formalization: that the strategy-making process can be programmed by the use of systems rather than the vision and learning of those deeply involved in the business.

Business leaders in the 1970s and 1980s also became disillusioned with formal strategic planning processes. John Harvey-Jones (1987: 8), a former chief executive of ICI, for example, described the implementation of strategic planning at its height:

> In many organisations planning became the job and responsibility of an increasingly specialised planning department, who were divorced from the everyday business and sought to apply theoretical measures of a quantified type to the complexities of business decisions. All too often in those days one was faced with plans produced by the staff that seemed somewhat remote or at variance with one's own experience of the actual behaviour of the market in which one was operating. But another and even more worrying variant of the same problem arose when the plans laid would have been helpful in a business sense, but were not followed because of the illusive lack of commitment in a decentralised organisation.

Ohmae (1982: 3) even compared the state of strategic planning at the beginning of the 1980s with the kind of centralized planning of the Soviet economy:

> We have all witnessed the heyday of the giant enterprise, the days when it seemed that big US companies, and later big European companies, could really end up controlling the whole world. Something happened to prevent it. There has been a marked decline in the ability of large corporations to cope with the changes that confront them. In these companies, brains and muscles were separated, destroying the entire body's co-ordination. On the one hand there were the brains; on the other there was the muscle – the people of the enterprise. They were there to make the plan a reality, to carry out the brain's instructions... In effect, most large US corporations are run like the Soviet economy. Many are centrally planned for three to five years, with their managers' actions spelled out in impressive detail for both normal and contingency conditions. During the ongoing implementation process, each manager is 'monitored' on how accurately he has been adhering to the agreed objectives. Long study of communist and socialist regimes has convinced many observers that detailed long-range planning coupled with tight control from the center is a remarkably effective way of killing creativity and entrepreneurship at the extremities of the organisation.

These quotes suggest that the perceived failure of strategic planning in the late 1970s and 1980s was caused by the approach becoming top-down, technique ridden, led by planning and forecasting experts, and divorced from the day-to-day management process.

Steiner (1979) supported this position and argued that the problems were caused by:

- planning being delegated to planners and top management failing to spend time themselves on long-range planning;
- the process being over-formalized and driving out innovation;
- planning processes in use not being regularly monitored and reviewed;
- top managers ignoring the plan in practice and making intuitive decisions;
- poor quality goal-setting and failure to use the plan as a framework for reviewing management performance.

The impact of this kind of rigid approach in practice, the lack of consistent evidence for its effectiveness, theoretical difficulties in supporting strategic planning, and the increasing turbulence of the external environment led, in the 1980s, to strategy falling down the agenda of private sector companies. In a 1996 survey of 100 chief executives of top UK and US companies, 'future strategy' only ranked sixth on their agenda. Only 14 per cent put strategy at the top of their list.

Much of the focus in the difficult economic circumstances in the West in the early 1990s moved to cost-cutting programmes, such as business process re-engineering (Hammer and Champy 1993), downsizing and delayering, what Hamel and Prahalad (1994) call 'corporate anorexia'. The consequence of this shift over a significant period, according to Kare-Silver (1997), was that the art of future planning and strategy was lost and the in-house skills were no longer there to revive it. Kare-Silver argued that much of the difficulty with strategic planning and management was the use of models and tools that were out-of-date, having been developed for a different era.

Ralph D. Stacey (1993), professor in strategic management at the Business School, University of Hertfordshire, drawing on the insights of chaos theory, went further and argued that the fundamental assumptions underlying traditional strategic planning, based on cybernetics, the study of artificial or natural systems which store information and use feedback mechanisms to guide and control their behaviour, are fundamentally flawed. He argued that the system that managers have to cope with is now too complex to allow them to instigate fully the future strategic direction of their organization. In other words, the complexity of the system is such that new strategic direction can only emerge, which is closer to the concept of incremental learning.

THE LEARNING SCHOOL

Quinn's work, mentioned above, is often described as being in the Incremental or Learning School. Adherents to these Schools are not convinced that the classical, rational, deliberate approaches to strategy formation represented by the Design, Planning and Positioning Schools represent the truth as to how strategy is actually developed in organizations.

It was research in the public, rather than the private, sector, by Lindblom (1959), published as *The Science of Muddling Through*, that initiated the Incremental or Learning School. In this work Lindblom suggested that, in the public sector, policymaking is not a neat rational linear process, but a messy one in which policymakers struggle with making sense of a world that is very complicated. Key to this school is a descriptive rather than prescriptive approach. The adherents to this approach suggest that major strategic moves rarely occur as a result of a structured strategic planning process, but can rather be traced back to small actions or decisions by actors who may not even be senior in the organization. This suggests a definition of strategy (see Chapter 2) as 'pattern' (Mintzberg 1994) rather than 'plan'.

From interviews with the chief executives of large companies in the US, Quinn (1980) concluded that planning did not describe how they formulated their strategies either. In contrast, he coined the expression 'logical incrementalism', drawing on Lindblom to describe the process where,

> real strategy tends to evolve as internal decisions and external events flow together to create a new, widely shared consensus for action among key members of the top management team. In well-run organizations, managers pro-actively guide these streams of actions and events incrementally towards conscious strategies … successful managers who operate with logical incrementalism build the seeds of understanding, identity and commitment into the very processes that create their strategies. By the time the strategy begins to crystallize in focus, pieces of it are already being implemented. Through their strategic formulation processes, they have built a momentum and psychological commitment to the strategy, which causes it to flow toward flexible implementation. Constantly integrating the simultaneous incremental processes of strategy formulation and implementation is the central art of effective strategic management. (Quinn 1980: 15; 145)

Quinn, however, in keeping with the approaches of the Design, Planning and Positioning Schools, still viewed the senior managers and the CEO as the key actors in the strategy process.

Other writers have focused on the important role of innovation within an organization in driving strategy, what has been called 'internal venturing' or 'intrapreneurship' (Pinchot 1985), which involves the skills and initiative of people who act deep within the corporate hierarchy. Strategic initiatives, according to Burgelman (1980), often develop deep in the hierarchy and are then championed, or given impetus, by middle-level managers who seek the authorization of senior executives. He stresses the importance of these individuals at the operational level in the organization who often initiate the first step in the innovative process. Previous work on corporate strategy had tended to ignore their role by focusing almost entirely on senior management, particularly the CEO. In the Learning School, top management still has a crucial role in creating the environment where this internal venturing can flourish, where innovation could take place with the support of management, and where new corporate competencies can be developed.

Centralized formal strategic planning and the emergent learning perspectives, although often presented as being in opposition to each other, are not necessarily entirely contradictory. The central top-down umbrella strategy (Mintzberg and Waters 1997) may establish the space, support and culture within which the bottom-up experimentation and learning can take place and enable strategies to emerge and become key strategies for the future (Anderson 2000). In the words of Eccles and Nohria (1997: 61):

> Strategy is a messy combination of both these perspectives...rational, top-down 'strategic plans' *can* effectively set the context for individual action. But people in firms always pursue their own strategic agendas as well, and many of these autonomous initiatives can end up as an important part of firm-wide strategy. Formal plans must be flexible enough to accommodate these emergent actions, which typically rely on individual intuition, timing and circumstances.

While the rational prescriptive strategy schools are primarily about planning and control, this new emergent school is very much about learning at the individual, team and corporate level in an organization through experimentation and discovery (Bartlett and Ghoshal 1998) and is well reflected in the approach of many firms in the fast moving IT industry.

Mintzberg, in Mintzberg *et al.* (1998), has postulated a grassroots model of strategic formations. In this model, strategies grow like weeds in a garden: they are not cultivated like tomatoes in a greenhouse. They can take root in all kinds of places: virtually anywhere people have the capacity to learn and the resources to support that capacity. Such strategies become organizational when they become collective, that is when the patterns proliferate, consciously or unconsciously, to pervade the behaviour of the organization at large. New strategies, which may be emerging continuously, tend to pervade the organization during periods of change, which punctuate periods of more integrated continuity. To manage this process is not to preconceive strategies but to recognize their emergence and intervene when appropriate.

Literature on organizations as learning systems goes back to the early 1960s with Cyert and Marsh's (1963) *A Behavioral Theory of the Firm* and was further developed in the 1970s, particularly by Argyris and Schon (1978), who put forward the concepts of single and double-loop learning. Single-loop learning reflects the traditional approach to strategy where the only learning is how to take corrective action to ensure the implementation of agreed goals. Double-loop learning allows a much wider scope to learning which can result in fundamental changes to goals and values. They also suggest a third level, deutero-learning, which encourages enquiry into the learning system itself.

Building on the approach of Argyris and Schon, Peter Senge (2000: 4), argues that organizations that will truly excel in the future will be 'the organisations that discover how to tap people's commitment and capacity to learn at all levels in an organisation'. He suggests that the key elements of the learning organization are:

- systems thinking: recognizing that organizations are complex systems;
- personal mastery: not only the development of particular work-related skills, but also the transformation of individuals so they accomplish things they really care about;
- mental models: the organization's driving and fundamental values and principles;
- shared vision: the co-creation of a shared vision of the future;
- team learning: the process of dialogue and discussion, to explore new ideas creatively and then narrow them down to choose the best alternatives.

Senge generated a new interest in the concept of the learning company. He considered that there are three key roles for a leader in a learning company:

- as a designer of the mission, vision and values of the organization and the structures and policies that create learning;
- as teacher, in the sense of helping everyone to gain new insights;
- as steward: stewardship for the people they lead and stewardship for the wider mission of the organization.

In Senge's words (1990: 13) 'people's natural impulse to learn is unleashed when they are engaged in an endeavour they consider worthy of their fullest commitment', a perspective that would be endorsed strongly in many parts of the Third Sector.

Lampel, in Mintzberg *et al.* (1998), summarizes the main principles of the Learning School as follows:

- organizations can learn as much, if not more, from failure as from success;
- a learning organization rejects the adage 'if it ain't broke don't fix it';
- learning organizations assume that the managers and workers closest to the design, manufacturing, distribution and sale of the product often know more about these activities than their superiors;
- a learning organization actively seeks to move knowledge from one part of the organization to another;
- learning organizations spend a lot of energy looking outside their own boundaries for knowledge.

The Learning School perspective provides a useful counterbalance to the mechanistic approaches of the classic rational planning schools, and, as such, is a useful perspective for the Third Sector. However, there is also the danger of going too far in the other direction. The development of a large number of innovations and experiments can result in a lack of direction or shared vision or focus. In a crisis, in particular, muddling through without a clear unified vision of the future can be a disaster. There is also the danger of strategic drift where the organization, over time, moves away from an effective strategy towards a less desirable one, as a result of a series of small steps (for example, following inappropriate funding opportunities – what Charles Handy calls 'strategic seduction').

It is also important not to ignore the real issues of power and self-interest in an organization which may influence which innovations are promoted and which are not. Indeed the Learning School has been criticized for ignoring power issues and suggesting that a learning organization is 'a utopia to be ushered in through the pursuit of shared goals in a climate of collaborative high trust and a rational approach to the resolution of differences' (Coopey 1995: 199), whereas 'what is deemed worth learning has already been selected, because only those in power learn the right things' (Gherardi 1999: 106).

In the learning organization the legitimization of learning is determined by the criteria for organizational success (Garrick and Rhodes 1998). Staff are encouraged to identify with the goals of the organization and to give full commitment to learning to achieve these goals. This is a common aspiration of many Third Sector organizations. However, real learning may result in a questioning of the legitimacy, not only of these goals, but also of the dominant modes of thought in the organization. This is reminiscent of Argyris and Schon's double loop learning (1978).

THE RESOURCE–BASED SCHOOL

The resource-based view of strategy (Barney 1991; Ambrosini 2007) which has become popular since the 1990s has a number of useful insights which help to elaborate the simple technique of looking at the internal strengths of an organization.

The resource-based view distinguishes between resources which are the basic inputs/ assets of the organization, e.g. buildings, equipment, technology, finance, staff. These are the basic units of analysis along with capabilities (also sometimes called 'distinctive competencies' (Kay 1993) or 'core competencies' (Hamel and Prahalad 1994)), which include the collective learning of the organization and the distinctive ways that the organizational resources are coordinated and configured together in teams or bundles of resources (strategic architecture) to exploit the organization's unique characteristics in achieving its objectives (Grant 1997). This strategic architecture can also include how the organization is linked to other organizations, which can be critical in the success of a Third Sector organization and sometimes difficult to emulate.

It would be very rare that an organization's success was based on a single resource or even several individual resources. The resource-based view is therefore concerned with how the organization organizes the various resources in synergy to create a successful organization. Grant suggests a model of strategic analysis using the resource-based view, which can be adapted for use by the board and staff of Third Sector organizations:

1. Identify and classify the organization's resources. Appraise strengths and weaknesses relative to other organizations. Identify opportunities for better utilization of resources.

2. Identify the organization's capabilities. What can the organization do more effectively than other organizations? Identify the resources inputs to each capability, and the complexity of each capability.

3. Appraise the potential of resources and capabilities to meet need and/or generate resources.

4. Select a strategy that best exploits the organization's resources and capabilities relative to external opportunities.

5. Identify resource gaps which need to be filled. Invest in replenishing, augmenting and upgrading the organization's resource base.

Grant (1997) highlights the main problem in appraising capabilities: the difficulty in maintaining objectivity. He suggests that organizations fall victim to 'past glories, hopes for the future, and wishful thinking', which lead the organization to assume that they are better than other organizations in key areas, when in fact they are not. Obtaining an objective view from key stakeholders, as suggested above, can be a useful counterbalance to this tendency.

Creating distinctive capabilities is not just a case of assembling a team of resources: capabilities involve complex patterns of coordination between people and other resources. Such coordination requires the development of organizational routines (Nelson and Winter 1982), regular and predictable patterns of activity made up of a sequence of coordinated actions. These routines need to be learnt and embedded through repetition. The development of these routines can lead to organizational efficiency, but there is also often a trade-off with flexibility. A turbulent external environment usually requires a flexible response from an organization. It can be difficult to change rapidly deeply embedded organizational routines.

The language of competitive advantage is not one often used by Third Sector organizations. However, in the fields of social economy, fundraising or competing for contracts from a local authority, or in recruiting volunteers, it is hard not to recognize that the organization is competing with others, Third Sector and otherwise. In these circumstances, Third Sector organizations have no choice but to maximize the potential of their resources and capabilities and in a way that is sustainable for as long as possible. According to the resource-based view, this sustainability is based on four key factors:

1. Durability: the extent that internal resources are sustainable, i.e. do not depreciate. An expensive mobile screening unit for a medical charity may depreciate relatively quickly, for example. An organization's reputation may be much more durable. The skills of particular trustees or staff may be lost when they retire or move to another organization. This is a good example of where the capability of trustees or staff needs to be embedded in a way that is not lost, when a particular trustee, staff member or members leave.

2. Transparency: the extent that other organizations can assess the capability advantage that another organization has and can replicate it. Many activities of Third Sector organizations are public and therefore relatively easy to replicate. Therefore

an organization that gets first mover advantage in developing a new kind of fund-raising activity, for example, often does not have it for long as other organizations can see the success and easily emulate it. Many fundraising events therefore often have a short lifecycle.

3. Transferability: the extent that the resources and capabilities that one organization has can be acquired or developed by another. A new children's charity, for example, cannot easily develop the reputation of a Save the Children Fund, Barnardo's or the NSPCC. But they could develop the capacity to engage in a direct mail campaign (which is often outsourced). Geographical location can also be a significant factor in transferability.

4. Replicability: the extent that the distinctive resources and capabilities of a successful organization can be replicated by internal development. Some capabilities may be relatively easy to replicate by training a member of staff or trustee, for example. Others may be much more difficult to replicate, like an organization's ability to motivate staff and volunteers, or good decision-making by the board.

THE POLITICAL SCHOOL

As suggested above, a difficulty with the rational structural approach to strategic management is that it ignores the power realities within organizations and therefore the realities of decision-making. A different perspective is to focus on the nature of organizations as political structures whereby decisions are determined, not by rational analysis, but by negotiation between the various power blocks.

According to this paradigm (Cyert and Marsh 1963; Bolman and Deal 1991), strategic decision-making within an organization is little to do with the rational strategic management theories and all to do with this power-brokering within the 'alive and screaming' political arenas that are organizations. As Scottish sociologist, Tom Burns, has pointed out, most modern organizations promote various kinds of politicking because they are designed as systems of simultaneous competition and collaboration. People must collaborate in pursuit of a common task, yet are often pitted against each other in competition for limited resources, status and career advancement.

If strategic decision-making is purely about power-brokering, then this begs the question as to whether there is any value in any form of strategic planning, in the Third Sector or elsewhere, as it is normally understood. Being aware of the tendency towards political power-plays and empire-building can help to ensure that strategic thinking maintains, as far as possible, a focus on the rational interests of the organization and its beneficiaries. Hudson (1995) argues that strategy is particularly important in Third Sector organizations precisely because they are usually coalitions of diverse people with different aspirations that need to be integrated into a shared focus for the organization to be successful. Strategy planning can therefore be seen as the process of bringing the various stakeholders together to negotiate an agreed future for the organization. This can recognize the power of each of the stakeholder groups, but also promote an active participation of all stakeholders in a 'bounded rationality'.

CONTINGENCY APPROACHES

With the availability of so many different approaches to strategy, all with their proponents and detractors, it is difficult for those with responsibility for the management and development of their organizations to make decisions about which approach is best. It is likely, however, that there is no one-best-way. The Contingency School of strategic management may be helpful in getting away from an either–or dilemma between a traditional technocratic approach to strategic planning and the experimental emergent approaches of the postmodernists.

Ansoff and McDonnell (1990) try to show how different approaches to strategy can be appropriate in different situations, depending particularly on the extent of turbulence, novelty and complexity in the external environment. In a stable, relatively simple environment a traditional planning approach may be appropriate. In environments which are highly complex and discontinuous, a more experimental, spontaneous, learning approach may be more appropriate. This enables the various approaches to strategic management to co-exist in creative tension with each other (Joyce and Woods 1996), rather than one paradigm replacing another.

In the Third Sector it is likely that different kinds of organizations with more stable or more turbulent environments may require different approaches. This may change over time too. Even within a single Third Sector organization it may be that the approach to strategy in relation to resource acquisition, e.g. fundraising, or to a social economy subsidiary may need to be much more akin to the traditional strategic approach and language (target markets, competitors, return on investment, etc.) of private companies because of the high level of competition for funds. However, in relation to the provision of human services to a particular client group in a particular geographical area, especially where there is an element of mutual aid involved, the environment may be more stable with much less competition. In this kind of context, participation, collaboration, learning, capacity-building, internal negotiation, influencing, living the values and incremental development are likely to be the key aspects of strategy development.

NEW PRAGMATISM

The increasing realization, in all sectors, of the value of a strategic management approach which avoids the rigid, linear, technocratic and top-down models of the past has led to the development of a range of 'new modernist' or pragmatic approaches.

Van der Heijden, Professor of General and Strategic Management at the Graduate Business School, Strathclyde University, for example, argues in *Scenarios* (1996) for the importance of bringing people together to engage in 'the art of strategic conversation'. He suggests a process in which managers can share their own intuitive thoughts and ideas – their own visions and dreams – in a way that uses what has been learnt. They can explore various possible scenarios for the organization and allow a consensus to develop that will create a viable way forward for the organization that can be continually reviewed and adapted or transformed as appropriate.

It has been argued that the best metaphor for this new approach is jazz (Vaill 1990; Perry *et al.* 1993; Kao, quoted in Micklethwait and Wooldridge 1996). In contrast to an orchestra, where everyone plays exactly what is on the score to the strict direction of the conductor whose back is turned to the audience, a jazz group improvises around basic patterns, keys and rhythms. In jazz the emphasis is on participation, creativity, innovation and effective and immediate communication around a particular theme or motif.

This reinvention of strategic planning as 'strategic thinking', 'strategic learning' or 'strategic improvising' resulted in a major resurgence of interest in strategy in the second half of the 1990s, coinciding with a major period of growth in the economies of the USA and the UK. In 1996, *Business Week* announced that 'strategic planning is back', explaining that there is a new interest in strategic planning in today's boardrooms. In a survey of global companies by Bain & Co in 1998 (Grant 2003), more than 80 per cent of companies were engaging in strategic planning, with a satisfaction level of over 95 per cent, and 90 per cent also had mission and value statements in which a satisfaction level of 93 per cent was reported. A study of the strategic planning processes of eight large oil companies operating in turbulent environments (Grant 2003) found that suggestions that strategic planning was in terminal decline were seriously overstated. However, the study found that the processes tended to reconcile rational design and emergent processes in which strategic planning systems provided a mechanism for coordinating decentralized strategy formulation and fostered adaptation and responsiveness.

While retaining much of what is best about the traditional approaches to strategic management, the key characteristics of the new more pragmatic or 'new modernist' approach seem to be the following:

- wide participation of staff, trustees and volunteers in reflecting on strategic issues rather than a top-down approach (Hatten 1982; Bunker and Alban 1997);
- creating a continuous process of experimentation and learning (Argyris and Schon 1978; Senge 1990; Nonaka 1991; Burgoyne *et al.* 1994);
- building on the distinctive competencies/capabilities of the organization (Selznick 1957; Barney 1991; Ambrosini 2007);
- participation of a wider range of stakeholders (Freeman 1984; Bryson 1995);
- recognition of the need to negotiate between the various sources of power, inside and outside an organization (Pfeffer and Salancik 1978; Bolman and Deal 1991);
- focusing on key strategic issues, or change challenges (Ansoff and McDonnell 1990; Edwards and Eadie 1994);
- taking into account a range of potential future external scenarios (de Geus 1988; Schwartz 1991; van der Heijden 1996);
- creating strong motivating visions, i.e. strategic intent, which enables the organization and its people to 'live deeply in the future while gaining the courage to act boldly in the present' (Hamel and Prahalad 1994; Collins and Porras 1994);
- creating a clear value base for the ethical management of the company (Collins and Porras 1994; Jones and Pollitt 1998);
- strategic thinking as a continual process, not just an annual cycle (Taylor 1997);

- strategic processes which produce common-sense frameworks which will help managers to make decisions;
- innovation, experimentation and creativity are encouraged and supported (Quinn 1980; Pinchot 1985; Burgelman 1988; Senge 1990).

This approach is very different from some of the traditional mechanistic top-down strategic planning approaches, led by planning departments, that have been heavily criticized. It is also much more in tune with the culture and values of the Third Sector. Sharp *et al.* (2007: 6) argue that strategy development in the Third Sector 'works best when it is appreciative, reflective, participatory and outcomes-focused'. The challenge is to 'design a process that effectively engages the whole organisation in a dialogue about direction. This dialogue extends to key external stakeholders as well as internal groups (staff, managers and the board). The product of this dialogue is a consensus about ends (strategic objectives) and means for their achievement (strategies)' (Doherty *et al.* 2009: 57).

SUMMARY

This chapter has explored many of the critiques of traditional top-down strategic planning approaches often carried out by detached expert planners. In contrast, a number of other approaches including the Learning, Political and Contingency Schools have been explored. Recognition has been given to the fact that different approaches may be appropriate for different situations, even different parts of the same organization. Finally, the key characteristics of the 'new pragmatism' approach to strategic management are highlighted, which reflect much of the values and culture of the Third Sector.

QUESTIONS

1. What are the weaknesses of the classic rational approaches to strategic management?
2. What are the best ways that an organization can develop a learning culture?
3. To what extent is the learning school in conflict with the classic rational approaches?
4. What are the key principles underpinning the resource-based view of strategy?
5. What kinds of distinctive competencies, resources or capabilities might Third Sector organizations have to build a strategy around?
6. Where are the main power blocks in a Third Sector organization likely to be?
7. In what situations might different approaches to strategic management be appropriate?
8. What are the main characteristics of the pragmatic 'new modernist' approach to strategic management?
9. To what extent does the pragmatic 'new modernist' approach to strategic management reflect the culture and values of the Third Sector?

DISCUSSION TOPIC

To what extent is decision-making in an organization rational?

SUGGESTED READING

James C. Collins and Jerry I. Porras (1994) *Built to Last: Successful Habits of Visionary Companies*, Random House.

Gary Hamel and C. K. Prahalad (1994) *Competing for the Future*, Harvard Business School.

Mark Jenkins and Veronique Ambrosini (2007) *Advanced Strategic Management: A Multi-Perspective Approach*, 2nd edn, Palgrave Macmillan.

Henry Mintzberg, Bruce Ahlstrand and Joseph Lampel (1998) *Strategy Safari*, Prentice-Hall.

5 THE DEVELOPMENT OF STRATEGIC MANAGEMENT IN THE THIRD SECTOR

OVERVIEW

Strategic planning, which became very common in the private sector in the 1960s and early 1970s, did not begin to take off in the Third Sector until the very end of the 1970s, and even then only in the USA. However, in the 1980s and 1990s traditional strategic management became increasingly common for Third Sector organizations around the world. In addition to various practical 'one-best-way' guides, strategic planning in the Third Sector became subject to considerable debate on both its theory and practice in the sector and the academic literature. This chapter explores the development of the use of strategic management models and techniques in the Third Sector from the late 1970s to the present day and some of the constraints in its development. Research in the Third Sectors in the UK and USA on the use of strategic management models and tools is highlighted.

LEARNING OBJECTIVES

After studying this chapter, you should be able to:

- identify the factors that may constrain the development of strategic management in the Third Sector;

- describe the nature of the literature on strategic management in the Third Sector;

- identify some of the strategic management tools and techniques used by Third Sector organizations; and

- describe the extent and nature of strategic management in Third Sector organizations.

MANAGERIALISM IN THE THIRD SECTOR

With the transfer of substantial functions, previously run by government agencies (particularly the provision of social care services), in the 1980s to voluntary non-profit organizations came major changes in what was expected of those organizations and the relationship between the public and voluntary non-profit sectors (see Kramer 1992;

Smith and Lipsky 1993; Rochester 1995; Lewis 1996; Deakin 1996; Gann 1996). This in turn started to have a very major impact on how these organizations were managed.

The main factors influencing this 'flood' away from the public sector towards the voluntary non-profit sector were described by Hudson (1995) as:

- a political philosophy that believed state-run organizations are neither efficient nor responsive to people's changing needs;
- the consequent separation of the functions of the purchaser (to specify standards and desired outcomes) and the provider (to deliver services efficiently and effectively, responding quickly to changes in the external environment), what Osborne and Graebler (1992) describe as separating rowing from steering;
- a desire to give local managers greater control over the management of their organizations;
- tighter control over public expenditure coinciding with increased social need;
- a belief that competition between suppliers can lead to efficiency gains, even though the notion of competition in the provision of basic services is deeply uncomfortable, particularly to professionals in these services.

Gann (1996), also writing in the context of the UK, reinforces the importance of most of these external factors and adds several additional ones:

- a reduction in the amount of 'untied' funds available to local authorities;
- a shift towards project or programme-based funding of development work by national government through local authorities (e.g. through Economic Development Corporations, Urban Programme, City Challenge and Single Regeneration Fund schemes);
- an increased secularization of society, while much voluntary work continued to be provided by religious groups;
- an increased emphasis on the use of modern management techniques in local government (see also Joyce 1999), leading to similar expectations of voluntary non-profit organizations funded through contracts by local authorities (e.g. in the use of monitoring and evaluation, staff appraisal, strategic and development plans).

The brief case study in Box 1.2 of Action for Children highlights an organization, initially founded on the basis of Victorian philanthropy, which has adapted to the contract culture and is now frequently contracted by statutory social services to provide care services to children and their families. In contrast, Save the Children made the strategic decision not to go down this route and divested itself of the management of service delivery in the UK. Mencap, in the learning disability field (case study in Part VI), has also developed a proactive approach to contracting services on behalf of government bodies.

Some people have suggested that the contract culture has resulted in statutory organizations becoming increasingly managerial and controlling, and voluntary non-profit organizations becoming more like the statutory bodies they are in contract with and whom, in some cases, they replaced as a primary provider of welfare services. Maria Brenton, in her study of nonprofits in the United States and the Netherlands, suggests that 'the process of development of the voluntary sector to the role of monopoly or major provider with the aid of state funds seems inevitably to follow a path similar to that taken by our statutory services – the path toward professionalisation and bureaucracy' (Brenton 1985: 206).

This difference of view is very relevant to the general discussion of whether voluntary non-profit organizations should adopt professional management approaches and techniques.

Government departments and agencies that fund voluntary non-profit organizations have been increasingly holding the organizations accountable through monitoring and evaluation processes for the outcomes of that funding (see pp. 112–16). These monitoring and evaluation processes often impose a framework which is similar to the management approach that is dominant within the statutory body itself and which emphasizes the articulation of goals, objectives, outcomes, performance indicators and budgets as well as the establishment of monitoring and control mechanisms.

The development of contractual relationships between voluntary non-profit and public sector organizations (Cairns et al. 2005) has also led to the position where certain voluntary non-profit organizations, particularly those which are in a contractual relationship with statutory bodies, are considered 'public bodies' in relation to particular statutory requirements such as the Human Rights Act 2000. This has already resulted in these bodies (housing associations, for example) being required to carry out the 'Best value' processes, initially only a requirement of statutory bodies. 'Best value', the Labour Government's successor to Compulsive Competitive Tendering, requires the adoption of a strategic management approach involving the organization's stakeholders. The Coalition Government, through its Modernizing Commissioning agenda, has increased the emphasis on Third Sector organizations bidding for public sector contracts.

An alternative perspective is that the introduction of competition for contracts and funding is pulling voluntary non-profit organizations into the culture of the for-profit sector rather than that of government. Voluntary non-profit organizations are increasingly required to compete against other voluntary non-profit organizations, as well as public and private sector organizations, for attention, funds, people (staff and volunteers) and commercial contracts (Clutterbuck and Dearlove 1996) and are therefore required to demonstrate that they are as effective and efficient as private companies. Gutch (1992) argues that contracting will result in voluntary non-profit organizations becoming larger, more professionalized and more like private companies, with a reduced influence of management committees, volunteers and service-users.

These views may not be as far apart as they appear, as the public sector itself has taken on board much of the new managerialism (Pollitt 1990; Joyce 1999), also known as 'market-based public administration' (Lan and Rosenbloom 1992) and 'entrepreneurial government' (Osborne and Graebler 1992), with the encouragement of government, government advisors from the private sector, and large consultancy firms. In turn, these statutory bodies are requiring voluntary non-profit organizations they fund, and particularly those they contract with, also to adopt these new managerial approaches. Powell and DiMaggio (1983) would describe this as an example of institutional isomorphism where, because of pressures in the field caused by professional training, regulations and standards, organizations in all three sectors are becoming more similar to each other.

A study of UK local government (Flynn and Talbot 1996) suggests that not only did the majority of local authorities engage in formal strategic planning, but also that it was perceived as providing a wide range of benefits. Research into the strategic management challenges facing the voluntary non-profit sector in the UK by Aston University (Lubelska 1996: 3) suggests that:

> boundaries are definitely blurring between voluntary organisations and the private sector...while the contracting-out of central and local government services...has resulted in voluntary organisations becoming more like local authority operations...voluntary sector managers these days are running organisations that are businesses and public bodies at one and the same time.

THE START OF THE USE OF STRATEGIC PLANNING IN THE THIRD SECTOR

Around the time that strategic planning was starting to be perceived in the private sector with less than the enthusiasm it had become used to in the late 1960s and early 1970s, the Third Sector began to explore the potentialities of its models and techniques.

In 1976, Charles Hofer, a leading scholar in the field of strategic management, published a review of research on strategic planning and throughout remarked on the lack of research into 'non-business organizations'. However, with the emerging use of strategic management models and techniques in the Third Sector in the 1970s, literature on strategic planning in the non-profit sector started to appear in the late 1970s, particularly in the USA. A range of publications and articles were produced which exhorted the sector to adopt the strategic planning and management techniques that have been used (successfully they argued) in the private sector (Selby 1978; Firstenberg 1979; Keating 1979; Steiner 1979; Drucker 1980; Greenberg 1982; Unterman and Davies 1982; Hatten 1982; Steiner *et al.* 1994). Karger and Malik (1975), for example, having demonstrated, as they saw it, the effectiveness of formal integrated long-range planning in the private sector, confidently predicted that 'future research will show the importance of such planning in both the private and non-profit sectors. Much of this literature reflected a preoccupation with the similarities and differences between the private (profit) and voluntary non-profit sectors (Cyert 1975).

The difference in the timing of the development of literature on management techniques in the private and Third Sectors is interesting and would suggest a time lag between the two of approximately 20 years. The literature on Management By Objectives (MBO), for example, developed in relation to the private sector from 1955 onwards (see Drucker's *Managing for Results* (1964)). Twenty years later, in 1975, McConkey published *MBO for Nonprofit Organisations* in the USA. The literature on strategic planning in the private sector developed in the mid-1960s and equivalent literature in relation to the non-profit sector began in the mid-1980s.

Unterman and Davies (1982) in their study of 102 Third Sector organizations in the US and their boards of trustees, concluded that many non-profit organizations have not even reached the strategic planning stage of development that private sector companies achieved 15–20 years ago, let alone the current strategic management stage.

Ayal (1986: 51) suggested that the reason for the long time lag between the use of strategic planning techniques in the private sector and the non-profit sector was the fact that:

> the mission for many nonprofit organisations is rather diffuse, and goals and objectives are multiple and more difficult to define; nonprofit organisations, more than the typical business firm, have multiple constituencies, frequently with conflicting goals. Resolution and decision making is usually 'political' in nature, and thus less amenable to formal planning; and leadership in many nonprofit organisations is volunteer, changes frequently, and though usually highly devoted, frequently lacks the time, staff, and other resources required for a proper strategic planning job.

Wilcox (2006) suggests that the reluctance to embrace strategic management in the Third Sector is due to certain ingrained thoughts and habits, including:

- Business is evil: the profit-driven corporate world is the enemy. Business models and tools are not therefore appropriate for the Third Sector.
- Professional management is not needed: sophisticated management approaches were not needed to get the organization set up during the successful entrepreneurial phase. Just because the organization has grown, why should they be needed now?
- It's customary to pay lip service to business management: it is often recognized that funders, evaluators and some board members think that strategic and business plans are important, so they are produced, but not with any commitment to ensuring that strategic management is at the heart of the development of the organization.

Newman and Wallender (1978) identified a number of factors which had constrained the development of rational planning in Third Sector organizations:

1. Service is intangible and hard to measure. This difficulty is often compounded by the existence of multiple service objectives (see also Kanter and Summers 1987).
2. Customer influence may be weak. Often the enterprise has a local monopoly and payments by customers may be a secondary source of funds. Third-party funders may be more important than its beneficiaries (see also La Piana 2005).
3. Strong employee commitment to professions or to a cause may undermine their allegiance to the enterprise.
4. Resource contributors may intrude into internal management – notably fund contributors and government (see also Wortman 1981).
5. Restraints on the use of rewards and punishments result from 1, 3 and 4 above.
6. Charismatic leaders and/or the mystique of the enterprise may be important means of resolving conflict in objectives and overcoming restraints.

Others have pointed to the difficulties presented by the existence of multiple stakeholders in Third Sector organizations (McLaughlin 1986; Bryson 1994; Rochester 1995). These barriers very much reflect the discussion in Chapter 1 about the perceived differences between the private and Third Sectors.

In considering the differences between the private and Third Sectors (discussed in Chapter 1), many writers and researchers have suggested that strategic management techniques are, indeed, relevant to the Third Sector, but need to be adapted to the particular circumstances and values of the sector (Setterberg and Schulman 1985; Steiner *et al.* 1994; Bryson 1995; Chauhan 1998; Kearns 2000; Lindenberg 2001). Others have gone further, however, and suggested that the differences between the sectors means that the general concept of formal planning may have limited use for voluntary organizations which have value-based aims (Gerard 1983). Walker (1983) suggests that following a traditional model of planning in the Third Sector may be dysfunctional because of the adherence to strong ideological belief systems in the sector.

Salipante and Golden-Biddle (1995) argue that the enduring nature of needs and the missions of Third Sector organizations make strategic planning approaches inappropriate because they imply that there is scope for substantial organizational change. Private sector organizations can change to producing very different products or services if they think it will be more profitable, but, they suggest, this is inappropriate for Third Sector organizations which are much more constrained by their founding documents and missions:

> Fundamental differences with the for-profit sector, and that sector's own experiences, make it unwise for nonprofit leaders to adopt business organizations' externally focused approach to strategic change. Theories of organizational survival and punctuated equilibrium models of change and continuity, as well as the authors' research, suggest that planning aimed toward matching the organization to changes in its environment has limited value...Due to the relative constancy of societal needs and nonprofits' missions and the importance of society's demands for reliable, accountable performance, nonprofits should greatly value continuity... Potential organizational change should be approached cautiously with a strong regard for traditionality. (Ibid.: 3)

Drucker (1990) has suggested, however, that it was the Third Sector that created the key strategy concepts of mission, vision and values, which have been copied by the private sector, not the other way round. Other researchers have pointed to the changes that have taken place in the approaches to strategic management in the private sector, which have moved much closer to the ethos of the Third Sector in relation to values such as social responsibility, multiple stakeholders, ethical values, non-executive directors and participation (see the discussion of the new modernist, pragmatic approach to strategy discussed in Chapter 4).

There is an extensive literature (referred to above), particularly from the USA, which argues for the benefits of using strategic management techniques, developed in the private sector, in the Third Sector (see Kearns 2000 for a more recent example). While much of the early literature on strategy in the Third Sector challenged the sector to examine its approaches to management and planning and to adopt more professional management methods, it was not backed up with sound empirical evidence. It tended to make the assumption that the Third Sector could and should uncritically copy the models and techniques of the profit-making sector without an analysis of the appropriateness of the models and tools to the Third Sector.

'HOW–TO' LITERATURE

A body of 'how-to' literature on strategic planning in the Third Sector was developed in the 1980s and 1990s which draws particularly on the techniques and models used in the private sector. This literature showed a considerable consensus in its use of strategic planning models and concepts, in particular SWOT analysis, PEST analysis (Political, Economic, Social and Technological), mission, vision, values, aims, objectives, performance indicators, and key results areas. Other techniques have been particularly adapted for use in the Third Sector (see Chapters 6–8), including:

- Ansoff's matrix (Courtney 1996);
- Porter's industry analysis (Oster 1995);
- the portfolio analysis of the Boston Consultancy Group (Gruber and Mohr 1982; Nutt and Backoff 1992; Lawrie 1994; Bryson 1995; Courtney 1996; Roller 1996; Bovaird and Rubienska 1996);
- the Balanced Scorecard (Kaplan 2001; Niven 2003).

Bryson (1988), Professor of Planning and Public Affairs at the University of Minneapolis, has highlighted three other techniques that are particularly useful in the public and non-profit sectors:

- mandate analysis, which looks at the written mandates that the organization has from legislation, constitutions, trust deeds, legislation, public policy documents, research reports, funding agreements, etc.;
- stakeholder analysis (Freeman 1984), which explores the expectations of the organization's beneficiaries, funders, volunteers, staff, regulatory bodies, etc. and what needs to be done to meet these expectations;
- identifying strategic issues that may have an impact on the ability of an organization to meet its aims and which therefore requires urgent action (Bryson 1988; Ansoff and McDonnell 1990; Nutt and Backoff 1992; Edwards and Eadie 1994).

These tools and techniques are discussed in detail in Chapters 6 and 7 when we analyse the organization and its external environment. Other strategy tools have been specially developed or adapted for use in the public and/or the non-profit sector.

Some of the early publications that practically advised Third Sector organizations on how they should be planning and managing their own futures included Wortman (1979), Hatten (1982), Ring and Perry (1985), Setterberg and Schulman (1985), Barry (1986), Bryson (1988) and Koteen (1989).

These are all American publications. A British guide to the literature on the management of Third Sector organizations, *Organising Voluntary Agencies* by Harris and Billis (1986), makes no mention of strategic planning for the sector. The UK literature really only began to come into its own in the 1990s with the publication of Web (1990), Barnard and Walker (1994) and Lawrie (1994), which are mainly by consultants working in the non-profit sector in Britain. Various books were also published in the UK by practitioners and consultants working specifically in the non-profit sector which focused more broadly on voluntary sector management, including Hudson (1995), Courtney (1996), Hind (1996) and Osborne (1996).

The time lag between a strategic planning approach being used by Third Sector organizations in Britain and the USA is similar to the time lag for British private sector organizations to adopt strategic planning approaches developed by American writers, such as Ansoff, Andrews and Porter in the 1960s and 1970s, and indicates that much of the formative thinking in this area comes from academic institutions and business schools in the USA.

RESEARCH EVIDENCE

In a comprehensive review of the international strategic planning research literature as it relates to Third Sector organizations (mostly in the US) Stone *et al.* (1999) conclude that a number of key things were known, at that stage, about strategic management in the Third Sector:

FORMULATION

1. Many Third Sector organizations have not adopted formal strategic planning (Jansson and Taylor 1978; Brown and Covey 1987; Crittenden *et al.* 1988; Odom and Boxx 1988; Stone 1989; Jenster and Overstreet 1990; Wolch 1990; Tober 1991).

2. For those that do adopt formal strategic planning, primary determinants are organizational size, characteristics of the board and management, prior agreement on organizational goals and mission, and funder requirements to plan.

3. Principal outcomes of formal planning are changes in organizational mission, structure, and board and management roles.

4. The relationship between formal planning and performance is not clear but seems to be associated with growth and with who participates in the process.

CONTENT

5. The determinants of strategy are largely driven by characteristics of resource environments and existing funder relationships.

6. Little attention has been paid to determinants expressing changing demands for services or shifts in client needs.

7. Third Sector organizations pursue both competitive and cooperative strategies, and the outcomes associated with each differ substantially.

IMPLEMENTATION

8. Exogenous turbulence affects organizational structure and the relationship between strategy and structure.

9. Important determinants of implementation activities are leader behaviour, the structure of authority, values and their interactions.

10. Inter-organizational systems or networks are critical to strategy implementation.

It is likely, however, that there has been a considerable increase in the use of formal strategic planning and in analyses of the earlier studies in both the UK and the US since 1999.

USE OF STRATEGIC PLANNING TOOLS IN THE UK THIRD SECTOR: WHITEHILL CLARKE STUDY

To find out to what extent voluntary organizations in the UK make use of strategic planning tools and techniques, the accountancy firm Whitehill Clarke undertook a survey of members of the Association of Chief Executives of National Voluntary Organisations (ACENVO; now ACEVO) – which therefore tended to be the larger Third Sector organizations in Britain, with the majority having an annual turnover in excess of £1 million.

The research found that the vast majority (82 per cent) of respondents had a strategic, corporate or business plan, and another 15 per cent intended to prepare one during the next 12 months, which contradicts the findings of Stone *et al.* (1999) that many Third Sector organizations have not adopted strategic management. The conflict may be due to the typological differences between Third Sector organizations in the US (most of Stone *et al.*'s studies) and the UK (the ACENVO study). It also may reflect the difference in time, as the Stone *et al.* studies mainly concern the 1980s, whereas the ACENVO study was conducted in the 1990s, by which time the prescriptive literature on the value of strategic management in the non-profit sector may have had more time to take effect.

The research also found that the arrival of a new chief executive in an organization was the most common reason given for preparing a strategic plan (40 per cent), followed by a request from the trustees (22 per cent) and the organization's financial situation (20 per cent).

Content of plans

The majority of plans included strategic objectives, a mission statement, financial plans/implications, detailed objectives, strategic priorities and organizational values. A minority (between half and a quarter) also included a vision statement, resource/skills needs, detailed action plans, competitive analysis and critical success factors.

Strategic planning processes used

Respondents were also asked to indicate which strategic planning tools and techniques were used in the preparation of the plan, how satisfied they were with each of them, and whether they would use them again. By far the most popular tool was SWOT (discussed in Chapters 6 and 7) which was used in the vast majority of cases. On average, organizations using it were 'somewhat satisfied' and most would use it again. The second most common tool was gap analysis (one-third), which received a satisfaction rating just over halfway between 'neither satisfied or dissatisfied' and

Table 5.1 Table of strategy tools used and satisfaction levels

	Usage (%)	Satisfaction	Would use again (%)
Zero-based budgeting	15	3.15	92
Scenario planning	14	3.75	75
Force field analysis	13	3.91	100
Portfolio analysis	11	2.44	78
Five forces analysis	11	3.33	56
Life cycle analysis	8	3.14	86
Value analysis	8	3.71	57

'somewhat satisfied', although three-quarters would use it again. Third most common was cost–benefit analysis (30 per cent) which produced an even lower satisfaction rating, close to 'neither satisfied or dissatisfied', although the majority said they would use it again. The fourth most used technique was PEST (an environmental appraisal looking at the potential impact of Political, Economic, Social and Technological trends), to be discussed in Chapter 6. Satisfaction ratings for PEST were similar to cost–benefit analysis, and three-quarters said they would use it again. Table 5.1 shows other tools and techniques that were used.

Table 5.1 indicates that of the less common techniques at least scenario planning and force field analysis could be made more use of. This is reinforced by the comparatively small number of techniques used, on average, by the voluntary organizations in the survey (an average of 2) compared with the private sector (an average of 6). The mandate analysis and stakeholder analysis techniques developed which have been adapted by Bryson (1988) specifically for the public and Third Sectors were not included in this survey.

Impact of strategic planning

Asked about the impact of their strategic plan on the organization's overall success, almost two-thirds of respondents felt that the plan and its implementation had a 'strong influence' on the organization's overall success (although when asked, half of the chief officers stated that they referred to the plan only quarterly or less). Unsurprisingly, a similar proportion (two-thirds) felt that the time and money spent on the strategic plan was 'very worthwhile' and a further quarter felt that it was 'somewhat worthwhile'.

The Whitehill Clarke study gives an interesting snapshot of strategic planning in some of the larger Third Sector organizations in the UK. It indicates that the various strategic management models, techniques and tools have been making a very major impact on the Third Sector (at least on national voluntary organizations) in the UK.

However, the study may also indicate two particular areas of potential concern. Firstly, the level of consultation with non-managerial staff, customers, clients, users, funders, suppliers and supporters is very low, which may have reduced both the quality of the plan produced and the sense of ownership, and therefore the commitment to the implementation, of the plan. Secondly, the level of actual satisfaction with most of the tools and techniques is not particularly high. Indeed none of them achieved a better rating than 'somewhat satisfied'. Despite this, most of the same tools and techniques would be used again, which may indicate the lack of alternative tools and techniques for use in the Third sector. Scenario planning and force field analysis, however, which were used by only a minority of organizations, received relatively high satisfaction ratings and could perhaps be made greater use of in the sector.

UK PERFORMANCE HUB SURVEY

A more recent study (Jackson and Irwin 2007) of 248 British Third Sector organizations produced the following findings.

Usefulness of strategic planning

More than half of the organizations surveyed found that strategic planning had particular benefits, including:

- helps to clarify where the organization would like to be;
- helps the organization to understand risks;
- helps the organization to prioritize;
- helps to motivate staff, volunteers, etc.;
- helps with fundraising;
- helps to coordinate different aspects of the work;
- creates opportunities for internal communication.

Techniques used

As with the Whitehill Clarke study, by far the most common strategy technique used was SWOT analysis, used by 72 per cent of organizations, of whom 55 per cent found it useful or very useful. Outcome and project evaluations, although not strictly strategic planning tools, were used by around half of the organizations, and 34 and 40 per cent, respectively, found them useful or very useful. Around 40 per cent used PEST (28 per cent finding it useful or very useful). Core competencies were used by 33 per cent (23 per cent finding it useful or very useful). Around 30 per cent used cost–benefit analysis (18 per cent finding it useful or very useful), stakeholder analysis (18 per cent finding it useful or very useful), an internal health check (27 per cent finding it useful or very useful), or mind mapping (16 per cent finding it useful or very useful). Approximately 20 per cent used strategy mapping (14 per cent finding it useful or very useful) or scenario planning (14 per cent finding it useful or very useful). Around 7–12 per cent used market share analysis (6 per cent finding it useful or very useful), the balanced scorecard (10 per cent finding it useful or very useful), portfolio analysis (6 per cent finding it useful or very useful), force field analysis (3 per cent finding it useful or very useful) or life cycle analysis (4 per cent finding it useful or very useful). SWOT and the balanced scorecard received a satisfaction rating of 75 per cent or higher by those who had used them. Outcome and project evaluations, PEST, cost–benefit analysis, core competencies, market share analysis, strategy mapping, Ansoff's matrix,

SWOT evaluations, PEST and stakeholder analysis were the techniques that received the highest 'very useful' ratings.

Involving people

Ninety per cent of organizations involved staff and the board in strategic planning; 48 per cent involved clients/beneficiaries; 46 per cent involved volunteers; 30 per cent involved funders; and 26 per cent involved consultants or advisors.

SUCCESSFUL STRATEGIES: ACTION RESEARCH FINDINGS

In parallel with the Jackson and Irwin survey highlighted above, the Performance Hub commissioned an action research project (Sharp *et al.* 2007) to engage five small and medium-sized organizations in strategic planning and evaluated the processes for the lessons learnt. The key conclusions were:

- ensure there is a clear and up-to-date vision and mission;
- connect strategy to the values of the organization;
- ensure a focus on outcomes;
- be appreciative, i.e. focus on the distinctive strengths and qualities;
- acknowledge and celebrate what the organization does well;
- plan and manage the process;
- ensure collaboration in the process of strategy development;
- be clear about your stakeholders;
- encourage active user involvement in strategy development;
- step off the beaten track: try out new methods to promote conversations;
- visit another organization to gain inspiration;
- consider new and unmet needs;
- acknowledge tensions and address diversity;
- see the big picture first then share out the tasks;
- use existing thinking to inform thinking and planning;
- establish a monitoring and evaluation framework for the strategy;
- find a critical friend.

STRATEGIC MANAGEMENT IN NORTHERN IRELAND

A doctoral research study (Courtney 2005) examined the use of strategic management tools and techniques amongst 128 medium to large-sized Third Sector organizations in Northern Ireland. The findings are discussed below.

Strategic plan

Almost three-quarters of the respondents' organizations had a current strategic plan. Over 90 per cent either had one or were currently actively developing one. This indicates that larger Third Sector organizations (those with an annual turnover of more than £100,000) in Northern Ireland have strongly adopted the recommendations in the prescriptive literature on management in the Third Sector, namely that such organizations should have a strategic plan. This finding appears to further contradict the findings of Stone *et al.* (1999), based on a review of 21 research studies on strategy in the US Third Sector (including Odom and Boxx 1988; Stone 1989; Tober 1991; Wolch 1990), that many Third Sector organizations do not use strategic planning and are more likely to rely on a variety of planning methods such as operational planning (e.g. annual goal setting), some elements of long-range planning, and/or informal planning. The difference may be due to the fact that the research reviewed by Stone *et al.* was carried out at least ten years earlier, with many of the studies in the 1980s, or because the research reviewed is mainly from the United States. It is also possible that the characteristics of the Third Sector organizations that were featured in the studies reviewed in relation to organizational size were different from the present study, due to the cut-off used here of annual turnover of organizations being over £100,000.

Less than a quarter of the organizations surveyed in Northern Ireland had had a strategic plan in place for more than ten years, reinforcing the perception that the adoption of strategic planning is a relatively recent phenomenon. It may provide the reason why the percentage of organizations in this current study using strategic planning/management techniques is significantly higher than the earlier studies.

The strategic plans identified were most likely to include the classic strategic planning elements, namely: a mission statement; long-term aims/goals/objectives; a statement of values/principles; a vision statement; performance indicators/measures of success; and strategy(ies) for achieving the aims/goals. A significant minority also had used critical success factors and/or multiyear budgets.

Strategic analysis processes

The most popular strategic analysis processes used by the organizations were SWOT, identifying strategic issues, visioning, mandate analysis, identifying core competencies/unique selling points, an appraisal of strategic options, a needs/market assessment, stakeholder analysis and an analysis of external trends. These were all carried out in some way by the majority of organizations. However, none of the above was carried out in an in-depth formal way by the majority of organizations, which may suggest a fairly superficial engagement in strategic analysis. Of other strategic analysis processes, around one-third of organizations only engaged in informal, superficial processes of stakeholder analysis, analysis of external trends, scenario planning, needs/market assessment, and analysis of roles and relationships with other organizations.

Strategic implementation processes

Of strategic implementation processes, more than three-quarters had an annual financial plan and budget, annual operational plans, indicators of success/performance indicators and a timetable for the frequent monitoring of the achievement of objectives in the plan.

Size of organization and strategic management

Prior to the research it was hypothesized that size of organization (by turnover) may be a significant factor associated with the use of strategic management techniques (Stone *et al.* 1999). Larger organizations may, for example, be better able to afford the time and resources to engage in sophisticated strategic analysis processes and engage a consultant (Young and Sleeper 1988), or they may have more sophisticated executive directors (Wolch 1990). The study did not, however, find that, overall, larger organizations in the survey were more likely to engage in more sophisticated strategic management. The finding might have been different if the research had included much smaller organizations, particularly those with no staff or only one staff member.

Drivers to engage in strategic management

The literature (see for example Feinstein 1985; Webster and Wylie 1988; Stone 1989; Wolch 1990; Tober 1991; Stone *et al.* 1999) suggests that Third Sector organizations only plan when they have to, namely when they are faced with a major drop in funding or in response to pressure from funders. To test this finding the research explored the various factors that led to the organizations becoming engaged in strategic planning. The research found that 'pressures' to engage in strategic management were at least as much internal (such as pressure from staff) as external (such as pressure from funders). The most prominent three drivers were primarily internal, two positive and one negative. They were rapid growth (more than half of organizations), the appointment of a new chief executive (one-third of organizations) and the fact that their survival was threatened (one-third of organizations). External drivers were the next two most prominent factors: an external evaluation (one-third, although in some cases this may have been instigated and funded by the organization itself) and pressure from funders (one-quarter). Internal pressure from staff was also a factor in just over one-quarter of cases. There was a lack of perceived pressure from trustees (even from a new chair), or from other volunteers, or from service-users, to engage in strategic planning.

This does not necessarily mean that external factors may not be significant in the decision to engage in strategic management. For example, although rapid growth is primarily internal it may also be influenced by external factors, including increased support from funders. The fact that the survival of an organization is threatened may well be accompanied by a drop or threatened drop in external support and/or funding. An external evaluation may be commissioned by an organization itself in response to internal pressures, but it may also be imposed by a funder and therefore be primarily externally instigated.

There is also a difference between these findings and those of the ACENVO/ Whitehill Clarke study (Caudrey 1995), discussed above, which did not mention organizational growth as a factor at all. The impact of a new CEO and pressure from trustees were more important for the British national charities than in the current study.

Perceived benefits of strategic management

In the view of the respondents, strategic planning/management had a range of positive impacts, of which by far the most important were:

- creating a clearer organizational focus (more than three-quarters of respondents);
- increasing organizational unity (half of respondents).

More than a quarter also reported that it improved: financial planning; programming and monitoring of performance; the quality of services; organizational structure; the sense of ownership by the staff; professionalism; and funding/fundraising and the likelihood of long-term survival. It also assisted creative thinking and making the organization more business-like.

What is interesting about this list is also what is missing. Only one in five of the respondents thought that strategic planning enabled the organization to:

- meet more of the need;
- help make difficult decisions (although this increases with the length of time that the organization is involved in strategic planning/management);
- increase the range of services.

Only 15 per cent reported that it resulted in an increased extent of services, in improved governance or in major changes. A similarly small number considered that it improved the public image of their organization or its reputation with decision-makers. It is also noteworthy how few respondents perceived any negative consequences of strategic planning/management.

KEY FACTORS FOR THIRD SECTOR LEADERS

In a survey of leaders of US Third Sector organizations (Katsioloudes and Butler 1996) conducted in the mid-1990s, the following were rated as the highest level of importance in strategic planning:

- review of the organization's mission and values;
- notification of all managers of broad long-term objectives;
- review and approval of the strategic planning document by the board;
- notification of all managers of specific short-term objectives;
- using the plan as the basis for ongoing monitoring of organizational performance by senior management and the board;
- involvement of the professional staff in the strategic planning process;
- a search for continuous improvement of internal activities;
- the formulation of strategies by the management team and the employees involved in the strategic planning process;

- involvement of a strategic planning committee or ad hoc task group of the board in the strategic planning process;
- regular meetings with managers to discuss the overall strategic planning process issues.

Other issues and tools, such as performance appraisal, SWOT analysis, organization structure, using external consultants, market research, financial projections and competitive analysis, were considered of low importance.

Also looking at the USA, Szabat and Simmons (1996) carried out a survey of small to medium-sized Third Sector organizations in Greater Philadelphia and a sample of grant makers to explore their attitudes to different elements of strategic planning and what happened in practice. They found that both the organizations themselves and the grant makers considered that all of the following main elements of strategic planning were considered to be very important (between 69 and 90 per cent):

- a strategic plan written in document form;
- a clearly articulated and agreed upon mission/purpose;
- an understanding of external trends, internal capacities and their impact on Third Sector organizations;
- generally understood one-year initiatives;
- a process to evaluate and modify a strategic plan.

However, in practice only the mission statement existed in the overwhelming majority of cases. Half had a written document; 42 per cent had initiatives; 30 per cent had objectives, strategies, action plans; only around a quarter had external trends, internal capacities and an evaluation process. The authors suggest that further research would be useful on those areas where there is a gap between perceived importance and actual practice and whether this is having an impact on the success of Third Sector organizations.

CONCLUSION ON STRATEGIC MANAGEMENT IN THE THIRD SECTOR

To conclude this analysis of the theory and practice of strategic management in the Third Sector, it is clear that strategic management tools and techniques that originated primarily in the private sector have been making significant inroads into the Third Sector in both the UK and the USA.

What is not clear, however, is the extent to which these strategic management tools and techniques represent the classical top-down rigid strategic planning approaches used in the private sector in the second half of the 1960s and throughout the 1970s and which came into disrepute in the 1980s, or whether the approaches now being used by the Third Sector reflect the current more inclusive and pragmatic approaches to strategic management now being recommended, which are closer to the culture and values of the Third Sector.

SUMMARY

This chapter has highlighted the use of strategic management in the Third Sector and some of the difficulties in applying strategic management approaches to the Third Sector, particularly the lack of a clear bottom-line and the large number of stakeholders. The literature on strategic management in the Third Sector has been explored, much of it exhorting Third Sector organizations to adopt private sector strategic management techniques and outlining specific strategic planning frameworks. Research in the UK and the USA which analyses the experience of strategic management in the Third Sector has also been highlighted.

QUESTIONS

1. What are the most commonly used strategic management tools and techniques in the Third Sector?
2. What are some of the barriers to a strategic management approach in the Third Sector?
3. Why was the Third Sector slower than other sectors to adopt a strategic planning/ management approach?
4. What factors in a Third Sector organization make it more likely that it will adopt a strategic management approach?
5. What are the potential benefits for a Third Sector organization of adopting a strategic management approach?

DISCUSSION TOPIC

To what extent can strategic management tools and techniques be transferred from the private sector to the Third Sector?

SUGGESTED READING

Michael Allison and Jude Kaye (2005) *Strategic Planning for Nonprofit Organizations*, Wiley.

John Bryson (2011) *Strategic Planning for Public and Nonprofit Organizations*, Jossey-Bass.

Mark Lyons (1996) 'On a clear day … strategic management for VNPOs,' in Stephen P. Osborne (ed.), *Managing in the Voluntary Sector*, Thomson Business Press.

Sharon Oster (1995) *Strategic Management for Nonprofit Organizations*, Oxford University Press.

Performance Hub Reports (2007) *Successful Strategies* and *Tools for Strategic Planning*, NCVO.

6 IS STRATEGIC MANAGEMENT EFFECTIVE?

OVERVIEW

From the discussion above, there are clearly different perspectives on the concepts of strategy and strategic management: different academics, consultants and practitioners advocate a diverse range of models, tools and techniques to help organizations become more successful (in whatever way that is defined). What most organizational leaders want to know, however, is whether any of it actually works. What is the evidence for the success of organizations and companies who have adopted any of the techniques and models advocated? In this chapter the evidence of the impact of strategic planning/management on organizational performance is examined, both from private and Third Sector perspectives. The difficulties in determining the relationship between the extent to which an organization has engaged in strategic management and organizational effectiveness will also be explored.

LEARNING OBJECTIVES

After studying this chapter, you should be able to:

- explain the difficulties involved in defining effectiveness;
- outline the evidence for the effectiveness of strategic management in the private sector;
- describe the evidence for the effectiveness of strategic management in the Third Sector;
- explain the need for further research in this area.

EFFECTIVENESS IN THE PRIVATE SECTOR

It is one thing to expound a particular approach to the management and development of organizations, but it is quite another to prove that this will, in fact, make an organization more effective – to improve its performance. Most famously, within five years, two-thirds of the 'excellent' companies in the sample used by Peters and Waterman had slipped from the USA's top company listings (some did return later)

(O'Toole 1986). Fannie Mae was researched as one of Jim Collins's 'Good-to-Great Companies' (Collins 2001). By August 2008, the company's shares had fallen by 90 per cent and was put into conservatorship (receivership).

Assessing the evidence on the success or otherwise of strategic management models and techniques in relation to any sector is somewhat problematic for a number of reasons:

1. How should success be defined? Even in the private sector there is a range of options for how performance can be measured:

   - pre-tax profits;
   - long-term asset growth;
   - return on Capital invested;
   - earnings per share;
   - increase in share price;
   - profit margin;
   - net asset turnover;
   - solvency;
   - liquidity;
   - market share;
   - share value.

   It is hard to find agreement on universal criteria to assess organizational performance in the private sector (T. Smith 1992). Agreement in the Third Sector is likely to be even harder to come by (see pp. 197–244).

2. What planning activities are being assessed? Every organization's planning processes will be different. Which processes should be considered to be the important ones to research? Might subtler influences, such as organizational culture, be more or less important than the use of hard tools and techniques?

3. Which companies/organizations should be chosen for comparison purposes? Should they be randomly selected, or, as Collins (2001) did, should pairs be chosen from organizations in a similar field? Even deciding what the total population to choose companies/organizations from is not simple: should it be those who are members of a particular institution or umbrella body?

4. What time period should be considered? Short-term success may be at the expense of long-term achievement.

5. How can causation be demonstrated, as opposed to simply correlation? That is, even if an organization is successful on key results indicators and has well developed strategic planning processes that does not prove that it was the planning that caused the success. It may indeed be that only successful organizations can afford to employ consultants and planners to develop sophisticated strategic planning processes; or it may be that both things may be the result of a third factor altogether.

Mintzberg (1994: 94) concludes that 'the assumption that the final number on some bottom line has an identifiable and therefore measurable relation to some process the organization happens to use – one among hundreds – would appear to be, if not extraordinarily arrogant, then surprisingly naïve'.

However, various studies have attempted to assess the link between formal strategic planning and financial performance in the private sector. The results of a range of studies in the 1970s and 1980s on the relationship between strategic planning and financial performance have been described as 'inconclusive' (Bresser and Bishop 1983) and 'inconsistent and often contradicting' (Pearce et al. 1987).

Despite early studies that seemed to indicate very positive correlations (Thune and House 1970; Ansoff et al. 1970; Herold 1972; Karger and Malik 1975), for every study in the 1980s that produced positive findings, such as Glueck et al. (1982) which indicated a correlation between the phase in strategic management and a company's profitability, there was another study that seemed to indicate no correlation.

In 1983, Pearce et al. (1987) studied 97 small US manufacturing companies and studied the relationship between strategy and performance using subjective evaluations of return on assets, return on sales, sales growth and overall performance. They found that increased planning formality was consistently linked to improved financial performance.

Greenley (1989) reviewed nine previous studies which had looked at manufacturing firms in the UK and the USA. He reported that five of them had found a relationship between the use of strategic planning and performance; the other four did not find such a relationship.

Boyd (1991), who reviewed 49 journal articles and book chapters, concluded that the correlations were 'modest' and that the overall effect of planning on performance (was) 'very weak'.

More recent studies, however, using more sophisticated definitions of planning, suggest that a strategic planning process that adheres to the key elements of the conventional strategic management paradigm (including the development of mission statements, long-term goals, action plans and controls) do seem to support organizational performance, although the formalization of these processes in plans and manuals does not (Miller and Cardinal 1994).

Waalewijn and Segaar (1993) argued that in small companies profitability is associated with the extent that the company has progressed through the various phases of strategy development, i.e. financial planning, forecast-based planning, environmental planning, and integrated strategic management. Pekar and Abraham (1995) have shown that return on investment grows as strategic management sophistication grows. They conclude that the important issue is no longer whether a company should adopt a strategic management process, but what kind of process might be most appropriate and how best to manage and implement the process.

Several studies have looked at the impact of strategic planning on companies with different types of external environment. These studies have suggested that comprehensiveness of strategic planning does have a positive relationship with performance in stable industries, but a negative relationship in dynamic industries (Fredrickson 1984; Fredrickson and Mitchell 1984; Fredrickson and Acquinto 1989; Powell 1992; Miller and Cardinal 1994).

Anderson (2000), in a study of three separate industries, explored the impact both of strategic planning and autonomous actions nurtured and supported by managers, reflecting the Learning School. This study showed that in all three industries strategic planning has a positive relationship with economic performance. Autonomous actions only had a significant effect in the dynamic computer sector, not in the more stable banking and food industries. The interaction between the two was also important, showing that organizations that adopted both approaches simultaneously achieved higher levels of performance than organizations that embraced only one of the approaches.

Falshaw *et al.* (2006) drew attention to the lack of more recent research on the relationship between formal strategic planning and company performance and the almost complete lack of studies in the UK. In their study of 113 UK companies, they found no relationship between formal strategic planning and subjective company performance, although they recognized the limitations of the measurement validity and the fact that current success may be due to previous strategic decisions and planning processes, not current ones.

EVIDENCE IN THE THIRD SECTOR

As the ultimate measure of organizational success, there has been a significant number of studies which have attempted to operationalize the concept of effectiveness in the Third Sector as a way of assessing the impact of particular organizational characteristics. A number of these studies has focused on the impact of the boards of Third Sector organizations (Bradshaw *et al.* 1992; Murray *et al.* 1992; Siciliano and Floyd 1993; Green and Griesinger 1996).

However, of central concern here is the use of measures of effectiveness to assess the impact of strategic planning/management. Because of the difficulties in determining criteria to assess effectiveness in the Third Sector, the studies that have taken place have used a number of different methods or factors to assess their relationship to organizational effectiveness. These have included:

- income generation (Cameron 1982; Crittenden *et al.* 1988);
- financial strength, in terms of free reserves as a proportion of turnover, and financial efficiency (Van de Ven 1980; Glisson and Martin 1980; Siciliano 1997);
- reputation/satisfaction (as effective) with funders (Szabat *et al.* 1996; Green and Griesinger 1996);
- satisfaction (as effective) with CEO/staff (Siciliano 1997; Courtney 2005);
- assessment by experts (Green and Griesinger 1996);
- assessment (as effective) with all stakeholders (Herman and Renz 1996; Crittenden *et al.* 1988);
- community acceptance (Van de Ven 1980);
- goal attainment (Glisson and Martin 1980; Schumaker 1980; Cameron 1982; Byington *et al.* 1991; Sheehan 1996);
- service or membership growth (Odom and Boxx 1988; Crittenden *et al.* 1988; Jenster and Overstreet 1990; Bradshaw *et al.* 1992).

IMPACT OF STRATEGIC PLANNING ON EFFECTIVENESS

There have been a number of case studies of the impact of strategic planning and management in particular organizations and sections of the Third Sector, particularly in the USA. A number of these have related to church organizations (Wasdell 1980; Kohl 1984; Coghlan 1987); hospitals (Bart and Tabone 1998); a professional association (Ayal 1986); a profile of ten diverse 'excellent' non-profit organizations (Knauft *et al.* 1991); case studies of three very diverse non-profit organizations (Steiner *et al.* 1994); and a case study approach to three different types of non-profit organization (Chauhan 1998). These all purport to demonstrate how the use of various strategic planning and management techniques have been used beneficially in specific organizations and subsets of the Third Sector.

What is missing, however, from the literature on strategy in the Third Sector, is the rigour of academic empirical research (even with all the methodological difficulties of interpretation discussed above). Very few empirical studies have been carried out in relation to the effectiveness of strategic planning in either public or nonprofit organizations (Singh 1996). Stone and Crittendon (1993) describe it as a 'noticeable gap' in the literature. Lubelska (1996: 3) in a review of strategic management challenges in the UK Third Sector concluded:

> We need much more research into strategic management in the sector. We need to study the links between process and outputs and outcomes and how this relates to the organisation's type, size, etc. We need to know what strategies work – to assess success. We need to ask – what stops an organisation from being effective? What can be done about it? We need to know when, where and how to apply global success factors from other sectors. We need to know to what extent *general* good practice measures apply across the whole of the sector to achieve performance and to what extent *specific* factors are more important.

There have, however, been several attempts to study strategic planning and its outcomes more widely in the Third Sector in the USA. Webster and Wylie (1988) tried to examine the content of plans in terms of recommended organizational changes. However, they did not assess the extent to which recommendations were implemented or the impact of the process on organizational performance. Van de Ven (1980) studied childcare community projects and showed that those that used a formal programme planning model had significantly higher levels of efficiency and community acceptance than those that did not.

Odom and Boxx (1988) found that planning sophistication, categorized as informal, operational, and long-range planning, was positively related to church growth rate of Sunday school attendance, total additions and baptisms. Crittenden *et al.* (1988) also studied religious organizations and concluded that the select use of individual strategic planning elements, particularly having a formal written planning process in place, was sufficient, in many cases, to maintain stakeholder satisfaction, which in turn ensured a continued flow of resources.

Siciliano (1997), in a study of 240 YMCA organizations, showed that, regardless of size, those organizations that use a formal approach to strategic planning had higher levels of financial and social performance than those with less formal processes.

Jenster and Overstreet (1990) attempted to correlate strategic planning with selected measures of organizational performance of particular credit unions studied in the research. They concluded that formal planning is related to multiple institutional performance measures: that credit unions that plan were found to have significantly greater goal clarity, more effective communications, more timely and effective decision-making, and higher growth rates, although they report that their research findings did not enable them to assess the strength of the relationship or the extent to which strategic planning 'caused' the better performance (a problem identified earlier when looking at research in the private sector).

Crittenden (2000) in a three-year study of 51 Third Sector social service organizations in the USA found that organizations with little strategic direction and without a clear funding strategy were more likely to demonstrate poor or faltering financial performance.

A study of a wide range of medium to large-sized Third Sector organizations in Northern Ireland (Courtney 2005) found a significant correlation between participation in strategic management and perceived organizational effectiveness, but that this may be a product of organizational size rather than any causal relationship. The findings also suggest that the perceived benefits of engaging in strategic management were different from the criteria that chief officers who participated in the research used to define organizational effectiveness. The top four benefits of strategic management were perceived to be:

- clearer organizational focus;
- increased organizational unity;
- improved financial planning;
- improved programming and monitoring of performance.

In contrast the top four criteria for defining organizational effectiveness were:

- the impact the organization has on need;
- the extent that lives are changed in a positive way;
- the quality of services provided;
- the level of satisfaction of service-users.

Therefore, in assessing the effectiveness of strategic management it is critical to be clear about how effectiveness is defined, as well as measured.

Kearns and Scarpino (1996: 436) highlight many of the weaknesses in the literature on strategic planning in the Third Sector and conclude that:

> We should make the effort to assess the extent to which strategic planning actually affects organisational behaviours and the extent to which those behaviours achieved the desired results. The effort must begin with research on the actual content of strategic plans. But we must go further to obtain information on the extent to which recommendations in a formal planning document are actually implemented and the extent to which those actions achieved the desired result: What was the intended purpose of the strategic plan and what recommendations were made? When does implementation break down? To what extent did the implementation of recommendations achieve the desired effect on organizational performance?

SUMMARY

This chapter has highlighted some of the difficulties in carrying out research into strategic management and organizational effectiveness. It has explored some of the conflicting evidence for the effectiveness of strategic management in the private sector, including a number of increasingly sophisticated studies. The limited research on the effectiveness of strategic management in the Third Sector has also been analysed, which indicates a positive relationship. The need for further research in this area has also been highlighted.

QUESTIONS

1. Why is measuring effectiveness important?
2. What measures of effectiveness does the private sector use? To what extent are they unambiguous?
3. To what extent has the effectiveness of strategic management been proved in the private sector?
4. How should effectiveness in the Third Sector be defined?
5. What measures of effectiveness can be used by Third Sector organizations?
6. How might different stakeholders view the concept of organizational effectiveness of Third Sector organizations?
7. To what extent has the effectiveness of strategic management in the Third Sector been proven?

DISCUSSION TOPIC

Might strategic management be more effective in some Third Sector organizations or external environments than others?

SUGGESTED READING

D. P. Forbes (1998) 'Measuring the unmeasurable: empirical studies of non-profit organization effectiveness', *Non-profit and Voluntary Sector Quarterly*, 27(2), 159–82.

J. I. Siciliano (1997) 'The relationship between formal planning and performance in nonprofit organizations', *Nonprofit Management and Leadership*, 7(4), 387–403.

Melissa Stone, Barbara Bigelow and William Crittenden (1999) 'Research on strategic management in nonprofit organizations: synthesis, analysis, and future directions', *Administration & Society*, July.

PART II
STRATEGIC THINKING

7 STRATEGIC ANALYSIS: THE EXTERNAL ENVIRONMENT

OVERVIEW

Third Sector organizations do not exist in a vacuum, but in a changing (in some cases turbulent) external environment which can have profound implications for them and their future. This external environment can provide important opportunities for the organization to develop, but also crucial threats to its future. This chapter explores the tools and techniques used by Third Sector organizations to analyse the external environment in which they operate and the implications of that environment for future strategy.

LEARNING OBJECTIVES

After studying this chapter, you should be able to:

- explain the importance of understanding trends in the external environment before making strategic decisions;
- describe ways of scanning and analysing the external environment and its potential impact;
- outline the limitations of some of the tools and models.

EXTERNAL ASSESSMENT

Third Sector organizations exist in a complex, often dynamic and uncertain environment. At any one time, while one aspect of the environment may be relatively stable, another may be in a perpetual state of flux. The success of any organization depends on how it adapts to and interacts with this external environment, which in turn depends on developing a clear understanding of what is happening in the external world.

Pettigrew and Whipp (1993) in a three-year study found that involvement in environmental assessment at the top of an organization, involving all its functions, was one of five key success factors in the highest performing companies they studied.

Third Sector organizations exist to make a change in the world, not to perpetuate themselves, provide employment for the staff or make profits for shareholders (although some social enterprises may make limited payments to investors). Their beneficiaries exist in the world external to them. Having an understanding of their lives and the influences and trends that affect their lives is crucial if they are to respond effectively to their needs and aspirations.

Third Sector organizations are also not only passive players blown about by changes in the external environment, but are often very active in public education, advocacy and campaigning – actually trying to influence the external environment (see the major case study of Greenpeace in Part VI).

The external environment of Third Sector organizations also provides the resources to enable them to thrive. These resources might include donations, grants, contracts, sales, goodwill, volunteers, staff and physical resources. Understanding the external environment in which these resources exist is, therefore, crucial in planning how best to acquire the resources needed by the organization.

A number of useful tools and techniques have been developed to enable organizations to analyse what is going on in this environment, which are examined in this chapter. Many of these are very relevant to the Third Sector.

OPPORTUNITIES AND THREATS

The final two parts of SWOT – OT – refer to the Opportunities and Threats that may exist for an organization in the external environment (Weihrich 1982). It can be a very powerful and simple technique to ask the key stakeholders, especially board members, staff and volunteers, in an organization to look outside of it and suggest what trends or changes in the external environment might constitute opportunities for the organization to take advantage of in future, or alternatively what might constitute threats to the organization achieving its vision, which the organization may need to try and avoid or manage.

However, even the ever-popular SWOT analysis has been the subject of criticism (Haberberg 2000) for the following reasons:

- being too imprecise;
- failing to evaluate the strategic importance of any of the suggested strengths or weaknesses;
- assuming a static external environment;
- providing no assistance in assessing products or services that might become strengths in the future if only they were developed a bit further.

SWOT has been criticized (Fahy and Smithee 1999; Hill and Westbrook 1997; Valentin 2001; Ip and Koo 2004) for not being able to distinguish between important and unimportant opportunities and threats. For example, simply listing the potential threats and opportunities doesn't indicate how important each of them might be, how likely they are to happen, or what the impact would be if they did happen. It also doesn't help in assessing the impact of a combination of the factors.

It is therefore important to prioritize the external factors suggested in order to focus attention on those which are most likely and would have the greatest impact (see pp. 93–108), and also to consider what actions need to be taken in light of these priority issues. More sophisticated techniques have been developed to analyse the risks (another word for Threats) that organizations face, or in order to create or maintain a risk register which is now a legal requirement for most Third Sector organizations in the UK. SWOT has also been criticized for stifling creativity and vision (Patrickson and Bamber 1995). Johnson *et al.* (2008) suggest that SWOT analysis should not be used as a substitute for more rigorous, thinking.

Cooperrider and various colleagues have developed an alternative to SWOT analysis – SOAR – which uses an asset-based rather than a deficit-based approach. SOAR keeps the consideration of Strengths and Opportunities, but replaces Threats and Weaknesses with Aspirations and Results. It is based on the concept of 'appreciative enquiry' (Cooperrider and Whitney 1999) which attempts to bring out the best in people, organizations and the world around them. It involves the art and practice of asking questions that strengthen the system's capacity to apprehend, anticipate and heighten positive potential.

SCENARIO ANALYSIS

One of the key criticisms of strategic planning is that in general it is impossible to predict the future. Often strategic plans articulate a set of assumptions about the external environment. Significant unexpected changes in the external environment, can, however, seriously derail an organization's plans. A planning technique developed in the oil industry to deal with this issue is scenario analysis (Schwartz 1991; van der Heijden 1996), whereby a number of different plausible future scenarios are generated and the potential impact on the organization's future is considered, as well as an assessment being made of the likelihood of each scenario coming true. This enables the organization to avoid strategies becoming derailed because assumptions about the future turned out to be unreliable.

Such scenario planning provides the organization with the opportunity to develop its plans in ways that will take most advantage of the possibilities provided by the most positive scenarios and also to devise strategies to deal with the more negative scenarios in case they came about. This avoids the limitations of strategies that are frequently developed on the basis of only one set of assumptions about the future and also enables the organizations to track some key features in the external environment to provide an early warning that a particular scenario may be developing.

The process commences in a traditional way with a listing of the external drivers of change that the organization needs to consider (see p. 118). These external factors are then prioritized on the importance of the factor and the extent of its uncertainty. Two axes are chosen for the two most important and uncertain factors in order to create a four-box model. A pen picture is drawn up of the future based on each box and the implications for the organization and its plans if that pen picture were to become a reality. A relevant example of scenario planning is shown in Box 7.1.

BOX 7.1 THE DEVELOPMENT OF SCENARIOS FOR CIVIL SOCIETY

In 2006 the Carnegie UK Trust set up an Inquiry into the Future of Civil Society in the UK and Ireland, using futures thinking to identify potential threats and opportunities for the sector, as a whole, looking towards 2025. The process first of all identified the (social, political, technological, economic, environmental and organizational) drivers of change for the sector, including core uncertainties. These were clustered under four key headings: the limits of economics, personal values, shifting activism, and the state and the individual. Four key potential scenarios for the future were identified:

Local life: resource scarcity and energy costs lead to the regeneration of local life, with civil society at the vanguard, but there is insularity and competition between localities.

Athenian voices (electronic age): technology and innovation lead to greater involvement in politics and inclusive debate, but technology also encourages atomization and individualism.

Diversity wars: cultural, economic, religious and ethnic diversity and environmental scarcity lead to conflicts between and within communities.

Global compact: the security state constructed for the war on terror is no longer considered effective. Civil society leads the campaign against exploitation inherent in cheap goods and monitors labour practices. Migrant labour is another story.

The implications of each of these scenarios were explored to identify seven key questions that need to be addressed by civil society and the potential implications for different kinds of civil society organizations.

The process used by the Inquiry into the Future of Civil Society provides a very useful model and individual tools that individual Third Sector organizations can use in considering their own future, as well as providing ideas that may be relevant to specific organizations.

A similar scenario approach was used by ACEVO in 2007 to help Third Sector leaders consider the future of the sector. The two axes that they chose after deliberation on a range of external factors were the wealth of the country (rich or poor) and cultural values (individualism or altruism).

(See Scenarios for Civil Society 2007, Carnegie UK Trust; Third Sector Leadership in 2007, ACEVO)

Scenario analysis is a useful tool for strategic development for four key reasons:

- it enables assumptions that people hold about the future to be articulated and confronted;
- it recognizes degrees of uncertainty, enabling organizations to work with what they don't know;
- it widens perspectives, by gathering information from various viewpoints and identifying and addressing blind spots;
- it helps to identify and resolve conflicts and dilemmas.

One of the weaknesses of the technique is that only two axes can be chosen. Furthermore, other critical uncertain factors may not be addressed, which later prove to be vital.

PROBABILITY IMPACT ANALYSIS GRID

With concern about the limited usefulness of simply listing the external factors which might impact on the organization in the future, a Probability Impact Analysis Grid can help ensure that each external factor is assessed against the likelihood of occurrence, and the impact if it did occur. This enables an organization to give most attention to those external factors which are most likely and/or might have the greatest impact. An impact analysis matrix is presented in Table 7.1.

Table 7.1   Probability impact analysis grid

		Impact		
		High	**Medium**	**Low**
Likelihood	**High**	Priority action	Action	Monitor effects
	Medium	Action	Contingency plan	Track
	Low	Contingency plan	Track	Track

PEST

Another common technique for exploring the external environment is to analyse external trends under a number of different headings. A common set of headings is known as PEST analysis: Political, Economic, Social, Technological.

In PEST analysis, the various trends and drivers for change in each area, and what the potential impact of each might be on the organization, are explored. This can be done in a participative way (as a brainstorm or with focus groups with organizational stakeholders, including board members and staff), or by expert research of the relevant literature, or using the Delphi technique to enrol experts to refine the external analysis over a series of stages to achieve consensus. The PEST framework has also been adapted as PESTLE to include legal and environmental issues (see Box 7.2).

BOX 7.2 PESTLE ANALYSIS

In 2011 nfpSynergy used a PESTLE analysis to suggest the following socio-economic trends affecting charities:

Political factors:
- declining statutory funding;
- declining confidence in the political system;

▶

- the evolution of EU influence;
- increased privatization and local strategic partnerships.

Economic factors:
- the impact of the recession;
- low interest rates;
- the slump in house prices and volatile stock markets.

Social factors:
- the evolution of the family;
- the ageing population;
- cultural diversification.

Technological factors:
- transformation of the technology and communications sphere.

Legal factors:
- the growth of equalities legislation;
- the growth of privacy and data protection regulations;
- the growth of political campaigning among charities.

Environmental factors:
- climate change and sustainability.

They suggest that charities should consider the following in response to these trends:
- make people believe in your charity and give people confidence to give;
- stop depending on the government;
- watch the markets;
- understand the families who make up your supporters;
- the over 65s are overlooked;
- make giving the new leisure activity;
- use new media to spread the word cost-effectively;
- use the new targeting opportunities that all media present;
- use freedom of information.

(Guild and Saxton 2011)

Other issues that are likely to be of particular importance to the voluntary sector might include changing needs, changing attitudes (the public, funders, users) and funding.

An alternative acronym that might be more appropriate for the complex environment of the Third Sector is PLANET DEFOE: Public policy, Legislation, Attitudes, Need, Expectations (of users and other stakeholders), Technology, Demography, Economy, Funding, Other organizations, Environment. See Box 7.3 for an example of an analysis of external trends by a Third Sector organization.

BOX 7.3 EXAMPLES OF EXTERNAL CHANGES FOR A CANCER CHARITY

Cancer:
- breast cancer deaths decreasing;

- cancer to overtake heart disease as the no. 1 killer;
- lung cancer overtaking breast cancer;
- increasing research into cancer (causes, cures, prevention);
- life expectancy and quality of life of people with cancer is increasing;
- more awareness of cancer: people can talk about it;
- increased awareness of men's cancers;
- more overweight people: increase in cancers.

Demographics:
- people living longer (higher expectations);
- increased percentage of elderly in the population.

Health service:
- increasing use of voluntary organizations to deliver services;
- increasing waiting times in NHS for detection and treatment;
- specialization of medical services;
- ageism in health services;
- impact of healthy living centres.

Attitudes:
- younger generation;
- more proactive about their health;
- less likely to put up with poor service;
- patients more empowered/taking more control and wanting choice;
- increasing acceptance of complementary therapies;
- changing attitudes towards charities (increasing awareness of waste, administration and overlap);
- more awareness of gender issues.

IT:
- internet: wider access to information;
- on-line giving;
- a lot of conflicting information available to the public.

Funding/fundraising:
- increased fundraising competition for funds and volunteers;
- greater accountability for donations (administration costs);
- more competition for funds and volunteers;
- tighter statutory financial regime.

(*Source:* notes by the author of a facilitated strategy workshop
of a UK cancer charity)

NEEDS ASSESSMENT

Critical to the success of any Third Sector organization is clear information on the needs the organization is concerned with. It is an important aspect of planning services and also engenders support from funders and donors. A needs assessment requires the organization to be very clear about the precise population that it wishes to benefit (e.g. all homeless people, whether single, young or with families, in London) and what aspects of the target population you are concerned with. For example, if the target population is people who are homeless in London, is your primary area of concern their physical health, their employability, alcohol or drug dependence, family relationships, etc.? It is then important to find appropriate sources of data or credible ways of measuring the needs in the relevant population. It must be clear what is being measured and how it can be measured in a way that is reliable and valid. There may already be good quality up-to-date data available, which can be accessed to provide a clear picture of the needs your organization is concerned with. If not, it may be necessary to carry out, or commission, appropriate research. There is a large literature available on research methods, to help guide those engaged in social research.

BOX 7.4 COMMUNITIES THAT CARE (CTC)

Communities that Care was developed and is widely used in the USA, and is operated in the UK by the Social Research Unit at Dartington. It provides a systematic methodology for assessing the needs of, and risks facing, children and young people in a specified geographic area, and then enabling the local community to identify evidence-based programmes that can be adopted in order to address the needs/risks that have been identified.

The CtC process works at both a local community and strategic level. Analysis of the particular risks influencing children and young people, using a standardised questionnaire, leads to a strategy where genuine priorities are targeted for action, allowing informed decisions to be taken about existing services and the most effective way of delivering them. Gaps in provision are identified and filled by introducing new interventions which have clear outcomes and a track record of success, having been evaluated using robust impact evaluation methods (typically randomized controlled trials). CtC advises sites to use the Blueprints database, which provides details of interventions which are known from robust research evidence to be effective (or at least promising) in reducing risk factors and enhancing resilience and other positive attributes.

Research shows there are influential risk factors in children's lives that increase the chances they will develop health and behavior problems as they grow older. Equally important, there are protective factors that help to shield young people from problems in circumstances that would otherwise place them at risk.

Using a school survey and a step by step approach, CtC makes it possible to map factors in the lives of local children that are making it more or less likely they will experience: school failure, school-age pregnancy and sexually transmitted diseases, or become involved in drug abuse, violence and crime.

CtC aims to enhance the level of protection and to reduce the risks of antisocial behavior and adolescent problems - making it less likely that children will be driven towards the margins of society as they grow into young adults.

CtC offers a comprehensive programme of training and technical support to local co-ordinators.

CtC is one of the first practical methodologies through which systematic use has been made of the research knowledge about overlapping risk and protective factors to target individuals, families, schools and communities. Through an holistic approach, communities learn how to measure and map the major risk and protective factors such as youth crime, drug abuse, school-age pregnancy and school failure in their neighbourhoods and how they can effectively be addressed. The CtC School Survey has been used in a UK-wide study of levels of risk and protection factors, 'Youth at Risk', as well as in specific local communities. Findings of the survey can be used to benchmark local data sets.

CtC offers a support service that includes resource assessment and strategic planning to local partnerships.

(For further information:
www.sdrg.org/ctcresource/index.htm
HYPERLINK "http://www.dartington.org.uk"www.dartington.org.uk)

Communities that Care is an example of a specific methodology that has been developed in the US, and now also used in the UK, to assess the needs of young people in a community, using a school-based survey, which has the advantage of capturing virtually all the young people in an area. The Communities that Care approach is highlighted in Box 7.4.

Increasingly, social research projects have been moving away from a deficit-based approach to social issues, i.e. focusing on problems and the negative aspects of the target population, towards an asset-based approach which emphasizes their strengths, rights, aspirations and potential and how these positive qualities can be reinforced and utilized.

In relation to community needs and assets there have been various attempts to create a suitable framework to assess the state of a geographical area. The Young Foundation Local Wellbeing Project, for example, developed a Wellbeing and Resilience Measure (WARM) (Mguni and Bacon 2010) to obtain insights into both assets and vulnerabilities in relation to self, supports, and systems and structures, in a local area. The framework uses surveys and statistical data to assess and benchmark community assets and vulnerabilities in relation to the following:

- self: life satisfaction, education, health and material well-being;
- supports: strong and stable families;
- systems and structures: local economy, public services, crime and anti-social behaviour, and infrastructure and belonging.

Some of the benchmark information used in WARM might include questions from frequently used surveys such as the General Health Questionnaire, which probes whether respondents:

- are capable of making decisions;
- enjoy day-to-day activities;
- have problems overcoming difficulties;
- have the ability to face problems;
- are losing confidence.

Other information, which can be benchmarked against national averages, is also collected from respondents, such as:

■ percentage employed;
■ percentage unemployed;
■ percentage retired;
■ percentage expressing overall job satisfaction;
■ health problems: anxiety, depression, etc.;
■ financial situation;
■ change in financial position in the last year;
■ financial expectations for the year ahead;
■ whether respondent saves from current income;
■ confidence;
■ frequency of meeting people;
■ whether living with a spouse or partner;
■ caring for someone disabled;
■ frequency of talking to neighbours;
■ whether respondent likes present neighbourhood.

The information analysed can then be used to identify ways to build on community assets and respond to vulnerabilities.

An approach to understanding local communities, based on the concept of social capital, has been developed by CENI (Community Evaluation Northern Ireland) (Morrissey *et al.* 2005, 2008; DSD 2006). This assesses the social assets of a local community based on:

■ community capacity: the number of community-based groups in the area.
■ community capability:
■ the ability to draw in funding and resources;
■ managing funding and resources;
■ carrying out programmes and activities based on need;
■ working with other groups and communities;
■ being representative of the entire population of the area.

This approach attempts to measure three aspects of social capital:

■ Bonding: the level of trust between groups and individuals within the community (the degree to which members of the community are empowered, as measured by educational attainment and economic activity; the degree to which members of the community are connected with each other, as measured by crime data, single person households and lone parent households; the level and quality of community infrastructure, as measured by the number of groups, organizations and amenities).

- Bridging: the level of trust and relationships with individuals and groups in other communities (engagement with other communities, as measured by residential segregation and social class mix; being accessible to other communities, as measured by the average travel to work distance and the number of users of health centres; being innovative in the sense of being open to new ideas, as measured by educational attainment (see above) and capacity to attract funding).

- Linking: the quality of relations between communities and decision-makers (resources, as measured by relationships with funders and funding acquired; influence, as measured by membership of partnership bodies and fora, and the assessment of decision-makers about their influence).

VISIBLE COMMUNITIES

Another approach to assessing the assets and needs of a particular community is to benchmark a community against a set of quality standards. Community Matters has developed a set of licensed quality standards, using the acronym VISIBLE, which is related to the following principles:

- A VOICE to represent issues of local concern: community organizations provide a voice for local concerns and for people whose views may not always be heard;

- An INDEPENDENT and politically neutral organization: community organizations are independent and politically neutral with a powerful commitment to democratic principles;

- A SERVICE provider for local people: community organizations deliver services to local people;

- An INITIATOR of projects to meet locally identified needs: community organizations initiate new projects and services that respond to local needs;

- A BUILDER of partnerships with other local organizations and groups: community organizations build partnerships with other local organizations and groups;

- A strong LOCAL network of people and organizations: community organizations provide a strong local network of people and organizations working together and supporting each other;

- A way to ENGAGE local people to become active in their communities: community organizations provide ways of engaging people to become active in their communities.

There are various quality standards related to each of these principles at a single level, by which a community can benchmark itself against the standards. There are versions of the standards for small community groups (Visible Review) and one for larger community groups with staff and premises (Visible Accredited Standards).

MANDATE ANALYSIS

Mandate analysis focuses on the policy context of the external environment. It has been developed by Bryson (1995) for use specifically in the public and non-profit sectors.

A mandate is 'support for a policy or course of action' (*Concise Oxford Dictionary*). Mandate analysis is a process of exploring the written documents that exist that support the mission of the organization. Mandates for a Third Sector organization might include the following kinds of documents:

- UN conventions and declarations of rights;
- EU legislation or policy documents;
- government legislation or policy documents;
- government statements;
- election manifestos;
- regional or local government policy documents;
- research reports;
- evaluations of the organization's work;
- the organization's constitution or founding document;
- quotes about the organization's work by significant individuals.

These documents can be used by the board and staff to explore the fundamental bases for the organization's mission, to understand the extent and nature of the need that the organization is concerned with, and to reflect on the distinctive competencies of the organization. These are all important in considering the appropriate strategies for the future. The key challenge with mandate analysis is to summarize and quote the key mandates which justify the organization's future strategy in a way that is coherent, concise and convincing.

ORGANIZATIONAL MAPPING

For all organizations, one of the most important issues is to consider what other organizations exist which are involved in similar work and how they might impact on the work of the organization. For Third Sector organizations it is likely to be important to avoid overlapping services and for each organization to have its own distinctive contribution to make. This distinction might be based on:

- the specific geographical area being served (e.g. Glas Cymru/Welsh Water or Coin Street Community Builders in Part VI);
- the particular client group (e.g. Behind the Mask (see the website case study) and Box 1.2: Action for Children);
- the distinctive nature or quality of the service provided (e.g. My Time CIC on the website shows how one organization has specialized in the provision of culturally sensitive counselling and training services);
- the cost, i.e. providing a free service to individuals who cannot avail themselves of a service for which they would normally be charged, or providing a service at a much lower cost than other organizations (Greenwich Leisure Limited (website case study) have been able to access alternative sources of finance and provide council leisure services at a lower cost than the councils would charge themselves).

La Piana (2005) argues that Third Sector organizations should not be reticent about the idea of competing with other organizations. In his view resources should flow to those organizations which are most effective and efficient, from those which are less so. Being upfront about this challenge, he would suggest, helps organizations to focus on how they can be more effective and efficient than the other players in the field.

The substantial development of social enterprises brings the Third Sector much more into the competitive trading environment where knowledge about the other organizations and their products and services within the marketplace is absolutely vital if the enterprise is to succeed. What products and/or services are they providing? What prices are they selling their services/products at? What is the quality of the products/ services?

Opportunities for collaboration or strategic alliances – in order to improve the impact on the mission, or to improve efficiency or organizational capacity – are also crucially and increasingly important to many Third Sector organizations in achieving their visions of social change (Hudson 2005). Despite the literature which suggests that 'partnership rhetoric' is often confused and understates the implications of overindulging in 'partnerships', given their demands in terms of time, commitment and trust (Rees *et al.* 2011), other literature suggests that partnerships can bring economies of scale, economies of scope (using the different capabilities of the different organizations), and opportunities for mutual learning (Bovaird 2004).

For all these reasons it can be very useful to carry out an organizational mapping exercise which compares the organization with each of the other organizations which might be considered similar. The comparison should clarify both the similarities and differences.

In developing a future strategy, this analysis of other players can help in enabling the organization to focus on those things in which it has a distinctive role to play and perhaps adapt or withdraw from services which overlap with other agencies.

PORTER'S COMPETITIVE ADVANTAGE

Although 'competition' is often an uncomfortable concept in the Third Sector, Porter's competitive strategy concepts can be relevant to the sector (Phills 2005), particularly in considering the impact of other organizations, such as those heavily involved in social enterprises, fundraising or trying to obtain or keep contracts with statutory bodies. Lindenberg (2001), however, found problems in trying to apply Porter's framework to a particular international Third Sector organization, meeting resistance from both a cultural and mechanical/conceptual perspective. Managers in the organization found the language of market and competition problematic and found it difficult to know where to place donors, for example.

Oster (1995) has adapted Porter's model for the Third Sector. She suggests the following six forces as relevant to the Third Sector 'market':

- relations amongst existing organizations;
- the threat of new entrants;

- the threat of new substitutes (competition from alternative services);
- the number and power of the user group;
- the power of the funding group, which typically increases with the proportion of revenues;
- the power of the supplier industry, especially the staff and volunteers of Third Sector organizations.

Although the meaning and relevance of Porter's industry analysis framework for the general Third Sector has been described as 'dubious' and 'not very useful' (Goold 1997), Oster (1995) describes in some detail how the future strategies of Third Sector organizations can be very significantly affected by the following factors:

- other organizations moving in and providing a better or cheaper service;
- the development of substitutes (e.g. the development of fostering rather than children's homes, or community care rather than residential homes or hospitals);
- the power of funders to, for example, grant or not grant a service contract which could result in the destruction or contraction of the organization;
- the power of users, e.g. organizational members of an umbrella Third Sector agency may have considerable power to determine the future of the agency.

La Piana (2005) has developed a detailed methodology for Third Sector organizations to use to assess and measure relatedness to other organizations, using a market research process. These other organizations may be:

- direct competitors, delivering the same kinds of service to the same client groups in the same geographical area;
- substitute competitors, who meet the same need, but in a different way;
- indirect competitors, who compete for funds, volunteers, trustees, etc., but not in service delivery;
- potential competitors, which do not currently compete in service delivery, but may move into the same field.

In assessing organizational relatedness La Piana recommends including the following in assessing an organization against competitors, in order to identify the top competitors:

- Customers: market share in terms of turnover, number of clients and sites where the service is delivered; future trends in need and demand; type of client.
- Programme/service delivery: experience and quality of, and reputation in, delivering the service; changes in programme focus, past and future.
- Leadership: quality of leadership, staffing and volunteers.
- Finances: financial stability; unit costs and charges; fundraising; diversity of funding.
- Marketing/communications: quality of marketing and public relations.

La Piana has developed a matrix of 12 generic strategies (both competitive and collaborative), which can be chosen depending on whether: your own organization is in a strong competitive position; there are many or few competitors in the market; and trends in the market suggest that it is shrinking or expanding.

ENVIRONMENTAL SCANNING

Another model that has been developed to analyse the external world is known as environmental scanning, which is rather akin to a submarine echo sounder which detects other crafts or objects, which might be relevant to the mission of the submarine, and shows them up on a radar screen. The environmental scanning makes a judgement as to how imminent or distant the potential impact is, by its closeness to the centre of the radar screen, and how big the impact might be, by the size of the image on the screen.

The strength of this model is being able to represent external influences visually. The weakness is that it doesn't provide any methodology to determine what factors should appear on the screen, or how large or close to the centre they should be (see Figure 7.1).

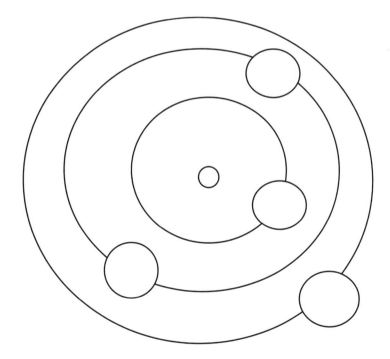

Fig 7.1 Environmental scanning

SUMMARY

This chapter has highlighted the importance of understanding the changing external environment in making strategic decisions. It has explored a number of tools and techniques that can be used to help analyse this external environment, including Opportunities and Threats; PEST; PLANET DEFOE; environmental scanning; scenario planning; needs assessment; mandate analysis; and organizational mapping.

QUESTIONS

1. What external factors are likely to drive and/or inhibit the achievement of an organization's mission?
2. What tools are available for a Third Sector organization to analyse its external environment?
3. Considering an organization you know, list the main external factors that need to be taken into consideration in the development of its future strategy.
4. Considering one organization you know, list the documents (mandates), especially in public policy, that provide support to the organization's strategy.
5. What are the characteristics of an organization that would suggest that it should be considered as a competitor?
6. What are the characteristics of an organization that suggest that it should be considered a potential partner/collaborator?
7. Think about one organization you know; list the organizations that are similar; and then describe the similarities and differences between these organizations and the organization you know.
8. What areas of work within the Third Sector do you think it would be easy for a new organization to enter? Which would be difficult? And why?

DISCUSSION TOPIC

What external trends are likely to affect most Third Sector organizations over the next five years? How many of them can be described under the headings 'political', 'economic', 'social' and 'technological'?

SUGGESTED READING

John M. Bryson (2011) *Strategic Planning for Public and Nonprofit Organizations*, Jossey-Bass.

Sharon Oster (1995) *Strategic Management for Nonprofit Organizations*, Oxford.

D. La Piana (2005) *Play to Win: The Nonprofit Guide to Competitive Strategy*, Jossey-Bass.

8 STRATEGIC ANALYSIS: THE ORGANIZATION

OVERVIEW

The 'rubber band theory' of how organizations develop suggests that if an organization can clearly articulate where it is now, as well as the vision of where it wants to go, that vision will catapult the organization accordingly. In this chapter, ways of defining where an organization is at present will be examined. Unlike a couple of decades ago, organizations can now choose from a range of useful frameworks designed for the board and staff to review their Third Sector organizations. Alternatively they can use some of the more general well-tested tools and techniques (some of which have already been mentioned above) that are available as a result of previous thinking and practice in other sectors about strategic planning.

This chapter explores some of the ways that the board and staff of Third Sector organizations might review themselves as part of their strategic analysis. Review tools that have proved useful in other sectors as well as a number of tools that have been specifically designed for the Third Sector and public sectors will be examined.

LEARNING OBJECTIVES

After studying this chapter, you should be able to:

- explain the importance of carrying out an internal review;
- describe some common tools for carrying out an internal review;
- outline some of the limitations of the various tools of internal analysis.

INTERNAL REVIEW TOOLS AND TECHNIQUES

It is crucial, for an organization in planning its future, to have a very clear and honest understanding of where it is now. The following are some of the models and tools that have been developed by strategic planning practitioners and writers over the last 30 years to help evaluate organizations and their environments, starting with some of the simpler tools.

STRENGTHS AND WEAKNESSES

The SW (Strengths and Weaknesses) of a SWOT analysis, although used frequently in a variety of contexts, is still a straightforward and invaluable way of bringing out views of what an organization is currently good and bad at, and which can be carried out without external facilitation or audit. This enables the organization to build on its unique strengths so that the strategy eventually adopted reflects what the organization does particularly well. It also enables the organization to develop strategies to work on, or manage, the things that it currently does less well, or indeed to withdraw involvement in those areas and leave it to others who will do it better.

The kinds of strengths that a Third Sector organization might have include:

- a well-known name and image (brand capital);
- significant financial reserves (financial capital);
- effective income generation (financial capital);
- strong user participation (social capital);
- a high level of expertise in relation to the service/user group (intellectual capital);
- technology skills and systems (intellectual capital);
- being highly innovative (intellectual capital);
- a well developed and evaluated service methodology (intellectual capital);
- have strongly committed and motivated staff and volunteers (human capital);
- have well-known people associated with the organization (human and brand capital);
- use volunteers extensively (human capital);
- have well developed policies, systems, procedures, databases, etc. (structural capital);
- strong collaborative relationships with other organizations in the non-profit, private and/or public sectors (relational capital);
- ability and flexibility to develop new programmes quickly in response to need (adaptive capability).

Size and competitive strengths

Research in the UK by nfpSynergy (2010) found that key strengths that can help Third Sector organizations get a competitive advantage include:

- ability to demonstrate success and achievement;
- constant innovation and development;
- keeping close to the needs of stakeholders;
- strong organizational values and beliefs;
- having a unique purpose and activities;
- ensuring a breadth of income sources;
- investing in a highly skilled workforce;

- strong branding and corporate positioning;
- high level of public awareness;
- emotive issue on which to fundraise;
- large database of loyal supporters.

Interestingly the things that provided competitive advantage varied according to the size of the organizations. Smaller organizations (those with a turnover under £500,000) tended to focus on (in order of priority):

- keeping close to the needs of stakeholders;
- ability to demonstrate success and achievement;
- constant innovation and development;
- strong organizational values and beliefs;
- ensuring a breadth of income sources.

Medium-sized organizations (those with a turnover of between £500,000 and £5 million) tended to consider the following as their approach to achieving competitive advantage (in order of priority):

- ability to demonstrate success and achievement;
- strong organizational values and beliefs;
- keeping close to the needs of stakeholders;
- ensuring a breadth of income sources;
- having a unique purpose and activities;
- investing in a highly skilled workforce.

Large organizations (those with a turnover of over £5 million) tended to consider their strengths in relation to competitive advantage as (in order of priority):

- ability to demonstrate success and achievement;
- strong branding and corporate positioning;
- having a unique purpose and activities;
- investing in a highly skilled workforce;
- high level of public awareness.

These findings suggest that the ability to demonstrate success and achievement is critically important for all sizes of organization, which may imply that success has the potential to breed success; and it is not enough to be successful – it is also important to find ways of measuring and demonstrating that success.

Keeping close to stakeholders was vital for smaller organizations, but seemed to become less important, the larger the organization. Large organizations particularly valued strong branding and corporate positioning, in addition to a high level of public awareness.

Strong organizational values and beliefs were very important for small and medium-sized organizations, but less so for large organizations, which valued more having a unique purpose and activities. Constant innovation and development was

Table 8.1 Confrontational SWOT matrix

	O1	O2	O3	O4	T1	T2	T3	T4
S1								
S2								
S3								
S4								
W1								
W2								
W3								
W4								

particularly important for smaller organizations, but much less so for the medium and large-sized organizations, which believed that investing in a highly skilled workforce was more important in terms of competitive advantage.

Ensuring a breadth of income sources was particularly important for small and medium-sized organizations. Large organizations may already have breadth of income sources, so may not have considered this so highly.

Having completed all four aspects of a SWOT analysis, the various internal and external factors can be put into a confrontational matrix, with Strengths and Weaknesses on one axis and Opportunities and Threats on the other. A score can be given to each box to indicate the importance of each box, so that the most important factors (combining the SWOT findings) can be identified and addressed. Table 8.1 shows a confrontational matrix with the most important of the Strengths, Weaknesses, Opportunities and Threats.

EVALUATION

One of the most common ways for Third Sector organizations to review how it is doing is to carry out, or commission, an evaluation. This can be done by internal review (self-evaluation) at one end of the spectrum or by an entirely independent person or company at the other. It may be initiated by the organization itself, or in some cases it is an evaluation of the organization carried out, or commissioned, by a core funder. The UK government's 'Scrutiny' initiative resulted in major external evaluations of many Third Sector organizations every five years. Oster (1995: 144) suggests that, because of concerns about objectivity, external evaluations are especially helpful in non-profit organizations.

Whether it is the initiative of the organization and is entirely controlled by the organization, or is imposed by a funder or some negotiated compromise, evaluation is frequently the first step and trigger to the move towards a more strategic approach to the management and development of the organization. Evaluation has been defined

(Weiss 1998: 4) as 'the systematic assessment of the operation and/or outcomes of a programme or policy, compared to a set of explicit or implicit standards, as a means of contributing to the improvement of the programme or policy'. Evaluations can be at the level of programme/project or the whole organization. Programme evaluations may be carried out to:

■ test a new programme idea;

■ make mid-course corrections to a programme;

■ choose the best of several alternatives;

■ decide whether to continue funding a programme;

■ decide whether to expand, contract, divest, mainstream or end a programme.

However, as Weiss points out, such evaluations are also sometimes instigated as:

■ a PR exercise for the organization: to make it look good;

■ to justify further funding to an external funder;

■ to duck responsibility for taking a difficult decision, e.g. to close the programme or remove a problematic member of staff;

■ to postpone a decision.

A survey of Third Sector organizations (CENI 2010) found the following as the most important ways an evaluation was used (in order of priority):

■ learn about what is working;

■ evidence benefits/outcomes;

■ improve work;

■ inform service planning and strategic planning;

■ assist with funding bids;

■ improve reporting to funders;

■ promote work;

■ inform development of practice in the field;

■ inform policy development in the field.

In contrast, however, funders emphasized the value of evaluations in 'providing accountability for projects', 'ensuring project objectives/targets are met' and 'ensuring programme/policy objectives. This difference in perspective has resulted in research findings in the evaluation arena that 'third sector organisations and funders experience a great deal of frustration and tension due to a mismatch of expectations and poor communications' (Arvidson 2009).

Evaluations determined by the needs of funders are often considered by Third Sector organizations to be 'meaningless and uninteresting at best, or inappropriate and damaging (misrepresentation of achievements, forcing organisational change) at worst' (ibid.: 12–13) and a resource drain and distraction from what they should be doing (Carman and Fredericks 2008). They are also often unclear how the funders are using the information from evaluations to aid decision-making. Behrens and Kelly (2008) argue that, as well as negotiating between the competing requirements of stakeholders, a series of, what they call, false choices or misconceptions needs to be addressed:

- evaluations that give clear answers versus evaluations that examine complexity without single cause-and-effect relationships;
- evaluations for learning and inquiry as opposed to evaluations that determine accountability to results;
- real-time data for day-to-day decision-making, as opposed to determination of causality of outcomes.

They call for improved understanding of how evaluation processes can transcend these 'false choices'.

Scope of Third Sector evaluations

Evaluations can be carried out in many different ways and focus on different aspects of the organization, depending on who has commissioned the evaluation and who is carrying it out and their particular interests and skills. An evaluation of a Third Sector funded organization might cover the following areas, in addition to providing a general description of the organization:

1. Aims and objectives of the organization:
   - how these can contribute towards the attainment of government/the funders' policy objectives, partnership approaches and use of volunteers;
   - whether the current activities of the organization are in line with its aims and objectives;
   - relevance of aims and objectives to assessed need in the organization's field of interest;
   - the strategic direction of the organization.

2. Effectiveness of services – some effectiveness issues which might be considered are:
   - consumer satisfaction, feedback from service users and professional partners;
   - quality standards, existence of and adherence to standards in organizational and professional activities;
   - the skills, knowledge and commitment of staff and volunteers;
   - relevance to need and evidence of effective targeting of resources;
   - consumer participation and extent to which service users are involved in decisions about issues affecting them;
   - methods of redress for service users and existence of complaints and representation procedures;
   - non-service activities and effectiveness in influencing, promoting and advocating the interests of the user group;
   - community impact, including long-term and unintended outcomes.

3. Effectiveness in meeting objectives:
   - regional and local planning processes;
   - ability to set and meet targets;

- evidence of progress and achievements;
- systems of review;
- the organizational culture, e.g. communication, participation, consultation.

4. Efficient and effective use of departmental grants:
    - staff salaries, volunteer costings, terms and conditions of service;
    - administrative and secretarial support;
    - use of buildings, vehicles and equipment;
    - cost of services;
    - financial strategies and resourcing within the organization.

5. Adequacy of organizational systems for meeting need and monitoring efficiency and effectiveness:
    - management information systems;
    - systems for self-monitoring and review;
    - employment practices, staff monitoring and support;
    - commitment to total quality approaches;
    - financial accounting and audit;
    - policies and procedures, including equal opportunities and non-discriminatory practice, health and safety policies and procedures, child/vulnerable person protection policies.

The Logic Model and theories of change models highlighted in Chapter 12 are often used in organizational evaluations to articulate the logic between organizational inputs and activities, and outputs and outcomes.

The CENI survey (2010) highlighted a number of issues that tended to impact on the satisfaction of Third Sector organizations with evaluations, including:

- the evaluator's understanding of the Third Sector;
- the nature of the relationship with the evaluator;
- the approach adopted by the consultant;
- the usefulness of evaluation in terms of providing objective review and giving direction;
- the relevance of recommendations;
- the limited size of the evaluation budget.

The survey also highlighted some skills gaps in the sector in relation to evaluation, including (in order of frequency):

- measuring and reporting outcomes (more than 50 per cent);
- using ICT systems (more than 50 per cent);
- using data collection systems;
- measuring and reporting performance;
- understanding terminology;
- understanding and implementing evaluations;
- identifying anticipated outcomes;
- commissioning and managing external evaluation.

Evaluation Support Scotland has developed a range of resource materials and case studies to help organizations and funders plan evaluations.

The idea, however, that evaluations and impact assessments are objective and value-neutral has been challenged in the literature (see Arvidson 2009). Issues of power and the competing interests and values of different stakeholders suggest an alternative frame from which to view evaluations, particularly those commissioned by a powerful stakeholder, e.g. main funder (vertical accountability). Barman (2007: 103), writing about the British Third Sector, argues that such measurement frameworks are 'historically situated and socially constructed'. According to Arvidson (2009: 10), understanding evaluation means not just mastering the technical aspects of producing and analysing data, etc., but a 'recognition that it needs to be placed in the context of a political arena, where values, power and resources constitute bases for differing interpretations and potential conflicts'.

Patton (2008) has highlighted that one of the major problems with evaluations is that the findings are often not implemented. He recommends an approach he calls Utilization-focused Evaluation which focuses from the beginning on why the evaluation is being carried out and how the findings will be used.

PEER REVIEW

An alternative approach to formal evaluation is peer review. Peer review can be internal or external, one-way or reciprocal, based on a specific quality framework (e.g. PQASSO) or can be one-off or part of a continuing process. It has been used extensively in the public sector, but less so in the Third Sector. In a pilot of a peer review model for the UK Third Sector, Purcell and Hawtin (2010) outlined a process whereby individuals, with a wide range of specialisms from various organizations, would, following training, review a particular aspect or aspects of an organization and provide a report with recommendations. The principles they suggest include:

- the 'host' organization, i.e. the organization to be reviewed, is in control of the process and which aspects of the organization the reviewers look at (the scope);
- the report from the reviewers is for the organization alone, i.e. there is no upward accountability to funders, etc.;
- there needs to be agreement beforehand on what standards the reviewers are using;
- reviewers need appropriate training to carry out the review effectively;
- there needs to be an intermediary body to organize a peer review process involving a range of organizations.

PORTFOLIO ANALYSIS

This technique was developed by the Boston Consulting Group, normally considered to be in the Positioning School, as discussed in Chapter 3. It is a way of evaluating

Table 8.2 Boston Portfolio Matrix

		Market Share	
		High	Low
Market growth	High	Stars	Question marks
	Low	Cash cows	Dogs

the programmes that an organization currently runs in preparation for deciding what place they have in its future plans (see Table 8.2).

In its simplest form portfolio analysis involves allocating each programme of the organization to one of the following categories:

- *Rising star*: the kind of innovative programme that is generating or increasing interest from the public and funders;
- *Cash Cow*: a popular programme that receives significant support and funding;
- *Question mark*: a programme that needs re-evaluating to see which of the other categories it best fits;
- *Dog*: a programme that has clearly past its sell-by-date and should be divested.

On the basis that most products and services, including those provided by the voluntary sector, follow the life-cycle of a normal distribution curve (Hudson 1995), at any point in time it is likely that any service will be at one of the following stages:

1. growth stage (rising star) and needs to be invested in;
2. is at a mature stage (cash cow) and currently requires little attention – the income should be harvested;
3. is in decline (dog) and should probably be divested or wound up;
4. it is not clear what category the activity should fall into (question mark) and therefore requires further investigating.

The Boston Matrix has been criticized (Slatter 1980; Ohmae 1982; Seeger 1991; Baden-Fuller and Stopford 1992; Whittington 1993; de Kare-Silver 1997) on the following grounds:

- being too simplistic in taking the two key categories of the Design School (external environment and internal capabilities) and selecting only one dimension of each and dividing each programme simply into high and low;
- basing too much emphasis on cost, ignoring differentiation;
- having a too narrow emphasis on market share and market growth;
- not providing any real tools to determine what strategy would lead to competitive advantage;
- depending on industry boundaries which in fact are hard to define;
- depending on being able to see where a product or organization is in the life-cycle.

The model has been adapted for use by the non-profit sector (Gruber and Mohr 1982; Nutt and Backoff 1992; Bryson 1995; Courtney 1996; Bovaird and Rubienska 1996; Krug and Weinberg 2004; Sargeant 2009) using different dimensions, e.g. social value (Gruber and Mohr 1982), tractability and stakeholder support (Nutt and Backoff 1992), demand for the service and capability to deliver the service (Courtney 1996), and internal appropriateness and external attractiveness (Sargeant 2009). Krug and Weinberg's model (2004) is a three-dimensional model with three axes: contribution to mission, contribution to resources ('money'), and contribution to quality/performance ('merit'). MacMillan (1983) also developed a much more sophisticated three-dimensional matrix which considers: programme attractiveness internally and externally; competitive position, i.e. the capacity to deliver the programme; and alternative coverage, i.e. extent of competition from other agencies.

STAKEHOLDER ANALYSIS

One of the most powerful and relevant techniques that can be applied in the Third Sector is stakeholder analysis, also developed by John Bryson (1995) for public and Third Sector organizations from the work of Freeman (1984). 'Stakeholders' are all those who are affected by the activities of the organization or who have expectations of the organization. It is not only concerned with internal analysis, however, as the stakeholders will include both internal and external players, and who will have views about both the internal aspects of the organization and the implications of changes in the external environment. It is therefore a moot point as to whether stakeholder analysis should be located within Chapter 7 on the external environment or within this chapter on assessing the organization. However, it is a process for identifying the views of external and internal stakeholders on the organization and where it should be going. As such it can be invaluable in assessing the views of important internal and external stakeholders about the current state of the organization, whose support may be critical in enabling the organization to change in the way it wishes to.

Typically the first step in the process is for the board and staff to identify exactly who these stakeholders are in relation to the organization and to prioritize them in relation to their importance to the organization. The second step is to determine what the needs and expectations of each of the most important stakeholders are in relation to the work of the organization. This can be done by the board and staff of the organization engaging in thoughtful guesswork, but a much more valuable approach is to identify a process to ask directly the key stakeholders what they think and expect of the organization and how it is currently doing. This is central to social auditing (see pp.119–24), and is often part of an evaluation process. It is also crucial to quality management initiatives.

The third step is identifying the extent to which each stakeholder has power over, and interest in, the organization. Eliot and Pottinger (2008) have developed a simple matrix for identifying which stakeholders have a high or low level of power, and which have a high or low level of interest in the organization, and therefore how the organization should respond (see Table 8.3).

Table 8.3 Stakeholder mapping

	Low interest	High interest
High power	Keep satisfied and build their interest	Manage closely (maximum effort)
Low power	Monitor (minimum effort)	Keep informed

The fourth step involves deciding on those actions which will help the organization to fulfil the expectations and aspirations of the stakeholders.

Kennerley and Neely (2001) have developed a Performance Prism based on the needs and requirements of key stakeholders and the processes and capabilities required by the organization to meet these requirements. They have developed a bank of over 200 performance measures that can be used by companies to assess performance in all different aspects of an organization. There does not appear to be any significant use of the Performance Prism model by Third Sector organizations.

BOX 8.1 TYPICAL LIST OF STAKEHOLDERS OF A THIRD SECTOR ORGANIZATION

- beneficiaries/service-users/clients;
- customers (social economy);
- members;
- statutory funders;
- individual, charitable and corporate donors;
- staff;
- volunteers;
- board of management;
- agencies who refer clients or to whom the organization refers clients;
- regulatory bodies;
- partners;
- the general public.

SOCIAL AUDITING

Following on from the concept of stakeholder analysis, the concept of social auditing, developed by the New Economics Foundation in England, alongside similar approaches developed in Scandinavia and Canada (including social accounting – see Quarter *et al*. 2003), puts the evaluation of organizations within the context of the needs and expectations of all its stakeholders. It provides a framework whereby the extent to which an organization is making progress towards meeting these needs and expectations can be regularly assessed by establishing key performance indicators and putting in place a social book-keeping system that assesses progress towards achieving performance targets and involves stakeholders in reviewing the performance indicators. A recent survey (CENI 2010) within the UK found 17 per cent of Third Sector organizations using social accounting/auditing.

Social auditing is based on the following eight principles:

- Inclusive: any accounting process must reflect the views of all stakeholders, not only those who have historically had the most influence over the evolution of the organization's formal mission statement.

- Comparative: the performance of the organization must be compared over time or with external benchmarks drawn from the experience of other organizations, statutory regulations or societal norms.

- Complete: no area of the organization's activities can be deliberately or systematically excluded from the assessment.

- Regular and evolutionary: an organization's 'social footprint' cannot be assessed in any one-off exercise. Issues vary over time as do the composition and expectations of key stakeholder groups.

- Embedded: the organization must develop clear policies covering each accounting area as well as procedures that allow the accounting to be regularized and the organization's awareness and operationalization of policies and commitments to be assessed and influenced through auditing.

- Communicated: disclosure of information must be routed in meaningful dialogue, not just consultation by publishing a document.

- Externally verified: external verification of the social audit ensures accountability and legitimacy, in the same way as a financial audit.

- Continuous improvement: the approach must identify whether the organization's performance has improved over time in relation to its values and objectives and those of its stakeholders and support future improvement.

The key stages of the social auditing process are as follows:

1. Planning:
    - establish commitment and governance procedures;
    - identify stakeholders of the organization;
    - define and review objectives, policies and values.

2. Accounting:
    - identify issues upon which performance is assessed;
    - determine scope of process;
    - identify indicators of performance;
    - collect information;
    - analyse information, set targets and develop improvement plan.

3. Auditing and reporting:
    - prepare reports;
    - audit the report;
    - communicate results and obtain feedback.

4. Embedding:
    - establish and embed systems for continuous improvement.

The Furniture Resource Centre (FRC) Social Audit (see Box 8.2 below) and that of Cosmic Ethical IT (see Box 12.5) reflect two quite different approaches to social auditing. The FRC social audit is based primarily on the measurement of a range of quantifiable indicators of progress, such as employment and qualifications. On the other hand, the Cosmic Social Audit is focused almost entirely on the satisfaction levels of a wide range of stakeholders (clients, partners, staff, etc.), drawing on various stakeholder surveys.

BOX 8.2 FURNITURE RESOURCE CENTRE IMPACT REPORT

The Furniture Resource Centre (FRC) Group provides low-income households with furniture and a removals service to help them create homes. It was founded in 1988 as a small furniture recycling charity. It came about in response to poverty in inner-city Liverpool. It was set up to:

- provide furniture for disadvantaged people;
- recruit and train the long-term unemployed;

It developed into a social business in 1994. Since then it has grown and now has a multimillion-pound turnover. Through its activities it creates work for 68 people. It offers salaried training to the long-term unemployed. Initially the service addressed the needs of disadvantaged people in Liverpool. The FRC Group is still based in that city but it has now extended its services to other parts of the country.

The group now consists of two different business enterprises: The Furniture Resource Centre, a one-stop furnishing service to over 100 registered social landlords; and Bulky Bob's, which collects unwanted large waste items, mainly focused on recycling furniture and making 'pre-loved' furniture available to low-income families.

Through all its activities the FRC Group integrates the long-term unemployed into the workforce. It aims to train them in useful transferable skills and offers them salaried, year-long employment contracts. In this way, it seeks to build up people's confidence and employability to help them get jobs when they leave the FRC.

The group has charitable status. It is governed by a board of volunteer non-executive directors. They ensure that the group achieves its charitable purposes and wisely uses the organization's resources. Since developing into a social business in 1994, the FRC has made significant changes and achieved some important outcomes:

- the payroll rose from 17 people to 80 in 2006/07;
- during 2011/12, 77 per cent of previously unemployed people received training and went into employment or further education after completing the FRC Group's training programme.

Through its Impact Report, the group tries to assess its impact on the unemployed and those on low incomes, as well as its influence on policymakers and the environment. The FRC has scored highly on customer satisfaction surveys and with the majority of council and registered social landlords.

The FRC has achieved more than half a dozen awards including:

- in 2010, the FRC Group was the 'Social Impact Champion' at the inaugural SE100 Social Enterprise Index;
- the Guardian Award for Innovation and Sustainability;

▶

- 2006 Enterprising Solutions Award for UK Social Enterprise;
- being listed by the *Financial Times* as one of the 50 best workplaces in 2005 and 2007;
- the Edge Upstarts trainee of the year award in 2006;
- Groundwork's award for resource efficiency with the public sector in 2007.

(Further information is available from the FRC website www.frcgroup.co.uk and the Improvement and Development Agency website www.idea.gov.uk.)

The Association of Chief Officers of Voluntary Organisations in Britain and the New Economics Foundation carried out a study (Raynard and Murphy 2000) into social auditing with Third Sector organizations (the SAVO project) to test the applicability of the social audit methodology in UK Third Sector organizations. The study was carried out by the New Economics Foundation. The conclusions of the 13 case studies of organizations which participated in the study included:

- Social auditing is a very useful tool in improving the accountability of Third Sector organizations and building trust with stakeholders.
- It can assist with the development of social objectives, strategic planning, evaluation, building trust in stakeholder relationships, and the demonstration of accountability and transparency.
- There are a number of particular strengths of the process: the emphasis of stakeholder dialogue as opposed to straight consultation; an opportunity to examine their social objectives and assess performance against these; the emphasis on developing indicators that were stakeholder led in order to assess performance; the verification of the process and outcomes – this process encouraged organizations to be open about their performance in the final report; the emphasis on communicating the results in a meaningful way to external audiences, including specific stakeholder groups; the emphasis on setting meaningful and measurable next steps for continuous improvement.

The report suggests that the social auditing process could be developed further in relation to internal management and leadership processes and can learn from the EFQM (European Foundation for Quality Management) Excellence model and Investors in People in these areas (see pp. 125–7).

The experience of the participating groups also suggest that including all stakeholders on all issues at once can be too much to do effectively and it might be better to focus on a smaller number of stakeholders or issues each year, with a view to ensuring that all stakeholders and areas are covered over a period of time. The resource limitations of the organization, both financially and in terms of time, can also be a barrier.

The project also found that sometimes stakeholders were not sufficiently informed to make informed judgements and, therefore, part of the process may need to involve building the capacity of stakeholders to contribute to the process. To be effective, too, the social audit recommendations need to be fed into the organization's planning systems and then be effectively implemented.

With the development of social auditing and a number of similar approaches in Scandinavia and Canada in particular (see Box 8.3 for an example of social auditing in PLAN, a Canadian Third Sector organization), and concerns expressed about some of the social auditing reports in the private sector, which have been accused of being mainly PR gloss with little real substance (Doane 2001), the need for quality standards for such ethical accounting, auditing and reporting processes became apparent. To address this, an organization called AccountAbility developed a quality framework, Accountability 1000 Standard (AA 1000), as a foundation standard in social and ethical accounting, auditing and reporting.

BOX 8.3 PLAN SOCIAL AUDIT

PLAN (Planned Lifetime Advocacy Network) is an organization dedicated to securing the future for people with disabilities and their families. Created in 1989 by families in British Columbia, PLAN is a not-for-profit charity that assists and supports families in responding to all aspects of the safety, security and well-being of people with disabilities, particularly after their parents become infirm or die.

PLAN's work aims to enhance the quality of life and security of people with disabilities by building a safety net of diverse programmes – secured networks of family and friends, increased financial independence, and avenues for true contribution and citizenship – that can withstand the death of their parents as well as unpredicted changes in government-funded support services.

PLAN's vision is a good life for all people with disabilities and their families. Its mission is to secure the future for people with disabilities and to provide them and their families with peace of mind. This would mean ending isolation and loneliness, creating financial security, enabling everyone to make a contribution, ensuring choice, and creating genuine homes.

In their work to secure good lives for people with disabilities and their families, PLAN is guided and inspired by four core values:

- relationships are the key to safety, security and a good life;
- contribution equals citizenship: PLAN works to ensure the people it serves are seen for their unique contributions;
- self-sufficiency: diversity of revenue sources and independence from government funding enable PLAN to advocate on behalf of individuals and families without fear of consequence;
- family direction: PLAN is structured to ensure it will always be directed by and accountable to families.

In 2002 PLAN became the first non-profit organization in Canada – and one of the few in the world – to conduct an externally verified social audit. The social audit is PLAN's way of holding itself accountable to those who they consider matter most: members, the people they serve, staff, facilitators, funders, network members and community supporters. It provides a transparent view of the organization, reporting on both successes and challenges in a candid way.

The board of PLAN implemented the social audit to ensure that the values around which PLAN is constructed are maintained long into the future and to measure how well PLAN is serving and supporting families. The audit has four specific goals:

1. to evaluate how well they are living their core values – being family-driven, being self-sustaining and keeping relationships at the centre of everything they do;
2. to strengthen organizational relationships;

3. to consider how well they are serving their members;

4. to explore how growth and change are impacting on the organization.

They believed that undertaking the social audit in 2002 strengthened the organization and learned a great deal about what they did well and what they must learn to do better. They therefore decided to repeat the social audit in 2005, this time including network members and associates in the survey. The 2005 Accountability Report identified many areas of strength for PLAN: growth was considered to be thoughtful and positive; personal support networks remained at the very heart of their work and, after 16 years, they were considered to be stronger and more vibrant than ever, making a significant difference in people's lives; relationships seem to be thriving; families seem to have a great deal of confidence in PLAN and more peace of mind; network members value their relationships. The findings demonstrate that people involved with PLAN share core values and a common vision and want to share it with others. They believe in the public policy work to create a good life for people who have disabilities; and families continue to be confident that they determine PLAN's goals, objectives and strategies. They felt that the social audit was an opportunity for them and other stakeholders (network members, facilitators and staff) to evaluate the effectiveness of the work and guide the future growth of the organization.

This 2005 social audit completes the first full cycle of PLAN's accountability process. In the 2005 social audit, PLAN reports on the progress towards 22 targets identified after the completion of the initial audit in 2002. These targets formed part of PLAN's strategic planning process. Completion of this subsequent social audit supports the effectiveness of the strategic plan that was put in place and the veracity of the benchmarks set in the first audit.

Of the 22 targets set by PLAN's board in the 2002 social audit process 17 were achieved. The most significant area for development remains in the areas related to funding and self-sufficiency. They have continued to pursue the remaining five targets and identify new challenges as PLAN'S board has embarked on the next phase of its strategic planning process.

(See *PLAN* 2005 *Social Audit Report* accessed via www.socialaudit.ca/
2005/Process2005/Process2005-whatissa.htm)

CUSTOMER SERVICE EXCELLENCE

One of the tools that the UK government has used over the last 15 years to drive up the performance of government agencies in delivering customer service was the Charter Mark – a kite mark based on a single set of standards of customer service. This scheme was reviewed in 2006 (Herdan 2006) and in light of the recommendations of the review the scheme was replaced with a new government scheme, Customer Service Excellence, which, like the Charter Mark, is externally accredited in order to award a kite mark. The new scheme has 57 single level standards, under five categories (15 subcategories), against which organizations providing a service to the public are assessed:

■ customer insight: customer identification, engagement and consultation; customer satisfaction;

■ the culture of the organization: leadership, policy and culture, and staff professionalism and attitude;

- information and access: range of information, quality of information, access, cooperative working with other providers, partners and communities;

- delivery: delivery standards, achieved delivery and outcomes, deal effectively with problems;

- timeliness and quality of service: standards for timeliness and quality, timely outcomes, achieved timely delivery.

INVESTORS IN PEOPLE AUDIT

The Investors in People (IIP) framework may also be useful in assessing the extent to which the organization has: a clear vision that staff and volunteers understand; a framework to assess and meet the training and development needs of the trustees, staff and volunteers in helping them to achieve this vision; a process to evaluate the extent to which the training actually achieves the purpose for which it is designed; and a process to encourage the participation of staff in decision-making. The IIP audit explores three key principles and ten indicators. The standard outlines between three and six evidence requirements for each indicator.

The results of the initial IIP audit enable the organization to draw up an action plan to address any weaknesses in any of the areas above. This action plan can then be integrated into the organization's strategic plan. Once the organization is satisfied that it complies with the evidence requirements of the ten indicators it can apply to be assessed for an IIP award. A survey of Third Sector organizations (CENI 2010) found that IIP was used by 29 per cent of respondents, the most popular of any of the quality frameworks, followed by Investing in Volunteers at 15 per cent.

Research on the impact of IIP (Centre for Business Performance at Cranfield School of Management 2010) provided evidence of investment in management capabilities and on business profitability. The study, which combined case studies, a survey of over 400 employers and analysis of financial performance information, found that working with IIP increases profitability by enhancing managerial skills, knowledge

BOX 8.4 INVESTORS IN PEOPLE STANDARD

Developing strategies to improve the performance of the organization

Principle: an Investor in People develops effective strategies to improve the performance of the organization through its people:

1. a strategy for improving the performance of the organization is clearly defined and understood;
2. learning and development is planned to achieve the organization's objectives;
3. strategies for managing people are designed to promote equality of opportunity in the development of the organization's people;
4. the capabilities that managers need to lead, manage and develop people effectively are clearly defined and understood.

▶

> **Taking action to improve the performance of the organization**
>
> Principle: an Investor in People takes effective action to improve the performance of the organization through its people:
>
> 5. managers are effective in leading, managing and developing people;
> 6. people's contribution to the organization is recognized and valued;
> 7. people are encouraged to take ownership and responsibility by being involved in decision-making;
> 8. people learn and develop effectively.
>
> **Evaluating the impact on the performance of the organization**
>
> Principle: an Investor in People can demonstrate the impact of its investment in people on the performance of the organization:
>
> 9. investment in people improves the performance of the organization;
> 10. improvements are continually made to the way people are managed and developed.

and experience, improving the effectiveness of management development practices, and increasing the performance of managers at all levels. The study also found that IIP inspired a high-performance management culture and an effective learning environment, both of which helped to improve business performance.

However, an IIP audit only relates to the organization's internal processes as they concern the development of staff in achieving the organizational goals. It does not assess other aspects of the organization, e.g. financial, the impact on users, or public awareness.

EUROPEAN EXCELLENCE MODEL

The EQFM Business Excellence Model, discussed in Chapter 12 (see pp. 235–7), in relation to measuring effectiveness, was not particularly designed for the Third Sector (as neither was IIP). However, the Quality Standards Working Group established by the National Council for Voluntary Organisations in England (NCVO), which undertook a major review of the issue of quality in the Third Sector in Britain and the whole range of models that are currently available, concluded that the EQFM Excellence Model represents the best overarching model for Third Sector organizations to use to assess their organizations and put in place measures to improve the quality of what they do. The Excellence Framework (see pp. 235–7) provides a very powerful assessment process to enable organizations to see to what extent the commitment to meet user and stakeholder needs and expectations is being delivered and to encourage continuous improvement. The key areas involved in an EQFM assessment are:

Enablers:
- leadership;
- policy and strategy;

- people;
- partnerships and resources;
- processes.

Results:
- customer results;
- people results;
- society results;
- key performance results.

Like IIP, the Business Excellence Model assessment process is supported by a self-assessment questionnaire. The NCVO Quality Standards Working Group (QSTC), working with the British Quality Foundation, have developed very useful materials to help non-profit organizations carry out assessments under the Excellence Model (QSTC *Excellence in view* 2000a; QSTC *Self-assessment workbook – measuring success* 2000b). There is a wide range of literature about the EFQM model. Particularly useful is a paper on 'Guidelines for self-assessment' by McCarthy *et al.* (2002).

PQASSO

PQASSO is a set of quality standards specifically developed by and for the Third Sector in the UK. They are the most commonly used quality standards in the Third Sector in the UK. The quality standards are specific, concise statements and associated measures, which set out aspirational, but potentially achievable, markers of quality.

PQASSO is built on 12 topics or quality areas. These are the building blocks an organization needs in order to be able to operate to a high standard.

Quality area 1: Planning
Having a clear overall purpose and planning ahead are essential for any sound organization. This quality area is about defining the organization's mission, aims and values, based on understanding what users and other stakeholders need. Organizations then plan what you will do and agree outcomes, set targets, and systematically review progress. Where relevant, involving users.

Quality area 2: Governance
Board members have overall legal responsibility for the organization. This quality area is about how the Board provides the strategic direction for the organization, how it ensures the organization meets all legal requirements and is governed effectively, and how the Board is accountable to its stakeholders. The Board reviews its practices, ensuring it has the right skills and experience.

Quality area 3: Leadership and management
Organizational leaders provide inspiration and direction, both internally and externally. Managers are responsible for planning and organizing resources, and supporting people to get the results the organization wants. This includes responsibilities for legal and financial matters, policies, systems and procedures. Managers also need to communicate well and encourage a constructive working environment.

Quality area 4: User-centred service
Third Sector organizations exist because of the benefit they can bring to their users. This quality area is about how to get to know who users are and what they need, and how to inform and involve them in order to achieve better outcomes for them. There also needs to be effective ways of collecting and reviewing user feedback.

Quality area 5: Managing people
Staff and volunteers are an organization's most vital resource. This quality area is about how to recruit and manage them so that the organization flourishes. It is also about how to value and support them so that they are motivated and effective.

Quality area 6: Learning and development
Learning opportunities are essential for the development of the organization and its people. This quality area is about how people get the information and skills they need to work well. This includes having an organized approach to training and the other opportunities for learning.

Quality area 7: Managing money
For an organization to survive, it must manage money competently. This quality area is about how to attract money to support the work, and then manage it effectively.

This includes meeting legal responsibilities and having a planned approach to getting the most out of financial resources.

Quality area 8: Managing resources
This quality area is about how to manage non-financial resources – for example, equipment, premises and information – for the benefit of the organization and its aims. This includes maintenance, health and safety, and environmental sustainability issues.

Quality area 9: Communications and promotion
Raising an organization's profile and being clear about what the organization wants people to know is essential in order to promote the work and represent the needs of users. This quality area is about how to raise awareness of services and activities externally. It is also about how to communicate with external stakeholders and influence change.

Quality area 10: Working with others
Working with other organizations, in partnership or simply to gather information, can help an organization to meet its aims. This quality area is about how to link with other organizations, how to give and get information, and how to systematically strengthen the work through partnership.

Quality area 11: Monitoring and evaluation
To ensure the best possible health and performance of an organization, it is necessary to systematically gather information and review it. This quality area is about the systems used for monitoring and evaluation. It is about ensuring that people

understand them and are using them effectively to learn from and improve what the organization does.

Quality area 12: Results
This quality area is about the results of an organization's processes, activities and services, and the quality of information about them. It covers: *user results* – to what extent the organization achieves positive outcomes for its intended users; *people results* – the commitment and job satisfaction of staff and volunteers; *organizational results* – whether the organization resources and delivers good quality services and activities as planned and within budget; and *community results* – how the organization contributes to the wider community. Where possible, demonstrating that results are improving.

PQASSO breaks down each topic into three levels. This enables organizations to assess how they are doing and plan a clear path for development in each area.

Each area includes a series of indicators which show broadly what the organization should be doing to meet its desired level of PQASSO. Self-assessment involves different people in the organization discussing how well the organization is doing against the indicators and whether any improvements are needed. Each area also includes examples of sources of evidence which offer some ideas about where an organization might look for evidence to demonstrate that your organization has met the indicators.

PQASSO offers a staged approach to implementing quality through three levels of achievement. All organizations should cover the requirements of Level 1. More established or complex organizations may then decide to move on to Level 2 and then Level 3. In each quality area, the standard itself is clearly defined and applies to all organizations. To work through the quality area, an organization should ask itself if it meets the indicators at the relevant level, and set out plans to make any necessary improvements.

PQASSO may be used in other ways, including as an organizational health-check or to help guide organizational development and growth. Organizations implement PQASSO by assessing themselves against standards and indicators using evidence to support judgements made. PQASSO also offers an external accreditation: the PQASSO Quality Mark.

In a Scoping study – *Quality Assurance in the Voluntary and Community Sector* – (Brodie, Anstey, Vanson and Richard Piper 2012), PQASSO was viewed positively for encompassing both organizational processes and outcomes. It was seen as being good for smaller organizations, particularly those which are embarking on a period of growth, whereas not as appropriate for the very large Voluntary or Community Organizations.

There are various other good practice frameworks developed for specific areas of work. Action with Communities in Rural England, for example, has developed (i) The Acre Good Practice Quality Standard, which uses a similar approach to PQASSO with nine areas of good practice, each at three levels, for Rural Community Councils and (ii) the DTA Healthcheck created for use by Development Trusts.

VENTURE PHILANTHROPY PARTNERS/MCKINSEY CAPACITY ASSESSMENT GRID

Following a study of 13 Third Sector organizations in the US, consultancy firm Venture Philanthropy Partners worked with international consultancy firm McKinsey & Co. to develop a freely available tool by which Third Sector organizations could assess their internal capacity (McKinsey 2001). It has some similarities to the PQASSO approach and covers aspirations, strategy, organizational skills, human resources, systems and infrastructure, organizational structure, and culture. Each of these capacity areas is broken down into more detail. The Grid provides a brief description of four levels (PQASSO has three levels) of competency in each detailed area, by which organizations can assess themselves and see a brief description of what the next level looks like.

The Grid is available free from www.vppartners.org/learning/reports/capacity. An updated version of the McKinsey Assessment Grid has been developed by The Marguerite Casey Foundation (and is available free from www.caseygrants.org).

THE BIG PICTURE

The Big Picture is an organizational self-assessment and development framework developed for the Scottish Council for Voluntary Organisations (SCVO) for all sizes of Third Sector organizations in Scotland. It draws on aspects of other models. Like PQASSO it is user friendly and focused on the needs of the Third Sector. Like the EFQM Excellence Model, it distinguishes clearly between enablers and results. Like EFQM, too, it is a scored continuous improvement system, rather than stating fixed

Table 8.4   The Big Picture quadrants

Direction	Stakeholder satisfaction
■ Governance	■ People we help
■ Purpose	■ Paid staff
■ Strategy and policy	■ Volunteers
■ Staffing	■ Funders
■ Culture	■ Partners
■ Legislation and regulation	■ Influencers
Processes	**Positive impact**
■ Planning	■ Strategic outcomes
■ Managing people	■ Financial health
■ Managing money	■ Evidence of standards
■ Managing other resources	■ Development
■ Managing activities	■ Public profile
■ Monitoring and review	■ Impact on society

standard levels. Like the Balanced Scorecard it is based on four quadrants, which in the Big Picture are two enablers – direction and processes – and two results sections – stakeholder satisfaction and positive impact. Each quadrant is then further broken down as shown in Table 8.4.

Each of these 24 strands is explained in two pages and organizations can then score themselves against each of these strands. The model provides useful suggestions for quality improvement under each strand. SCVO has produced a range of support materials and have trained peer supporters who can help organizations facilitate review sessions.

VOLUNTARY SECTOR CODE OF PRACTICE

Although not strictly a framework to review voluntary organizations, this code, developed by the Joseph Rowntree Foundation, provides a useful list of policies and practices that Third Sector organizations ought to have in place under the following headings:

1. effectiveness;
2. accountability;
3. standards;
4. user involvement;
5. governance;
6. voluntary action;
7. equality and fairness;
8. staff management.

The working group which devised the code recommended that voluntary organizations adopt a code of practice that includes the following commitments (the numbers in brackets relate to the eight areas above which these commitments refer to). We will:

- state our purpose and keep it relevant to current conditions (1);
- be explicit about the needs that we intend to meet and how this will be achieved (1);
- manage and target resources effectively and do what we say we will do (1);
- evaluate the effectiveness of our work, tackle poor performance and respond to complaints fairly and promptly (1, 2);
- agree and set out for all those to whom we are accountable how we will fulfil these responsibilities (2);
- be clear about the standards to which we will work (3);
- be open about our arrangements for involving users (4);
- have a systematic process for making appointments to our governing body (5);
- set out the role and responsibilities of members of our governing body (5);
- have clear arrangements for involving, training, supporting and managing volunteers (6);

- ensure that our policies and practices do not discriminate unfairly or lead to other forms of unfair treatment (7);
- recruit staff openly, remunerate them fairly and be a good employer (8).

The Charity Commission for England and Wales have produced similar guidance (the Hallmarks of an Effective Charity). It suggests six Hallmarks:

- **Hallmark 1**: clear about its purpose and direction – an effective charity is clear about its purposes, mission and values and uses them to direct all aspects of its work.
- **Hallmark 2**: a strong board – an effective charity is run by a clearly identifiable board or trustee body that has the right balance of skills and experience, acts in the best interests of the charity and its beneficiaries, understands its responsibilities and has systems in place to exercise them properly.
- **Hallmark 3**: fit for purpose – the structure, policies and procedures of an effective charity enable it to achieve its purposes and mission and deliver its services efficiently.
- **Hallmark 4**: learning and improving – an effective charity is always seeking to improve its performance and efficiency, and to learn new and better ways of delivering its purposes. A charity's assessment of its performance, and of the impact and outcomes of its work, will feed into its planning processes and will influence its future direction.
- **Hallmark 5**: financially sound and prudent – an effective charity has the financial and other resources needed to deliver its purposes and mission, and controls and uses them so as to achieve its potential.
- **Hallmark 6**: accountable and transparent – an effective charity is accountable to the public and others with an interest in the charity (stakeholders) in a way that is transparent and understandable.

JIM COLLINS'S MEASURES OF SUCCESS

Collins (2006), author of the business book Good to Great (Collins 2001), was invited to use a similar methodology to examine nine successful American associations, including professional associations and Girl Scouts of the USA, to determine what it is that these associations do that other, less successful bodies don't do. He concluded (Collins 2006) that the following were the distinguishing factors of excellent associations:

- Commitment to purpose: a customer service culture – customer service excellence to individual members, but also structures and interactions that respond to members' needs and expectations; alignment of products and services with mission – pruning services and products that don't progress the mission of the organization.
- Commitment to analysis and feedback: data-driven strategies – tracking members' needs and issues as well as the wider environment to drive improvement; dialogue and engagement with staff and volunteers – contributing together to a shared vision and values; CEO as a broker of ideas – stimulating ideas, energy and engagement.

■ Commitment to action: organizational adaptability – consistently implementing their priorities, while responding effectively to a changing external environment; alliance building – working collaboratively with others to pursue its mission.

Four Core Components of Capacity Model

In assessing the efforts by charitable foundations in the US to build the capacity of Third Sector organizations, Connolly and York (2003) developed a model of organizational effectiveness (see Figure 8.1). The model contains three concentric circles. The outer ring reflects the external environment, based on the traditional PEST model. The circle inside the outer circle highlights the key resources which are required to support most directly programmes and services. The inner circle is the organization itself. It has organizational culture at its core, with spokes spreading outwards for structure, rituals, values, beliefs, history and language. The inner circle (the organization) requires four key capacities in order to be effective (reflected by the four oval shapes):

■ Adaptive capacity: the ability to monitor, assess and respond to internal and external changes, through assessing organizational effectiveness, evaluation, planning and networking.

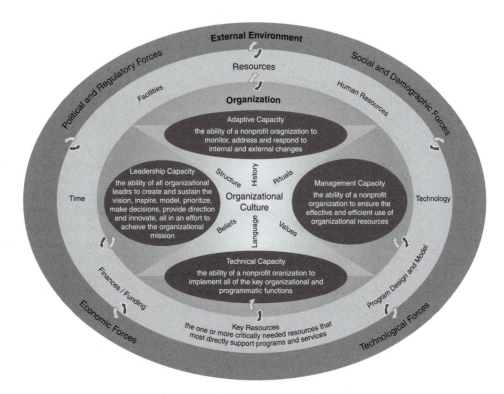

Fig 8.1   Four Core Components of Capacity Model

Source: Reproduced with permission of the TCC Group.

- Leadership capacity: including visioning, inspiring, prioritizing, directing, innovating, modelling and decision-making.

- Management capacity: ensuring effective and efficient use of resources.

- Technical capacity: the ability to 'do' the work and deliver the programmes and services, including technology, budgeting and accounting, fundraising, facilities management, marketing/communications, evaluation/research and legal.

According to Connolly and York, it is the adaptive capacity that is the most critical capacity for Third Sector organizations, though most effort is put into improving the technical capacities. The idea of adaptive capacity was introduced by Letts *et al.* (1998) and developed by Carl Sussman in *Making Change: The Role of Adaptive Capacity in Organisational Effectiveness* (2003). Connolly and York (ibid.: 4) suggest that adaptive capacity:

> entails explicating goals and activities and the underlying assumptions that link them, evaluating organizational and programmatic effectiveness and programs, and flexibly planning for the future. Adaptive capacity also encompasses improving the level and quality of creating alliances, collaborating and networking with others in the community, and increasing knowledge sharing with colleague organizations.

SUMMARY OF FORMAL ASSESSMENT FRAMEWORKS

The more formal models are summarized in Table 8.5. The first two models (JRF and Customer Service Excellence) have a single level of standards, which the organization is expected to achieve over a period of time through continuous improvement). After that, the organization is expected to maintain the standard (quality assurance). PQASSO and VPP/McKinsey provide three and four levels respectively, so the organization continuously improves to the next highest level. The Big Picture and the EFQM Excellence model are rating schemes which also encourage the organization to improve continuously.

The JRF, PQASSO, Big Picture and EFQM are concerned with the whole organization. IIP and Customer Service Excellence are concerned with important aspects of the organization, but not the whole. Some can result in an award or kite mark, others do not. Some of the models are free, others require a fee. Some are supported by advisors, others are not. Some were designed with the Third Sector in mind, others were not.

The choice of framework to use depends on the needs of the organization. The criteria which an organization may wish to consider in choosing which framework is most appropriate at a particular time might include:

- cost;
- the availability of support to work through the framework;
- the value of a kite mark or award;
- the reputation of the relevant scheme, kite mark or award;
- which aspects of the organization need most attention;

Table **8.5**   Matrix of assessment frameworks

Organizational assessment framework	Number and levels of standards	Kite-mark/ award	Aspects of the organization covered	Sector	Cost to access the standards	Support available in UK
JRF Voluntary Sector Code of Practice	1 level 12 standards in 8 categories	No	Whole organization	Third Sector	Free	No
Customer Service Excellence	1 level 57 standards in 5 categories	Yes	Services to clients or customers	Public and Third Sector	Free	Yes
Investors in People	1 level 10 indicators under 3 principles	Yes	Processes that support the development of staff	Private, public and Third Sector	Yes	Yes: trained and licensed mentors
PQASSO	3 levels 12 categories	Kitemark awarded by CES for achieving levels 1, 2 or 3	Whole organization	Third Sector	Yes	Yes: CES in England, CENI in Northern Ireland
VPP/ McKinsey	58 standards x 4 levels in 7 categories	No	Whole organization	Third Sector	Free	Not in UK
Big Picture	Scored rating; 24 areas in 4 sections	No	Whole organization	Third Sector	Yes	Scotland only: SCVO
EFQM	Scored rating against 32 standards in 9 categories	Yes	Whole organization	Private, public and Third Sector	Yes	Yes: from quality centres

- the level of complexity the organization would be able to deal with;
- the time available to carry out assessments and implement actions.

RESEARCH ON OTHER ORGANIZATIONAL ASSESSMENT MODELS

There is a range of other similar schemes available, particularly in North America, for assessing an organization. For example, Murray and Balfour (1999) examined 19 systems for reviewing a Third Sector organization, available in North America (only one of which is discussed above), including:

- the Balanced Scorecard;
- the Drucker Foundation 'self-improvement tool';
- the Balridge National Quality Award (similar to the EFQM Excellence model);
- ISO 9000 quality assurance framework;
- the 'high performance non-profit organisations' system of Letts *et al.* (1998);
- the outcome funding system of the Rensselaerville Institute;
- the American Institute for philanthropy 'charity rating guide';
- the United Way 'outcome funding' approach;
- the Canadian Comprehensive Auditing Foundation 'framework for performance reporting'.

They concluded that there is inadequate research on the impact of any of the models considered; however, they thought that the Balanced Scorecard combined with the Canadian Comprehensive Auditing Foundation 'framework for performance reporting' showed most promise. The others that were rated highly were the 'high performance non-profit organisations' system of Letts *et al.*, the outcome funding system of the Rensselaerville Institute, and the United Way 'outcome funding' approach.

Paton (2003) examined the use of a range of schemes by Third Sector organizations in the UK (including Best Practice benchmarking, PQASSO, EFQM Excellence model, ISO 9000, Social Return on Investment, the Administrative Costs to Expenditure ratio, and social auditing), using a case study approach in the context of the academic literature. Rather than concluding that any of the schemes were better than others, he argues that they all have potential benefits, costs and pitfalls. On the benefits, he concludes that all the frameworks can be used to good effect, for example:

- Measurement systems can be used at the design stage to surface issues around underlying purposes and different meanings of performance to clarify goals and to communicate priorities.
- Ossified systems of reporting based on counting activities and outputs can be challenged and simplified. The performance information generated may provide a better basis for demonstrating achievements and for giving recognition.
- Act as a crude filter to direct scarce managerial attention where it is most likely to be needed.

- Inform planning and decision-making, identify trends, examine the impacts of new practices or provide a challenge requiring that an issue be addressed or an anomaly explained.

- Provide a basis for dialogue with stakeholders and for increasing the understanding of issues.

- The existence of a functioning system may in itself reassure funders and purchasers.

However, Paton, along with Wilkinson and Wilmott (1995) and Clark and Newman (1997), argue that there are clear limitations, difficulties, pitfalls and costs associated with any assessment and measurement scheme, which often delivers less than promised. These drawbacks include:

- there can be significant costs in terms of time and resources in using any detailed scheme;

- it is not possible to have simultaneously both focus and comprehensiveness, or reliable validity and non-intrusive simplicity;

- focus on the requirements of any scheme may mean that other crucial aspects of the organization's performance and changes in the external environment may be ignored;

- they can create cynicism amongst managers and staff, who may complain about initiative overload;

- it can be seen as another way for managers to control professionals.

The reasons a particular framework is adopted and how it is introduced are critical to the value that it may provide to the organization (Paton 2003). In assessing schemes that provide a kite mark, such as IIP, Customer Service Excellence and ISO 9000, for example, the award can be achieved in a way that makes as little impact on the activities and performance of the organization as possible. At the other end of the spectrum it is possible genuinely to make the changes to organizational systems and culture and ignore the badge. Many organizations achieving one or more of the kite marks do so because they genuinely want to improve the organization and outcomes for its beneficiaries (see the case study of the Cedar Foundation in Box 12.6). In those organizations, there is an integration of the award into the motivation and activities of the organization – it lives the award. But the scheme may be imposed by senior management or the board and thus introduced reluctantly. Piloting of a scheme within one part of an organization, which can be helpful in learning lessons for applying it elsewhere in the organization, can sometimes result in competition and resentment within the organization.

As well as reassuring key external and internal stakeholders, self-assessment, continuous improvement models, such as PQASSO and the EFQM Excellence model, can have important benefits in the dialogue they create and the new thinking triggered by the self-assessment process. The structure and content of the models provide an integrative map or overview of managerial issues that many users of the schemes value highly (Paton 2003). However, they can also involve substantial commitments of management time and attention. It can be challenging to integrate the continuous improvement processes with the normal decision-making and planning processes.

Subsectoral schemes

There are also many organizational assessment, evaluation and quality assurance schemes that have been developed for particular subsectors of the Third Sector for different purposes. These can provide a focus on the particular standards required, for example to serve effectively a particular client group in addition to more generic organizational standards.

SUMMARY

This chapter has explored a range of tools and techniques that have been used to help Third Sector organizations to analyse their internal environment. These tools include methods developed for the Third Sector such as evaluation, stakeholder analysis, social auditing and quality frameworks such as PQASSO, The Big Picture, the VPP/McKinsey Capacity Assessment Grid and the Joseph Rowntree framework. They also include tools that are frequently used in the private sector such as Strengths and Weaknesses (usually part of a SWOT analysis), the Boston Matrix Portfolio Analysis, the EFQM Excellence model and Investors in People. Research on the use of these schemes in the UK and similar schemes in the US have been examined.

QUESTIONS

1. List the distinctive or core competencies of a Third Sector organization you know.
2. List the key stakeholders of a Third Sector organization you know and what you think they expect from the organization.
3. What criteria would you use to assess that a particular programme in an organization is a 'dog' and should be ended?
4. What are some of the 'rising star' issues in the Third Sector?
5. What criteria should be used to evaluate a Third Sector organization?
6. Should Third Sector organizations aim for externally accredited quality frameworks with a kitemark?
7. What are the criteria you would use to define a Third Sector organization as excellent, and why?
8. What is the difference between evaluation and audit?

DISCUSSION TOPIC

What makes for an effective organization and why?

SUGGESTED READING

John M. Bryson (2011) *Strategic Planning for Public and Nonprofit Organizations*, Jossey-Bass.

J. Cutt and V. Murray (2000) *Accountability and Effectiveness: Evaluation in Non-Profit Organizations*, Routledge.

Sharon Oster (1995) *Strategic Management for Nonprofit Organizations*, Oxford.

R. Paton (2003) *Managing and Measuring Social Enterprises*, Sage.

PART III
STRATEGY CHOICES

9 STRATEGIC OPTIONS

OVERVIEW

Having explored the history and concepts of strategic planning, strategic formulation and strategic management in some depth, the question of the *content* of strategies, as opposed to strategy concepts, models and processes, has yet to be considered. It is often not clear from many strategic plans that any real strategic options were considered as to how the organization might achieve its mission and make important steps towards its vision of the future. Some writers consider that it is not possible to talk about generic strategies: every organization is different with different capabilities or competencies. The environment of each organization is also different. Does it therefore make sense to talk of generic strategies or configurations of strategy? This chapter examines the concept of generic strategic options and various approaches that have been suggested for describing the choices that are open to Third Sector organizations and the circumstances that it might be appropriate to adopt particular kinds of strategy.

LEARNING OBJECTIVES

After studying this chapter, you should be able to:

- describe the generic strategy options of Ansoff and Porter;
- explain different ways of categorizing the strategic choices available to non-profit organizations;
- outline different types of growth strategies for Third Sector organizations.

GENERIC STRATEGIES

Kearns (2000) argues that there are only basically three choices for a Third Sector organization when deciding on an appropriate strategy: growth, retrenchment and stability. However, reality is more complicated and within these options there are a number of more detailed choices. For example, within the fundamental growth strategy, there are the options of concentrating on, and expanding, existing services and programmes (horizontally or vertically) by increasing the capacity to serve more users or expanding geographically; or to diversify into new, related or unrelated services.

Growth can also happen in a number of different ways (ibid.):

■ by internal expansion, i.e. by expanding the existing organization;

■ by setting up a joint venture, partnership, licence arrangement or strategic alliance with another organization, or a consortium of organizations, which may be in the Third Sector or in the private or public sectors;

■ by merging with, or taking over, another Third Sector organization.

Crittenden (2000) has noted that growth options in Third Sector organizations are an infrequently researched topic.

ANSOFF'S MATRIX

Ansoff (1965), founder of the Planning School, suggests that there are two key dimensions of strategy for any company: the market and product/service. Companies only have a limited number of options: market penetration; product/service development; market development and diversification. Ansoff's Matrix has also been used as the basis for exploring the options that are available to non-profit organizations (Courtney 1996):

■ Extend existing services to cover a new target group of potential beneficiaries. Sometimes called 'market extension' (which is similar to Kearns's description of horizontal integration concentration strategy). Osborne (1998) describes this approach to organizational change as expansionary.

■ Develop new services with the existing target group in the current geographical area. This is sometimes described as product/service development. (Osborne 1998 describes this approach as evolutionary; Kearns 2000 describes it as concentric diversification.)

■ Develop new services with a new target group in a new geographical area (described by Osborne 1998 as total organizational change and by Kearns 2000 as conglomerate diversification). Crittenden (2000) warns, however, that voluntary non-profit service organizations need to stay focused on their product/service offerings and avoid adding numerous related or unrelated product/service offerings as these can diffuse management's attention and make it more difficult to send a clear message to funding sources.

■ Extend existing services to the current target group in existing areas (Osborne 1998 describes this as a 'developmental approach').

■ Extend existing services to the current target group into new geographical areas.

■ Develop new kinds of services in new areas.

■ Reduce or close existing services (similar to Kearn's retrenchment strategy).

■ Improve existing services (see Oster's 'quality leadership' on p. 145).

■ Wind up the organization.

In Osborne's study of innovation (1998), only the first three above qualify as being innovative strategies as they involve discontinuities over the past. The others are forms of organizational development, decline or stagnation.

VALUE DISCIPLINES

Treacy and Wiersema (1995) claim that there are three generic strategies, what they call 'value disciplines', that deliver value to customers. Organizations should choose between the three strategies, as follows:

- operational excellence: aiming for optimal running costs through efficiency and standardization and therefore offer products/services of a consistent good standard at low prices;
- product/service leadership: being the first to deliver the new products/services using the best technology – the emphasis is on research, development and design;
- customer intimacy: offering long-term relationships and the best solutions for customers through being dependable and responsive to customer needs.

PORTER'S GENERIC STRATEGIES

In the Positioning School, Porter also suggests that there are only three possible generic strategies:

- cost leadership: being the lowest cost producer in the industry;
- differentiation: developing unique products, relying on brand loyalty;
- focus: developing knowledge and competence in a narrow market segment.

Others (Gilbert and Strebel 1988; Miller 1992; Baden-Fuller and Stopford 1992), however, have criticized Porter's assertion that a company's strategy has to be one of these three and cannot be a combination.

In the Third Sector, using an adapted version of Porter's five forces industry analysis (Oster 1995, see p. 144 above), it is possible to suggest a number of similar generic strategies for non-profit organizations:

- *Cost leadership*: achieve the same objectives as other Third Sector organizations in the same field, but at a lower cost, therefore enabling the organization to compete more effectively for contracts. However, it has been argued that non-profits are not well equipped to engage in a narrow efficiency competition with private companies (Frumkin and Andre-Clark 2000; Anheier 2000).
- *Quality leadership*: provide a better quality of service for the users than other organizations.
- *Differentiation*: provide a service that is unique and develop a loyalty to that unique service and/or to the organization (Nicholls 2006). Anheier (2000) argues that the complexity of Third Sector organizations makes them natural born niche-seekers.
- *Focus*: develop the knowledge, credibility and competence in a very narrow area (geographical or type of beneficiary).

The differentiation and focus strategies are clearly very similar and may be better seen as a single kind of strategy.

Hudson (2005) suggests from his experience with the Third Sectors in Britain and the US that there are only four generic strategies that can increase impact:

- diversify service range (or into other activities, such as campaigning or to serving related groups of people);
- specialize service range: improve and enhance existing services;
- scale up geographically: replicate successful approaches;
- scale deep in a limited geographical area and well-defined user group to have a greater impact: build local relationships and brand.

MILES AND SNOW'S STRATEGIC TYPES

Miles and Snow (1978) suggest four main strategic types based on the rate that companies change their products/services and markets:

- *Defenders*: seek stability (see also Kearns 2000) by producing a limited range of products/services directed at a narrow segment of the potential market. They tend to defend their turf aggressively to keep out the competition by efficiency measures, competitive pricing, creating relationships with key decision-makers or concentrating on the high price, high quality end of the market. They tend to develop by market penetration and limited product development. Defensive strategies tend to be most appropriate when the external environment is stable. Osborne's (1998) study of innovation describes this approach as traditional as opposed to innovative or developmental.
- *Prospectors*: almost the opposite of defenders, their strength is in finding new product and market opportunities. The focus is on innovation, market research to identify gaps in the market and flexibility. The prospector strategy tends to be most appropriate when the external environment is dynamic/turbulent.
- *Analysers*: try to combine the strengths of both defenders and prospectors. They seek to minimize risk and maximize profit but also to innovate. However, the innovation tends to be on the basis of products or services that have been tried out by prospectors first. Analysers tend to follow prospectors with a superior or cheaper product. The strategy of the analysers is most appropriate in a changing but not turbulent external environment.
- *Reactors*: these tend to be companies that in Porter's words are 'stuck in the middle'. It is not clear which kind of strategy they are following, if any, and they tend to react to the latest whim or change in the external environment.

Boschken (1988) in a study of USA port authorities, and Boboc (2005) in a study of Romanian NGOs, demonstrated the applicability of Miles and Snow's typology to the public sector.

ACAR'S CONTINGENCY–BASED FRAMEWORK

Nutt and Backoff (1992) suggest that only two of these strategies are in fact viable ones: defender and prospector. Acar (1987) developed a contingency-based framework which suggests effective strategies for each of the possible environmental conditions:

- *Custodian*: this is similar to the defender strategy of Miles and Snow. It assumes a stable environment and market. Custodians maintain the distinctive competencies of the organization and nurture historical markets. They tend to ignore competitive threats, limit risk as far as possible and accept slow growth rates. They tend to seek protection from regulatory authorities.

- *Stabilizer*: appropriate where markets are seen as stable with many aggressive competitors (a 'clustered-placid environment'). Each cluster in the market is recognized as having different characteristics and the demand and market share can shift, requiring appropriate response in relation to that cluster through steps such as cost-cutting or efficiency measures.

- *Developer*: in a disturbed environment developers take action in response to moves from their competitors, often emulating their new products or services.

- *Entrepreneur*: in turbulent environments entrepreneurs seek to capture changing markets by aggressive action. Entrepreneurs read weak market signals and take risks and innovate with new products and services often leading to rapid growth and profitability.

MILLER'S ARCHETYPES OF STRATEGY FORMATION

Danny Miller at the Ecole des Hautes Etudes Commerciales (University of Montreal) and McGill University developed a strategy framework based on four dimensions: innovation, market differentiation, breadth and cost-control strategy. Miller (1976, 1979) suggests ten archetypes of strategy formation from his study of companies. These included four of failure and six of success, including:

- *stagnant bureaucracy*: where the previous placid environment has lulled the firm to sleep, unable to respond when major changes to the market or technology take place;

- *headless giant*: where there is a set of businesses with weak central authority to provide guidance and direction;

- *the aftermath*: where a transformational strategy, a turnaround, is required but the new team have inadequate resources or experience;

- *the dominant firm*: which is well established, controls key patents, has strong traditional strategies and is immune from serious challenge;

- *the entrepreneurial conglomerate*: an extension of the kind of approach used by a visionary entrepreneur in starting a company;
- *the innovator*: smaller firm with a simple structure and undiversified product line, with much product innovation.

In 1986 Miller suggested that there are four basic strategic configurations which are associated with particular organizational structures:

1. *Niche marketers*: who focus on a specific type of customer, service or geographical area. The structure tends to be simple with little formalization or bureaucratization, dominated by a chief executive. A common scenario in the Third Sector.

2. *Innovators*: who constantly invest in research and development in new services and products to stay ahead of other organizations in the field. The structure is often organic (Burns and Stalker 1961), sometimes called 'adhocracies' (Mintzberg 1979), with few rules and structures. Power tends to be decentralized.

3. *Cost leaders*: who tend to operate in relatively stable environments and standardize the production of a product or service so as to deliver it at the lowest possible cost. The structure tends to be a rigid mechanistic (Burns and Stalker 1961) machine bureaucracy.

4. *Divisionalized conglomerates*: which tend to operate unfocused diversified strategies. The structure tends to be divisionalized and bureaucratic. Each division being responsible for one product or service, or one group of products or services, which may be quite different from each other. There are various examples of Third Sector organizations that have developed a range of only tangentially related services to diverse beneficiaries (see the case study of Bryson Charitable Group in Part VI).

NUTT AND BACKOFF'S MATRIX

Nutt and Backoff, in their handbook on strategic management for public and non-profit organization leaders (1992), recognize the importance of the political arena for public and Third Sector organizations. Their framework has two dimensions: the extent of pressure for action to tackle needs and the need for external responsiveness and collaboration with other agencies. They suggest a positive and negative strategy that can be adopted in each segment of the matrix:

- High pressure for action, low external responsiveness required: *director strategy*. Assumes a moderate to high action orientation with a moderate accountability. Where the organization tries to operate with no accountability (a *dominator* strategy), it tends to run into difficulties.

- Low pressure for action, but high external accountability required: *accommodator strategy*. In a stable environment this strategy demonstrates an adequate responsiveness to a particular constituency. When there is no real action the strategy can become one of *posturer*.

- Low pressure for action and accountability required: *bureaucrat strategy*. This depends on routinized programmes and standardized procedures in a stable environment to carry out modest action in relation to specific needs with limited accountability and little innovation. At its most negative the strategy becomes that of a *drifter*, with little direction or accountability, achieving little.

■ High pressure for action and accountability required: *mutualist strategy*. The most proactive of the archetypes which is particularly appropriate to deal with a turbulent environment and respond to diverse and changing needs in an effective and collaborative way with other agencies. In response to calls for action to respond to a number of needs the *compromiser* strategy will try to play off constituencies against each other, often only responding to the needs of the most important or the most needy.

MARKETING STRATEGIES

nfpSynergy (2010) argue from their research that there cannot be one coherent thread that runs throughout a Third Sector organization. The only thing that could be described as a generic strategy in the Third Sector, in their view, is a marketing strategy 'which provides all of the fundraising, communications and brand activities of an organization with the direction and synergy necessary to achieve competitive advantage or superior performance' (ibid.: 36). They suggest there are four possible competitive marketing strategies for Third Sector organizations:

■ *Externally driven*: income primarily from legacies, investments, or statutory grants or contracts.

■ *Differentiation*: creating a perceived uniqueness:

  ● Audience-based: creating a direct and lasting bond with a target constituency (e.g. Behind the Mask – see website case study; Christian Aid; Trochaire; Muslim Aid; Ramblers Association; many medical and disability charities).

  ● Product-based: a distinctive and branded way of supporting a voluntary organization (e.g. Habitat for Humanity, Comic Relief, and Fairtrade – see Part VI case studies; Wikimedia – see website case study; Samaritans; membership of the National Trust; Amnesty International; museums; or child sponsorship).

  ● Beliefs-based: organizations with a distinctive set of values or beliefs (e.g. Greenpeace – see website case study; the Big Issue – see Part VI case study; Tear Fund).

■ *Niche*:

  ● Emotion or issue-based strategy: focusing on a single issue with emotional power; aiming for the organization to be recognized as owning that niche (e.g. RSPB, Cats Protection, Water Aid, National Trust, Help for Heroes).

  ● Geographically based: most people prefer to support initiatives that help the local area they identify with, which might be anything from a housing estate to a country (e.g. local community associations; Coin Street Community Builders, the Eden Project – see Part VI case studies; National Trust Scotland; Welsh National Opera).

- Awareness/market leadership: large competitive organizations promoting a high level of brand awareness through their media profile, e.g. RSPCA, Salvation Army, Oxfam, Barnardo's, NSPCC, Macmillan Cancer Support, British Heart Foundation, and Comic Relief (see case study in Part VI).

RUBIN'S STRATEGY METAPHORS

Rubin (1988), from his study of public sector organizations, characterizes types of strategic actions as the following metaphors:

Saga: depicts a historical perspective focusing on the heroic exploits, achievements and traditional values of the organization to defend itself from change. Within the Saga orientation, Rubin suggested three different strategies may operate:

- *restorative strategies*: which bring the organization back to where it was before changes were imposed by the external environment;
- *conservatory strategies*: which protect the values of individuals and particular organizational arrangements;
- *reformative strategies*: which will modify existing policy and mandates which are no longer seen to be appropriate.

Quest: this metaphor suggests leaders who focus their efforts and resources around a compelling vision and it captures the sense of adventure and test of courage in search of something of value. Within the quest metaphor Rubin suggests there can be three kinds of strategy:

- the *new agenda strategy* which involves creating a coalition of people around a new agenda which deliberately brings actors together with different priorities;
- the *grand visioning strategy* which develops a clear image of what the future state of the organization can become and which attracts support around it;
- an *alternative course strategy* which is designed to deal with a particular burning issue and to focus attention on resolving this key problem.

Venture: a venture is an action that responds to particular opportunities or needs in the present or near-future, particularly in relation to emerging issues where the appropriate long-term response is not clear. The strategies may include:

- the *target strategy* which improves the organization's capacity before an emerging issue can be addressed;
- the *trial strategy* which involves short-term experiments and temporary arrangements to deal with an emerging issue;
- the *compact strategy* which involves short-term arrangements with other organizations concerned with the issue or need which can be renegotiated later.

Parlay: a parlay is used by organizations to exploit an opportunity to position itself for a better opportunity. This can be useful when it is difficult to read the pattern of trends and events. It draws on Quinn's (1980) incremental approach where small actions may result in learning which will feed into further actions. The strategies involved may include:

- A *hedging strategy* where there are several likely future scenarios. Prioritization of programmes is deliberately avoided to give scope for action when the situation becomes clearer.

- A *leveraging strategy* using the development of social contacts and networks that will build up social credit and goodwill that can be cashed in when required at a later date.

- An *advancing strategy* which uses a windfall opportunity to reduce risk.

BARRY'S NON-PROFIT STRATEGIES

Barry (1986) is one of the few writers who have addressed the particular strategy configurations of Third Sector organizations:

- Large Third Sector organizations, in particular, often choose growth and diversification of services and funding sources as a way of gaining control over their environment. The major case studies in Part VI of Bryson Charitable Group, and Boxes 12.16 (the Cedar Foundation) and 1.2 (Action for Children), for example, reflect this kind of combined expansion strategy.

- Non-profit organizations may choose to team up with each other through mergers, collaborations, joint ventures, etc. The HIV/AIDS charities in Britain have recently gone through a period of merger, to ensure their long-term ability to survive in the context of a changing external environment (see also the Age UK case study on the website).

- With financial constraints, Third Sector organizations may choose to downsize or have it imposed on them.

- Third Sector organizations may choose to focus on a particular area or issue and specialize in that area. The major case study of Coin Street Community Builders in Part VI discusses a Third Sector organization which has chosen to focus in terms of geographical area; Emmaus, Habitat for Humanity, Fairtrade Foundation and PATHS (see Part VI case studies) have all chosen to focus in terms of the issue to be addressed.

- Non-profit organizations may use social economy initiatives, i.e. developing an activity which is income-generating in order to subsidize an activity which needs resources (see the case studies of the Bryson Charitable Group, Emmaus, Five Lamps and the Big Issue Foundation in Part VI; the Furniture Resource Centre in Box 8.2; and My Time CIC on the website for examples of charitable organizations that have very effectively developed social economy businesses).

- Third Sector organizations can seek contracts, especially in the health and social services field. The Bryson Charitable Group and Mencap (see Part VI case studies), for example, have developed extensive contracts with social services for a range of services over the past 20 years.

- Third Sector organizations may choose to professionalize their activities by upgrading their staffing. This is very common after the first entrepreneurial phase of a Third Sector initiative that is started by volunteers, sometimes supplemented by placements or trainees. As the organization develops, professional staff are appointed. (See, for example, the early days of Greenpeace on the website.)

- Third Sector organizations can also deprofessionalize using volunteers, peer education, community development strategies, etc.

- Third Sector organizations can also decide to wind up (or allow themselves to be taken over by another organization – 'mercy mergers' – if they decide they are no longer of value or are not economically viable).

One approach to expanding or scaling up the work of a Third Sector organization is through social franchising (Dees *et al.* 2002; Bradach 2003; Johnson *et al.* 2007). This strategy can be successful where the organization has a successful business model which is suitable for franchising through a licensing arrangement. The licensing organization generates income from a licence fee, the sale of programme manuals and other resources, and training and coaching of licensee staff/volunteers. The licensor needs to have a way of ensuring the contract is fulfilled and there is fidelity to the original programme.

An additional approach to the development of services being used, particularly in the public sector, is co-production, whereby organizations and citizens make better use of each other's assets and resources to achieve better outcomes and improved efficiency (Bovaird and McKenna 2011). This can be in the co-commissioning or co-delivery of services. Voluntary organizations or community groups might partner with a public sector body in co-production. A larger voluntary organization may also engage in co-production with a local community group.

STRATEGIES FOR SCALING UP SOCIAL ENTERPRISES

Lyon and Fernandez (2012) have examined the growth strategies of early years providers and identified the following strategies for scaling up social enterprises:

- Growth within the organization: maximizing the social impact of existing provision; diversification; in-house growth of existing programmes/services; starting programmes/services on new sites; taking over existing organizations or programmes/services; winning contracts from commissioners (a strategy being supported by the UK Government through its Modernizing Commissioning initiative).

- Scaling up through formalized relationships with other providers: spin out new organization(s); social franchises; kitemarks and quality standards.

- Open access sharing and disseminating good practice: training and accredited courses; networks established to share good practice; provision of open source material and encouraging learning.

MIXED SERVICE AND ADVOCACY STRATEGY

Crutchfield and Grant (2008), having closely examined a dozen successful US Third Sector organizations, concluded that great social sector organizations both 'advocate and serve', i.e. as well as providing services to a particular client group, engage in public policy advocacy to bring about change in statutory policies, practices and financial allocation. Although the provision of services and engaging in policy advocacy can be seen as separate strategic options, Crutchfield and Grant argue that engaging in both provides important synergy. They argue that providing direct services programmes generates greater impact on the ground, grassroots support and channels for implementing ideas, which all support policy advocacy. In turn, policy advocacy generates greater impact through legislation, government funding, increased credibility and influence.

BOX 9.1 MERGERS IN THE THIRD SECTOR HEALTH FIELD

In the private sector there has been considerable evidence of consolidation taking place in various industries, through mergers and acquisitions. Until recently there has been little sign that the Third Sector would follow suit. However, in the health field in the UK there have been significant moves towards mergers, particularly in relation to HIV/AIDS and cancer.

Following a period of financial difficulties caused by competitive contracting in the Health Service and a drop off in public interest in HIV/AIDS, two key mergers have been taking place in the HIV/AIDs field.

In April 2000, the National AIDS Trust, a leading HIV charity, focused on policy and prevention, and Red Ribbon International, which has led the campaigning around World Aids day with the red ribbon, as well as other campaigning work, merged. The two organizations see combining the two campaigning/policy organizations (neither provide direct services to people with HIV) as a way of strengthening their ability to improve the lives of people with HIV and protect communities vulnerable to infection in the UK and developing countries.

In October 2000, two of Britain's leading HIV/AIDS organizations, the Terence Higgins Trust, which had already merged with a number of regional HIV/AIDS charities in the previous year, and London Lighthouse joined forces to form a single organization, the Terence Higgins Trust Lighthouse. The combined organization will have a turnover of £8 million. They hope that merging will enable savings to be made of around £1.2 million through efficiency and streamlining of activities. They also hope that the two organizations will, in the longer term, be able to generate greater income, in this difficult fundraising field, as a single entity.

The two organizations are complementary in their particular strengths. The Terence Higgins Trust has been traditionally strong in relation to campaigning, health promotion, direct marketing, major donors and corporate fundraising, while Lighthouse is very well regarded by those who use their services, which have been effective in cause-related marketing and

▶

committee-led fundraising. A study of this merger (Harris and Hutchison 2002) concluded that: the interests and concerns of staff and other stakeholders require close attention during the implementation phase of the merger; during the implementation phase the vision of the new organization needs to be held in balance with an awareness of the organizational history of the constituent parts; and that partners to the merger should not underestimate the cost of merger in terms of money, human resources and time. In 2008, The International HIV/AIDS Alliance and Health & Development Network agreed to merge.

In the cancer field the plethora of large cancer charities has been confusing for the public who find it hard to distinguish the roles of the various charities and therefore to be confident that they are not duplicating services unnecessarily. In 2000, MacMillan Cancer Relief and Marie Curie Cancer Care, two leading UK cancer charities, discussed merging, but decided against it because of doubts as to whether a combined organization would be more effective than two single organizations working apart. In 2002, The Cancer Research Campaign and the Imperial Cancer Research Fund successfully merged, driven particularly by the medical research side, believing that a combined organization is more likely to find a cure for cancer.

In 2008, after three previous failed attempts, Help the Aged and Age Concern agreed to merge to become Age UK (see major case study on the website).

An interesting approach that bridges the Third and private sectors has been developed by Henry Mintzberg, one of the leading figures in modern thinking on strategy in the private sector, and Frances Westley, who had originally trained in the sociology of religion. They looked at the strategies that the main world religions had used to survive over such a long time period, despite enormous changes externally. They suggested three key types of strategy (in the sense of pattern rather than plan):

- *Enclaving*: this involves the carefully controlled integration of learning from within the existing structures. The change is conceived in an enclave of the organization. Rather than destroying the effort, the organization tolerates it (however minimally), isolating it to avoid challenge to, or contamination of, the rest of its activities. At some point, however, whether because the movement has moderated its radicalism or the larger organization finds itself in crisis and so has the need of the change (or perhaps, more commonly, both together), the change is accepted, legitimized and then allowed to infuse the rest of the organization and so effect a broader shift (Mintzberg and Westley 1992).

- *Cloning*: this involves the splitting off of groups into separate organizations or units, allowing for the expression of a variety of interpretations and a range of innovations. There are many examples of Third Sector organizations that spin off new organizations either in a new geographical area or from an emerging activity from within the organization. Kearns (2000) discusses divestment strategies for non-profit organizations but assumes that it is only appropriate in negative circumstances, requiring retrenchment. Many Third Sector organizations, however, adopt the positive strategy of developing new initiatives and if they are successful then floating them off as independent organizations.

■ *Uprooting*: this is a way of trying to keep the original vision and enthusiasm fresh by preventing the organization becoming bureaucratized and safe, by plunging the organization, or part of it, into a new context. Mao Zedong's Cultural Revolution was an example of how Mao tried to revitalize the Revolution by uprooting large numbers of Chinese from their homes. As in this example, the question is at what cost.

The founder of the Simon Community that works with people who are homeless in Britain and Ireland had a deliberate policy of occasional retrenchment in the 1970s, which involved the closure of its houses for people who were homeless to allow for a period of reflection on the vision and purpose of the organization.

STRATEGY CHOICES AND ORGANIZATIONAL LIFE CYCLES

Of the important issues to consider, which has been alluded to at various times, but not yet addressed directly, is the issue of organizational life cycles. An organizational life cycle is the life cycle of an organization from its creation to its termination. Based on a classic sigmoid (or bell) curve, many authors have suggested that organizations (as well as particular products or services) follow a similar life cycle to natural organisms:

■ inception/birth;

■ growth;

■ maturity;

■ decline;

It may even result in the death of the organization.

These stages are represented in Figure 9.1.

Donnelly-Cox and O'Regan (1999) examined the resourcing of organizational growth and development in the Third Sector in Ireland and concluded that it is important to

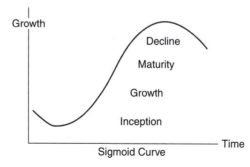

Fig 9.1   Sigmoid curve of the organizational life cycle

recognize that organizations are not static entities, but are constantly in flux. Drawing on open systems, resource-dependence and institutional theories, as well as the life cycle model, they argue for a typology involving three types of Third Sector organization:

- emerging;
- established;
- institutionalized.

The stage the organization is at will be reflected in resource issues (need legitimacy, organizational legitimacy, finance and human resources), and suggests, as organizations grow, where crises may occur over time.

Other models, however, do not assume the inevitability of institutionalization, decline and death. Daft (2010) suggests there are four stages in an organizational life cycle:

- entrepreneurial stage;
- collectivity stage;
- formalization stage;
- elaboration stage.

Greiner (1998) (see Figure 9.2) assumes the potential for growth, but suggests that there is likely to be a crisis every four to eight years, based on five key dimensions:

- an organization's size;
- an organization's age;
- an organization's stage of revolution (turmoil and change);
- an organization's evolution;
- the growth rate of the industry.

Based on these dimensions he identified five growth phases:

- growth through creativity;
- growth through direction;
- growth through delegation;
- growth through coordination;
- growth through (internal) collaboration.

He has since identified a sixth:

- growth through alliances.

He postulates that as the organization grows through each phase it is likely to face a crisis which will challenge further growth and result in turmoil and substantial change:

- At the end of the growth through creativity phase there is likely to be a leadership crisis, as the entrepreneurial founders struggle to manage a larger, more complex organization. A strong business-focused manager may be brought in at this stage who brings in more formal hierarchical structures, policies and systems. The

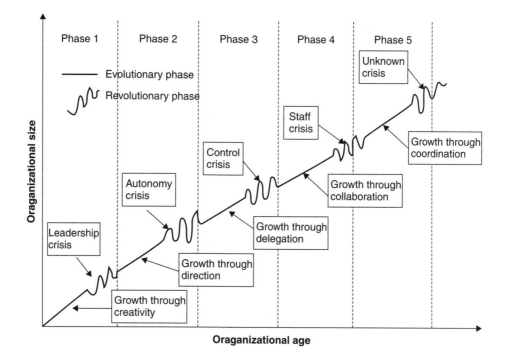

Fig 9.2   The five phases of organizational growth
Source: Adapted from Greiner (1972).

founders may adapt, leave or be pushed out (see Block and Rosenberg 2003 on 'founder's syndrome' and Hernandez and Leslie 2001 on the difficulties of succeeding a charismatic leader).

- At the end of the growth through direction phase there is likely to be an autonomy crisis, as lower-level managers feel frustrated with the tight control at the top despite their knowledge of the services and beneficiaries, leading to greater delegation throughout the organization.

- At the end of the growth through delegation phase there is likely to be a control crisis, as top managers feel they are not in control of what is happening in the organizations as decisions are made by lower level managers where parochial attitudes develop, leading to the development of more effective coordination mechanisms, including in their structures and formal planning processes.

- At the end of the growth through coordination phase there is likely to be a red tape crisis, where the organization feels stuck in bureaucracy and lacking in flexibility, leading to a more collaborative approach, based on cross-functional tasks and problem-solving teams and a simplification of control structures.

- At the end of the growth through (internal) collaboration phase there is likely to be a growth crisis, where the only growth options are through external mergers and collaborations.

The organization avoids the decline and death phases of the sigmoid curve by overcoming each of the crises, which enables it to create a further upward curve.

Ichak Adizes (1999) has suggested ten stages of the corporate life-cycle:

- *courtship*: the initial development or creation of the group/organization;
- *infancy*: after the launch, the start of active provision of the service/product;
- *go-go*: frantic energetic early growth and sometimes chaos;
- *adolescence*: still developing but more established and defined;
- *prime*: organization at its fittest, healthiest and most competitive, popular and profitable;
- *stability*: still effective and popular and can still be profitable, but beginning to lose the leading edge – vulnerability perhaps creeping in;
- *aristocracy*: strong by virtue of market presence and consolidated accumulated successes, but slow and unexciting, definitely losing out to competitors and new technologies, trends, etc.;
- *recrimination*: doubts, problems, threats and internal issues overshadow the original purposes;
- *bureaucracy*: inward-focused administration, cumbersome, seeking exit or divestment, many challenges;
- *death*: closure or mercy merger.

All the life-cycle models have some theoretical and analytical power; however, there are limitations in the value of a life-cycle approach, regardless of model. There is no necessity for an organization to move from one stage to the next. It may remain in one stage or it may jump phases. In Greiner's model it is not clear when the organization is likely to hit one of the crisis points. The models also, generally, do not indicate how long any particular stage might last. Organizations will want to develop a successful second wave (Ross and Segal 2002) before it reaches the stage where the curve begins to plateau out, before it starts to decline. The challenge is to know when you are reaching that point. A second wave at a later point may be too late. The models, therefore, may be more useful when looking backwards, than looking forwards. It is also useful for examining the life cycle of particular products or services, which is the basis of the Boston Matrix (see Chapter 8).

Regardless of how the stages of a Third Sector organization's development are described, for the purposes of this book the interesting issue is how the stages might relate to the kinds of strategies the organization might adopt at the different stages of development. Greiner's model focuses more on the internal challenges that an organization may face at different stages than what kinds of growth strategies might be appropriate. A common sequence of strategies in light of the changing life stages of an organization might look something like the following:

1. At the entrepreneurial stage, the founders are likely to have a simple proposition in relation to a particular service for a particular target group, e.g. the need for a zebra crossing to protect children on a housing estate; the need for a nightshelter for people currently sleeping rough; the need for counselling for adults facing emotional problems. It is unlikely that this is written down as a strategic plan until required

by a funder or potential funder. The Community Action Network (see Part VI case study) reflects the crucial role of such social entrepreneurs.

2. To achieve its initial objective young Third Sector organizations often struggle to acquire the resources they need to both survive and have an impact on their initial objectives (see the case study of the Emmaus Community in Part VI). Funders tend to expect a degree of formalization of plans, policies and governance.

3. As the initial idea takes off, both in meeting a real need and generating sufficient income, the organization tends to become more formalized, perhaps with paid staff. The target group is likely to stay the same, but the strategies may tend to become more sophisticated, i.e. the service offer becomes diversified. This is sometimes called 'scaling deep'. The community group that wanted a zebra crossing may want to set up a youth centre in the area; the nightshelter group might want to provide resettlement support; the counselling project might want to provide group therapies. The Big Issue (see Part VI case study) has developed from training and supporting homeless people to sell the Big Issue to a range of support and development functions for the same client group.

4. As the organization achieves success and becomes more formalized, the kinds of strategy the organization may consider can vary, including:

   ■ Expanding the geographical boundaries of its work, going more to scale by replicating the successful model elsewhere, e.g. the community group might expand to include a nearby estate; the nightshelter group might set up a second nightshelter elsewhere; the counselling project may negotiate a satellite centre to deliver its counselling. The Cool2Care social enterprise model (Box 1.3) demonstrates the geographical expansion of a successful model.

   ■ Expanding the range of clients/customers that the organization serves, e.g. the community group might set up a parent and toddlers group; the nightshelter group might develop a special project for young homeless people; the counselling project might negotiate to work in schools. My Time CIC (website case study), for example, began with simple counselling services and has developed related services for couples, families, employees, etc. Cool2Care (Box 1.3), which began with befriending support for children and young people with disabilities, has now moved into a befriending service for disabled adults in some of its areas.

5. As the organization continues to grow, the strategies are likely to become even more sophisticated and articulated in a formal strategic plan, which might include a mixture of:

   ■ Developing further new services to meet the needs of existing clients/customers. Mencap (Part VI case study), for example, has over the years expanded the range of services for people with a learning disability and their families.

   ■ Providing current or related services to new client groups. Black Sash (Part VI case study), for example, after the end of apartheid, adapted to the new environment and used their advice and advocacy skills to help the poor in tackling other forms of injustice and inequality.

   ■ Geographical expansion: going more substantially to scale by further expanding the existing boundaries and/or developing work in entirely new geographical areas. The Emmaus Community movement and Habitat for Humanity (in Part VI) reflect well the idea of going to scale with a model that was successful in one area until it has been extended across the globe.

- Campaigning on issues relevant to the organization and its clients/customers. Médecins Sans Frontières (website), for example, became increasingly outspoken about the actions and inactions of governments in areas it was working.

6. As the organization expands, and it develops new programmes and projects, perhaps through contracts, one of the likely strategies is quality assurance and improvement, i.e. policies, procedures and training to ensure that the standards of the services provided are consistently high and continuously improve (see Bryson Charitable Group in Part VI and Box 12.16 Cedar Foundation). In addition, a strategy of cost-efficiencies become more important when competing with private sector companies tendering for public sector contracts.

7. Over time, the original services may no longer be meeting client needs or generating sufficient income, e.g. changes in the bus service have removed the need for the zebra crossing; the limitations of nightshelter provision have created the need for it to be replaced with independent flats; the original counselling service which was grant funded has been put out to tender and won by another organization. New service developments may therefore replace old ones, or it may need to retrench, merge or close. Action for Children (Box 1.2), for example, moved from a model focused on providing children's homes, more to one based on adoption and fostering, as the limitations of residential care became more apparent.

INCOME GENERATION STRATEGY

In parallel with the strategies highlighted above is the challenge of income generation, which is relevant at all stages. The precise nature of the income generation the organization is likely to engage in will very much depend on the nature of the cause and the background and skills of the key players. For example, causes where the beneficiaries are seen to be innocent (e.g. children, animals), where the consequences of them not receiving help are perceived to be severe (e.g. life threatening diseases, overseas disasters), the impact of financial support is obvious (e.g. a capital appeal for a building) and/or there is a direct impact on, benefit for, individuals (e.g. churches, diseases, disabilities, old age, fine arts) are likely to follow a strategy of obtaining donations and other support from individuals:

- where those directly affected include some wealthy people (e.g. fine arts, church or school capital appeals), the strategy may include cultivating those individuals for big gifts;
- organizations that can engage a large number of volunteers are more likely to adopt a strategy of fundraising events (e.g. Comic Relief and Habitat for Humanity);
- causes which are a statutory responsibility (e.g. Action for Children – Box 1.2, Mencap and PATHS – see Part VI case studies) are more likely to emphasize getting grants or contracts from public bodies;

Table 9.1 Matrix of strategic choices for Third Sector organizations

	Client/customer group	Services/products	Geography
Retrench	Reduce, divest or close services to particular client/customer group(s)	Reduce, divest or close particular services/activities	Reduce, divest, or close services in a particular geographical area
Reduce costs	Reduce costs of services to particular client group(s)	Reduce costs of particular service(s)	Reduce costs of services in particular geographical area
Maintain	Continue services to existing client groups	Continue existing services	Continue services in existing areas
Improve quality	Improve the quality of services to particular client group(s)	Improve the quality of particular service(s)	Improve the quality of services in particular area(s)
Empowerment	Increase the participation, control and skills of clients/customers	Develop a particular service/product/process which increases the control of clients/customers	Increase the power and skills of clients/customers in a particular geographical area
Experiment	Pilot service(s) to a new client group	Pilot new kind of service(s)	Pilot service(s) in a new geographical area
Quantitative expansion	Increase the number of clients served	Increase the extent of provision of a particular service(s)	Increase the provision of services in a particular area
Expand boundary	Extend the boundary of a particular client group(s)	Extend the amount of particular service(s) that is provided	Extend the boundary of the geographical area covered
Expand boundary through social franchising	Extend the boundary of a particular client group(s) through social franchising	Extend the amount of particular service(s) that is provided through social franchising	Extend the boundary of the geographical area covered through social franchising
Switch to new related strategy	Switch services to a related client group	Switch to delivering a related type of service/activity	Switch to delivering services in a related geographical area
Switch to radical new unrelated strategy	Switch services to an unrelated client group	Switch to delivering an unrelated type of service/activity	Switch to providing services in an unrelated area
Unrelated expansion	Expand to provide services to an unrelated client group	Expand to provide unrelated types of service/activity	Expand to provide services in unrelated area(s)
Social economy	Develop fee-earning services to a particular customer group to earn income to subsidize other programmes	Develop a particular fee-earning service(s) to subsidize other activities	Develop fee-earning service(s) in a particular geographical area to subsidize other activities
Partnering	Develop a closer partnership with another agency in relation to particular client group(s)	Develop a closer partnership with another agency in relation to particular service(s)	Develop a closer partnership with another agency in particular geographical area
Merge	The same or complementary client group	The same or complementary services	The same or complementary geographical areas
Blue Ocean/ disruptive strategy	Any	Develop a new service concept/offering that satisfies new needs/demands of clients/customers	Any

- social enterprises are more likely to emphasize building a successful profit-making business (e.g. Bryson Charitable Group – see Part VI case study, Cosmic, Ethical IT – Box 12.5, Furniture Recycling Centre) through some combination of geographical expansion, new products/services and new clients/customers.

In terms of income generation, the stage of development of an organization is also likely to have an effect on the kind of income generation it may engage in. For example:

1. at the entrepreneurial stage, income generation may start with a fundraising event, like a sponsored walk, or a one-off small grant application to the local authority or a charitable trust, or the development of a simple social enterprise;
2. as the organization develops and the staffing required to run the services increases, the one-off funding application may turn into applications for longer-term funding and the development of other fundraising ideas or the expansion of the social enterprise;
3. as the service offer develops and the organization expands, the organization may be: making multiple grant applications; submitting tenders for the delivery of various public contracts; making approaches to individuals for donations and legacies; approaching companies for sponsorship; organizing more sophisticated fundraising events.

The various models and taxonomies of strategic options suggests a complex matrix of strategic choices for Third Sector organizations (see Table 9.1).

PREFERRED STRATEGY CHOICES

The preferred strategy choices of Third Sector organizations in the UK has been researched (Courtney 2005). In the study, respondents were asked to indicate the activities that had been a significant part of the organization's strategy over the previous three years from a defined list of 18 drawn from the literature. The types of strategies which respondents' organizations were most likely to have adopted in the previous three years were:

- improving the quality of services (three-quarters);
- providing new services (just over half);
- collaborating more closely with statutory bodies and/or with voluntary bodies;
- increasing user/member/client empowerment;
- increasing fundraising;
- working with new types of clients;
- working in new geographical areas;
- increasing public awareness;
- improving efficiency (more than a third);
- increasing campaigning/lobbying (more than one-quarter).

Clearly, quality improvement and growth strategies of various kinds (new services, new clients, new geographical areas) were key strategies adopted by the respondents' organizations, supported by increased fundraising, public awareness and campaigning/lobbying. However, the extent of collaborative strategies (both with the public sector and with other Third Sector organizations and to a lesser extent with the private sector) was also substantial and worthy of further research. Strategies to increase user/member/client empowerment – a distinctive value for many Third Sector organizations compared with the private sector – were also common and worthy of further research.

APPRAISING STRATEGIC OPTIONS

Various ways of defining the options that are open to Third Sector organizations have been highlighted above. The various case studies in Part VI demonstrate a wide variety of strategies. However, what is of interest to organizations is less about looking backwards, but looking forwards. A key issue is how organizational leaders should assess the possible options open to them to help them make strategic decisions. In the private sector this analysis is primarily concerned with the potential of the strategic options to make a profit for the company. In a Third Sector social enterprise, the issue of profitability is also important, if the enterprise is to be viable and perhaps subsidize non-profit-making activities which are important to the mission of the organization.

Haberberg and Rieple (2008) suggest using the RACES framework to assess strategic options:

- Resources needed to implement the option must be available, or the organization must be able to obtain them quickly;
- it must be Acceptable to powerful internal and external stakeholders;
- it must be Coherent with other proposals and existing strategies;
- it must be Effective in resolving issues that it is intended to address;
- it must contribute to the Sustainability of the organization.

More detailed criteria for assessing strategic options in the Third Sector are likely to include:

Suitability

- Mission alignment: to what extent will the strategic option progress the achievement of the organization's mission?
- Values alignment: to what extent is the strategic option consistent with the values and desired culture of the organization?
- Competency alignment: to what extent does the strategic option reflect the distinctive skills and knowledge of those within the organization (if not, how easy are they to acquire)?
- Strategies alignment: is there synergy between the strategy option and other strategies the organization has adopted or is contemplating?

Feasibility

- How likely is it that the organization can make the strategic option work?
- How likely is it that the strategic option will achieve the desired results?
- How likely is it that the strategic option will enable sufficient resources to be generated/acquired to implement the option?
- What are the risks involved and can they be managed?

Acceptability

- To what extent is the strategic option acceptable to the organization's internal stakeholders (e.g. staff, volunteers, trustees, members)?
- To what extent is the strategic option acceptable to the organization's external stakeholders (e.g. funders, partners, the public)?

SUMMARY

This chapter has explored the difficulty in determining generic strategies and whether it is even possible to talk about them. A variety of different possible ways of categorizing generic strategic choices that Third Sector organizations face have been explored. Potential criteria for appraising the strategic options have been examined.

QUESTIONS

1. In what ways do Third Sector organizations compete with each other?
2. How many different generic strategies are there that Third Sector organizations can adopt? Are some more effective than others?
3. According to Ansoff, what are the growth strategies available to Third Sector organizations?
4. In which ways can an organization scale up without expanding the organization itself?
5. Is growth always a good thing for Third Sector organizations?
6. To what extent is innovation a good thing for Third Sector organizations?
7. Should Third Sector organizations divest/spin off good projects that could be independent?
8. What different types of collaboration are there with other organizations?
9. Which criteria should a Third Sector organization use to assess the range of possible strategies it should adopt?

DISCUSSION TOPIC

Should Third Sector organizations working in a similar field and geographical area merge?

SUGGESTED READING

Kevin P. Kearns (2000) *Private Sector Strategies for Social Sector Success*, Jossey-Bass.

H. Mintzberg, B. Ahlstand and J. Lampel (1998) *Strategy Safari: A Guided Tour through the Wilds of Strategic Management*, Prentice-Hall.

Sharon Oster (1995) *Strategic Management for Nonprofit Organizations*, Oxford University Press.

PART IV

FORMULATING A STRATEGIC PLAN

10 STRATEGIC FORMULATION: CONTENT

OVERVIEW

Having analysed both the organization and its external environment, it is then possible for the board and staff of a Third Sector organization to begin putting together a framework for making decisions about future development. In doing so it is important to use the needs and expectations of the stakeholders, the changing trends in the external environment, developments with the other key players, and the distinctive or core competencies of the organization discussed above to help form the backdrop to the plan. But crucially the plans need to be formed from a clear, shared and inspirational sense of mission, vision and values. In this chapter the classic strategic planning framework used by a large number of Third Sector organizations to develop and describe their strategic direction will be explored. The theory behind each element of the framework and how they are interrelated will also be outlined.

LEARNING OBJECTIVES

After studying this chapter, you should be able to:

- describe the basic structure of a classic strategic planning framework;
- outline the purpose of, and difference between, mission, vision and values;
- describe the relationship between values and culture;
- outline the purpose of, and difference between, aims, priorities and objectives.

MISSION

According to Collins and Porras (1994), in their very successful book *Built to Last: Successful Habits of Visionary Companies*, the two most fundamental questions that any organization needs to ask in a changing world are: What do we stand for and why do we exist? They argue that encapsulating the answers to these questions in a statement of purpose or mission which taps into the intrinsic motivations of the people in the organization is crucial to the creation and development of an enduring and successful organization. As a concept, of course, the idea of mission comes from the Third

Sector, not the private sector; for centuries many faith organizations had a mission to spread their religion to non-believers.

Phills (2005: 22), in an examination of mission and strategy in the Third Sector in the US, describes mission as:

> the psychological and emotional logic that drives an organization. It is why people get up in the morning and go to work in a nonprofit; it is why donors support non-profits... because they are motivated to do so by the mission. Mission is the fuel that provides the psychological energy that motivates and inspires people to contribute their time, their energy, and their money to the organization. Mission is the source of passion; it is what people care most deeply about... Mission does all this by defining the social value that the organization creates. The key feature of social value – whether it is spiritual, moral, societal, aesthetic, intellectual, or environmental – is that it transcends economic value. Thus it is inextricably linked to fundamental human values, which are the basis of intrinsic worth or importance.

Such a mission statement which 'captures the soul of the organization' is more important for Third Sector organizations – which are not driven by making a profit, but by some particular sense of purpose or mission – than for the private sector. Drucker, who is very clear that 'the mission comes first' (1990) quotes a private sector CEO who served on various Third Sector boards who said 'the businesses I work with start their planning with financial returns. The nonprofits start with the performance of their mission' (Drucker 1990). Knauft *et al.* (1991) in *Profiles of Excellence* argue that a 'clear, agreed-upon mission statement' is one of the four primary characteristics of successful Third Sector organizations.

Sitting down with the key players within an organization and the key external stakeholders to explore the various possible answers to the basic question of what the purpose of the organization is can be a very salutary experience, as it is discovered how different the answers to that question can be, even in an apparently united organization. It can immediately raise some of the key strategic issues, dilemmas and choices that the organization needs to consider. It is also a very powerful question, as it quickly gets to the heart of what motivates each person to commit him or herself to give their time, energy and/or money to the organization.

The end product of these discussions should be a clear, concise and motivating statement of purpose (or mission statement) which covers all aspects of the organization's work. At its heart a mission statement normally contains at least two core elements: an infinitive verb that indicates a change in status (e.g. increase, decrease, eradicate, end, prevent, transform) in relation to the beneficiary population; and an identification of the problem to be addressed or condition to be changed (e.g. the impact of a particular disease, the lack of play facilities in an area). It should also communicate a sense of what is distinctive about the organization and what it is trying to achieve.

Oster (1995) argues that a mission statement serves three main purposes:

- it describes the boundary of the organization;
- it motivates staff, volunteers and donors and creates a sense of unity and focus for all stakeholders;
- it helps in the process of evaluation of the organization.

Goodsell (2006: 631) says that 'mission is the basis for agency self-identification, staff motivation, programme coherence, organizational pride, and political support. Likewise it stimulates a conscious level of intentionality that keeps the organization on track and mobilises the resolve needed to resist capture by special interests'. This strong sense of mission has been called 'mission trajectory' (Phipps and Burbach 2010) in the face of competing external forces.

Drucker (1990) argues that a mission statement should be based on three things:

- the things that the organization does well: the organization's strengths or competencies;

- where the organization can make the biggest difference in tackling the needs;

- what the people in the organization really believe, i.e. what they are really committed to.

The mission is crucial in guiding the future of the organization and its ability to respond to a changing external environment. Levitt (1960), like Drucker (1990), stresses the crucial importance of continually asking: What business are we in? Evans and Saxton (2004) ask, for example, 'are cancer research charities in the "cancer research" business, or "stopping people dying of cancer" business?'. The answer to the question may have a crucial impact on the future of the organization and its ability to innovate. Examples of the mission statements of some Third Sector organizations are given in Box 10.1.

BOX 10.1   MISSION STATEMENTS

'The RSPCA is a charity which will, by all lawful means, prevent cruelty, promote kindness to and alleviate suffering of animals.'

'Reduce crime, change lives.' (NACRO)

'To help the most vulnerable children and young people break through injustice, deprivation and inequality, so they can achieve their potential.' (Action for Children)

'Greenpeace is a global campaigning organization that acts to change attitudes and behaviour, to protect and conserve the environment and to promote peace.'

'Our mission is to provide guide dogs and other mobility services that increase the independence and dignity of blind and partially-sighted people. We campaign for improved rehabilitation services and unhindered access for all blind and partially-sighted people.' (Guide Dogs)

'To undertake research and action focused on preventing and ending grave abuses of the rights to physical and mental integrity, freedom of conscience and expression, and freedom from discrimination, within the context of its work to promote human rights.' (Amnesty International)

'Our mission is to challenge blindness by empowering people who are blind or partially-sighted, removing the barriers they face and helping to prevent blindness.' (RNIB)

'Our mission is to inspire breakthroughs in the way the world treats children, and to achieve immediate and lasting change in their lives.' (Save the Children [SCF])

'To serve our members by carrying on business as a co-operative in accordance with co-operative values and principles.' (The Co-operative Group)

Examination of the mission statements in Box 10.1 suggests that they can serve at least five purposes. They can:

- highlight commitment to core values (e.g. Amnesty International's commitment to the Universal Declaration of Human Rights, such as freedom of conscience and expression; the Co-operative Group's commitment to cooperative values, etc.);
- clarify the target group of beneficiaries, e.g. RNIB's 'people who are blind or partially sighted';
- highlight the changes that the organization wants to see in relation to the target group of beneficiaries, e.g. NACRO's 'create a safer more inclusive society';
- clarify the means that the organization uses to achieve its purpose, e.g. 'to provide guide dogs' (Guide Dogs) or 'undertake research' (Amnesty); clarify the geographical boundaries of the organization's work, e.g. SCF's (Save the Children Fund now Save the Children) 'worldwide'.

The mission statements of Third Sector organizations, although designed to be long term, often change over time as the organization develops and the values and language used within the sector or subsector changes. Sometimes, however, an organization begins with a clear sense of a distinctive mission, but over time, with changes in the external environment – such as new trustees and staff, incremental decisions to develop new or innovative services or serve new groups of beneficiaries, or under financial pressures – a process of 'mission drift' or 'mission creep' takes place, which gradually moves it away from its distinctive mission, until it doesn't know what it stands for. Around the original core of uniqueness, 'encrustations' (Porter 1997) may be added incrementally. Like barnacles, however, Porter suggests they need to be removed to reveal the underlying strategic positioning. The challenge, in his view, is to refocus on the unique core and realign the organization's activities with it. However, an alternative perspective on such changes is that the organization has adapted to a changing external environment, allowing innovations to emerge, until it reaches the point where deliberately creating a new sense of mission may be important, which is likely to be different from the earlier one.

The breadth of scope of an organization's mission is crucial. Bryson Charitable Group (see Part VI case study), for example, has become a diverse multifunctional organization. Its mission statement reflects this: 'We are committed to identifying and developing sustainable responses to existing and emerging social need.' Habitat for Humanity (see Part VI case study), on the other hand, has remained focused on its distinctive ideology and methodology for tackling housing issues. Its mission reflects this

> Habitat for Humanity works in partnership with God and people everywhere, from all walks of life, to develop communities with people in need by building and renovating houses so that there are decent houses in decent communities in which every person can experience God's love and can live and grow into all that God intends.

Although the process of strategy development is primarily about looking to the future, Porter argues that an organization's history can also be particularly instructive. He suggests that organizations should ask themselves the question: What was the vision of the founder? and What were the features that made the organization successful in the first place? He suggests that it is possible to re-examine the original strategy to see if it is still valid, although he recognizes that it may need to be implemented in a modern way, consistent with today's technologies and practices. He suggests that this sort of thinking may 'lead to a commitment to renew the strategy and may challenge the organization to recover its distinctiveness' (Porter 1997: 76).

VISION

Alongside developing a mission statement, many Third Sector organizations also now have a vision statement. This is a word picture of the state of affairs that the organization would ideally like to see, if its work was successful. Evans and Garvey (2006) describe an organization's vision as its 'guiding star'.

Mintzberg (1994: 272 and 416) argues that 'many of the great strategies are simply great visions…only when we recognize our fantasies can we begin to appreciate the wonders of reality!'. Bennis (1985 in Kennedy 1996: 32) defines leadership entirely in terms of vision, as 'the capacity to create a compelling vision and translate it into action and sustain it'. Mary Parker Follett (Fox and Urwick 1973: 244) one of the great (and neglected) early writers on management, who took a much more human view of it than Taylor or Fayol, argues that 'the most successful leader of all is one who sees another picture not yet actualized'.

Bryson (1995) argues that an organization should have a vision for the future which:

- clarifies the organization's direction and purpose;
- is relatively future orientated;
- reflects high ideals and challenging ambitions;
- captures the organization's uniqueness and distinctive competence as well as desirable features of its history, culture and values;
- is short and inspiring;
- is widely circulated;
- is used to inform organizational decisions.

Phills (2005: 46) suggests that 'vision is the place to be inclusive, expansive, enthusiastic, poetic and passionate. Vision has to be compellingly rich, evocative'. Evans and Garvey (2006), in their study of vision statements of over 80 British charities, give the following advice on creating powerful vision (and mission):

- start with the heart and soul of your organization;
- good vision statements act as a polar star in the darkness;
- vision statements are for everyone;
- be unique and distinctive (every charity wants to be caring, dedicated and friendly);
- secure widespread ownership, but don't write by committee;

- less is more: omit redundant words;
- live it, breathe it, be it.

Pascale and Athos (1981) having explored the success of Japanese companies, argue for the value of the Japanese approach to vision statements which are 'dynamic, vivifying *modus operandi* rather than pallid or generic statements of corporate intent' (Crainer 2000: 182). Examples of the vision statements of some Third Sector organizations are given in Box 10.2.

BOX 10.2   VISION STATEMENTS

'To end cruelty to children in the UK.' (NSPCC)

'Samaritan's vision is that fewer people die by suicide.'

'The RSPCA's vision is to work for a world in which all humans respect and live in harmony with all other members of the animal kingdom.'

'That NACRO leads the way in ensuring comprehensive preventive and resettlement services are available across England and Wales by 2015.'

'Our vision is of a world where all children and young people have a sense of belonging and are loved and valued, a world where they can fulfil their potential, shape their destiny and experience the joy of life.' (Action for Children)

'The National Childbirth Trust wants all parents to have an experience of pregnancy, birth and early parenthood that enriches their lives and gives them confidence in being a parent.'

'Guide Dogs wants a world in which all blind and partially-sighted people enjoy the same rights, opportunities and responsibilities as everyone else.'

'Our vision is of a world in which every person enjoys all the human rights enshrined in the Universal Declaration of Human Rights and other international human rights instruments.' (Amnesty International)

'Our vision is of a world in which blind and partially-sighted people enjoy the same rights, freedom, responsibilities and quality of life as people who are fully sighted.' (RNIB)

'Our vision is a world where people with a learning disability are valued equally, listened to and included. We want everyone to have the opportunity to achieve the things they want out of life.' (Mencap)

'VSO's vision is of a world without poverty in which people work together to fulfil their potential.'

'To build a better society by excelling in everything we do.' (The Co-operative Group)

'Our vision is a world in which every child attains the right to survival, protection, development and participation.' (Save the Children)

'The Vision of the Big Issue Foundation is to extend our support to vendors throughout the UK and in doing so to create a brighter future in which vendors are happier, healthier and safer.'

'Imagine a world in which every single person on the planet is given free access to the sum of all human knowledge'. (Wikipedia)

Most of the vision statements in Box 10.2 provide inspiring statements of how the organization wants the world they are concerned with to look like ideally. Most focus on what they would like to see for their particular beneficiary group. Some social enterprises follow the private sector perspective on vision by focusing on the future success of the enterprise and the customer experience. Cool2Care's vision statement, for example, is:

> To be the leading provider of one-to-one matching services for disabled young people and their families in the UK, incorporating trained volunteers, care-workers, personal assistants, befrienders, buddies, and professionals.

The NACRO vision statement, highlighted in Box 10.2 earlier:

> That NACRO leads the way in ensuring comprehensive preventive and resettlement services are available across England and Wales by 2015.

This statement is particularly interesting because it contains three different elements:

- a vision of the external world, i.e. comprehensive preventive and resettlement services are available across England and Wales;
- a vision of the leadership role of NACRO in ensuring this is achieved;
- a date by which this will be achieved.

Some Third Sector organizations have mission statements which read as vision statements and vice versa. Others have developed vision statements for each aspect of their work. Greenpeace, for example (see Box 10.3), as well as having an overall vision, has developed visions for each of its campaigning areas: climate, forests, oceans and a peaceful world.

BOX 10.3 THE GREENPEACE VISION

Our vision
The underlying goal of all our work is a green and peaceful world: an earth that is ecologically healthy and able to nurture life in all its diversity.

Our vision for the climate

We want climate solutions that will help us prosper without damaging the planet. We're working to replace our hugely inefficient and carbon polluting energy system with a clean energy one so that our air will be clean and our climate will be stable and healthy.

Our vision for the world's forests

We're working to protect the world's ancient forests and the plants, animals and peoples that depend on them. The Earth's rainforests should be doing the job they were made for: regulating the climate, providing rain and enabling plants, animals and people to thrive. We are exposing the causes of forest destruction and working to transform industry practices to protect the world's remaining rainforests.

Our vision for healthy oceans

We want oceans that are protected and full of abundant, healthy marine life; oceans that are carefully managed, and sustainable fishing practices that don't put marine species at risk. We are

▶

working for a global network of marine reserves across the world's oceans – sea sanctuaries where no fishing or polluting industries will be permitted and to eliminate destructive fishing practices. This is vital to protect battered ecosystems and give threatened species time to recover.

Our vision for a peaceful world

Governments and industry around the world must ensure that the Earth's finite resources are shared fairly, so people have what they need to live peacefully. That way there is simply no need to fight over dwindling food, gas, oil, and water, or to develop weapons of mass destruction. We tackle the root causes of global insecurity and promote a vision of green development which is vital for living peacefully on a finite planet.

(www.greenpeace.orgSee)

The gap between the current reality and the vision articulated in the vision statement is what Sheehan (2010) calls the 'mission gap', which is what drives an organization to create a strategy, with strategic stretch goals (see p. 183) which will 'catapult the organisation to higher levels of performance'.

VALUES

The third element of a fundamental description of what an organization is about is often a statement of values, principles or philosophy which underpins the whole work of the organization. Thomas Watson Jr (1963: 1), a former CEO of IBM observed:

> Consider any great organization – one that has lasted over the years – I think you will find it owes its resilience not to its form of organization or administrative skills, but to the power of what we call beliefs and the appeal these beliefs have for people.

Peters and Waterman (1982) argue that shared values are one of the seven key elements of an excellent company and devoted a whole chapter to them in *In Search of Excellence*. Collins and Porras (1997: 48; 88) also state that one of the key principles of a visionary company is the existence of a core ideology that gives guidance and inspiration to its people.

Bryson (1995) argues that only strategies that are consonant with the philosophy, core values and culture of an organization are likely to succeed. He also argues that clarifying its values will enable an organization to maintain its integrity, by turning down opportunities which might damage this integrity. Hudson (1995) suggests that while organizations in other sectors may have values, Third Sector organizations must really cherish their values.

Evans and Garvey (2006) found from their research that the best value statements were those that truly captured the ideological orientation of the organization. The importance of values is not a new phenomenon in relation to organizations. Chester Barnard as far back as 1938 recognized that all acts of individuals and organizations are interconnected and interdependent, and argued (in the language of the times) that 'the distinguishing mark of the executive responsibility is that it requires not merely conformance to a complex code of morals but also the creation of moral codes for others' (Barnard 1938: 279).

Some of the mission and vision statements quoted already include statements of key values. For voluntary organizations which are, by definition, value-led it is particularly important to be concerned with not only what it does but also how it does it. The headings of typical statements of values in the Third Sector are shown in Box 10.4.

BOX 10.4   TYPICAL VALUES

Integrity

Confidentiality

Putting the needs of the users first

Effectiveness

Quality/excellence

Partnership

Inclusion

Compassion

Learning

Openness

Accountability/probity/efficiency

Empowerment

Valuing people

Teamwork/working together/partnerships

Dynamism/innovation

Diversity

Sustainable development/self-reliance

Equal right to achieve potential

Respect

Equal opportunities/equality

Challenging discrimination

Trust

Passion

Hope

A real example of a statement of values from Save the Children is shown in Box 10.5. The case study of Wikimedia in Part V shows how they have developed some quite distinctive values that drive both its strategy and resource acquisition approach.

Some organizations base their values on universal declarations of rights, such as the International Rights of the Child or the UN Declaration of Human Rights. Most, however, develop their own, some of which may be rights-based. Some may be very general in scope and others may be very specifically focused on the concerns of the particular organization. Box 10.5 is an example of a more detailed value statement from a leading Third Sector organization engaged particularly in policy, advocacy and innovation in relation to children.

BOX 10.5   SAVE THE CHILDREN VALUES

Our values are:

Accountability: We take personal responsibility for using our resources efficiently, achieving measurable results, and being accountable to supporters, partners and, most of all, children.

Ambition: We are demanding of ourselves and our colleagues, set high goals and are committed to improving the quality of everything we do for children.

Collaboration: We respect and value each other, thrive on our diversity, and work with partners to leverage our global strength in making a difference for children.

Creativity: We are open to new ideas, embrace change, and take disciplined risks to develop sustainable solutions for and with children.

Integrity: We aspire to live the highest standards of personal honesty and behaviour; we never compromise our reputation and always act in the best interests of children.

Values are the articulation of the desired culture of the organization, both its beliefs about its beneficiaries (about their rights for example) and 'how things are done around here'. Culture has been defined as 'the shared beliefs and values guiding the thinking and behavioural styles of members (Cooke and Rousseau 1988: 1), and

> the social and normative glue that holds an organization together…the values or social ideals and the beliefs that organization members come to share. These values or patterns of belief are manifested by symbolic devices such as myths, rituals, stories, legends and specialized language. (Smircich 1983: 344)

All organizations have a culture, regardless of whether they have a statement of values or not. Indeed different parts of an organization may reflect different cultures. The values and culture of people involved in finance or fundraising in a Third Sector organization may be different, for example, from those providing human services, community development or campaigning. Young professional staff may have different values from older more traditional volunteers or trustees. This diversity, as well as being a rich source for dialogue, can sometimes give rise to conflicts within organizations. At least identifying the differences, and the reasons for them, can help at least to clarify, if not resolve or transform, them.

Johnson (2001) developed a Cultural Web to help organizations think about aspects of the culture of an organization (see Figure 10.1).

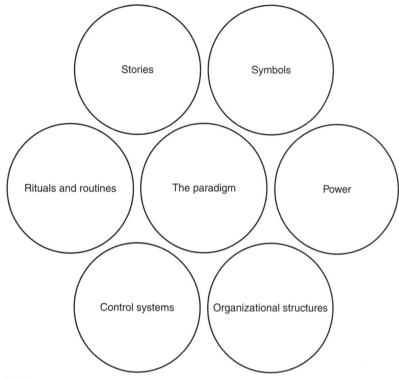

Fig 10.1 Cultural Web

Source: Adapted from Johnson and Scholes 1993.

Organizations can use the Cultural Web to reflect on the current culture and envisage the one that they would like to see in future. Box 10.6 highlights some of the words that might be used to give an indication of the actual culture, or values in use, of a Third Sector organization.

It is important to distinguish between values in theory and values in practice (Argyris and Schon 1974) and to identify and try to narrow the gap between the two. There is considerable evidence that publicly espousing a particular value or view is likely to result in behaviour which is more consonant with that value or view than if there had been no public espousal (Payne 1996). However, there are many organizations with charters or statements of values or beliefs that bear little relationship with how the organization actually works and deals with customers/clients in practice. This can result in cynicism both internally and externally.

Bartlett and Ghoshal (1989: 204) argue that culture, what they call 'organizational psychology', can be 'developed and managed just as effectively as the organizational anatomy and physiology', although many major change programmes which have attempted to fundamentally transform the culture of an organization have shown how difficult this can be. It has been suggested that it takes at least five years to change fundamentally the culture of an organization.

It is important to put in place processes to assess the extent that the values stated by the organization are being applied in practice and, therefore, to help ensure that

BOX 10.6 WORDS THAT HELP TO DESCRIBE AN ORGANIZATIONAL CULTURE

What words describe the organization as it is now?
What words would you like to describe the organization in future?

Well-structured	Far-thinking	Makes do
Hierarchical	Determined	Accessible
Flat-structured	Outward-looking	Public-focused
Collegiate	Inward-looking	Consensual
Strong volunteer ethos	Persuasive	Autocratic
Dynamic	Opportunity-focused	Shy
Stable	Confident	Reflective
Risk averse	Cosy	Modest
Influential	Results-driven	Inspirational
Respectful of tradition	Strategic	Motivating
Strong leadership	Constantly learning	Blame-culture
Research-driven	Disciplined	Predatory
Movement-builder	Entrepreneurial	Aggressive
Collaborative	World class	Chaotic
Partnership-focused	Competitive	Muddles through
Responsible	Innovative	Lean
Radical	Evidence-based	Controlled
Decisive	Creative	Skilled
Leader in its field	Democratic	Ethical
Responsive to feedback	Flexible	Pragmatic
Technologically driven	Continuously improving	Outspoken
Responsive	Focused	Rebellious
Victimized	Participative	Knowledgeable
Leading edge	Consultative	Giving
Public policy focused	Excellence-focused	Altruistic
Open	Highly organized	Brand-aware
Relaxed	Client obsessed	Cumbersome
Efficient	Empowering	Controlling
Effective	Outcome-focused	Commercially driven
Fair	Intuitive	Unquestioning
Equitable	Assertive	Action-focused
Diverse	Vocal	Trendy
Interdependent	Funding-driven	Community
Rights-focused	Hard-working	Vibrant
Charitable	Welcoming	Intellectual
Enterprising	Well-organized	Caring
Businesslike	Laid back	Victorian
Accepting	Authoritarian	Rudderless
Delegating	Exclusive	Friendly
Hard-nosed	Questioning	Open
Secretive		

they are values in practice as well as values in theory. This can be done through: induction and training; leaders setting a good example ('the actions and behaviour of senior managers are vital as examples and statements of commitment' (ibid.: 177)); regularly referring to the values; and adopting policies and strategies for implementing the values (e.g. equal opportunities, confidentiality, quality, health and safety); regularly asking stakeholders how the organization is doing in living up to its stated values; setting performance indicators around each of the values and regularly measuring the indicators.

The distinctive culture and values of an organization often tend to derive initially from the influence of a charismatic leader, usually the founder, who defined the basic beliefs, values and patterns of behaviour that epitomize good citizenship (Schein 1992). These may, consciously or unconsciously, still be important many years after the leader has gone. Often, in the early stages of the establishment and development of an organization, such a strong sense of vision and values formed the basis of an entrepreneurial strategy (Mintzberg and Waters 1997), which is very much in the control and direction of one person. Many successful organizations are the result of the strong sense of vision and values of a powerful founder (see the case studies of Community Action Network in Part VI). However, the environment, or key parts of it, need to be open in some way to this vision, otherwise the organization would not survive or develop. When this strong sense of vision and values becomes accepted by a group of people, usually the trustees and staff of an organization, it can be described as an ideological strategy (ibid.). As the trustees and staff of Third Sector organizations are often committed to making a particular change in the world in a particular way, they can also be very resistant to pressures to change from outside.

Although much of the literature on culture and values is about the positive aspects of organizations having, and living up to, these shared values, as Hamel (2000) has pointed out, there can also be a dark side. Organizations may be faced with a rapidly changing external environment, including changing attitudes of key stakeholders, such as funders, service-users and/or the public, which strongly conflict with the traditional values of the organization. Many older Third Sector organizations, for example, were founded on Victorian values of charity and philanthropy, of looking after the deserving poor in large separate institutions. In contrast, much of the current philosophy around social care is based on the concepts of rights, of empowerment, integration and equal opportunities. This often gives rise to conflict between professional managers who have increasingly been appointed to Third Sector organizations from outside and long-serving trustees who feel a strong desire to remain true to the historic principles of the organization and of the founder. This conflict can be particularly strong where relatives, descendants or friends of the founder (even the founder him or herself) are still on the board of management. Hamel (2000) has also argued that when values are 'endlessly elaborated, overly codified and solemnly worshipped' they can become the manacles that shackle the organization to the past.

An organization's distinctive value-base can be a powerful driver of the organization's strategy. Frumkin and Andre-Clarke (2000: 159) argue that:

> it is all but certain that values may be the right starting point for either aggressive growth or product differentiation strategies. No matter how this translation is made from values to specific strategy, thinking about the relationship between values and an organization's ultimate ability to perform is an important task. It is this fundamental tension that frames both strategy and identity within the nonprofit sector.

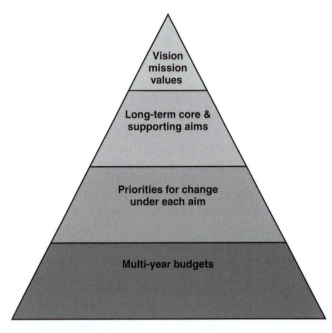

Fig 10.2   Strategic planning pyramid

The mission, vision and value statements, discussed above, provide the pinnacle of a pyramid through which the strategic plan of the organization can be cascaded (see Figure 10.2).

LONG–TERM AIMS

Mission, vision and values statements, by their very nature, tend to be aspirational, long-term and very broad. To give the strategic plan a coherent framework there is commonly a number (usually between four and ten) of long-term core aims (sometimes called goals or strategic objectives) which cover each of the main strategic areas (sometimes called critical success factors) that the organization will need to engage in, over the whole period of the plan, if it is to make progress towards achieving its mission and vision. These long-term aims typically cover the main strategic options that were identified from an analysis and appraisal of the strategic options for achieving the aims and vision.

Greenwich Leisure Services' aims (see the case study on the website), for example, are to:

- encourage community involvement;
- promote healthy living;
- increase levels of physical activity by delivering sport and health programmes that reach all sectors of the community;

- ensure its financial viability;
- meet its charitable objectives;
- increase employee participation;
- maintain and expand services;
- endeavour continually to exceed customers' expectations.

Collins and Porras (1994) in their influential book *Built to Last: Successful Habits of Visionary Companies* argue that organizations should create what they call 'B'Hags' (Big Hairy Audacious Goals!), what Ross and Segal (2002) call 'breakthrough goals', which go beyond providing some stretch. These are designed to provide real challenge and motivation for all those involved in the organization. This is consistent with Hamel and Prahalad's (1994) concept of 'stretch' – the sense of real ambition which creates energy and commitment around a consistency of effort and purpose over the long term. They argue that the problem with many larger older organizations is that they have become complacent and have lost the original sense of ambition or stretch and are often overtaken by new smaller organizations which have a hunger or ambition to achieve more audacious goals. (See the aims of the British Red Cross in Box 10.7.)

BOX 10.7   BRITISH RED CROSS AIMS

Emergency response and recovery

When an emergency strikes we will respond.

Resilience

We will make people and communities more resilient by helping them prepare for and withstand disasters.

Health and social care

We will help vulnerable people recover from health and social crises, and live with dignity and independence in their homes.

Supporting the movement

We will increase the International Red Cross and Red Crescent Movement's impact on the lives of the most vulnerable.

Volunteers and staff

We want to make volunteering for us the best experience money can't buy.

Positioning

We will make sure people and groups know what we do and why – and how they can help.

►

Organisational development

We will ensure those who use our services, and who support us in other ways, trust us and have confidence in how we work.

Funding the strategy

We will maximize our net income as cost-effectively as possible.

(British Red Cross Corporate Strategy 2010–15)

STRATEGIC PRIORITIES

All of the above (mission, vision, values, long-term aims), which form the top half of the strategy pyramid, are still very visionary, idealistic and broad. It is important however for an organizational plan to move towards some more specific goals that the organization can work towards achieving within the period of the strategic plan (often three or five years). In the UK Vision example in Box 10.8, for example, what are the subgoals or priorities for change that need to be achieved if the three core aims are to be achieved?

BOX 10.8   UK VISION STRATEGY

The UK Vision Strategy brings together people with sight loss, users of eye care services, eye health and social care professionals and statutory and voluntary organizations, in order to produce a unified framework for action on all issues relating to vision.

The UK Vision Strategy has been developed in response to the World Health Assembly VISION2020 resolution to reduce avoidable blindness by the year 2020 and improve support and services for blind and partially sighted people. The UK Vision Strategy works to achieve equal and timely access to the UK's eye health and sight loss services, address the exclusion of blind and partially sighted people and increase understanding about the importance of eye health. A determined and united cross-sector approach will make these changes a reality. Three strategic outcome areas are identified to achieve this::

1. Improving the eye health of the people of the UK

Five-year aim: To raise awareness and understanding of eye health among the public, including those people most at risk of eye disease, to allow every individual to develop personal responsibility for eye health and to achieve maximum eye health for all. To raise awareness of eye health among health and social care practitioners, and to ensure the early detection of sight loss and prevention where possible.

2. Eliminating avoidable sight loss and delivering excellent support for people with sight loss

Five-year aim: To improve the coordination, integration, reach and effectiveness of eye health services, and services and support for those people with permanent sight loss.

3. Inclusion, participation and independence for people with sight loss

▶

Five-year aim: To improve the attitudes, awareness and actions of service providers, employers and the public towards people with sight loss and to remove significant barriers to inclusion, so that people with sight loss can exercise independence, control and choice. To achieve improved compliance with disability discrimination legislation.

The UK Vision Strategy is underpinned by the following values:

- Fair and equitable access for all members of society to eye health, eye care and sight loss services.

- Person-centred delivery of excellent services and support in the most appropriate way for each individual.

- Evidence-based policies and services to guide resource allocation and effective services.

- Awareness of and respect for people with sight loss and full compliance with equality legislation.

The UK Vision Strategy implementation plans have clear objectives which are monitored to ensure that progress is maintained across the Strategy's five-year span. This includes reviews every five years. In November 2012 a consultation about the UK Vision Strategy took place and the refreshed UK Vision Strategy will be launched in June 2013.

The delivery of the UK Vision Strategy requires a united eye health and sight loss sector, speaking with one voice to strongly influence the future direction and prioritization of eye health and sight loss. Implementation needs the same collaborative approach that enabled the development of the UK Vision Strategy. It must also respect the divergence of priorities and arrangements between the countries within the UK.

Tangible examples of what the UK Vision Strategy has achieved to date by working together include:

- The Department of Health Public Health Outcomes Framework for England launched by the government in 2012 includes a Public Health Indicator on eye health that will track the rates of three major causes of avoidable sight loss: glaucoma, age-related macular degeneration and diabetic retinopathy.

- The chair of the Scottish Vision Strategy Advisory Group is a member of the working group implementing Scotland's new £6.6m electronic referral scheme, which will roll out across each of the 14 regional Health Boards over the next three years. The working group involves senior government and health board representatives alongside Eyecare Scotland, Optometry Scotland and ehealth.

- The Bridging and Gap document, available in Wales, Scotland, Northern Ireland and England, sets out the support available to young people in the transition from school to higher or further education and work.

- The REACT talking sign system, which uses a trigger fob to activate speaker units to aid navigation, is being installed as part of Belfast City Council's Streets Ahead project.

These achievements have only been made possible by organizations and individuals getting together behind the outcomes of the UK Vision Strategy.

Maintenance of a united and cooperative stance will be the cornerstone for achieving the UK Vision Strategy outcomes. It has a power that cannot be ignored and will be the key to its success.

(UK Vision strategy report http://www.vision2020uk.org.uk/ukvisionstrategy/;
A VISION 2020 UK initiative led by RNIB)

One useful step in this direction is to establish some key priorities for change, or main thrusts under each long-term aim, that the organization will focus on over the three or five years of the plan. The aims (which they call objectives) and priorities (which they call actions) of Marie Curie Cancer Care are highlighted in Box 10.9. Regardless of the names that are given to the different levels within a strategic plan, the same hierarchical/pyramid principle applies.

BOX 10.9 MARIE CURIE CANCER CARE STRATEGIC PLAN: PUTTING PATIENTS AND FAMILIES FIRST VISION

Everyone with cancer and other illnesses will have the high quality care and support they need at the end of their life in the place of their choice.

Core value

We put patients and families first.

Key objectives (aims) and actions (priorities) over the next three years include:

Better care

1. Delivering the right care, in the right place, at the right time

We will ensure high quality care is provided to people in the greatest need at the end of their lives, giving them the choice to die at home. Our care will be available to people with cancer and other illnesses free of charge and will be easier to access.

Key actions

- Those in greatest need will be given priority. Marie Curie Nurses will take responsibility for determining the level of care and support provided by the charity.

- Patients and families will be able to contact us directly to request a nurse.

- We will provide practical training and support for families caring for the dying, and we will pilot a service offering follow-up visits after the death of a patient.

2. Hospices being the hub of their communities

Our hospices will reach out to more patients and families and will improve end of life care in the communities they serve.

Key actions

- Our hospices will be working in partnership to improve care for patients, support for families and training for healthcare professionals in their local communities.

- We will explore sharing services with other hospice care providers to improve efficiency and save costs for all.

- Our new hospice in the West Midlands will be open, and a programme to improve our hospice facilities across the UK will be in place.

▶

3. *Always improving quality*

We will continuously improve all our services for patients and families, whatever the economic environment, so that they receive the highest quality care and support.

Key actions

- We will have Quality Markers in place for all our activities in hospices and the Marie Curie Nursing Service. These will be continuously improved.

- Whatever the economy, we will not provide services below our quality benchmark.

- We will improve the quality of care delivered to patients and families by ensuring that our research findings directly impact on the care we deliver.

Wider reach

4. *Research and development to improve end of life care for everyone*

We will be known as a leader in end of life care research and development that brings direct benefits to patients and families. We will provide a significant increase in funding.

Key actions

- On an annual basis, we will provide an analysis of end of life care across the UK, providing clarity on where services are most needed.

- We will deliver credible economic evidence demonstrating the economic cost and impact of different approaches to end of life care in different settings.

- We will increase our investment in developing, testing and implementing new services in partnership with others.

5. *Being better known and understood*

We will raise our profile at local and national level to reach more patients and families, to influence health policy in all four countries and to grow our fundraising and support.

Key actions

- We will be represented on influential groups where our expertise in end of life care can have a positive impact for patients and families on the NHS and governments.

- All major fundraising campaigns will be supported with investment in marketing that increases our income.

6. *Helping communities build better local care*

We will support and encourage local communities and initiatives to improve the availability and quality of end of life care for people at home.

Key actions

- We will have a network of Marie Curie volunteers across the UK with an active interest in care of the dying in their local communities.

- Our website will be a recognized source for local support and practical information for people at end of their lives and their families.

- We will be involved in more local partnerships that deliver and promote high quality care at the end of life and will enhance our reputation as a good partner.

> **Stronger foundations**
>
> There are additional objectives and actions in relation to fundraising, volunteer support, and improving efficiency and effectiveness.
>
> (www.mariecurie.org.uk; Marie Curie Cancer Care 2011–2014 Strategic Plan)

Strategies can also be developed collaboratively in order to have greater impact by uniting behind agreed aims. The UK Vision 2020 strategy (see Box 10.8), led by RNIB, involved the engagement of a range of organizations in developing an agreed set of aims and values.

SUMMARY

This chapter has explored the classic elements of a strategic plan and their relevance for the Third Sector. In particular the need for clear statements of mission, vision and values, as well as ambitious long-term aims and priorities, have been highlighted. A pyramid model of strategic planning has been presented.

QUESTIONS

1. What different purposes do mission statements serve?
2. What criteria could you use to determine if a mission statement is a good one or not?
3. What is the difference between a mission and a vision statement?
4. Write mission and vision statements for an organization you know.
5. Write the values that you think underpin an organization you know.
6. What is organizational culture and what is the relationship between organizational values and culture?
7. Describe the culture (values-in-practice) of an organization you know.
8. What is an aim? List the aims of an organization you know.

DISCUSSION TOPIC

To what extent should organizational values remain the same or change over time?

SUGGESTED READING

Michael Allison and Jude Kaye (2005) *Strategic Planning for Nonprofit Organizations*, Wiley.
John M. Bryson (2011) *Strategic Planning for Public and Nonprofit Organizations*, Jossey-Bass.

11 STRATEGIC FORMULATION: PROCESS

OVERVIEW

In the previous four chapters various tools and models for analysing the external environment and the organization were discussed, generic strategic options were considered and the common elements of a strategic plan identified and examined. What has not yet been addressed is the process or processes an organization could or should use to do this strategic thinking and to draw up an appropriate strategic plan. This chapter will therefore explore who should be engaged in the process of strategic thinking and the formulation of a plan and the kinds of processes that might be used. The implications of different approaches will be explored.

LEARNING OBJECTIVES

After studying this chapter, you should be able to:

- identify the stakeholders of a particular Third Sector organization;
- describe a strategic planning process;
- explain the implications of different levels of participation in strategic thinking and planning processes.

STRATEGY PROCESS

Many organizations treat strategy development as a technical exercise, sometimes drawn up by just one person, to produce a written document that can be given to funders. Arguably, the process of creating and implementing an organization's strategy is as important as the content of the strategy. Figure 11.1 outlines a model of the whole strategic management process.

STAKEHOLDERS

In various sections of this book the concept of stakeholder and the value of a stakeholder approach have been discussed. These groups, who have a strong interest in the

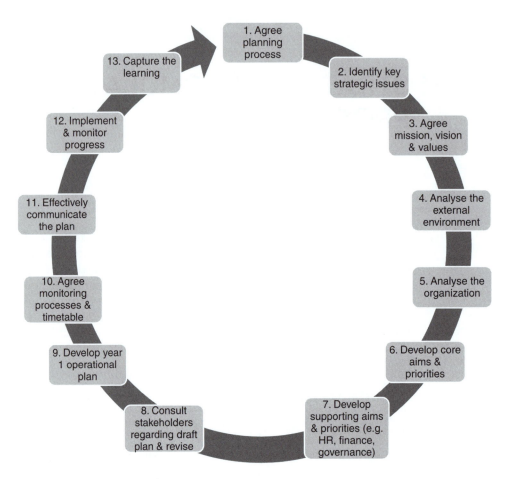

Fig 11.1   Strategic management cycle

future development of the organization, and hence in any strategy processes, might include:

■ beneficiaries (clients, customers, etc.);

■ members;

■ the board of directors/trustees;

■ the chief executive;

■ senior managers;

■ middle managers;

■ front-line staff;

■ support staff;

■ volunteers;

■ funders;

- policymakers;
- partner organizations;
- the general public.

Each of these stakeholders has a potential claim to participate in the strategic thinking and formulation processes of an organization they are involved with.

RESEARCH FINDINGS ON PARTICIPATION IN STRATEGY PROCESSES

The ACEVO Whitehill Clarke UK study (Caudrey 1995) conducted in the 1990s found that the chief executive took the lead in the preparation of the strategic plan in 89 per cent of cases, and trustees in 14 per cent. The only groups consulted during preparation and drafting stages, by the majority of organizations, were trustees, directors and senior managers. The level of consultation with 'all staff' was low (see Table 11.1), as was the consultation with funders. The extent that the strategic planning processes were very internally focused is particularly highlighted by the very low level of consultation with customers, clients, users, and supporters both during the preparation of a draft plan and in relation to the draft plan before it is finalised (see Table 11.1). These same groups were also a very low priority when it came to communicating the final agreed plan.

The lack of participation by various stakeholders in strategy process is at odds with the research literature on human motivation (see Chapter 14, pp. 262–78), which suggests that participation enhances commitment to the goals agreed and staff feelings of commitment and well-being. It also contradicts the suggestion that participation is generally considered to be a particularly strong value in the Third Sector. This may indicate that, in adopting strategic planning techniques developed in the private sector, the Third Sector has also adopted the lower emphasis on participation that has traditionally been a characteristic of the private sector. However, as noted earlier, the culture of participation may be in the process of significant change in the private sector, as reflected in many of the more recent writers on management and strategy.

Table 11.1 Participation in strategic planning

Stakeholder	Participation in preparation of a draft plan	Participation at draft plan stage
All staff	11%	6%
Funders	15%	12%
Customers	13%	5%
Clients	11%	8%
Users	19%	12%
Supporters	8%	4%

Source: Whitehill Clarke (Caudrey 1995).

The UK Performance Hub Survey (Jackson and Irwin 2007) of 248 British Third Sector organizations found that 90 per cent involved staff and the board in strategic planning; just under half (48 per cent) involved clients/beneficiaries; almost as many (46 per cent) involved volunteers; three in ten (30 per cent) involved funders; one-quarter (26 per cent) involved consultants or advisors.

In Courtney's 2005 Northern Ireland research into Third Sector strategic management, the extent to which various organizational stakeholders and any external consultant were involved in strategic management processes was also explored, distinguishing between 'involved' and 'involved in-depth'. It found that only a small number of other stakeholder groups tended to be involved in an in-depth way in strategic management processes. In the majority of the organizations, the only categories of participants who had an in-depth involvement were the chief executive and other senior staff. In almost two-thirds of the organizations, all trustees had a significant involvement, but in only 45 per cent of cases was this in-depth. In 44 per cent of the organizations there was a strategic subcommittee of trustees (in 31 per cent of the organizations this involvement was in-depth). The limited in-depth involvement of trustees in the majority of cases may have significant implications for the issue of governance. If the trustees do not feel a sense of ownership of organizational strategy, they may be unlikely to ensure appropriate mechanisms are in place to monitor it effectively and instead may want to be involved in operational aspects of the organization (Cornforth 2003). In 70 per cent of organizations the front-line staff had a significant involvement, although in only 47 per cent was this in-depth. The involvement of volunteers (other than trustees), service-users, funders or other external agencies was all very low, which is consistent with the ACENVO/Whitehill Clarke study.

ROLE OF CONSULTANTS

Each of the UK research studies on strategic management, highlighted above, shows a similar picture. In the Whitehill Clarke study, almost half of the organizations also made use of a consultant, particularly to advise on the process and as a sounding board. In one-third of cases however, the consultant actually wrote the plan. In the Courtney study, although the majority of organizations relied on their own resources to plan and manage the process, 42 per cent had used an external facilitator. More than a quarter had used the services of a consultant to write the strategic plan, which may reduce the sense of ownership of it within the organization. In the more recent UK Performance Hub Survey, 26 per cent involved consultants or advisors.

There are four main options for using consultants in strategic planning:

- commissioning a consultant to carry out an external environmental scan/audit;
- commissioning a consultant to review/evaluate the organization;
- commissioning a consultant to facilitate a strategic planning process, including facilitating focus groups and the planning group;
- commissioning a consultant to write a strategic plan for consideration by the organization (perhaps following some interviews and focus groups).

The literature would suggest that the more the consultant is involved in writing the strategic plan, the less those within the organization will feel a commitment to implementing it. The advantage of engaging a consultant to facilitate the planning process (but not to influence the content) is that key internal players are freed up to concentrate on the content, rather than having to worry about the process.

SIZE OF ORGANIZATIONS

The level and nature of engagement of different groups of stakeholders may vary according to the size of the organization. The processes in an organization where all the volunteers, staff and board members/trustees can easily meet together in one small room are likely to be very different from those of a national organization, with hundreds, even thousands, of beneficiaries, staff and volunteers, let alone the other stakeholders.

STAGES OF PARTICIPATION

The stage at which the various stakeholder groups are invited to engage in the strategic thinking and/or formulation processes can also have a significant impact. Very commonly, for example, a draft strategic plan is drawn up by a small group, even one person (e.g. the CEO or a consultant). Particular stakeholder groups are then asked to comment on the draft plan, in some form of consultation process. The results of such consultation processes are often perceived to be unsatisfactory because:

- few people respond to the consultation;
- stakeholders often believe that their views will make little difference, because the plan has already been decided and divergent views would not be welcomed;
- there is little sense of owner ship of the finally agreed strategic plan.

For these reasons, many Third Sector organizations put in place more sophisticated strategic thinking and formulation processes, before the development of any draft plan, that engage stakeholder groups from the beginning of the process, encouraging stakeholders to address the most fundamental questions (discussed in Chapters 7–10) about:

- the purpose of the organization;
- its vision of where it should be going;
- its culture and values;
- the key strategic issues that need to be addressed;
- the changing needs and expectations of the beneficiaries;
- the requirements and expectations of powerful stakeholders, such as funders;
- the implications of the changing external environment;

- the distinctive strengths of the organization and how these can be used for comparative advantage;
- the weaknesses of the organization that need to be addressed.

Some of the processes used to gain stakeholder views include:

- a needs assessment (e.g. a survey of needs as identified by members of a local community);
- a member, customer or beneficiary satisfaction survey;
- individual interviews with key stakeholders, such as funders;
- open meetings/workshops for members, beneficiaries, staff or volunteers (applying some of the tools and models discussed in Chapters 7–10).

These processes provide materials and ideas to assist the organization in its strategic thinking; however, on their own they do not enable an organization to make decisions around key strategic issues and formulate a strategic plan. It is therefore likely that a smaller planning group (perhaps 8–12 people), including ideally the chief officer, senior managers, some board members/trustees and representatives of staff and volunteers. The nature of the membership of this group is vitally important, for two key reasons:

- The individuals who are involved in this group will feel the strongest commitment to ensuring the achievement of the strategic plan that emerges from its discussions and become its champions.
- The decisions that will be made about the future of the organization, and parts of it, will be strongly affected by who is in the room in these discussions. If, for example, a key strategic issue is whether to close a particular programme or project, or outsource a particular service, the presence of a staff member or manager who might be made redundant as a result of such a decision, in the planning team which would be making such a recommendation to the board, may affect its ability to come to a rational decision.

TIMESCALE

One of the key issues concerning strategic thinking and formulation processes is the time available to engage in the processes in sufficient depth. Typically, many organizations only start such a process very close to the end of the financial year, leaving insufficient time to carry out the processes in any in-depth way or to engage effectively all the stakeholders appropriately. Some larger organizations with sophisticated strategic management processes commence the strategic planning processes 9–12 months prior to the start of the new planning cycle.

Box 11.1 outlines the strategic planning process of one medium-sized Third Sector organization during the final year of its current strategic plan.

BOX 11.1   EXAMPLE OF A STRATEGIC PLANNING TIMETABLE

Month 1 Draw up and agree a planning policy and procedure.

Month 2 Appoint a planning group.

Agree survey designs.

Month 3 Carry out and analyse member/beneficiary needs and/or satisfaction survey(s).

Month 4 Carry out and analyse staff and volunteer satisfaction surveys.

Month 5 Interview key stakeholders, e.g. funders.

Invite independent experts in your field to speak to the planning group (or wider), as a critical friend, to share their view of the organization and where it should be going.

Month 6 Organize and write up a series of workshops for beneficiaries, staff and volunteers.

Month 7 Identify the key external drivers and uncertainties that the plan needs to respond to. Identify the key strategic issues/dilemmas that the strategic plan needs to tackle.

Develop draft mission, vision and values statements.

Month 8 Draw up and agree a draft strategic plan.

Board governance review session to identify governance priorities and operational objectives.

Month 9 Consult stakeholders on the draft strategic plan.

Start work on the operational plan for year 1.

Month 10 Finalize strategic plan in light of the consultation responses.

Work on operational plan for year 1.

Consider the human resource implications of the strategic plan (e.g. staffing complement and structure, training and development).

Month 11 Agree year 1 operational plan (with SMART objectives).

Agree organizational budget for year 1.

Month 12 Agree personal objectives to contribute to achieving the strategic and operational plans (and training and development needs) with each staff member through the appraisal system.

Agree the reporting and monitoring process and timeframe.

SUMMARY

This chapter has explored the potential processes a Third Sector organization may use in order to develop a strategic plan. Some of the implications of the different levels of participation, the potential roles of a consultant, the size of the organization and the timescale required have been examined.

QUESTIONS

1. How and when should an organization's stakeholders be involved in strategic planning?
2. What time period should an organization allow for a strategic planning process?
3. How might the size of an organization effect the strategic planning process used?
4. Should consultants be brought in to help with strategic planning? If so, how?
5. What are the advantages and disadvantages of front-line staff and/or volunteers participating in the planning group?
6. Write out a strategic planning process and timetable for a Third Sector organization you know.

DISCUSSION TOPIC

Who are the most important stakeholders for a Third Sector organization? What is it they expect from Third Sector organizations?

SUGGESTED READING

M. Allison and J. Kaye (2005) *Strategic Planning for Nonprofit Organizations*, 2nd edn, Wiley.

J. M. Bryson and F. K. Alston (2011) *Create your Strategic Plan: A Workbook for Public and Nonprofit Organizations*, 3rd edn, Wiley Jossey-Bass.

A. Lawrie (2007) *The Complete Guide to Business and Strategic Planning for Voluntary Organizations*, 3rd edn, Directory of Social Change.

12 MEASURING PROGRESS

OVERVIEW

In Chapter 8, some of the different methods of evaluating a Third Sector organization were explored. This included an examination of some organizational assessment models which are used to measure how a Third Sector organization is getting on, i.e. whether it is being effective. In this chapter we return to this theme and how a Third Sector organization can measure its performance and the impact of its agreed strategy. We will explore the concepts of measuring organizational effectiveness and the various models that have been put forward, under three main headings: the rational-structural frame; the human resources frame; and emergent approaches. In relation to each model the discussion will try to clarify the concept, the conceptual and operational difficulties presented by these models, and examine whether there is a way forward in considering the concept of organizational effectiveness that is both academically sound (as far as any model or theory can be) and pragmatically useful in the Third Sector.

LEARNING OBJECTIVES

After studying this chapter, you should be able to:

- explain the factors increasing the demand for measurement of performance;
- identify the difficulty in measuring effectiveness in Third Sector organizations;
- outline the rational goal approach to measuring effectiveness and its limitations;
- explain the stakeholder approach;
- describe the Balanced Scorecard, its strengths and limitations;
- outline the various other over arching models that are available.

DEMANDS TO DEMONSTRATE EFFECTIVENESS

Every day we make judgements about the performance of organizations. We usually have no difficulty in coming to a view as to whether organizations we know well, e.g. the provider of the local train service, are effective or not. It is important, too, for organizations themselves, not to mention their funders and users, to get a clear idea about the effectiveness of the organizations with which they are involved, or fund, in order to identify what needs to be improved.

The pressure on Third Sector organizations to account for their effectiveness has been increasing. Public bodies themselves are subject to increasing pressures to demonstrate 'value for money' or 'best value' and are in turn requiring substantial accountability for funding given, often under a detailed written contract or service agreement detailing expected outputs and outcomes.

In the USA, this demand for increased accountability culminated in legislation (the Federal Government Performance and Results Act of 1993) requiring a significant level of performance measurement. This increased with the passing of the Sarbane-Oxley Act in 2002, in the wake of the Enron and Tyco private sector scandals, which states are increasingly using as a template for financial accountability in non-profit organizations. In Britain, the Government's 'Scrutiny' report (Home Office 1990), a series of Charities Acts, and changes in the charity accounting regulations (SORP) have heralded a new level of accountability to be applied in the funding and regulation of Third Sector organizations. Hudson (2005) argues that the trend towards greater accountability will further increase and that leading edge organizations 'expect more demanding funders' and act accordingly.

Third Sector organizations, themselves, conscious of an increased demand for services and often fierce competition for contracts and funding, realize they need to be able to demonstrate to funders and potential funders the particular effectiveness of the organization (Lubelska 1996; Lyon and Arvidson 2011). Their concern is that unless they take measuring organizational effectiveness seriously Third Sector organizations will tend to be perceived as a 'kind of therapy: warm but illusory feelings of momentary comfort' (Matthews 1996: 18).

The general public, too, has become more sceptical about Third Sector organizations generally, in the wake of particularly well publicized scandals and accusations of unreasonably high administrative costs. These are leading to an increasing demand for greater transparency, accountability and administrative efficiency and effectiveness.

Lyon and Arvidson (2011) found the main motivations to measure impact came from: grant-making agencies; commissioning agencies; from within the organization for learning and marketing purposes. They also found that external drivers to measure impact often created resistance based on the feeling that it was being imposed. Even attempts to measure impact driven internally can create resistance in staff within the organization.

It has been argued that the concept of effectiveness is at the heart of organizational analysis and is the ultimate dependent variable in organizational research (Au 1996). As a result, for over 50 years, the academic community has been investigating the concepts of organizational effectiveness and performance to try to clarify what it means and how they might be operationalized.

In the private sector the concepts of profit, return on investment and share value have provided widely used measures of organizational success, which can be used to assess the effectiveness and efficiency of an individual firm. A single measure of profitability can evaluate how well it is satisfying customer needs, as well as enabling firms from very different sectors to be compared. While the profit concept is far from free of controversy, and wider measures are increasingly being introduced (Kaplan and Norton

1992; Eccles and Nohria 1992; Meyer and Gupta 1994), at least these measures provide the private sector with commonly used indicators of effectiveness with which to assess their own organizations and compare with others in the same or different industries.

Because of the quasi-public nature of the services provided by Third Sector organizations, frequently at no cost to the consumers, the Third Sector, generally, has no such agreed measures, although profitability can be very important for social enterprises. Herman and Renz (1999) argue that the fundamental reason that developing a single measure of Third Sector organizational effectiveness is an impossibility is that the crucial exchange that such organizations help to enact is not measured in monetary terms but in moral or value terms. The key question for the Third Sector is, therefore, succinctly put by Drucker (1990): 'what is the bottom line when there is no bottom line?'. Or put another way: is it even possible to develop indicators of effectiveness for the Third Sector at the organizational or sectoral level?

There is, of course, the crucial question of why Third Sector organizations might want to measure performance. There are possibly at least 11 different reasons for Third Sector organizations to use performance measurement systems and processes (adapted from Hailey and Sorgenfrei 2003; Moxham 2009):

- *The legacy role*: measuring and documenting changes that have taken place in order to demonstrate impact.
- *The internal communication role*: communicating achievements internally to motivate staff, volunteers and board members.
- *The beneficiary communication role*: motivating beneficiaries by helping them to recognize the progress they are making.
- *The external communications role*: communicating achievements to external stakeholders to encourage them to further invest in the programme/organization.
- *The governance role*: ensuring internal accountability to the board and senior management by monitoring the achievement of agreed goals and objectives.
- *The learning role*: gathering and analysing information and data on changes that have taken place, in order to learn for the future and improve services.
- *The public accountability role*: ensuring accountability to external stakeholders by recording the achievement of agreed aims and objectives.
- *The public policy role*: gathering and analysing information and data on changes that have taken place, in order to demonstrate how the programme/organization is furthering government aims and priorities.
- *The public policy advocacy role*: gathering and analysing information and data on changes that have taken place, in order to inform and bring about changes in public policy and practice.
- *The financial reporting role*: which is increasingly required to include non-financial aspects.
- *The operational control*: helping the CEO and senior managers control what is happening at the grass-roots level.

It is useful to recognize the motivation behind choosing to introduce a performance measurement system. Who is it being introduced for and why? The answer to that question might have important implications for both the measures chosen and the mechanisms for measuring the processes. In the current context, we are particularly interested in ways of measuring progress that has been highlighted in a strategic plan.

ACHIEVING MISSION/GOALS

The early explorations of the concept of organizational effectiveness tended to revolve around a rational, structural, closed-system paradigm that postulates that organizations are rational goal-seeking entities that process inputs to create outputs to achieve these goals (Georgopoulos and Tannenbaum 1971; Gouldner 1971; Scott 1992). This model has been described as 'purposive-rational' (Pfeffer 1982) and as the 'managed systems' model (Elmore 1978). The origins of this approach can be traced back to the earlier proponents of scientific management, such as Taylor and Fayol, discussed earlier.

March and Simon (1959) suggest that the following principles underlie the rational model:

- organizations have one or more formal goals;
- those who decide what the organization will do choose activities aimed at achieving these goals, and they take steps to measure the effectiveness of these activities;
- when these measures indicate that progress towards goal achievement is unsatisfactory, 'problems' are defined for decision-makers;
- decision-makers can follow rational procedures to solve these problems: gather information on causes, identify alternative solutions, estimate the relative costs and benefits of the alternatives, choose the optimum alternative, and evaluate the impact of its implementation.

The particular effectiveness models suggested within this paradigm have included 'mission accomplishment' (Ford and Ford 1990; Sheehan 1996; Brudney and Golec 1997), 'objective fulfilment' (Zuluaga and Schneider 2006) and 'goal attainment' (Lillis and Shaffer 1977; Glisson and Martin 1980; Schumaker 1980; Byington *et al.* 1991; Green and Griesinger 1996). From this perspective, the more that an organization achieves its mission or the goals and objectives that it has set itself, the more effective it is. How their achievement is assessed can be either qualitative – e.g. a zebra crossing is built on a busy road near a school; a cure is discovered for a particular disease; a particular piece of legislation is passed (setting SMART objectives is discussed on p. 255) – or quantitative – e.g. child literacy in a school improves to the national average; the number of young people in an area not in employment, education or training has reduced to less than 10 per cent (methods of measuring an organization's performance in relation to its mission and goals are discussed below).

PRODUCTION OF WELFARE MODEL

Kendall and Knapp (1998) also favour a rational-structural model. They base their approach on addressing organizational effectiveness on the economist's 'production of welfare' model (Knapp 1984). This model was described by Osborne and Tricker

(1995) as an excellent framework to use in considering service delivery in human services. It clearly distinguishes amongst inputs, process, outputs, outcomes and impacts on the external environment, thereby creating a 'theory of change' as to how each of these components relate to one another, e.g. what inputs are required to carry out the agreed activities? What activities will lead to the desired outcomes? Brown (1996) developed a similar 'input-process-output-outcome framework'.

Some of the detailed models based on this approach include additional levels of outcomes, e.g. immediate outcomes, intermediate outcomes, final outcomes, long-term (including unanticipated) impacts. In the Theory of Change of approach, there is a clear unambiguous 'so that' link between each of the stages in the model, starting with a long-term goal to be achieved, then a backwards mapping exercise which identifies the preconditions necessary to achieve that goal, followed by the interventions the organization will perform to create these preconditions, and then an addressing of what indicators will be required to measure the performance of these interventions.

This kind of approach is used extensively with NGOs in the world development sector under the title of Logical Framework Analysis, or Log Model for short (see Figure 12.1), and also by some foundations (see Box 12.1). An example of a Logic Model is highlighted in Table 12.1.

A similar approach – ZOPP (Zielorientierte Projektplanung) or GOPP (Goal Oriented Project Planning as it is sometimes translated in English) – is used and promoted by the Deutsche Gesellschaft für Technische Zusammenarbeit (German Technical Cooperation) for overseas development projects. The ZOPP approach provides a systematic structure for identification, planning and management of projects, developed again in a workshop setting, with principal interest groups. The ZOPP's output is a planning matrix – the logical project framework – which summarizes and structures the main elements of a project and highlights logical linkages between intended inputs, planned activities and expected results. The ZOPP approach is used for essentially all German funded projects and is a prerequisite for funding approval.

The logic model, similar to the concept of the value chain which includes external organizations, particularly suppliers, has been adapted to create various rigorous processes for tackling social issues. The Logic Model is often a core element of results-based management adopted by NGOs working in developing countries, which also includes:

- the identification of objectives;
- the identification of performance indicators or measures for the objectives;
- setting targets for each of the indicators;
- monitoring systems to collect regularly the information;
- the comparison of results with the targets set;
- the integration of evaluations to provide complementary performance information;

| Inputs → | Activities → | Outputs → | Intermediate outcomes → | Final outcomes |

Fig 12.1   Logical framework

BOX 12.1   ATLANTIC PHILANTHROPIES

Atlantic Philanthropies was established by American billionaire Chuck Feeney, who made his money from duty-free shops. He decided that he was going to give away all his money before he died and founded the Atlantic Philanthropies in 1982. For most of its history, the foundation operated deliberately incognito. Organizations could not apply for funding and beneficiaries, few of whose staff would know the origin of their gifts, were required to sign agreements acknowledging that funding would be stopped if its source were revealed. Feeney has said that aside from his own wish for anonymity, this was in part to leave 'space' for other philanthropists who would want naming rights in return for their gifts, something which notably arose with both USA and Irish universities.

In 2002 Atlantic Philanthropies made a series of crucial strategic decisions:

- to spend down its entire endowment over the following ten to fifteen years;
- to allow recipients of grants to acknowledge the source of the grants;
- to stop funding higher education and to focus grant-giving on four programme areas: ageing (Bermuda, USA and Ireland), disadvantaged children and young people (Bermuda, USA and Ireland), human rights and reconciliation (USA, South Africa and Ireland) and public health (Vietnam and South Africa);
- to adopt a Logical Model (inputs, activities, outputs and outcomes) approach to its grant giving particularly in its children and youth programme.

The use of the Logical Model approach created the potential for a more rigorous approach to service design, drawing on the best international evidence of what works, and to evaluation, as outcomes could be much more clearly defined. As a result of this change, for example in Ireland, where there had only ever been one random control trial evaluation (the gold standard of quantitative evaluation approaches) in the social policy area (as opposed to medical trials), the foundation's Disadvantaged Children and Youth Programme provided funding for the development, implementation and evaluation of over 20 programmes to create a better understanding in Ireland and beyond of the effectiveness of a range of promising programmes for disadvantaged children and young people. This potentially provides, for the first time, a robust knowledge-base for decision-makers to be able to make policy choices on the basis of real evidence of what has been shown to work.

In its 2008/09 review of its programme strategies, the foundation agreed social justice as an overarching principle for all of its work. Conscious that public policy decision-making does not only operate on a rational basis, but is deeply influenced by the pressure that is exerted by the various pressure groups and the media, it was decided that much of the future work of the foundation would focus on improving the advocacy capacity of progressive aspects of civil society in each of the agreed programme areas. The Children and Youth Programme in Ireland continued to make use of the Logic Modelling approach. In 2012, with the departure of its chief executive, the foundation revisited its strategy and how it might best optimize and demonstrate its impact before it closes its doors several years after giving its last grants in 2014.

(Conor O'Clery (2007); Atlantic Philanthropies website: www.atlanticphilanthropies.org)

Table 12.1 Aspire Programme Logic Model

Inputs	Activities	Outputs	Intermediate outcomes	Final outcomes
Grant support to fund: ■ coordinator and programme staff; ■ programme costs; ■ governance and management costs; ■ evaluation. Contribution from the two primary school principals to chair the steering group and ensure partners liaise effectively with the schools. Contribution from each of the partners to participate in the steering group and deliver the agreed programmes. Contribution from parents and children to participate in the various elements of the Aspire programme.	The Aspire programme will have the following elements: ■ early intervention support services for both children and parents to deal with crises that may limit their ability to achieve their potential; ■ incredible years; ■ Pyramid Plus; ■ parent and infant programme; ■ Parenting programmes (Sink or Swim; PAMP; What if; Parenting Apart); ■ 1:1 parents advice outreach service for parents.	Incredible Years parent programme (10–12 parents for 12 weeks x 2.5 hours per week, two terms yearly). Incredible Years Readiness Programme (10–12 x 2 parents for four weeks each term). Pyramid Plus (10–12 children, two 10-week clubs each year). Parent and infant programme (one 1-term programme each year). Hero Books (8 parents/children, 6–8 sessions x 1–2 hours each term). Parent support outreach service (four appointments each week). Parenting programmes (one programme of eight parents for eight weeks each year).	■ Increased parental involvement in the schools and their children's learning. ■ Increased parental confidence in dealing with child's behaviour. ■ Improved children's behaviour. ■ Raised aspirations of parents and children within the target area. ■ Improved educational outcomes for children within the target area. ■ Reduced anxiety of engaging with the other community. ■ Increased willingness of parents to make links with parents from other communities.	■ Improved educational outcomes for children. ■ Improved life outcomes for children. ■ Increased social cohesioAn and sharing.
⇑	⇑	⇑	⇑	

- the use of performance information for both external reporting and accountability and internal accountability, learning and performance improvement.

The Logic Model has been criticized for being too rigid, mechanistic and top-down to reflect the complex cultural realities of rapidly changing development projects (Gasper 1999).

Using a more detailed version of a logic model, Mark Friedman (2002) developed what he called 'results-based accountability' to help improve the well-being of children and families in the US, and it is now used, in whole or in part, in 40 states and in six other countries. It is a methodology or approach which is equally applicable to other social problems. Friedman has tried to create a common language of ideas that can be applied to a social problem. The heart of his approach is to apply a series of plain English questions to an issue, such as the following:

- *Population*: What is the population that you are concerned with? (e.g. all children aged 0–5 in Scotland.)
- *Results*: What are the results in terms of well-being we would like to see exist for this population? (e.g. healthy, ready and able to learn, emotionally well developed.)
- *Experience*: How would we recognize these results in our day-to-day lives in the community? (e.g. children communicating effectively, children playing with other children.)
- *Indicators*: How could we recognize these results in a measurable way? (e.g. number of visits to the doctor, weight, reading grades, school tests.)
- *Baselines*: How can we measure where the target population are now in terms of these issues? (e.g. carry out a baseline survey with parents in a SureStart scheme, use existing data.)
- *The story behind the headlines* (epidemiology): What are the causes and forces at work behind the results of the baseline findings? (e.g. poverty, lack of high quality childcare, literacy problems amongst parents.)
- *Partners*: Who are the players that have a role in the results for the target population? (e.g. parents, relatives, nurseries, childcare centres, SureStart schemes, childminders, funders.) Who has most impact?
- *What works*: What do we know from the evidence about what actually works in improving the results we want to see? (e.g. what programmes have been subject to rigorous random control trial evaluations and shown to make a significant difference to the results for our target population?)
- *Criteria*: Agree a set of criteria to apply to a long list of programmes to help choose which to choose (e.g. the amount of improvement the evidence suggests will result from using the programme; the cost; the extent it fits with our values) and make a decision.
- *Performance accountability*: Be clear about what is to be measured in terms of the programme to be introduced and how.
- *Action planning*: Develop an action plan and budget, negotiate resources and implement.

Using the Logic Model framework, Poole *et al.* (2000) developed and tested a Program Accountability Quality Scale, a theory-driven model to assess the quality of proposed measuring systems in order to determine the need for expert support in this area. The framework contains 21 items:

- Resources: identification of resources; comprehensiveness; match the type of programme.

- Activities: logical link to outputs; sufficient activities to achieve outcomes.

- Outputs: number of participants; number of events or processes; time frame.

- Outcomes: logical link to goals; change statements; outcomes rather than activities or outputs.

- Goals: intended effect on need and population; description of broad community impact.

- Indicators: specific and measurable terms; valid measures of outcomes; efficient measures; important to changes in need of measurement.

- Evaluation plan: data collection method; resources for implementation; efficient measurement of progress towards outcomes; realistic plan.

MEASURING OUTCOMES

In the Logic Model, measuring inputs (staff costs, premises, running costs, administration, etc.) and outputs (the number of people served, the number of training sessions organized, etc.) is a relatively easy exercise and can be important information for funders. A critical question, however, is how to measure the outcomes and impact (including unintended and/or negative consequences). Campbell (2003) identified the difficulty in linking organizational or programme outcomes with community impact indicators, which may be influenced by a wider range of factors and organizations. One approach to linking the two is to develop a collaborative consensus between organizations, including the relevant government agencies to agreed indicators that link organizational measures with community impact ones.

United Way of America, a leading funder of Third Sector organizations in the USA, has developed a sophisticated outcome-focused approach to funding. In *Measuring Program Outcomes: A Practical Approach* (United Way of America 1996), a Logic Model is presented, which is consistent with the approaches of Kushner and Poole, and Kendal and Knapp, discussed above, with six key elements:

- inputs;
- activities;
- outputs;
- initial outcomes;
- intermediate outcomes;
- longer-term outcomes.

3. Personal Growth								
20.	I am patient							
21.	I am unable to talk about my feelings							
22.	I find it hard to relax							
23.	I worry about what people think of me							
24.	I know how to keep healthy							
25.	I live a healthy lifestyle							
26.	I am aware of how I appear to others							
27.	I am willing to learn new things							
28.	I can face problems in my life							
29.	I want to succeed							

Source: Purvis *et al.* (2009) for the Department for Work and Pensions.

Rapp and Poertner (1992) suggest that performance indicators should ideally be final outcomes, e.g. how people's lives have changed as a result of the activities of the organization. However, these can often be difficult to measure, or it can be difficult to determine the extent that it was the organization itself that brought about the change (attribution). Often, therefore, organizations adopt intermediate outcomes, which may include more immediate outcomes for service-users, e.g. changes in skills, knowledge or attitudes, or the satisfaction level with the services provided. Performance indicators also often include outputs, i.e. ways of counting the extent of the service provided, such as the number of sessions run or the number of people who attended.

One of the methods that can be used to measure changes in an individual over time is the distance travelled methodology. An individual would complete a questionnaire before he or she commences a programme and then at certain points during and at the end of the programme (and potentially some time afterwards to see how long the effects last) to see in what ways he or she has changed (see Table 12.2).

Criteria for good performance indicators

Andrews *et al.* (1994) suggests that performance indicators (outcome measures) should comply with six factors:

- *Applicability*: addresses dimensions that are important for the service users and the staff/volunteers working in the organization, but also enable the collation of data.
- *Acceptability*: they are brief and user-friendly in terms of format and language.
- *Practicality*: simple to score and interpret, minimal cost to collect and analyse and require little training to collect.

Table 12.2 Example of a distance travelled questionnaire

Factor		5 Always	4 Often	3 Sometimes	2 Rarely	1 Never	Not applicable
1. Achievements							
1.	I am aware of my strengths & weaknesses						
2.	I can control my finances						
3.	I don't give up easily on things						
4.	I am able to work on my own						
5.	I can concentrate for 30 minutes						
6.	I can complete tasks on time						
7.	I find it hard to ask for help						
8.	I can keep appointments						
9.	I can complete complicated forms						
10.	I usually come over well at interview						
11.	I am confident about writing letters for different situations						
2. Social							
12.	I find conflict hard to handle						
13.	I take chances with my health						
14.	I can plan ahead						
15.	I am able to be assertive						
16.	I am tolerant of other people						
17.	I can take responsibility when things go wrong						
18.	I am good at listening						
19.	I am a confident person						

Please tick (✓)

3. Personal Growth								
20.	I am patient							
21.	I am unable to talk about my feelings							
22.	I find it hard to relax							
23.	I worry about what people think of me							
24.	I know how to keep healthy							
25.	I live a healthy lifestyle							
26.	I am aware of how I appear to others							
27.	I am willing to learn new things							
28.	I can face problems in my life							
29.	I want to succeed							

Source: Purvis *et al.* (2009) for the Department for Work and Pensions.

Rapp and Poertner (1992) suggest that performance indicators should ideally be final outcomes, e.g. how people's lives have changed as a result of the activities of the organization. However, these can often be difficult to measure, or it can be difficult to determine the extent that it was the organization itself that brought about the change (attribution). Often, therefore, organizations adopt intermediate outcomes, which may include more immediate outcomes for service-users, e.g. changes in skills, knowledge or attitudes, or the satisfaction level with the services provided. Performance indicators also often include outputs, i.e. ways of counting the extent of the service provided, such as the number of sessions run or the number of people who attended.

One of the methods that can be used to measure changes in an individual over time is the distance travelled methodology. An individual would complete a questionnaire before he or she commences a programme and then at certain points during and at the end of the programme (and potentially some time afterwards to see how long the effects last) to see in what ways he or she has changed (see Table 12.2).

Criteria for good performance indicators

Andrews *et al.* (1994) suggests that performance indicators (outcome measures) should comply with six factors:

- *Applicability*: addresses dimensions that are important for the service users and the staff/volunteers working in the organization, but also enable the collation of data.
- *Acceptability*: they are brief and user-friendly in terms of format and language.
- *Practicality*: simple to score and interpret, minimal cost to collect and analyse and require little training to collect.

Using the Logic Model framework, Poole *et al.* (2000) developed and tested a Program Accountability Quality Scale, a theory-driven model to assess the quality of proposed measuring systems in order to determine the need for expert support in this area. The framework contains 21 items:

- Resources: identification of resources; comprehensiveness; match the type of programme.
- Activities: logical link to outputs; sufficient activities to achieve outcomes.
- Outputs: number of participants; number of events or processes; time frame.
- Outcomes: logical link to goals; change statements; outcomes rather than activities or outputs.
- Goals: intended effect on need and population; description of broad community impact.
- Indicators: specific and measurable terms; valid measures of outcomes; efficient measures; important to changes in need of measurement.
- Evaluation plan: data collection method; resources for implementation; efficient measurement of progress towards outcomes; realistic plan.

MEASURING OUTCOMES

In the Logic Model, measuring inputs (staff costs, premises, running costs, administration, etc.) and outputs (the number of people served, the number of training sessions organized, etc.) is a relatively easy exercise and can be important information for funders. A critical question, however, is how to measure the outcomes and impact (including unintended and/or negative consequences). Campbell (2003) identified the difficulty in linking organizational or programme outcomes with community impact indicators, which may be influenced by a wider range of factors and organizations. One approach to linking the two is to develop a collaborative consensus between organizations, including the relevant government agencies to agreed indicators that link organizational measures with community impact ones.

United Way of America, a leading funder of Third Sector organizations in the USA, has developed a sophisticated outcome-focused approach to funding. In *Measuring Program Outcomes: A Practical Approach* (United Way of America 1996), a Logic Model is presented, which is consistent with the approaches of Kushner and Poole, and Kendal and Knapp, discussed above, with six key elements:

- inputs;
- activities;
- outputs;
- initial outcomes;
- intermediate outcomes;
- longer-term outcomes.

In an example of an education programme for expectant teenage mothers, each of the following possible outputs and outcomes could be distinguished and measured:

- outputs: the number of pregnant teenagers attending the programme and their attendance levels;
- initial outcomes: the teenagers' level of knowledge of prenatal nutrition and health, and proper care, feeding of and social interaction with, infants;
- intermediate outcomes: teenagers follow proper nutrition and health guidelines during pregnancy, deliver healthy babies and provide proper care, feeding and social interaction to their babies;
- longer-term outcomes: babies achieve appropriate 12-month milestones for physical, motor, verbal and social development.

In building on the production of welfare model, Kendall and Knapp (1998) suggest that the distinctive features of the Third Sector should be built into all indicators of effectiveness. In particular they suggest using the additional performance domains of choice/pluralism, social capital/participation, advocacy and innovation, all of which may be neglected by most traditional models. They recognize, however, the difficulty that can exist in trying to operationalize concepts like advocacy, choice and innovation.

Outcomes can be measured at four different levels:

- the individual;
- a particular programme;
- the organization;
- public policy impact (usually drawing on the performance of a range of organizations).

Changes in individuals

Rapp and Poertner (1992) suggest six outcome types related to what they call 'client status':

- the service-user's attitude towards themselves, e.g. level of self-esteem;
- the service user's level of knowledge about a particular issue;
- the service user's use of a particular skill, e.g. cooking, debt management, social interaction;
- changes in the service user's behaviour, e.g. reduction in substance use/abuse; talking to parents;
- changes in the service user's status, e.g. from unemployed to employed, homeless to housed, or ill to healthy;
- changes in the service user's environment, e.g. play facilities provided for children.

Patton (2008) also includes 'prevention', e.g. prevention of unplanned pregnancies, eviction, as an additional relevant outcome status.

- *Reliability*: the method of collecting the information should produce the same result regardless of who is collecting it.

- *Validity*: the indicator should measure what it is designed to measure and not something else.

- *Sensitivity to change*: the indicator must be sensitive enough to detect the relevant changes that have taken place.

The Urban Institute (2006) suggests six criteria:

- Specific: unique, unambiguous.

- Observable: practical, cost-effective to collect, measurable.

- Understandable: comprehensible.

- Relevant: measured important dimensions, appropriate, related to programme, of significance, predictive, timely.

- Time-bound: covered a specific period of time.

- Valid: provided reliable, accurate, unbiased, consistent and verifiable data.

Using the above criteria, the Urban Institute (2006) researched a range of Third Sector organizations from different subsectors in the USA to build a common framework of outcomes to measure non-profit performance. They suggested the following framework for participant-centred outcomes:

- Knowledge/learning/attitude:

  - skills (knowledge, learning): percentage increase in scores after attending; percentage that believe skills were increased after attending; percentage increase in knowledge (before/after programme);

  - attitude: percentage improvement as reported by parent, teacher, co-worker or other; percentage improvement as reported by participant;

  - readiness (qualification): percentage feeling well-prepared for a particular task/undertaking; percentage meeting minimum qualifications for next level/undertaking.

- Behaviour:

  - incidence of bad behaviour: incident rate; relapse/recidivism rate; percentage reduction in reported behaviour frequency;

  - incidence of desirable activity: success rate; percentage that achieve goal; rate of improvement;

  - maintenance of new behaviour: number of weeks/months/years continued; percentage change over time; percentage moving to next level/condition/status; percentage that do not re-enter the programme/system.

- Condition/status:

  - participant social status: percentage with improved relationships; percentage who graduate; percentage who move to next level/condition/status; percentage who maintain current level/condition/status; percentage who avoid undesirable course of action/behaviour;

- participant economic condition: percentage who establish career/employment; percentage who move to long-term house; percentage who move to safe and permanent house; percentage enrolled in education programmes; percentage who retain employment; percentage with increased earnings;

- participant health condition: percentage with reduced incidence of health problem; percentage with immediate positive response; percentage that report positive response post-90 days.

BOX 12.2   ACEVO MEASUREMENT PLAN

ACEVO is the Association of Chief Officers of Voluntary Organisations in England and Wales. There are equivalent bodies in Scotland and Northern Ireland. It provides various forms of support to Third Sector chief officers, including support work, peer support, information and training, press and policy work. In 2010, ACEVO commissioned New Philanthropy Capital (NPC) to examine its Logic Model and current ways of measuring how it is getting on. The review examined the strategic outcomes (e.g. members run their organizations better), intermediate outcomes (e.g. members feel part of a peer group) and enabling factors (ACEVO's support must be good) in relation to each of the four key areas of ACEVO's work and created a Logic Model. The review recognized that the nature of ACEVO's work makes it difficult to set quantitative measures, and so recommended a number of more qualitative indicators, which would be regularly measured, using the following:

- an annual survey of members;
- an annual survey of former members;
- survey of non-members;
- website and helpline analysis;
- press analysis;
- course and conference evaluations;
- case studies of ACEVO members;
- independent interviews with journalists and policymakers;
- impact anecdotes.

(ACEVO Measurement Plan, NPC February 2011)

The performance indicators chosen should be linked to the long-term aims (and ultimately to the mission) the organization has agreed. An organization running a youth centre might, for example, have a long-term aim that 'all the staff and volunteers have received the training and accreditation they need in youth and community work to provide a professional youth work service'. The performance indicators might be:

- the percentage of staff and trainees who achieve a recognized youth work qualification at a particular level;

- the level of satisfaction of staff and volunteers with the training received;

- the level of satisfaction of the young people using the centre with the skills and professionalism of the youth work service provided;

- positive changes in the young people attending the youth centre in terms of knowledge, skills, behaviour, relationships, accreditation/qualifications;
- the number of young people who set and achieve personal goals.

It is important not to create too long a list of performance indicators, as it can become unmanageable to actually try and regularly track and report on all the indicators. Each of the indicators do not have to be perfect indicators of success, but together they should provide at least a good indication as to whether the organization is making progress in the right direction. The important point is that at least each year there should be a review against each indicator. With experience, annual targets for these indicators can be set which can then be integrated into the annual operational plan (see pp. 254–5). The Balanced Scorecard and other Dashboard frameworks involve the creation of a small number of critical indicators of success that should be regularly monitored to assess how much progress the organization is making in achieving its mission and aims. Examples of the performance indicators for services provided by a medical charity are given in Box 12.3.

BOX 12.3 EXAMPLES OF PERFORMANCE INDICATORS FOR SERVICES PROVIDED BY A MEDICAL CHARITY

OUTPUTS

- the number of people using the early detection service;
- the number of men using the early detection service;
- the number of people from areas of high deprivation using the service;
- the extent that early detection clients are from all parts of the country;
- the number of people using the genetics counselling service;
- the waiting time to get an appointment for early detection screening;
- the time clients are kept waiting after their agreed appointment time;
- the waiting time from screening to receiving the results.

INTERMEDIATE OUTCOMES

- the satisfaction level of early detection clients with the service;
- the number of cancers detected;
- the number of other medical conditions detected that are referred on for treatment or further assessment.

FINAL OUTCOMES

- changes in death rates.

Visual presentation

For many client groups, a simple visual method of presenting information on the progress they are making can be helpful. For example, Kevin Callaghan developed an Evaluation Ladder (Callaghan 2009) for West Lothian Cyrenians' work with people who are homeless with drug-use problems. Each rung on the ladder represents progress (in relation to housing on one side and drugs on the other). Evaluation Support Scotland identified the Evaluation Wheel, amongst a number of visual tools, as being a particularly effective way of measuring and seeing change (see Figure 12.2).

The wheel can relate to an overall outcome, with each spoke relating to a particular indicator. Alternatively each spoke can relate to a particular outcome (the names of each of the spokes in Figure 12.2 are an example of potential outcomes for a particular client group). Persons in the target group mark where they think they are on each spoke. The exercise is most useful when it is repeated over time to check progress, with dots joined up to visually represent change. The wheel can be the same for all clients of a particular programme or it can be different for different clients.

A similar approach is the licensed Outcomes Measurement Star developed for St Mungo's in London, initially in relation to people who are homeless, which has now been adapted for use with various different client groups.

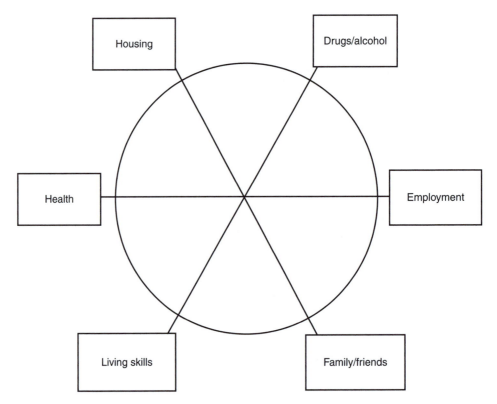

Figure 12.2   Evaluation Wheel

Objections to a goal approach to measuring progress

Unfortunately, despite the seeming logic of the goal approach, a range of conceptual and practical objections have been raised against it (Reimann 1975; Hannan and Freeman 1977; Jenkins 1977; D'Aunno *et al.* 1991; Scott 1977):

- How does an organization know whether the goals were the right ones in the first place? Surely, the argument goes, to be effective the organization must be effective in tackling the need (in the case of Third Sector organizations) and not just in meeting the goals set. These goals may have been set to be very easy to meet, or to address the least important, or least difficult to meet, need, or may not benefit the intended beneficiaries at all.

- The organization's activities may also have a range of other effects, positive and negative, which may be ignored by only focusing on the goals which were set.

- The question also arises as to who sets the mission or goals: the founder, the board, the chief executive, the staff, funders? And in practice are they all pursuing the same goals for the organization? If not, then for the purposes of organizational effectiveness which, or rather whose, goals are the relevant ones? Are the official goals the same as the actual goals being pursued by all parts of the organization?

- From a practical perspective, too, most mission statements and organizational goals are couched in very general terms, making it very difficult to provide any clear measure of success in achieving either.

- Are performance measurement systems, which are often imposed by funders/ donors or senior management, simply about power relationships and managerial control? Is what gets measured what is important to funders/donors and management rather than what is important to the beneficiaries?

- There is also an issue of timescale, and this is equally true regardless of sector. In making the judgements about effectiveness in achieving the mission or goals, what length of time should be considered? Britain has often been accused of taking too short a view, compared with, say, the Japanese. It is suggested that in the UK short-term results are given most prominence to the detriment of the long-term ones. In the private sector, those firms that forgo profits in the short term may be much more profitable in the long term. For the non-profit sector, too, there is a similar issue of what length of time should be considered reasonable to assess the effectiveness of an organization. Is it a year, three years, five years or longer?

- How does an organization know that it was its activities, or which of those activities, that produced the change the measurement system evidenced? This is called the attribution problem.

- Because measurement systems are used for accountability purposes, they can be threatening to staff and service-users who may feel under pressure to ensure the results are what the organization expects.

- Does choosing some measures which are easier to measure over others which are harder to measure mean that important, perhaps the most important, changes become less important to those delivering the service and to the service-users themselves? Does more effort therefore go into influencing the measurable outcomes, rather than influencing other outcomes which are less measurable?

- How much is what gets measured and how it gets measured determined by cultural factors? How much, for example, should what is measured in, say, a north African Muslim country, be determined by Western or Muslim culture and values?

- Is the cost of sophisticated measurement systems, in terms of money and staff time, required to capture complex changes, justified, when the resource could be focused on the provision of services?

Kanter and Summers (1987: 155) summarize concisely the weaknesses in the goal-attainment perspective. Third Sector organizations are:

> complex entities, the specification of whose goals is problematic. Organizations may have many goals, and they can be inconsistent, contradictory or incoherent; it is often unclear at what level or with respect to what units the goal should be measured...goals may even be a mystification.

THE 4ES

The kind of logical model highlighted above (inputs-activities-outputs-outcomes) can also be used to show how the 4Es (economy, efficiency, effectiveness and equity) relate to the relationship between each part of the service production process (inputs, activities and outputs):

- economy is related to the cost of inputs;
- efficiency is concerned with the relationship of the cost of inputs with the achievement of outputs;
- effectiveness is concerned with the achievement of outcomes;
- equity is normally concerned with the distribution of outcomes amongst the total population of concern, although there can be concerns of issue in each part of the framework.

Table 12.3   4Es and the Logic Model

Inputs	Economy	Activities	Efficiency	Outputs	Effectiveness	Outcomes	Equity	Impact
	The relationship between inputs and activities.		The relationship between inputs and outputs.		The relationship between activities/ outputs and outcomes.		The relationship between outcomes and impact.	
	Were the inputs acquired as cheaply as possible?		Were the resources used in the best way possible to achieve the outputs?		Do the activities result in the best possible results?		Were the benefits distributed as fairly as possible?	
⇨	⇔	⇨	⇔	⇨	⇔	⇨	⇔	

Efficiency/value for money

Within the structural-rational paradigm, an alternative measure of effectiveness gained popularity, particularly during the Reagan and Thatcher years of the 1980s. This was also concerned with outputs, but was equally concerned with inputs and the relationship between the two. This is sometimes called cost-effectiveness, efficiency or value for money. If two organizations had the same outputs, which organization produced them with the smaller amount of inputs? However, similar problems remain concerning the above of assessing outputs (or goal achievement), which may not be the same as the outcomes for the beneficiaries.

Tinkelman and Donabedian (2007) suggest a framework for evaluating the efficiency of Third Sector organizations using four factors:

- the proportion of revenues actually used in the current year;
- the proportion of the expenditures allocated to programmes;
- the units of output produced from that spending;
- the value of the units produced, expressed in terms of an index value.

An emphasis on efficiency as opposed to effectiveness, some would argue, results in aiming for a low quality of service, particularly for beneficiaries of the services of Third Sector organizations which often cannot choose an alternative provider. In practice it is also probably impossible to find even two Third Sector organizations that provide the same quantity and quality of a service to enable valid comparisons to be made.

Economy

An approach closely aligned with that of cost-effectiveness or efficiency is an emphasis on economy. In assessing economy the important consideration is the cost of the various inputs and particularly whether the cost could be, or could have been, reduced. Unlike the efficiency approach, no comparison is made with the number or quality of outputs or outcomes.

Equity

It has also been argued from a Third Sector perspective (Osborne and Tricker 1995) that measures that focus only on effectiveness as outputs/outcomes or efficiency ignore the value base of many Third Sector organizations which emphasize equity as much as the other two dimensions. In their view any measure of Third Sector effectiveness needs also to contain a measure of equity (Savas 1977), i.e. to what extent is the service meeting the expectations or needs of those in greatest need or those who tend to be socially excluded, because of gender, ethnicity, disability, sexual orientation, etc.? This usually requires significant monitoring of beneficiaries to assess the extent that equity has been promoted.

INTERNAL PROCESSES

Particularly where it is not possible to develop goal attainment output or outcome indicators, some researchers favour the development of internal process or quality measures of organizational effectiveness, other than efficiency or economy. Processes can include all the activities that translate the input resources into outputs and eventually outcomes. This can include: management, financial, quality, human resource and administration policies; systems and procedures; and management – any activity that is involved in carrying out the work of the organization.

Internal processes can be measured by assessing the organization against a set of quality standards (see Chapter 7 for a discussion of various models and tools for assessment of organizations against specific standards, or by benchmarking against other organizations).

Benchmarking

The development of benchmarking arrangements provides organizations with other organizations with which they can compare particular processes (usually organizations which are considered to be particularly advanced in the area that the original organization wishes to improve in). This can enable an organization to consider how these processes can be improved. Letts *et al.* (1998) suggest that benchmarking is one of the four key areas that Third Sector organizations need to address in order to develop their capacity to become high performing organizations.

Paton (2003) discusses the 'best practice' of process benchmarking in the Third Sector in the UK. He describes the key feature of this kind of benchmarking as:

- careful study of a defined set of activities, often an economically important, cross-functional, operational process, but which may also be a function or policy;
- a concern with the definition and measurement of performance, often using non-financial measures, cost-activity ratios and the like, in order to compare and track performance levels;
- identification of others from whom one might learn, because they carry out the process more effectively or efficiently;
- setting targets in relation to external standards, rather than past internal performance;
- a collaborative orientation to the sharing of performance data and/or process methods through benchmarking partnerships, clubs, study visits, etc.;
- adopting and adapting ideas used elsewhere to achieve improvements in performance;
- formation of a project team to carry out the study and champion the introduction of changes.

Neely (2002) distinguishes between indicator benchmarking, which is focused on measurement, and ideas benchmarking, which is concerned with ideas for improving performance. Benchmarking can be:

- internal: comparing the performance in different parts of the same organization, or over time in the same part of the organization;
- competitive: comparing performance with direct competitors;
- functional: comparing practices and methods with similar functions in organizations outside one's own industry;
- generic: comparing one's own processes with those of organizations that are considered to be innovative or exemplary.

There is very little literature on the effectiveness of this kind of benchmarking. In his study of examples in the Third Sector in the UK, Paton (2003) concluded that:

- best practice benchmarking is very rarely used by social enterprises; those that do, or that intend to, are almost always the larger ones;

- Third Sector managers use the terms 'best practice' and 'benchmarking' to encompass a wide range of related, often informal, activities, which are used more frequently than best practice benchmarking itself;

- for most Third Sector managers, 'benchmarking' means performance comparisons, and this aspect of it is of genuine interest to them;

- the benchmarking activities that have actually been carried out have often been problematic or inconclusive;

- the concepts of good and best practice have enormous appeal for Third Sector managers, but they don't necessarily assume that they are implied by the concept of benchmarking;

- benchmarking can be used to good effect by Third Sector organizations, but it requires a very substantial investment of time and effort.

Lindenberg (2001) highlighted the difficulty in adapting traditional top-down benchmarking processes in a particular Third Sector organization, although it was reported that methods that mixed project manager self-rankings, self-improvement plans and high levels of participation had the greatest success.

In addressing internal processes, the organization can measure the extent that it is 'doing things right'. However, this approach has been criticized by those who point out that there is no way of knowing whether these internal processes, even done exceptionally effectively, will actually lead to the organization being effective externally in the achievement of its goals and the provision of services to its beneficiaries (Porter 1997). It may be doing things right, but is it doing the right things?

COMPLIANCE WITH VALUES

In light of the suggestion that it is their basis in values that makes Third Sector organizations distinctive, and the increasing importance placed on organizations from all sectors addressing the question of organizational values, John Hailey has suggested (Hailey 1999) that Third Sector organizations should develop measurable, clear and precise indicators of key organizational values. He suggests, for example, in relation to NGOs involved in overseas development, that assessing the capacity of Third Sector organizations does the following:

- promotes internal learning;
- engages in genuine participation in planning, monitoring and evaluation processes;
- is accountable and transparent in its dealings with the community;
- has local legitimacy and is embedded in local society.

He goes on to give some examples of what the specific indicators might look like. He recognizes that there are Third Sector agencies that concentrate on living their values, but levels of performance are low, and suggests that other forms of indicators should not be jettisoned, and that indicators of compliance with stated organizational values should complement other kinds of financial and social indicators.

RESOURCE ACQUISITION

The Production of Welfare and Logic Model approaches include the crucial issue of acquiring the resources needed to carry out the agreed activities. The Logic Model too highlights the role of inputs in achieving the eventual outputs and outcomes. The acquisition of these inputs/resources can relatively easily be measured. The systems-resource approach (Seashore and Yuchtman 1968) is based more on an organic open systems or population ecology approach than the goal-attainment model. The systems-resource approach argues that all organizations need to be adaptable and acquire resources from outside in order to survive. Their ability to acquire these resources is therefore an appropriate measure of effectiveness in sustaining their own functioning.

Survivability is therefore the ultimate measure of effectiveness in this model. However, as Kanter and Summers (1987) point out, survival may be completely unrelated, even negatively related, to the impact of the organization. Particularly in the Third Sector, where some would say the main job of these organizations is to do themselves out of a job by eradicating the social problem it was set up to deal with, survival may well not indicate effectiveness. Meyer and Zucker (1989) have commented on the persistence of Third Sector organizations despite their low performance, precisely because of a lack of measures of success or failure.

The resource acquisition model has some attractions for the Third Sector which is constantly aware of the need to obtain funding from statutory, private and charitable sources, as well as volunteers from the general public. However, as a measure of effectiveness it tells us little about how the money is used, i.e. what effect the resources had on the beneficiaries. Perhaps the organization has an effective fundraising and PR machine, but achieves little with it.

Although it is theoretically possible to compare the resources acquired by one Third Sector organization against another, it makes little sense to try and compare the resource acquisition of Oxfam, or a children's hospice, with that of a neighbourhood residents' association or an unpopular cause, such as a wet house for alcoholics with a mental health problem. There are also likely to be a range of other properties that are required for an organization to sustain itself, which are much more difficult to measure, such as morale, adaptability and cohesion (Quinn and Rohrbaugh 1983).

The danger is that if the adaptability and resource acquisition functions become dominant in an organization's strategic thinking, it can lead to the sort of strategic delinquency highlighted earlier by Charles Handy, where an organization cynically pursues any potential funding source regardless of the mission or values of the organization or any assessment of needs.

STAKEHOLDER APPROACH

It is clear that there are many different perspectives on organization effectiveness. In relation to any single organization there will be a range of internal and external stakeholders who will have different values, different reasons for being involved in the organization and therefore very different perspectives on what might constitute success or organizational effectiveness (Kanter and Summers 1987). Indeed research has shown (Herman and Renz 1998) that stakeholders often differ markedly in their judgements of effectiveness of the same Third Sector organization. The reputational or participant satisfaction approach seeks the views of various stakeholders as to the effectiveness of the organization (Jobson and Schneck 1982; Herman and Tulipana 1985; Smith and Shen 1996).

Bigelow *et al.* (1996), in reviewing the literature on Third Sector strategies, argue that the institutional pressures from funders and other stakeholders is particularly strong and therefore the management of stakeholders through some form of 'corporate political strategy' is particularly important for Third Sector organizations. Strategies that ignore the intrusive nature of these multiple stakeholders are likely to be inadequate. This has led writers in the field down three parallel channels:

- the multiple constituency approach;
- the political approach;
- the more post-modernist, social constructionist, contingent and symbolic frame approaches.

In the multiple constituency approach, the diversity of perspectives of the various stakeholders (clients, funders, board members, volunteers, staff, etc.) is recognized (particularly that of the dominant coalition) and is used positively to define the criteria with which the organization will be evaluated. This can then create a rich framework of indicators of effectiveness (Connoly *et al.* 1980; Bluedorn 1980; Kanter and Brinkerhoff 1981; Zammuto 1984; Tsui 1990; D'Aunno 1992).

Herman and Renz (1998) argue that the multiple constituency model should be part of any approach to understanding the effectiveness of Third Sector organizations. It also provides a useful theoretic underpinning for practices such as social auditing (Gonella *et al.* 1998), which has been defined as 'a means of assessing the social impact and ethical behaviour of an organisation in relation to its aims and those of its stakeholders', and which has been championed in the UK by the New Economics Foundation and been taken up by a significant number of socially minded private sector companies (although few in the top 100 UK companies), as well as Third Sector organizations (Raynard and Murphy 2000). Social auditing is discussed further in Chapter 12. Other similar approaches are constituency accounting, developed by Robert Hugh Gray (Dierkes and Bauer 1973), and ethical accounting (Pruzen and Thyssen 1990).

POLITICAL APPROACH

The weakness of the approach above is that it provides no way of determining the particular weight that should be given to any particular constituency or group of stakeholders. It assumes that it is possible to integrate the various different perspectives, which may in fact be in conflict with each other, and indeed may be mutually exclusive.

In contrast, the political approach (Perlmutter and Gummer 1994) starts from the bases of limited resources, conflicting priorities, unequal power and the formation and dissolution of coalitions. Organizations, as viewed through the political frame, are seen as 'alive and screaming' political arenas that house a complex variety of individual group interests.

There is some research evidence to support the importance of this frame for the Third Sector. Heimovitics *et al.* (1993) found that effective executives in the Third Sector, particularly when faced with external issues, are more likely to employ a political frame as part of a more complex multiframe perspective than executives who are identified as not effective. They also found in a later study (1995) that effective executives were more likely to accept responsibility for executing a political dimension to leadership, such as coalition building.

Bolman and Deal (1991) summarize the five main propositions of the political perspective as the following:

- organizations are coalitions composed of varied individuals and interest groups;
- there are enduring differences among individuals and groups in their values, preferences, beliefs, information and perceptions of reality (though such differences change slowly, if at all);
- most of the important decisions in organizations involve the allocation of scarce resources: they are decisions about who gets what;
- because of scarce resources and enduring differences, conflict is central to organizational dynamics, and power is the most important resource;
- organizational goals and decisions emerge from bargaining, negotiation and jockeying for position among members of different coalitions.

Gummer (1990; quoted in Au 1996), suggests that social services is:

> mainly a political arena in which money is tight and there are no commonly accepted rules for how resources should be allocated. Resources often go to those organizations skilled at competing for them, but not necessarily to those which deliver the most effective services. Furthermore, goals of a social welfare organization often reflect the interests of those powerful factions within and beyond the organization, rather than as products of rational choices themselves. As a result, effective organizations are those which can survive and adapt to these political dynamics while at the same time are able to exploit the environment for the scarce resources that they need.

From this political perspective the existence of conflict about priorities is the norm for any organization and not necessarily a bad thing. As Heffron (1989: 185) argues,

> a tranquil, harmonious organisation may very well be an apathetic, uncreative, stagnant, inflexible, and unresponsive organization. Conflict challenges the status quo, stimulates interest and curiosity. It is the root of personal and social change,

creativity and innovation. Conflict encourages new ideas and approaches to problems, stimulating innovation.

The political frame is a useful counterbalance to the rational-structural perspective as to how in practice organizational goals are determined, usually following a process of negotiation and bargaining between the various coalitions, which are internal and external to the organization. Understanding the relative power positions of each of these various stakeholders (often easier to do in hindsight) can often provide a salutary dose of reality to the process of determining organizational goals, the methods to achieve them and how achievement will be measured.

CONTINGENCY APPROACH

D'Aunno (1992) argues that the approach to the concept of organizational effectiveness should be dependent on the particular context of the organization, i.e. that the definition of effectiveness is contingent on a range of internal and external factors which need to be considered before agreeing the measures of effectiveness in a particular organization. It is not therefore possible to agree either any global criteria of effectiveness that can be applied to all organizations or any particular organization in advance of considering the external and internal factors which may influence the criteria of effectiveness appropriate to that particular organization.

SOCIAL CONSTRUCTIONIST APPROACH

The social constructionist approach (Pfeffer 1982), derived from institutional theory, takes this argument a step further and holds that definitions and assessments of effectiveness have meaning, but that the meaning is:

- created by the individual or organizational actors involved;
- specific to the context in which it was created;
- capable of evolving as the actors continue to interact (Forbes 1998).

From this perspective, according to Quinn and Rohrbaugh (1983: 363–4),

effectiveness is not a concept but a construct. A concept is an abstraction from observed events, the characteristics of which are either directly observable or easily measured. Some concepts, however, cannot be so easily related to the phenomena they are intended to represent. They are inferences, at a higher level of abstraction from concrete events, and their meaning cannot easily be conveyed by pointing to specific occurrences. Such higher-level abstractions are sometimes identified as constructs, since they are constructed from concepts at a lower level of abstraction. The problem is that no-one seems to be sure which concepts are to be included in the construct of effectiveness, or how they are to be related. The highly abstract nature of the construct and the lack of agreement as to its structure accounts for a major portion of the confusion in the effectiveness literature.

A similar approach is taken by narrative theorists (see, for example, Barry and Elmes 1997) who examine strategy as a form of narrative or story-telling. They emphasize the existence of the simultaneous presence of multiple, interlinked realities, linked to historical and cultural contexts.

Institutional theory (Meyer and Rowan 1977; Johnson and Greenwood 2007) highlights the tendency of organizations, which desire legitimacy, to adopt social rules and copy one another and become more similar over time, rather than independently adopt distinctive competencies or niches. The pressures to copy what are perceived as successful organizations, to comply with regulatory systems and the impact of professional training programmes, all reinforce the tendency within any field to become more similar. This suggests that some of the rhetoric of strategic management about competition and distinctive competencies are not the only influences that affect what strategies any particular organization may adopt.

These post-modernist perspectives, like the political and contingency ones, do not necessarily help in developing ways of defining or measuring the concept of organizational effectiveness, but it puts the discussion into a wider framework. The questions that arise from these post-modernist perspectives are more to do with who is asking the questions about organizational effectiveness and why. What are the power relationships? What is the meaning each of the players give to the concept? And how does this relate to the meanings that are important to the other constituencies?

From the above discussion of alternative approaches to measuring organizational effectiveness it can be seen that these emergent frameworks – multiple constituency, political, contingency and social constructionist – are complementary to each other and provide a wider perspective on the concept of organizational effectiveness which is particularly useful from a theoretical perspective. Together they suggest that:

> criteria for evaluating organizational effectiveness cannot be produced by some objective apolitical process. They are always normative and often controversial, and they are as varied as the theoretical models used to describe organizations and the constituencies that have some interest in their functioning. (Scott 1992: 361)

THE SYMBOLIC FRAME

The symbolic frame is more interested in exploring organizational myths, symbols, culture and rituals that legitimize the organization internally and externally. Quinn's comment on strategic planning as 'so much raindancing' would reflect a symbolic perspective. In this view, the concept of organizational effectiveness is a myth created through organizational ritual to help legitimize the organization internally and externally. In common with the social constructionist perspective, what an event means is more important than what happened – the same event can have completely different meanings for different people. In the symbolic frame, events and activities in an organization are inevitably ambiguous and uncertain. The greater the uncertainty the harder it is to use rational analysis and decision-making and therefore the participants (actors) tend to create symbols and ritual to resolve confusion and increase predictability and provide direction, helping the participants to find meaning and order (Bolman and Deal 1991). In relation to organizational effectiveness, the symbolic frame sees this as a powerful and useful myth:

> Ceremonial criteria of worth ... are useful to organizations: they legitimize organizations with internal participants, stockholders, the public and the state. The incorporation of structures with high ceremonial value ... makes the credit position of an organization more favorable. Loans, donations, or investments are more easily obtained. (Meyer and Rowan 1991: 351)

Unfortunately, the utility of these essentially post-modernist approaches in relation to measuring organizational effectiveness focus mainly on revealing the problems associated with defining and measuring the concept in a rational manner than on providing any solutions to these problems.

MULTIPERSPECTIVE PERFORMANCE MEASUREMENT MODELS

The above discussion of different approaches to measuring performance/effectiveness in the Third Sector suggests that more than one approach is likely to be valid. Triangulating the measurement of progress using various different kinds of indicators is likely to produce a much richer picture than the use of simply one approach. The indicators might include the following:

- achievement of goals/objectives;
- satisfaction of external stakeholders e.g. funders, members;
- satisfaction of service users;
- changes in the skills, knowledge, attitudes, status and/or feelings of service users;
- value for money including Social Return on Investment;
- generation of external resources;
- scores on a quality/evaluation framework.

Various models have been developed that try to bring together a range of perspectives in order to reduce the limitations inherent in any of the simple models. The various approaches and models discussed above are not necessarily conflicting. Various attempts have been made to develop an overarching model that can encompass a number of these different approaches. There is a strong argument that a triangulation of approaches is likely to result in a more accurate and useful picture than results that come from applying only one approach. Some of these models have been used as the basis for strategic performance measurement systems, i.e. concise sets of metrics that support the strategic decision-making processes of an organization by gathering, processing and analysing quantified information about its performance, from multiple perspectives, and presenting it in the form of a succinct overview (Gimbert *et al.* 2010). In other models it is not clear how the measures should be developed from the relevant model.

Customer perspective	Internal perspective
Innovation and learning perspective	Financial perspective

Fig 12.3 Balanced Scorecard framework

BALANCED SCORECARD

Another overarching framework which tries to encompass a number of the models above is the Balanced Scorecard, developed by Kaplan and Norton (1996). This has been used extensively by private sector companies around the world, which are looking for a broader approach to measuring organizational effectiveness than narrow financial indicators, and an increasing number of Third Sector organizations.

The Balanced Scorecard model, which can be used for the development of strategy as well as measuring and communicating its impact, comprises four main perspectives within which to develop objectives, measures, targets and initiatives:

- the customer: concerned with outputs and outcomes (goal attainment, multiple stakeholder and reputational models);
- learning and growth: concerned with both a human resource development model and an internal process model;
- internal processes: concerned with an internal process model;
- financial: which includes resource acquisition, economy and efficiency models, and a goal attainment model (even if the goal is not to incur a deficit).

According to Kaplan and Norton (1992), the Balanced Scorecard helps organizations to answer four key questions:

- How do customers see us (customer perspective)?
- What must we excel at (internal perspective)?
- Can we continue to improve and create value (innovation and learning perspective)?
- How do we view our shareholders (financial perspective)?

Organizations are then expected to set measurable objectives and targets for each of the four boxes. The strength of the model is its simplicity, though probably also its weakness. It doesn't include the human resource perspective (employee satisfaction), supplier performance, product/service quality, or an environmental or community perspective (Gupta *et al.* 2011). It also doesn't provide any mechanism for benchmarking performance against other companies. Niven (2003) has argued that the Balanced Scorecard is equally applicable in the Third Sector and has developed a step-by-step guide, although the mission of the organization and the customer perspective becomes even more important.

One of the founders of the Balanced Scorecard (Kaplan 2001: 369) has reviewed some of the uses of the model in the Third Sector and argues that:

> the balance scorecard has enabled the nonprofit organizations to bridge the gap between vague mission and strategic statements and day-to-day operational actions. It has facilitated a process by which the organization can achieve organizational focus, avoiding the pathology of attempting to be everything to everybody. The measurement system has shifted the organization's focus from programs and initiatives to the outcomes the programs and initiatives are supposed to accomplish.

Applying the Balance Scorecard to the Third Sector, however, presents some difficulties (Bozzo 2000), particularly for small organizations (Cutt 1998). A key issue is how appropriate the four perspectives are for Third Sector organizations. Niven (2008) suggests that because of the importance of the mission of Third Sector organizations, 'mission' could be a fifth overarching perspective to develop measures and targets. He also suggests that it may be appropriate to reword the existing perspectives to be more acceptable to the Third Sector. Kong (2008) argues that the Balanced Scorecard offers 'an inferior framework for the nonprofit sector'. Moore (2003) suggests the Balanced Scorecard is not an appropriate framework for non-profit organizations, for three reasons:

- Financial measures in a non-profit organization are a means towards achieving the mission, and are not an end in themselves.
- Customers: Third Sector organizations have third-party payers and upstream customers – except in social enterprises, there is not a two-way transaction between buyer and seller. There is usually a third-party payer, i.e. a funder or donor, who may be viewed as an upstream customer.
- Partnerships and collaboration should be important factors, rather than competitive advantages.

Bontis *et al.* (1999) suggest that the Balanced Scorecard is too restrictive for Third Sector organizations. Forcing organizations into the four boxes may mean that crucial issues, such as governance, fundraising or campaigning, may be missed. From an action research study in Brazil, Gomes and Liddle (2009) argue that the Balanced Scorecard is more valuable if separate scorecards are developed for each unit of the organization, rather than for the organization as a whole.

Cutt and Murray (2000), having reviewed a range of systems for evaluating performance and performance improvement, suggest that the Balanced Scorecard does show promise if combined with another system (they suggest the Canadian Comprehensive Auditing Foundation System – see p. 136). They consider, however, that the four perspectives (boxes) of the traditional Balanced Scorecard are inadequate to deal with the complexities of measuring the performance of most Third Sector organizations and suggest alternative versions of the Scorecard involving between seven and ten perspectives. It would also be possible, for example, to use the nine areas covered by the EFQM Excellence Model (see pp. 125–7) as scorecard perspectives, thereby integrating the two models. See Box 12.4 for an example of the use of the Balanced Scorecard in the Third Sector.

BOX 12.4 NACRO BALANCED SCORECARD

NACRO is the largest charity in England and Wales which works to make society safer by reducing offending. It has 300 projects in Britain supporting over 80,000 people. NACRO used the Balanced Scorecard approach in developing its 2008–11 Corporate Plan. In addition to developing statements of a mission, vision and core principles, the organization used the four perspectives of the Balanced Scorecard – stakeholder, finance, learning and development, and internal processes – to develop key strategic goals and objectives:

Stakeholder perspective

Key strategic goal: to align ourselves effectively with our service users, funders and with policymakers.

Objectives:

- service users: to grow our portfolio of services – working in partnership where this benefits our service users – to meet the needs of a greater number and wider range of service users and to improve levels of satisfaction and engagement experienced by our service users;
- policymakers: to be the rational and constructive voice in public discussion of crime policy;
- funders: to be the preferred national provider of resettlement and preventive services to offenders and those at risk of offending.

Finance perspective

Key strategic goal: to maintain our financial viability.

Objectives:
- to increase free or unencumbered reserves;
- to ensure full cost recovery on all contracts and activities;
- to control the cost base.

Learning and development perspective

Key strategic goal: to attract, retain and motivate our staff to deliver excellent services.

Objectives:

- to attract, develop and retain a diverse and motivated workforce;
- to achieve Investors in People status for NACRO as a single organization.

Internal process perspective

Key strategic goal: to have an internal structure and infrastructure that support the integrated and seamless delivery of NACRO services.

Objectives:
- to identify and manage risk through a rigorous risk self-assessment process;
- to secure funding to deliver coordinated services;
- to establish an integrated and robust IT system and automated finance and accounting procedures across the organization.

(NACRO Corporate Plan 2008–11)

Strategy Maps

Kaplan and Norton (2004), the creators of the Balanced Scorecard, have also developed the concept of a Strategy Map: a one-page visual representation of the strategy, showing how all the elements of it fit together. The map will tend to show: the vision, purpose and aims (usually at the top); the main expectations of the key stakeholders; the key themes. Each key theme will have its own strategic objectives, measures and stretch targets, which can be clearly communicated to staff, and strategic enablers, which support the achievement of the strategic objectives, e.g. finance, human resources, facilities (see Figure 12.4 for an example of a Strategy Map).

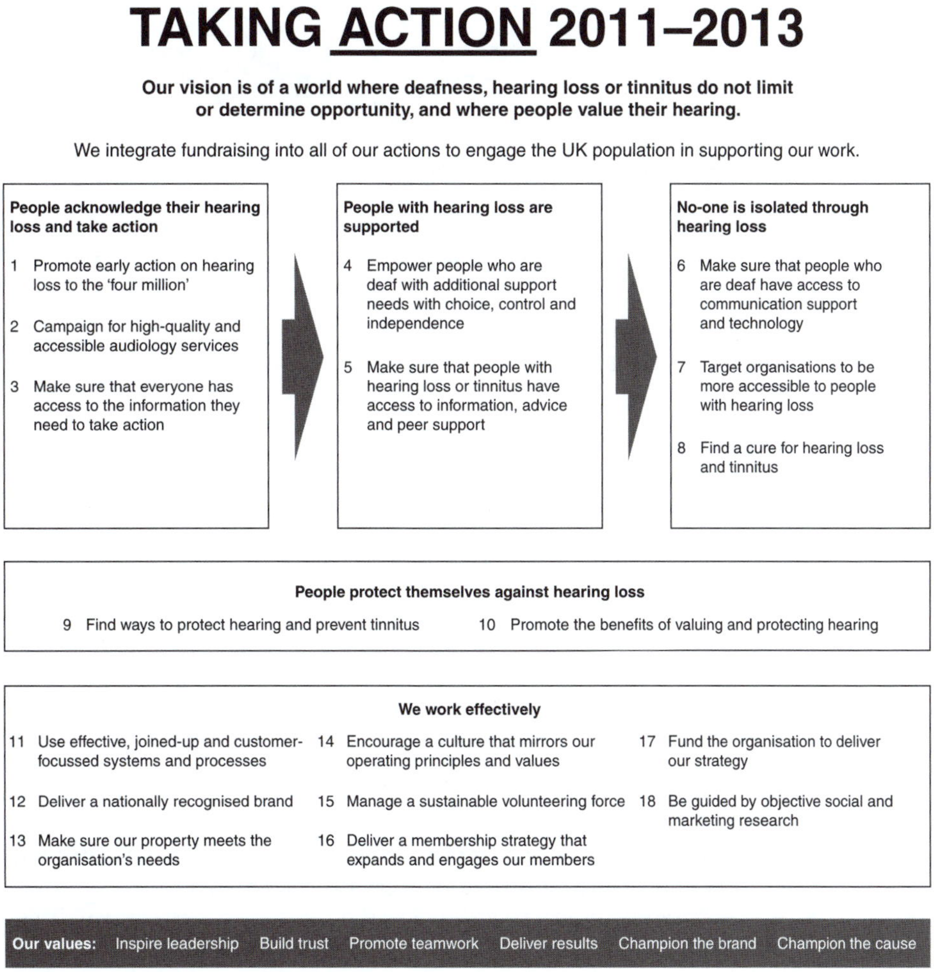

TAKING <u>ACTION</u> 2011–2013

Our vision is of a world where deafness, hearing loss or tinnitus do not limit or determine opportunity, and where people value their hearing.

We integrate fundraising into all of our actions to engage the UK population in supporting our work.

People acknowledge their hearing loss and take action

1 Promote early action on hearing loss to the 'four million'

2 Campaign for high-quality and accessible audiology services

3 Make sure that everyone has access to the information they need to take action

People with hearing loss are supported

4 Empower people who are deaf with additional support needs with choice, control and independence

5 Make sure that people with hearing loss or tinnitus have access to information, advice and peer support

No-one is isolated through hearing loss

6 Make sure that people who are deaf have access to communication support and technology

7 Target organisations to be more accessible to people with hearing loss

8 Find a cure for hearing loss and tinnitus

People protect themselves against hearing loss

9 Find ways to protect hearing and prevent tinnitus   10 Promote the benefits of valuing and protecting hearing

We work effectively

11 Use effective, joined-up and customer-focussed systems and processes

12 Deliver a nationally recognised brand

13 Make sure our property meets the organisation's needs

14 Encourage a culture that mirrors our operating principles and values

15 Manage a sustainable volunteering force

16 Deliver a membership strategy that expands and engages our members

17 Fund the organisation to deliver our strategy

18 Be guided by objective social and marketing research

Our values: Inspire leadership   Build trust   Promote teamwork   Deliver results   Champion the brand   Champion the cause

Fig 12.4   Action on Hearing Loss Strategy Map

PUBLIC VALUE SCORECARD

Moore (2003) suggests a triangular model, the Public Value Scorecard, reflecting three key calculations needed before committing the organization to a strategy:

- the value circle: the value provided through achieving social objectives;
- the legitimacy and support circle: earning its standing with third-party payers, e.g. funders and donors;
- operational capacity: the ability to achieve the desired goals.

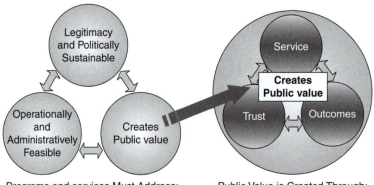

Fig 12.5 Public Value Scorecard
Source: Moore (1992).

PERFORMANCE PRISM

Andy Neely (2002), in close cooperation with the Centre for Business Performance at Cranfield School of Management and the Process Excellence Core Capability Group of Andersen Consulting, developed an alternative framework called the Performance Prism (see Figure 12.6), which takes as its starting point the reciprocal relationship with each stakeholder, i.e. both what the organization expects from the stakeholder and what the stakeholder expects from the organization, which will ideally lead to stakeholder satisfaction and loyalty. These two key stakeholder perspectives, then become central to three additional crucial factors in delivering stakeholder satisfaction:

- Strategy: what is the organization's strategy for delivering for the stakeholders and ensuring the stakeholders deliver what is expected of them?
- Processes: what organizational processes need to be in place to implement the strategy and ensure consistent delivery for stakeholders?
- Capabilities: what skills and knowledge are required to deliver the strategy for the benefit of stakeholders and ensure they deliver?

Figure 12.7 shows the interrelationship between the different elements of the Performance Prism.

The Five Facets of the Performance Prism

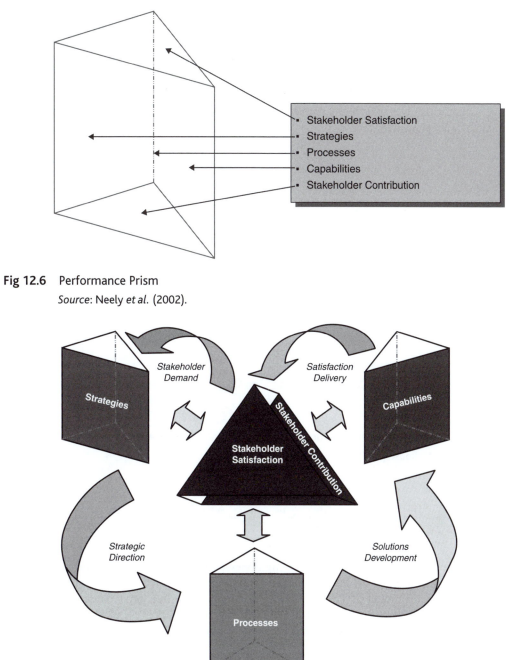

Fig 12.6   Performance Prism
Source: Neely *et al.* (2002).

Fig 12.7   Interrelationship between different elements of the performance prism
Source: Neely *et al.* (2002).

ROUSE'S MACRO–MICRO FRAMEWORK OF PERFORMANCE MEASUREMENT

Paul Rouse (2003) built on the basic inputs-activities-outputs model to include feedback loops, stakeholder expectations, strategic outcomes and benefits and related it to a strategic planning structure of vision/goals, objectives, plans and performance norms. The macro–micro framework applies equally well to a Third Sector context (see Figure 12.8).

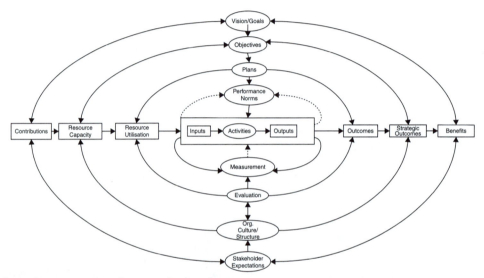

Fig 12.8   Rouse's macro–micro framework of performance measurement
Source: Rouse (2003).

GENERAL MODEL OF ORGANIZATIONAL EFFECTIVENESS

Kushner and Poole (1996), having reviewed the literature on organizational effectiveness, combined the logic model and stakeholder satisfaction approaches and suggested a general model of Third Sector effectiveness with five key elements: constituent satisfaction; resource acquisition effectiveness; internal process effectiveness; goal attainment; and organizational effectiveness (see Figure 12.9).

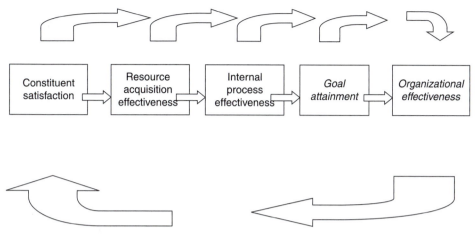

Fig 12.9 General model of organizational effectiveness

Source: Kushner (1994b, presented in Kushner and Poole 1996).

COMPETING VALUES MODEL

Quinn and Rohrbaugh (1983) developed a spatial model by using multivariate techniques on a range of criteria used by theorists and researchers to evaluate the performance of organizations. The axes of the model are internal–external and flexibility/control, which reflect common organizational dilemmas. The four quadrants contain four lenses with which to view an organization: the human resources model (flexible/internal); the open system model (flexible/external); the rational goal model (external/control); and the internal process model (internal/control). Organizational culture, as

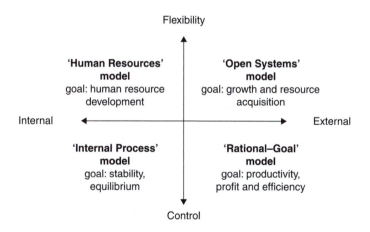

Fig 12.10 A competing values model of effectiveness criteria

Source: Quinn and Rohrbaugh (1983).

well as strengths and weaknesses, can be assessed in relation to each of the four lenses (see Figure 12.10).

Balduck and Buelens (2008) successfully applied Quinn and Rohrbaugh's competing values model of effectiveness, along with Sowa *et al.*'s (2004) two levels of analysis (management and programme), to measure the effectiveness of sports clubs.

TRIPLE BOTTOM LINE

Another approach to encourage companies to consider a wider range of performance measurement than just profitability is the Triple Bottom Line, developed by John Elkington (1998), in which success is judged in terms of being economically viable, environmentally sound and socially responsible, or in short 'people, planet, profit' (see Willard 2002; Savitz and Weber 2006). It was ratified in 2007 as the United Nations and ICLEI standard for urban and community accounting and has been adopted as part of the State Sustainability Strategy by the Government of Western Australia. Robbins (2006) highlights the difficulty of measuring the benefits of the Triple Bottom Line to society, the environment or individual organizations which adopt this approach. Henriques and Richardson (2004) produced an edited volume of papers examining the strengths and weaknesses of the Triple Bottom Line approach. Box 12.5 provides an example of a UK social enterprise that uses this approach.

BOX 12.5 COSMIC ETHICAL IT'S TRIPLE BOTTOM LINE

Cosmic is an ethical IT company, based in Devon, UK, housing web development, technology support, and training and consultancy under one roof. The staff have particular expertise in social media, search engine optimization, graphic design, hardware and web applications.

The aim of Cosmic Ethical IT is 'to improve other people's digital lives and by doing this we hope we can improve yours'.

Cosmic Ethical IT helps individuals, businesses, voluntary and community organizations and the public sector to solve IT challenges and help people to take advantage of new technologies. It provides:

- Cosmic website services: producing fully accessible, easy-to-use and simple-to-manage websites for every type of organization;
- Cosmic technical support: providing IT knowledge and support;
- Cosmic workshops and mentoring: letting people know how technology can change lives, even in a small way;
- Cosmic consultancy: bringing a diverse range of specialist research, project development, consultation and business planning skills to organizations.

Cosmic is a social enterprise and company limited by guarantee. It has been awarded the Social Enterprise Mark, is a nationally recognized Social Enterprise Ambassador and acts as Regional ICT Champions for the South West. Cosmic was recently shortlisted in the impact category of the RBS SE 100 Index.

Cosmic Ethical IT has a membership which is open to anyone passionate about its work and shares its values. The board of directors of eight people – both executive and non-executive – is elected by its members every year.

'Ethical IT' relates to the way Cosmic does business. As a social enterprise, Cosmic measures its success against a Triple Bottom Line – profit, people and the planet – using a social accounting approach, based on various stakeholder surveys. They are committed to incorporating ethics into the heart of their business, from the people they employ, the products they use and the way they work with customers. They always aim for fair and collaborative working relationships that allow for change and new ideas.

(Cosmic Ethical IT website: www.cosmic.org.uk.)

SOCIAL RETURN ON INVESTMENT

To try to provide a robust way of measuring the impact of social programmes, Social Return on Investment (SROI) has been developed using cost–benefit analysis techniques to place a monetary value on social outcomes, so that these can be compared to the cost of the inputs to create an SROI ratio. A ratio of 3:1, for example, means that for every pound spent on a social programme, £3 is generated in terms of social impact. Using this kind of approach, Nobel prize-winning economist, Jim Heckman, has shown that £1 invested in the best evidence-based early years programmes for young children is likely to produce £7 in later savings in things like mental health services, prisons and criminal justice services, and welfare benefits. Using this approach he was able to show that the later (in terms of the age of the children/young people) prevention and early intervention services are provided, the lower the ratio will be. This thinking has led to the development of social investment vehicles being actively promoted by the UK Government (HM Government 2012), such as Social Impact Bonds, which enable organizations to receive investment on the basis of the later financial savings.

The key Principles of SROI (Nicholls *et al.* 2009) are:

- *Stakeholder's perceptions*: understanding the way in which the organization creates change through a dialogue with stakeholders.
- *Scope and materiality*: acknowledging and articulating all the values, objectives and stakeholders of the organization, before agreeing which aspects of it are to be included in the scope, and determining what must be included in the account in order that stakeholders can make reasonable decisions.
- *Understand change*: articulating clearly how activities create change and evaluate this through the evidence gathered.
- *Comparative*: making comparisons of performance and impact using appropriate-benchmarks, targets and external standards.
- *Transparency*: demonstrating the basis on which the findings may be considered accurate and honest, and showing that they will be reported to and discussed with stakeholders.

- *Verification*: ensuring appropriate independent verification of the account.
- *Financial proxies*: using financial proxies for indicators in order to include the values of those excluded from markets in the same terms as those used in the market.

The following are the key stages in undertaking an SROI analysis (ibid.):

1. Understand and plan. Gain support for the process.
2. Stakeholders: identify stakeholders, their overarching goals and their specific objectives for the programme. Prioritize key stakeholders and objectives. Identify common or overriding objectives.
3. Boundaries: define the organization or programme, geographies covered and a time period. Explain how, if at all, income and expenditure are broken out into social and economic elements.
4. Analyse income and expenditure between social and financial elements.
5. Impacts and indicators. Identify how the programme works and how the programme affects key stakeholders (linking this to stakeholders' objectives). Capture this through an analysis of inputs, outputs, outcomes and impacts. Identify appropriate indicators for capturing inputs, outputs, outcomes and impacts. Identify monetary values for the indicators, using averages and estimates where information is not available. Use deadweight to take account of the extent to which outcomes would have happened without the intervention.

1. Prepare an SROI plan. Set out the timescales and resource requirements of an SROI process.
2. Implement the plan.
3. Projections: prepare projections of future costs and benefits.
4. Calculate the SROI: create a discounted cash flow model using gathered data and projections. Calculate the net present value of benefits and investment, total value added, SROI and payback period. Use sensitivity analysis to identify the relative significance of data.
5. Consider and present the results in a way that brings out the subtleties and underlying limitations and assumptions.

There are, however, various challenges in trying to implement an SROI process (Arvidson *et al.* 2010):

- The need for evidence and monitoring systems: there needs to be appropriate data to be collected and sophisticated systems for collecting and analysing it regularly.
- Judgement and discretion in setting the indicators: clear and appropriate impact indicators need to be established, some of which are much more difficult to measure than others.
- Focus on impact at the expense of understanding process: although SROI is claimed to tell a 'compelling story of change' (Nicholls *et al.* 2009), in fact SROI focuses on

calculating the ratio of costs to impact, not exploring the processes that resulted in the change.

- Competing principles and goals: because not everything can be measured, there is always a question as to whether the process is distorted by ignoring those things that can't be measured.

- Quantifying the value of benefits: SROI uses a monetary value as a proxy for the benefits for a social programme. Some kinds of benefits are relatively easy to ascribe a monetary value to, which is why SROI is more commonly used in certain social fields, e.g. learning disability, work with offenders, employability, rather than others. Putting a monetary value on social outcomes is not a value-free process.

- Valuing inputs: putting a price on volunteering presents particular challenges.

- Deadweight, displacement and attribution: it is often difficult to be sure which factors (and which programmes/organizations) actually lead to the projected outcomes (attribution). SROI therefore needs to assess what would have happened without the programme (deadweight), whether other people lose out as a result of the success of the beneficiaries (displacement), and a reduction in enthusiasm for and results of the programme over time (drop-off).

- Using and reporting SROI results: all the challenges of SROI mean that it can be a dangerous thing to compare the SROI results of one programme or organization with another. The strength of SROI, however, is the presentation of a simple ratio, which can be compared with the ratio of a comparable programme, making public decision-making and resource allocation easier.

- The high cost of conducting SROI assessments: SROI assessments can be expensive due to the high level of skills, as well as the internal systems, which may be required.

In addition to the Nicholls *et al.* Guide to SROI commissioned by the Cabinet Office, New Economics Foundation (NEF) (2008) has also produced a useful free guide, *Measuring Value: A Guide to Social Return on Investment (SROI)*.

EUROPEAN EXCELLENCE MODEL

The European Excellence Model has been developed by the European Foundation for Quality Management and promoted by the British Quality Foundation and various quality centres around Europe. This model has now been used extensively for continuous improvement by a large number of private sector companies and a few larger Third Sector organizations. It is similar to the Baldridge Quality award framework in the US (see Figure 12.11).

The EFQM Quality framework contains nine elements, five of which are described as enablers (leadership; people management; policy and strategy; partnership and resources and processes) and four results areas (people results, customer results, society results and key performance results).

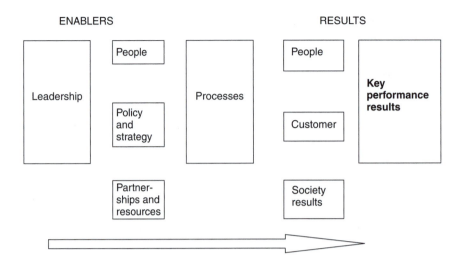

ENABLERS

People

Leadership

Policy and strategy

Processes

Partner-ships and resources

RESULTS

People

Customer

Society results

Key performance results

Fig 12.11 EFQM Excellence Model
Source: QSTG (2000a).

The Model's nine boxes represent the criteria against which to assess an organization's progress towards excellence. Each of the nine criteria has a definition, which explains its high level meaning:

- Leadership: excellent leaders develop and facilitate the achievement of the mission and vision. They develop organizational values and systems required for sustainable success and implement these via their actions and behaviours. During periods of change they retain a constancy of purpose. Where required, such leaders are able to change direction of the organization and inspire others to follow.

- Policy and strategy: excellent organizations implement their mission and vision by developing a stakeholder focused strategy that takes account of the market and sector in which it operates. Policies, plans, objectives and processes are developed and deployed to deliver strategy.

- People: excellent organizations manage, develop and release the full potential of their people at an individual, team-based and organizational level. They promote fairness and equality and involve and empower their people. They care for, communicate, reward and recognize in a way that motivates staff and builds commitment to using their skills and knowledge for the benefit of the organization.

- Partnerships and resources: excellent organizations plan to manage external partnerships, suppliers and internal resources in order to support policy and strategy and the effective operation of processes. During planning and whilst managing partnerships and resources, they balance the current and future needs of the organization, the community and the environment.

- Processes: excellent organizations design, manage and improve processes in order to satisfy fully, and generate increasing value for, customers and other stakeholders.

- Customer results: excellent organizations comprehensively measure and achieve outstanding results with respect to their customers.

- People results: excellent organizations comprehensively measure and achieve outstanding results with respect to their people.

- Society results: excellent organizations comprehensively measure and achieve outstanding results with respect to society.

- Key performance results: excellent organizations comprehensively measure and achieve outstanding results with respect to the key element of their policy and strategy.

These nine areas are further subdivided into 32 subcriteria each of which generates a set of scaled questions.

One of the positive advantages of the EQFM Excellence model is that the score(s) of one organization can be compared (benchmarked) with that of others in the same or a different industry or sector. An organization can also track its progress over time. It is also a fairly comprehensive framework that can incorporate most of the elements of the various models discussed above.

The link between use of the European Excellence Model and traditional measures of business performance has, however, been described as inconclusive (Ghobadian and Woo 1994) and concern has been expressed that the model has been used so extensively with so little research evidence for or against its efficacy.

Because of the plethora of quality models on offer, The National Council for Voluntary Organisations (NCVO) in Britain established a major review of quality models in the mid-1990s, with a view to either adapting one for general use by the Third Sector or the establishment of a new Third Sector quality model. The conclusion of this project after substantial consultation was that, of all the models, the EFQM Excellence Model could be most suitably adapted for use by the Third Sector. The project also produced some useful materials for Third Sector organizations wishing to use the Excellence Framework (QSTG 2000a).

Box 12.6 highlights how one organization providing services for disabled people has used the EFQM Excellence Model, SROI and other quality tools to manage and improve its services.

MULTIDIMENSIONAL AND INTEGRATED MODEL OF NON–PROFIT EFFECTIVENESS (MIMNOE)

In 2004, Sowa *et al.* developed their multidimensional MIMNOE model of non-profit effectiveness, founded on five principles:

- there are multiple effectiveness dimensions, with management and programme effectiveness being main dimensions;

- each primary dimension is composed of two subdimensions: capacity and outcomes;

- researchers should collect both objective and perceptual measures of effectiveness;

BOX 12.6   CEDAR FOUNDATION

The Northern Ireland Council on Orthopedic Development (NICOD) was established in 1941 to work with people with severe physical disabilities. Since the late 1970s it has focused on innovative development in relation to living options, services for children and young people, and training and employment services.

In the early 1990s, using traditional strategic planning tools and the Balanced Scorecard, the organization began a process of internal review and strategic development to ensure the organization remained relevant to the needs of people with disabilities. This resulted in a managed move from segregated provision such as employment workshops to community-based employment and training programmes, and the development of an increased range of choices with regard to community living. This included assisted 'living schemes' and 'supported living' in partnership with Habinteg Housing Association.

The increasing diversity of services meant the name NICOD was considered no longer relevant, and was also confused with the name of another disability organization which had chosen a name with a similar acronym, resulting in the name change in April 2000. 'The Cedar Foundation' was chosen as the organization felt that the cedar tree represented the characteristics of strength and renewal, which were appropriate for an organization committed to continuous improvement and a determined pursuit of its aims.

To manage and improve its services effectively, the organization began to engage with, and then pioneer, the application of a range of quality initiatives within the organization. It has successfully used a range of quality tools to drive its work forward. This has resulted in a substantial expansion in its work with a doubling in the number of clients in a five-year period, consistently high approval ratings by clients and staff, and the receipt of a series of quality awards.

Investors in People

During the 1990s, it committed to a process of continuous improvement and gained recognition as an Investor in People organization. The commitment to Investors in People continued over the following decade and in November 2007 the Cedar Foundation gained IIP Champion status at an award ceremony in London, which recognized the organization's commitment to the development of its people, acknowledging their value in continuing to develop and deliver high quality and innovative services for disabled people. This commitment to its people is also demonstrated by the Foundation's training services having won five National Training Awards.

Quality assurance

In order to ensure the consistent quality of these services, they put in place a documented, internally and externally audited, quality assurance system to ISO 9002 registration standard for their Assisted Living Scheme and subsequently made the transition to ISO 9001:2000, covering the whole of the organization in 2005.

Continuous improvement

A key continuous improvement tool used by the Cedar Foundation has been the use of the EFQM excellence model. In 2001 the organization scored 400–450 on their EFQM assessment. Every two years the assessment has been repeated and they were twice awarded the EFQM Mark of Excellence (2002 and 2004). By 2007 the organization's score had increased to 750–800. As a result they were awarded the prestigious Northern Ireland Quality Award, based

▶

on the EFQM Excellence Model, in January 2006, the first Third Sector organization in Ireland to do so, and in October 2007 it was awarded the EFQM European Excellence Award, Europe's most prestigious recognition for organizational excellence given to Europe's best performing companies and organizations.

Customer service

The Cedar Foundation achieved the Charter Mark for the quality of its customer services and was one of the first three organizations in Europe to be awarded the European Quality in Rehabilitation Mark (EQRM) in 2003.

Between 2007 and 2009, the Cedar Foundation carried out a Social Return on Investment study on its Community Inclusion Programmes, based on the Aspirations of Change (reflected in clearly defined outputs and outcomes) of six stakeholder groups, including participants, their families, residential homes, referral agencies and education and training providers. Indicators were identified for each output and financial proxies were selected to represent each indicator's value. Values were adjusted in light of accounting for attribution, displacement, deadweight, drop off and a sensitivity analysis. The SROI ratios ranged from 2.73:1 to 3.2:1. The saving of 6,077 day centre days saved the Health Trusts £428,166 over a two-year period, more than the Trusts' financial contribution over the period.

(Cedar Foundation website: www.cedar-foundation.org; Cedar Foundation Community Inclusion programmes SROI study April 2007–September 2009)

- the effectiveness model should allow for organizational and programmatic variations within a systematic structure;
- the analytical tool should capture multiple levels of analysis and model interrelationships between dimensions of organizational effectiveness.

The MIMNOE model could be represented as follows:

Nonprofit effectiveness:

- Organizational/management
- capacity (processes and structures): objective, perceptual;
- outcomes: objective, perceptual.
- Programme
- capacity (processes and structures): objective, perceptual;
- outcomes: objective, perceptual.

COMPOSITE MODEL FOR THIRD SECTOR ORGANIZATIONAL EFFECTIVENESS

Effectiveness in the Third Sector is clearly complex and contains a range of different elements, a number of which do not fit easily into any of the existing models, which were developed within a private sector context. The most distinctive of these elements

239

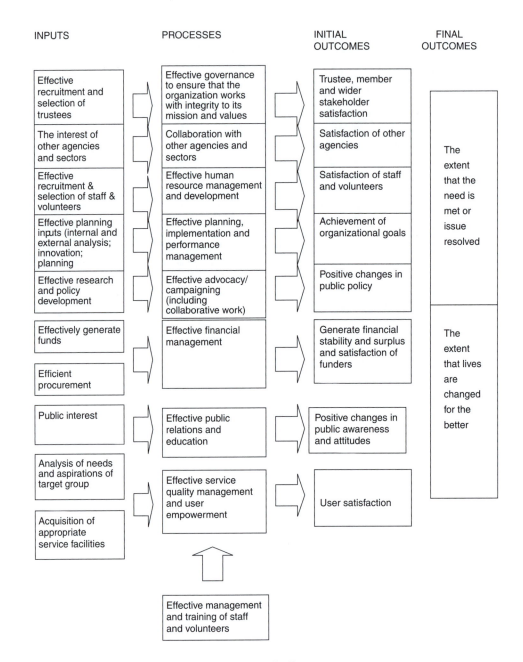

Fig 12.12   Composite model of Third Sector organizational effectiveness

(Courtney 2005) are the impact the organization has on need, the extent that lives are changed in a positive way, the extent that the organization works to its value-base, the extent that public policy is changed positively, the ability to generate public interest and support, and the extent that public attitudes are changed positively.

In terms of strategies adopted by Third Sector organizations, including quality improvement, user/member/client empowerment, collaboration with other agencies and sectors, fundraising, public awareness and campaigning/lobbying are also distinctive, although not unique to the Third Sector, which should also be reflected in any model if it is to be relevant to that Sector, in addition to the classic Ansoff strategies of providing new kinds of products/services, working with new types of clients and working in new geographical areas.

The research literature, highlighted above, in relation to the impact of strategic management in Third Sector organizations, included some of the factors used to define effectiveness, but also key internal processes, such as financial planning and programming and monitoring of performance, which should be included in a comprehensive model of organizational effectiveness.

The composite model (see Figure 12.12) draws on some aspects of other models, including the EFQM Excellence and the Production of Welfare/Logical Framework models, but also has features which highlight the distinctive nature of the Third Sector and the aspects of effectiveness that are most important to the sector itself. It is suggested as an appropriate model for Third Sector organizations.

The model suggests two key final outcome indicators:

- the extent that the need is met, or issue(s) resolved;
- the extent that lives are changed for the better.

Both of these are unlikely to be included in an equivalent model for a private company.

Contributing to the achievement of these two final outcomes are various initial outcomes:

- the satisfaction levels of users, trustees, members, staff, volunteers, funders, other agencies and wider stakeholders;
- positive changes in public policy;
- positive changes in public awareness and attitudes;
- achievement of organizational goals;
- generating financial stability and surplus.

These initial outcomes are achieved by the effective fulfilment of ten key 'upstream' internal processes:

- effective governance;
- ensuring the organization works to its mission and value-base;
- collaborating effectively with other organizations and sectors;
- effective human resource management and development;
- effective planning, implementation and performance management;

- effective advocacy/campaigning;
- effective financial management;
- effective public relations and campaigning;
- effective service quality management;
- user empowerment.

These ten processes in turn require various key inputs:

- effectively analysing the needs and aspirations of the target group;
- effective recruitment and selection of trustees, staff and volunteers;
- effective generation of income and public interest of the public and other agencies and sectors;
- acquisition of appropriate service facilities;
- planning inputs, research.

Research (Courtney 2005) has shown that the recruitment, selection, management and development of staff and volunteers are shown to contribute to more than one of the initial outcomes.

This model suggests eight key domains where there will be relevant inputs, processes and intermediate outcomes. These can be described as:

- governance;
- collaboration with other agencies and sectors;
- human resources;
- strategic and operational management;
- campaigning;
- income generation and financial management;
- public relations/education;
- service quality management.

The model has elements of the Production of Welfare model (Kendall and Knapp 1998), with its inputs, processes and outputs, as refined by Kushner and Poole (1996) with their constituent satisfaction (trustee, member, stakeholder, funder, staff and volunteer satisfaction), resource acquisition (effectively generate funds), internal process effectiveness (financial, human resource and service quality management), goal attainment (strategic and operational management), and organizational effectiveness (meeting need and changing lives positively). It includes elements of the EFQM Excellence model with its enablers (inputs and processes) and results areas. It also contains aspects of Quinn and Rohrbaugh's competing values model with its human resource model (effective human resource management and development, and staff and volunteer satisfaction), rational goal model (strategic and operational management), open systems model (effectively generate funds), and internal processes model (service quality and financial management). Finally it also encompasses the four core areas of the Balanced Scorecard: customers (user satisfaction and goal attainment), learning and growth (human resource development, research, strategic analysis and assessment of needs, staff training and development), internal business processes (effective service quality and human resource management), and financial (effectively generate funds, effective financial management, and financial stability and surplus). However, this new model also incorporates all the distinctive areas of organizational effectiveness defined by the respondents from the Third Sector strategic management research (Courtney 2005), and therefore suggests in more detail than most models where actions that affect organizational effectiveness need to be directed to affect particular outcomes.

Weaknesses in the model may include the danger that each of the eight domain areas is seen as separate from the others, and the management of the organization becomes compartmentalized into these silos. In reality they are interdependent and progress on achieving any of the outcomes depends on effective work in many of the other domain areas. The model also does not reflect the current interest in the concept of social capital as a possible outcome domain (Kendall and Knapp 1998).

The model is also consciously based on a rational logic model and therefore does not reflect the more post-modern perspectives, including the impact of power on decision-making or the symbolic meaning of actions.

HERMAN AND RENZ'S THESES

In 2008, Herman and Renz returned to review the literature on advancing non-profit organizational effectiveness that they had explored in a series of papers in the late 1990s, and came to nine conclusions:

The effectiveness of a non-profit organization (NPO) is:

- always comparative;
- multidimensional;
- related to board effectiveness (but how is not clear);
- related to the use of correct management practices but not in any simple 'best practices' way;
- a social construction.

They also concluded that:

- it is unlikely that there are any universally applicable best practices that can be prescribed for all NPO boards and management;
- organizational responsiveness (to stakeholders) is a useful organizational-level effectiveness measure;
- distinguishing among types of NPOs is important and useful;
- the level of analysis makes a difference in researching and understanding effectiveness.

243

BARRIERS TO PERFORMANCE MEASUREMENT IN THE THIRD SECTOR

Lester Salamon (2010), in the Johns Hopkins Listening Post Project looking at Nonprofit Innovation and Performance Measurement, identified the resource constraints, including staff time and expertise at engaging in sophisticated performance measurement. The vast majority of the respondents to his survey called for:

- better tools to measure quantitative impacts;
- less time-consuming measurement tools;
- tools with clearer definitions;
- additional resources to support their measurement and research functions;
- greater help from intermediary organizations in fashioning common evaluation tools;
- training for personnel in how to use the relevant tools.

SUMMARY

An underlying assumption is that strategic management is designed to make organizations become more effective. This chapter has explored what is meant by the concept of organizational effectiveness and how it may be able to measure its performance. It has explored: the rational goal-based approaches; input, process and output models that emphasize economy, efficiency, effectiveness and equity; and resource acquisition approaches and their limitations. Alternative perspectives which recognize that effectiveness is defined by different stakeholders in a different way according to their own interests, meanings and values have also been explored. Finally a number of overarching models which try to incorporate different models have been explored.

QUESTIONS

1. To what extent is measuring the achievement of an organization's stated goals or objectives a reasonable measure of success?
2. Is income generation a reasonable indicator of success? What are the pros and cons?
3. How important is it for Third Sector organizations to demonstrate value for money and how can this be done?
4. How can the effectiveness of an organization's internal processes be measured?
5. How can an organization's adherence to its values, such as equity, be measured?
6. Who are likely to be the stakeholders of a Third Sector organization? How can their perspectives on the effectiveness of a Third Sector organization be measured?

7. Does measuring quantifiable indicators of effectiveness take attention away from other equally important 'soft' aspects of effectiveness?

8. List the aspects of effectiveness that can be measured in an organization you know.

DISCUSSION TOPIC

What are the indicators that a Third Sector organization is being effective?

SUGGESTED READING

James Cutt and Vic Murray (2000) *Accountability and Effectiveness Evaluation in Non-Profit Organizations*, Routledge.

Robert D. Herman and David O. Renz (2008) 'Advancing nonprofit effectiveness research and theory: nine theses', *Nonprofit Management & Leadership*, 18(4), 399–415.

Rosabeth Moss Kanter and David V. Summers (1987) 'On doing well while doing good: dilemmas of performance measurement in nonprofit organizations and the need for a multiple-constituency approach', in W. Powell (ed.), *The Nonprofit Sector: A Research Handbook*, Yale.

Vic Murray and Bill Tassie (1994) 'Evaluating the effectiveness of nonprofit organizations', in Robert D. Herman and Associates (eds), *The Jossey-Bass Handbook of Nonprofit Leadership and Management*, Jossey-Bass.

Stephen P. Osborne (1996) 'Performance and quality management in VNPOs', in S. P. Osborne (ed.), *Managing in the Voluntary Sector*, Thomson.

Rob Paton (2003) *Managing and Measuring Social Enterprises*, Sage.

PART V

IMPLEMENTATION

13 STRATEGIC IMPLEMENTATION: MAKING IT HAPPEN

OVERVIEW

For some Third Sector organizations, the greatest weakness in relation to strategic planning is probably in the implementation phase, or rather the non-implementation phase. All too often, a one-off plan is drafted, even including many of the elements given above, but it then sits in a filing cabinet for a few years until someone, often an evaluator or a new chief executive or chair, comes along who thinks it is time for a new strategic plan, and so on. This chapter explores the various factors that ensure that the strategy of a Third Sector organization once it has been agreed will actually be implemented effectively. In particular the chapter will explore the issues of: organizational resources, physical, financial and human; operational planning; performance management; and structure.

LEARNING OBJECTIVES

After studying this chapter, you should be able to:

- describe the key elements of successful strategic implementation;
- outline how strategic planning processes affect the commitment to implementing a strategic plan;
- explain the importance of resource planning to ensure a strategic plan is implemented;
- describe the concept, and importance, of operational planning;
- explain the concept, and importance, of performance management;
- describe the importance of monitoring the implementation of the strategic plan;
- outline some of the options for organizational structure.

FORMULATION AFFECTS IMPLEMENTATION

Jack Walsh, chairman and CEO of General Electric, is quoted as saying: 'in real life, strategy is actually very straightforward. You pick a general direction and you implement like hell' (Gifford 2010: 1). Louis Gerstner, the man who rescued IBM, says that 'execution really is the critical part of a successful strategy. Getting it done, getting it done right, getting it done better than the next person is far more important than dreaming up new visions of the future' (Gerstner 2002: 230). A recent survey (Bodley-Scott 2010) of senior managers in European companies in the UK, however, found that more than three-quarters thought that their implementation could be improved. Poor implementation of a strategic plan is often not only a problem of the implementation processes, discussed below, but is also a problem of strategy formulation, because the planning process does not include a number of elements that are key to ensuring that the plan becomes part of the day-to-day management of the organization.

ENGAGEMENT OF STAFF AND VOLUNTEERS

It is clear that ensuring that a strategic plan is effectively implemented requires the commitment and motivation of the board, staff and volunteers. This commitment is only likely to exist if there is a high level of ownership of the plan. As Weisbrod (1987) says: 'people will support what they help to create'. This, in turn, will require ensuring that board members, staff and volunteers have all had a real opportunity to participate actively in the strategic planning process and put forward their own ideas.

> Some organizations manage the process by assigning responsibility to a single person, small group or external consultant; there is then little wider ownership of the plan, so that even if a plan is produced it may not be implemented and disillusion may result. (Sharp *et al.* 2007)

Failure to implement a strategy is often due to the staff responsible for delivering it on the ground perceiving, sometimes rightly, that the plan doesn't adequately reflect their views or the realities on the ground (Piercy 2002). Experience would indicate that the earlier in the process the board members, staff and volunteers are involved, the more committed they are likely to be to implement the final plan. Similarly, involving other key stakeholders, such as funders, in the strategic analysis and formulation process is likely to result in a much greater commitment, and support, from them in implementing the agreed strategy.

As highlighted in Chapter 10, the stage at which the various stakeholders are consulted is also important. Often this only happens once a draft strategic plan has been agreed. Stakeholders feel that, as a draft plan has already been created without their input, it is not really required, which results in a poor response rate and little commitment to the plan. Face-to-face involvement in the strategic analysis and formulation processes, at an early stage, as well as later in the process, helps the stakeholders to feel valued and that their contribution is important in shaping the plan. This then tends to create a much higher level of commitment to the plan amongst the stakeholder groups.

IMPLEMENTATION PROCESSES

There are also a range of other implementation processes, highlighted below, that need to be addressed if a strategic plan is going to be effectively implemented. As Bryson (1995: 166) states:

> creating a strategic plan is not enough. Developing effective programs, projects, action plans, budgets, and implementation processes will bring life to the strategies and create real value for the organization (or community) and its stakeholders.

Stone *et al.* (1999) point out, however, that there has been little actual research directly on implementation of strategic activities in the Third Sector context.

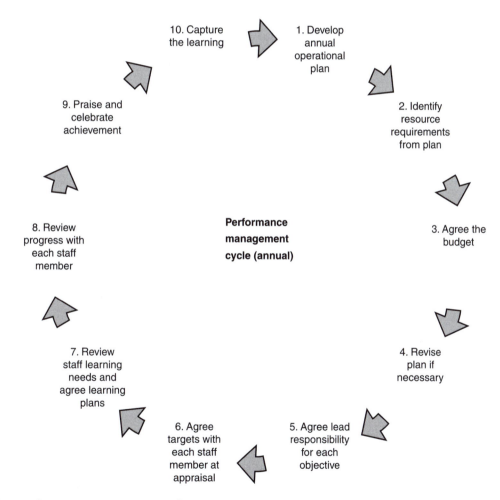

Performance management cycle (annual)

10. Capture the learning

1. Develop annual operational plan

2. Identify resource requirements from plan

9. Praise and celebrate achievement

3. Agree the budget

8. Review progress with each staff member

4. Revise plan if necessary

7. Review staff learning needs and agree learning plans

6. Agree targets with each staff member at appraisal

5. Agree lead responsibility for each objective

Fig 13.1   Performance management cycle

Bryson (1995) also points out the danger of implementation processes being too rigid and, thus, preventing adaptive learning from taking place (see the discussion on the learning organization in Chapter 4 above) when circumstances change or new knowledge becomes available, internally or externally. As Mintzberg (1994) points out realized strategies are (and should be) a mixture of what is intended and what emerges in practice. Figure 13.1 shows a typical performance management cycle to support the implementation of organizational strategy.

RESOURCE IMPLICATIONS

As highlighted in Chapter 2, one of the key criteria for a plan or decision to be considered as strategic is that it requires the commitment of significant resources. One of the first of the crucial elements in strategic implementation, then, is consideration of the resource implications of the plan that has been drafted, i.e. what resources will be required to ensure that the plan can be implemented fully? These resource implications are likely to include the following.

Physical resources, which may need to be purchased, rented/leased or obtained as a gift in kind, such as:

- buildings;
- vehicles;
- ICT hardware and software;
- equipment;
- furniture.

These in turn may become sources of net income for the organization if they can be rented to other organizations. Furthermore they all require annual financial costs (see below) to use, insure, maintain and ultimately replace the physical assets. Effective storage, security and cyclical/planned and reactive maintenance processes are also important in ensuring the resources are well looked after.

Human resources, such as:

- the number and type of staff, managers, volunteers, trustees, freelance consultants/contractors required to carry out the plans;
- the skills and knowledge needed by staff, managers, volunteers, trustees, freelance consultants/contractors to implement the plan effectively (knowledge resources);
- human resource policies and procedures which ensure that trustees, staff and volunteers receive the support and supervision they require;
- the appropriate salary and benefits structure are in place to ensure that good staff stay as well as enable the organization to recruit appropriate new staff;
- an appropriate organizational structure is in place to make sure the organization works effectively together (see pp. 258–60).

Systems and procedures, such as:

- personnel;

- finance;
- administration;
- training;
- quality assurance and improvement;
- communications (internal and external);
- governance;
- organizational policies and procedures.

Financial resources, which are the costs of the other resources outlined above, and may include:

- one-off capital costs;
- annual property-related costs;
- time restricted project costs;
- salary-related costs;
- annual programme costs;
- administration costs which can be allocated to specific projects/programmes;
- administration costs which cannot be allocated to specific projects/programmes.

The ultimate aim of considering the resource implications of the strategic plan under the above headings is often to create a multiyear budget which will clarify the specific financial resources and ultimately the funding/fund raising targets that need to be set and achieved within the plan to ensure these resources are acquired to achieve it. Alternatively, the creation of a budget for the organization's strategic plan may result in a revision of the plan in order to make it more realistic. This reinforces the need to allow enough time – from the drafting of a strategic plan to the creation of an organizational budget – for the plan to be adjusted, if necessary, and appropriate fundraising plans included in the strategic plan and the operational plan for the coming year. Bryson (1995) argues that budget decisions are critical to strategic implementation and often 'represent the most important and consequential policy statements that…non-profit organizations make'.

There is often a gap between the cost of achieving everything in the strategic and operational plan and the guaranteed income for the organization. Some of the objectives in the operational plan may be 'subject to funding'. This gap is the income generation target, which may have to be met from a range of possible sources, depending on the nature of the organization and the activities that need to be funded. These may include:

- grants from local, regional, national or international statutory bodies;
- successfully winning tenders from commissioning bodies;
- grants from charitable trusts or foundations;
- gifts or sponsorship from companies;
- gifts from company staff funds;
- gifts from wealthy individuals;

- gifts from associations/clubs, including the proceeds from events that others organize;
- legacies (difficult to plan for);
- one-off or regular gifts from individuals;
- income from raffles/lotteries;
- gifts in lieu of flowers or presents;
- selling goods or services to other organizations;
- selling goods or services to the public;
- fundraising events that the Third Sector body organizes.

Having developed a budget that puts a price tag on the strategic plan, the development of cash flow forecasts and effective, regular, usually monthly, monitoring of this budget requires appropriate financial management and reporting systems to be in place (Oster 1995); yet, as Anthony and Young (1984) suggest, the financial controls in many Third Sector organizations are woefully inadequate.

The resource aspects of the annual operational plan are sometimes referred to, or included as part of, a business plan (see p. 33).

The resource-based view discussed in Chapter 8 places resources at the heart of strategy and argues that they don't simply follow strategy, as the organization's distinctive resources are central to its success and around which the strategy needs to be built. The organization's distinctive resources will therefore be an important part of the review of the organization itself (see pp. 60–2). Some of the organization's resources may reflect particular strengths or unique competencies (for example, Greenpeace's boats have been a vital part of its campaigning activities) which should help to indicate where the organization's future strategy should lie.

ROLLING OPERATIONAL PLAN

The structure of the prescriptive planning processes recommended by Bryson (1995), Allison and Kaye (2005) and many others, requires a further step to be included in the process to ensure that it is implementable: the process of drawing up the detailed operational or business plan for each year based on the agreed mission, vision, values, long-term aims and priorities contained in the strategic plan. Schofield (1996: 113) states that 'business planning is about making strategic vision a reality and it does this by identifying the tasks which need to be completed and then allocating these tasks into particular organizational functions'. This process, which Jack Koteen calls 'bite-sized management' and Bryson describes as 'action planning', usually begins in the middle of the previous year's operational plan. In the middle of year one, therefore, the organization would begin the process of drawing up the year two operational plan. In the middle of year two the process of drawing up the operational plan for year three would begin.

The mission, vision, values and priorities, however, tend to remain largely the same each year, unless there is a major change in the focus of the organization or external environment over the three years, but typically the operational plan is created each year as it is rarely possible for an organization to be able to say exactly what it will be able to achieve over each of the three years of a strategic plan. Plans that do try and do this tend to look very sparse in year three! It is therefore common to create these much more specific operational plans which clarify, usually one year at a time, the progress the organization intends to make that year towards achieving its mission, vision, values and priorities.

The operational plan is normally based on creating objectives which are **SMART**: **S**pecific and stretching; **M**easurable and motivating; **A**chievable and agreed; **R**ealistic and robust; **T**ime-scaled and timely. Examples of objectives for an actual Third Sector organization are shown in Box 13.1.

BOX 13.1   EXAMPLES OF OBJECTIVES FOR A THIRD SECTOR ORGANIZATION

One of the organization's communication priorities is to communicate better with its members. The operational objectives are shown under the relevant three-year priority.

Communication with members
Aim: ensure effective two-way communication with members.

Operational objectives 2011–12:

- Listen to the views of, and feedback from, members: agree a members' satisfaction survey and process by August 2013; analyse and report on the 2011 members' satisfaction survey by September 2013.
- Ensure the website effectively meets the needs of members: agree a process and responsibility for regularly updating the website at least four times a year between April 2013 and March 2014.
- Make effective use of social networking to promote the organization and communicate with members: explore the potential of social networking to promote the organization and discuss in committee by December 2013.
- Produce a regular newsletter which meets the needs and expectations of members: produce at least four newsletters by March 2014.
- Ensure members receive timely information on relevant opportunities: agree a standard agenda item for each committee meeting on any forthcoming opportunities for members from April 2013 to March 2014.

As highlighted in Box 13.1, the operational objectives are usually established under each priority, which are grouped under each long-term aim. Taken together the objectives should make an impact on progressing the relevant priority, which in turn helps to achieve the relevant aim and, therefore, ultimately the mission of the organization.

Some of the common practices in the Third Sector in relation to operational planning, that can have significant negative consequences include:

- Losing the link between the structure of the operational plan and the strategic plan, so rather than building the operational objectives on the agreed aims and priorities in the strategic plan, some organizations build the operational plan around the departmental structure of the organization. This means that the operational objectives are not necessarily progressing the agreed aims and priorities.

■ Rather than developing the operational plan collectively, some organizations treat it as being the collection of work plans of the staff, or managers (in a larger organization). This reinforces a silo approach to the development of the organization and prevents a real dialogue between different parts of the organization as to how to progress the agreed aims and priorities in the strategic plan, in a particular year.

■ Setting completely unrealistic timescales for the operational objectives, so they are mostly unachievable, leaving the staff feeling very deflated, having failed to achieve the set targets.

■ Setting operational objectives that are too vague, e.g. improve relationships with social services, so when progress in achieving the plan is being monitored, it is impossible to determine with any authority whether the objective was achieved or not. Sometimes, this involves monitoring reports against such objectives as 'ongoing', rather than stating 'achieved' or 'not achieved'.

■ The objectives set are far too detailed, setting out every stage in the process of achieving an important target, rather than simply the final objective, or at least key milestones en route.

■ Not creating any objectives that are particularly relevant to particular groups of staff (often lower paid staff) or volunteers, so they do not feel involved in the implementation of the organizational plans.

■ Not including any governance objectives, which ensures that the governing body is continuously addressing ways of improving the governance of the organization.

MONITORING

Many strategic plans fail to be implemented simply because no framework was put in place at the beginning to control and monitor progress against the plan. As Cyert (1975) succinctly puts it, 'the declaration of desirable goals is not enough to guarantee immortality'. At its simplest it requires the board of the organization to agree a timetable for reports to be produced which describes the progress that has been made in achieving the objectives under each aim/objective and gives a report on progress against each of the operational objectives. It is obviously important to indicate if an objective has not been achieved, and why, and a new timetable established for its achievement if the objective is still relevant. It is also helpful if the monitoring report highlights objectives which are not on track to being achieved, so any corrective action can be agreed. It is also important to have a mechanism for reporting against the agreed quantifiable key performance measures (see Chapter 12 'Measuring Progress' pp. 197–245), even those where it has not yet been possible to set an operational objective/target against.

This process of regular monitoring of progress against the strategic plan provides a key agenda item for the board and ensures that it remains focused on implementing the agreed strategy, rather than on distracting detail. It also enables the board to feel much more in control of the outcomes of the organization. Depending on the nature of the plan and the changeability of the external environment, it may be appropriate for the board to consider a progress monitoring report quarterly or every six months.

> Some commentators have pointed out that although it is common to talk about management control in the private sector, because of the value-base of much of the sector, it is rare to talk about it in Third Sector organizations. (Hofstede 1981)

This may be because 'certain control strategies are incongruous with the personal psychological needs of adults' (Argyris 1952; Hofstede 1967; Newman 1975; Anthony and Young 1988; Hayes 1996). As discussed in Chapter 14 on motivating staff and volunteers, people generally like to feel in control of their own work. They do not like to feel they are being controlled, which can then give rise to challenges to these controls:

> control in an organization is not simply a process in which everyone shares with the same goal in mind; it is also a process in which there is resistance and counter control and pursuit of conflicting objectives. (Child 1984: 136)

It can also lead to dysfunctional behaviour, such as rigid bureaucratic behaviour or invalid data reporting (Lawler and Rhode 1976; Hayes 1996). Controls may be particularly problematic in the Third Sector context where (i) it is harder to establish credible and quantifiable measures to control and (ii) where there is the danger of easily quantifiable output measures driving out the more subjective outcomes (Sayles 1972; Newman and Wallender 1978). Chapter 13 highlights research which shows that people generally are more motivated to achieve targets they understand, which contribute clearly to a positive outcome for the organization and target beneficiaries, and which they were involved in setting. The research also suggests that people achieve more if they are working towards clear goals which provide stretch. However, the lack of effective controls or clear monitoring processes can also send a signal that these targets are not actually important to the organization. Anthony and Young's 1988 book on the subject of management control in the public and Third Sectors is a rare exception in directly addressing the issue of control in the Third Sector.

MANAGING INDIVIDUAL PERFORMANCE

The strategic plan will also come to nothing if it does not become part of the daily work of each of the individual staff and staff teams. In small organizations it may be enough to ensure that each of the objectives in the operational plan is allocated to a named individual. In larger organizations, each department or unit may develop its own subsidiary operational plan, which shows the more detailed sub-objectives that the department or unit needs to achieve to enable the objectives of the organization as a whole. The Balanced Scorecard process (see pp. 224–6) is designed so that each individual part of an organization develops its own Scorecard, which, in turn, feeds into the organizational Scorecard.

The cycle of performance appraisal or review with staff and volunteers should also be designed to relate to the operational planning cycle, so that the agreed operational objectives are cascaded down the organization. Relevant targets can be set with each individual and team (sometimes called action planning or work planning) which will in turn ensure the achievement of the department or unit's objectives (in a larger organization) or directly (in smaller organizations) the achievement of the organization's operational objectives.

Where there is a performance management system that is based on the organization's strategic and operational planning cycles, the review of the performance of staff should take place at the end of the annual operational planning period so it is possible to discuss the contribution that the individual made towards the organization's operational plan in the preceding 12 months, as well as to agree the targets, so as to contribute to the organization's objectives for the forthcoming 12 months.

The board also needs to consider the appraisal of the chief officer, which should also be based on how well the objectives in the organization's operational plan have been achieved. The appraisal of the chief officer may be done by the chair, or another board member with the relevant skills.

STRUCTURE

To deliver an organizational strategy effectively, there needs to be an appropriate structure through which the strategy can be delivered. Some of the issues that will influence organizational structure are:

- The legal status of the organization and the requirements of the constitution/memorandum and articles of association. This will be particularly important in relation to the structure of the board or management committee, as well as the relationship between sub-units/affiliates/members and the central/parent organization.

- The size of the organization: an organization of six staff will be very differently structured from one with one hundred staff. In particular, larger organizations will require additional layers of management and the relevant policies and procedures for supervision, appraisal and team leadership, as well as specialist skills in particular functions such as finance and human resources.

- The range and diversity of the kinds of work the organization is engaged in: Chapter 8 explored the issue of strategy choices and the extent that an organization should focus on a narrow niche or diversify to include a wide range of types of services, products and client/customer groups. These choices will have crucial implications for organizational structures.

- Geographical spread: are all the organizational activities in one geographical area? How spread out is the area, or does it operate in various distinct geographical areas? Geographical spread may have important implications for the structure of the organization.

- The complexity and difficulty of the tasks that the staff/volunteers need to undertake, and the implications of mistakes: this will affect the amount of supervision that is required and therefore the span of control of any manager.

- The level of collaboration, or competition, with other agencies: collaboration, in particular, can require the development of more sophisticated structures.

■ The similarity or diversity of different skills and knowledge that are required to carry out the various functions can have significant implications for the organization's structure. Staff or volunteers with similar skills or experience are often grouped together in a single team.

■ The extent that services are provided by permanent staff, or by volunteers or short-term placements, trainees, freelance consultants, etc., will also have implications for the organizational structure.

■ The financial stability of the organization may affect its ability to commit to permanent staff, or to staff at a particular skill and experience level.

Structural choices

Any organization has a number of basic choices about the main structure of the organization, as follows:

■ Geographical structure: many international agencies, for example, have directors and offices, even separate organizations, in each country or region they are working in. The nature of the relationship between regions and the central organization is often problematic. Depending on the organizational history, the need and demand for local control and the value of what is provided by the centre, the relationship can be:

  • a direct hierarchical relationship with strong central control;

  • a looser relationship with greater autonomy, perhaps a local advisory board;

  • closer to a franchise, with considerable autonomy, within the constraints of the franchise agreement, which must be met if the region wishes to be able to use the name and logo of the parent. Oster (1995) argues that this structure has significant advantages;

  • complete autonomy with no central control, with perhaps a federal membership structure, where the members collectively control the centre.

■ Client group structure: where the organization serves very different kinds of client groups, it may be structured around those different groups, e.g. an organization that serves children and young adults may have a separate children and young adults division.

■ Services structure: alternatively, where the kinds of services provided are very different from each other, it may be more appropriate to structure around the different kinds of services, e.g. an organization providing services for the homeless may have separate hostels, long-term housing and campaigning divisions.

■ Functional structure: where the structure creates a number of separate functional departments, e.g. finance, fundraising, human resources, communications, direct services. Boards sometimes mirror these functions by establishing sub-committees to oversee at least some of the particular functions (finance is most common).

■ Process/project structure: which is much more fluid than the other structures and provides the flexibility to create project teams for various periods to respond to particular opportunities (or threats), e.g. an international relief agency may put together specific project teams with the right mix of skills to respond to a particular disaster situation.

It is important to recognize that the issue of structure is not a static one. An organization life-cycle model is relevant here (see pp. 155–60). Particularly for organizations that are growing, the issue of structure will regularly come to the fore, as structures need to adapt to meet the current requirements of the organization.

When an organization is small and all on one site, the structure can be simple, with all the staff or volunteers meeting regularly together as a team. Expansion of the number of staff or volunteers often means the need to create a new structure with additional managers and separate teams. This can create the silo effect where organization departments tend to protect their own patch within the organization and engage in turf wars with other departments. Expansion into other sites can create further potential for conflict. Grossman and Rangman (2001) highlight some of the areas of difficulty when an organization has more than one site:

- How is income generated in the geographical area of an affiliate (sub-office, region, etc.) allocated?
- How well does that affiliate comply with quality standards and procedures established by the centre?
- Is the affiliate keeping within the mission and values of the organization and reflecting the appropriate brand image of the organization?
- Does the centre provide appropriate and valued services, commensurate with any affiliation fee?
- Is decision-making authority clear between the centre and affiliate (often between a national board and a local one)?

Some major organizations that have had a devolved structure with independent affiliates have successfully transformed the organizational structure to create a much stronger and unified one, e.g. the British Red Cross, The American Heart Association, The American Cancer Society, The American Diabetes Association. Others have given greater devolved authority, even independence, to geographical regions.

The success of restructuring to create more centralized organizations probably reflects (i) the success the national organizations had in winning the trust of the member organizations through a broadly inclusive decision-making process and (ii) the fact that the member organizations were persuaded that the restructuring would increase resources available for local programmes and services (Standley 2001).

Ultimately it is vital that the structure that is adopted enhances the ability of the organization to deliver the strategy that has been agreed. Clarity and simplicity of structure is probably the key. There has been an increasing awareness in the last two decades that too many levels in an organization and too complicated structures only diminish the ability of the organization to be effective. Too few levels can mean that particular managers have to manage too many staff or volunteers and fail to provide the necessary supervision and appraisal. All the teams and individual staff and volunteers need to be clear about the contribution that they are required to make to achieve the agreed organizational strategy. The structures should enhance the ability of individuals and teams to achieve the strategy.

SUMMARY

This chapter has highlighted the importance of implementation in the strategy process. It has explored the key elements of the implementation of the strategic plan, in particular: the analysis of resource requirements and the drawing up of budgets; the setting of operational objectives; the monitoring of the implementation of the strategic plan; the performance management systems to connect the individual staff (and volunteers) with the requirements of the strategic plan; the importance of relevant organizational structures; and the importance of wide participation in the strategic planning process to gain commitment to implementing the strategic plan.

QUESTIONS

1. How can the process of drawing up the plan assist in ensuring that it is effectively implemented?
2. What are the issues an organization needs to think about in creating a budget?
3. What makes for good objectives in an operational plan?
4. What are the main elements of performance management?
5. To what extent does the existing structure of an organization help determine the strategy? And the other way round?
6. What are the issues to consider in thinking about the structure of a Third Sector organization?
7. How should individuals be linked into the implementation of the strategic plan?
8. How can an organization ensure that an individual contributes to the achievement of the organizational strategy?

DISCUSSION TOPIC

To what extent should a strategic plan be based on the resources available?

SUGGESTED READING

John M. Bryson, Sharon Roe Anderson and Farnum K. Alston (2011) *Implementing and Sustaining your Strategic Plan*, Wiley/Jossey-Bass.

Richard L. Edwards, John A. Yankey and Mary A. Altpeter (eds) (1998) *Skills for Effective Management of Nonprofit Organizations*, NASW Press.

Mike Hudson (2009) *Managing without Profit*, 3rd edn, Penguin.

Stephen P. Osborne (ed.) (1996) *Managing in the Voluntary Sector: A Handbook for Managers in Charitable and Non-profit Organizations*, Thomson.

14 MOTIVATING STAFF AND VOLUNTEERS

OVERVIEW

Having an excellent strategy that reflects the unique competencies of the organization and the changing external environment, along with comprehensive implementation processes, will come to nothing if staff and volunteers are not enthusiastic about achieving the strategy. This chapter addresses the role of people (staff, volunteers and trustees) in the process of managing and developing organizations. It explores the various theories of human motivation in relation to work, which have been increasingly influential in the management of organizations generally and are particularly relevant in supporting the kind of management that many Third Sector organizations aspire to. The importance of human resources in a resource-based view of strategic management is also highlighted.

LEARNING OBJECTIVES

After studying this chapter, you should be able to:

- explain traditional approaches to motivation;
- outline some of the weaknesses in the traditional approach to human motivation;
- explain the weaknesses in performance-related pay;
- describe some of the key factors that motivate staff in work;
- identify suggested differences in staff motivation between Third Sector and for-profit organizations;
- explain the significance of people in the resource-based view of strategy.

TRADITIONAL APPROACHES TO MOTIVATING STAFF

In Chapter 3, the development of strategic management from the early work of Taylor and Fayol introduced a disciplined approach to examining how work is carried out. These early writers on scientific management emphasized the 'command and control' aspects of management. The assumptions underlying these approaches were:

- that the average human being has an inherent dislike of work and will avoid it if he or she can;
- most people have to be coerced, controlled, directed and threatened with punishment to get them to make an effort in the direction of the organization's goals;

■ the average human being dislikes responsibility and has little ambition, and prefers being directed and wants security first and foremost.

On the basis of this theory, which assumes that organizations are like machines (Morgan 1986), and therefore that the people are like parts of the machine, effectiveness can best be measured by systems like time and motion studies, and per capita productivity. Skinner (1938), from his work on learning in animals, developed the concept of instrumental conditioning, by which behaviour can be seen to be conditioned by the provision of positive and negative reinforcement. Hammer (1974) developed the reinforcement theory for the modern workplace and suggested rules for managers in applying operant conditioning techniques, i.e. providing rewards, in the workplace. Charles Handy (1988: 29) in his book *Understanding Voluntary Organisations* is particularly scathing about this view of managing people:

> Motivation has come to mean getting other people to want what you want them to want. Pigeons have been starved and then taught to dance for food. To treat pigeons like that is distasteful; to do it to humans and then to dignify it with names like reinforcement theory is akin to calling murder a form of genetic weeding.

WORK STUDIES

Studies of military and air force personnel and war-time manufacturing companies during and after World War II gave a major boost to all the human sciences including the scientific approach to the study of work, management and organizations. A famous study of a real organizational work setting by Elton Mayo (1945), known as the Hawthorne experiments, provided further evidence of the value of a scientific approach to studying work and workers, although not necessarily to the adoption of a traditional mechanistic or instrumental approach to the planning and organizing of work. These experiments began with the perspective of looking at how to tackle the tiredness and boredom at work that results from the 'scientific' approach to work as advocated by writers such as Taylor and Fayol. The research, as it developed, unexpectedly showed the importance of some very human factors in the working environment, in particular the influence of interpersonal and group relations. The study played a crucial role in the development of modern industrial psychology.

At around the same time as Mayo's experiments in the USA, Max Weber, a German sociologist, was examining the changes that were taking place in the industrial workplace and society and in particular the move towards specialization and standardization created by the 'scientific' paradigm, based on the analogy of a machine. He saw that what he called the bureaucratic approach had the potential to routinize and mechanize almost every aspect of human life, eroding the human spirit and capacity for spontaneous action.

HUMAN RELATIONS SCHOOL

An alternative frame (Bolman and Deal 1991) to view the motivation of staff and volunteers in work situations is the Human Relations School. Organizations are made up of people (staff and volunteers, including board members) with their own visions, needs, values and views. Third Sector organizations, in particular, exist to serve human needs (not the reverse). How the staff and volunteers within Third Sector organizations view work, the organization and the future are crucial to the strategic development of the organization.

Different approaches to management and effectiveness are influenced by different perspectives on human motivation, which according to Steers and Porter (1983) is the force that energizes (causes people to act), directs behaviour towards specific goals and sustains behaviour until goals are achieved.

MCGREGOR'S THEORY X AND Y

McGregor (1960) described the various mechanistic instrumental theories of human behaviour, including Skinner's, collectively as Theory X. In contrast he argued (along with Maslow 1970, who developed the concept of a hierarchy of needs – see pp. 265–6) that as organizations provide for the physiological and safety needs of their employees, the employees will seek to satisfy higher needs. However, if no opportunity is provided to satisfy these higher needs then the employees are likely to act in ways consistent with Theory X. He proposed an alternative theory of human behaviour (Theory Y) which assumes that:

■ physical and mental effort at work is as natural as rest or play;

■ the threat of punishment and controls are not the only ways of achieving the goals of the organization;

■ people do exercise self-control and self-direction if they are committed to these goals;

■ the average human being is willing to seek out and take responsibility under certain circumstances;

■ many people are capable of exercising a lot of imagination, ingenuity and creativity in solving the problems of the organization;

■ the way things are traditionally organized (based on Theory X), the average human being's brainpower is only partly used.

HERTZBERG'S MOTIVATORS AND HYGIENE FACTORS

Hertzberg (1968) developed a two-factor theory based on his research with groups of engineers and accountants. He argued that the factors which create job satisfaction are different from those that create dissatisfaction. The 'motivators' which create satisfaction tend to be factors such as achievement, recognition, responsibility, opportunity for advancement, and interesting work. The factors which create dissatisfaction, or 'hygiene factors', tend to be pay, working conditions, type of supervision, relationships with co-workers, and company policies. This theory suggests that if companies want to increase the motivation of workers, they need to tackle, and measure the satisfaction with, the softer needs issues such as making the work interesting, giving recognition and a sense of achievement. This approach has resulted in the development of many programmes to enrich jobs and undertake regular staff audits to assess satisfaction with both the motivation and hygiene factors.

Hertzberg's motivators and hygiene factors, however, have not found universal support in subsequent research (Schneider and Locke 1971). Dunnette *et al.* (1967) have suggested that it is only applicable to white-collar workers. A large-scale Global Strategic Rewards Survey 2007/8 involving over 13,000 employees, found that 31 per cent of employees put base pay in their top three factors that attract them to a job, and 33 per cent put it in the top three factors that retain them in a job. However, the nature of the work was more important in attracting them to a job than base pay.

Interestingly, for the Third Sector, Kohjasten (1993) looked at motivation in the private and public sectors using Hertzberg's model. He confirmed the importance of work achievements in the public sector as a motivator, but found that pay and job security were also motivators, not just hygiene factors, in the private sector. This would suggest that a sense of work achievement is also likely to be an important motivator in the Third Sector. This is confirmed by a research study comparing the meaning of work to employees in the private sector and Third Sectors in Ireland. This research found that, compared with those in the private sector, employees of Third Sector organizations:

- indicate a higher work centrality in their lives;
- identify more with the company/organization and the product/service;
- value more the society-serving aspect of their work;
- seek interesting work, learning new things, good interpersonal relations, a match between job and skills, autonomy of work, variety in work, and convenient working hours.

This study indicates a greater importance of the human resource perspective on motivation in the Third Sector than the private sector. Other researchers (Benz 2005; Devaro and Brookshire 2007) found that employees of Third Sector organizations experience higher job satisfaction and are more intrinsically motivated than their private sector counterparts.

MASLOW'S HIERARCHY OF NEEDS

Maslow's hierarchy of needs suggests that when lower order needs, such as physiological and safety needs, are met, the individual seeks fulfilment of higher order needs, such as love and esteem, cognitive needs and, ultimately, self-actualization (see Figure 14.1).

While appealing in theory, particularly to the Third Sector, which sees its key role as responding to human needs, Maslow's hierarchy has found little support in subsequent research (Rauschenberger *et al.* 1980; Miner 1984). Others have argued that the concept of need is too vague to be measured and ignores the crucial impact of environmental influences (Salancik and Pfeffer 1977). Maslow's hierarchy of needs has, however, been influential in the Third Sector particularly in relation the beneficiaries of care services. One organization, working with people who are homeless, even incorporated it into their value statement (Courtney 1992).

Fig 14.1   Maslow's hierarchy of needs
Source: Maslow (1943; 1987).

Alderfer (1972) developed a variation of Maslow's theory which proposes three types of needs:

■   Existence needs, similar to Maslow's physiological and safety needs;

■   Relatedness needs, which are met through social interaction, a key feature of Mayo's work;

■   Growth needs, to enable the individual to develop and achieve his or her potential.

Unlike Maslow, this ERG theory does not presume that the three types of needs are in a hierarchy. He suggests that we aspire to all three, and that failure to achieve one can be compensated by progress in another area. There has been little academic research into the evidence for or against this theory.

Clearly an organization that operates according to McGregor's Theory Y, Maslow's hierarchy of needs or Alderfer's ERG needs will tend towards a much broader power base – what Leavitt (1963) has called 'power equalization' – and will value the participation of employees in organizational decision-making (Schein 1988) and strategic management processes. It is this power equalization and desire for participation, which is common in many Third Sector organizations, that many managers who move from the private sector to the Third Sector find so difficult (Leat 1995). However, the research evidence (see pp. 24–5) in relation to strategic planning suggests that such power equalization is by no means universal in the Third Sector.

MCCLELLAND'S ACHIEVEMENT, POWER AND AFFILIATION THEORY

McClelland (1961) suggests that people tend to be motivated by different things. Some people are motivated more by a need for achievement, others by a need for power, and others by a need for affiliation. His theory emphasizes the importance of understanding the particular motivation of each individual, rather than trying to apply a blanket solution to problems of motivation. Robert Ardrey (1970), a paleoanthropologist, after studying animal behaviour, selected identity, security and stimulation as his three key needs that have to be satisfied in one way or the other.

ADAMS'S CONCEPT OF SOCIAL EXCHANGE

Adams (1965) developed the social psychology concept of social exchange to develop an equity theory of motivation in the workplace, whereby workers weigh up what it costs (what they have to give, materially and psychologically, to work in a particular job) and what they get out of it. These factors may be actual objective factors, such as hours and pay, or they may be factors where self-perception is more important, such as status. Dissatisfaction arises, according to the equity theory, when workers perceive that the balance between benefits and costs is inequitable. This may occur, not just as a result of a change in their own position, but as a result of what is perceived as better treatment of another group of workers, e.g. when others are promoted or given a pay rise. His, and other research (Martin and Peterson 1987; Perry 1993; Van Wijck 1994), indicates that when employees perceive the benefits they receive to be unfair, compared with those of other staff, they are likely to change their behaviour to create greater equity, such as reducing the amount or quality of work they do, seeking a salary rise or leaving. This may help to suggest why the research on performance-related pay (PRP), except in narrowly defined situations, rarely shows a clear positive link between PRP and performance, as the comparisons with other staff, which are used to assess performance in PRP schemes, are often perceived by the participants to be unfair.

VROOM'S EXPECTATION THEORY

Vroom (1964) argued that motivation is complex and highly subjective and depends significantly on what we expect. He used the three concepts of:

- Valence: how much the outcome of work is worth to the individual;
- Expectancy: how much work is required to complete the job;
- Instrumentality: the expectation of what will be the result of carrying out the work.

Van Eerde and Thierry (1996) found some general evidence in support of the VEI theory. Mastrofski *et al.* (1994) found the concepts of the theory consistent with their work with police officers related to arrest productivity. Thompson and McHugh (2002) found difficulties in the measurement of the concept and questioned the extent that people make rational cognitive decisions when making choices. They also criticized the lack of attention to the context in which the decisions are made.

SCHEIN'S PSYCHOLOGICAL CONTRACT

In concluding a discussion of motivation, Schein (1988) underlined 'the importance of the psychological contract'. He argued that whether people work effectively depends significantly on 'the degree to which their own expectations of what the organisation will provide to them and what they owe the organisation in return matches what the organisation's expectations are of what it will give and get in return' (ibid.: 99). The nature of what is actually exchanged tends to include:

- money in exchange for time at work;
- social need satisfaction and security in exchange for hard work and loyalty;
- opportunities for self-actualization and challenging work in exchange for high productivity, high quality work and creative effort in the service of organizational goals.

Schein further stressed that the psychological contract is constantly renegotiated throughout the organizational career, as both the organization's and the individual's needs change. This can make the change process particularly difficult. A developing Third Sector organization, for example, that has had largely the same group of staff for a number of years, may have developed a particular unwritten psychological contract with staff, which may include the idea that the staff have a job for life with the organization, if they want it. The loss of a major contract or funding source, for example, and the need to make even one member of staff redundant, can change the psychological contract, which may have a strong effect on all staff, not just on those being made redundant, because the contract between the organization and the staff is being broken.

LOCKE'S GOAL-SETTING THEORY

The goal-setting theory developed by Locke (1968) supports the active participation of staff (and volunteers) in strategic planning and objective setting. Research in relation to this theory has shown considerable support for Locke's theory that workers will achieve more if:

- they have clear challenging goals to achieve;
- they are involved in setting the goals themselves;
- are provided with feedback on progress en route to the goal (Locke *et al.* 1981; Erez and Arad 1986; Handy 1988).

These findings support the inclusive strategic planning processes that involve staff and volunteers, as well as the board, in developing clear shared plans for an organization and providing regular progress reports (see pp. 256–7). Argyris (1964) argues that when employees in an organization aren't given the opportunity to participate in defining their goals they become passive and dependent, experiencing 'psychological failure' and operating more in accordance with McGregor's Theory X.

HACKMAN'S JOB FACTORS THEORY

Hackman and his colleagues (Hackman and Lawler 1971; Hackman and Oldham 1975, 1979) developed a more complex and refined model which shows the core job conditions that lead to critical psychological states and produce desirable outcomes. The core job dimensions, they suggest, are:

- skill variety: the degree that the job requires the performance of activities that challenge a variety of skills and abilities;
- task identity: the degree to which a job requires completion of a whole and identifiable piece of work;
- task significance: the degree to which the job has a substantial and perceived impact on the lives of other people, which may be one of the key reasons that motivation levels of those in Third Sector organizations tend to be higher than those found in other sectors;
- autonomy: the degree to which the job gives the worker freedom, independence and discretion in scheduling work and in determining how it will be carried out;
- feedback: the degree to which the worker gets information about the effectiveness of his or her efforts.

This model suggests that these five job factors can create the situation where the employees experience the meaningfulness of work, responsibility for outcomes and knowledge of the actual results of work activities. This can then in turn create high internal work motivation, high quality work performance, high satisfaction with work and low absenteeism and turnover. However, the success of the model also depends on the employees having the appropriate skills, being happy with the basic organizational context (the hygiene factors) and being motivated by challenge and growth.

KATZ'S TIME–IN–JOB THEORY

Katz (1978) suggests that different factors will be important at different points in time. In the first six months in a job, task significance and feedback are important; from six months to five years, all the factors are important; after five years, pay and working conditions may become more important.

GROUP DYNAMICS

Research on group dynamics, which started in the 1940s and reached a peak in the 1960s, has indicated that increased involvement and participation are desired by most people and have the ability to energize greater performance, produce better solutions to problems and greatly enhance acceptance of decisions. It was found that such group dynamics worked to:

- overcome resistance to change;
- increase commitment to the organization;
- reduce stress levels;
- make people, generally, feel better about themselves and their worlds (McGrath 1984).

However, Janis (1972), analysing the US Government's response to the Cuban Bay of Pigs situation in the early 1960s, has shown that, particularly in a group with a dominant leader, there is a danger of a group descending into 'group think' where alternative perspectives on a problem are not voiced and poor decision-making can result. Groups can also reinforce deviant subcultures, such as working too hard as unacceptable to the group members, so ensuring that in order to be accepted new group members have to reduce their work rate to a similar level to the other members.

LAWLER'S DETERMINATES OF ORGANIZATIONAL EFFECTIVENESS

Lawler (1986) links research into the needs and expectations of individual employees with the need for organizational effectiveness. He argues from a human relations perspective that there are five major determinates of organizational effectiveness: motivation, satisfaction, acceptance of change, problem solving and communication, and that all of these can be positively affected by increasing the participation of the employees. Lawler also argues that increased participation reduces the resistance to change which so often undermines an organization's efforts to implement strategic plans.

Various studies have shown that increased participation at work leads to significant improvements in both morale and productivity at the same time (for a review of the literature see Blumberg 1968; Katzell and Yankelovich 1975). Increased participation may also lead to demands for other changes in the organization.

MOTIVATING THIRD SECTOR EMPLOYEES

Schepers *et al.* (2005) found that the motivation theories of Hertzberg, Hackman and Vroom were equally relevant to the Third Sector. They found that Third Sector employees were more likely, than their private sector counterparts, to be motivated by:

- altruism;
- personal growth;
- social contacts;

- working with and for people;
- opportunities to learn;
- intrinsic rewards.

Other studies have found worker satisfaction in Third Sector organizations to be high, even in the presence of low wage levels (Mirvis 1992; Benz 2005). Third Sector employees tend to be more satisfied, committed, loyal and driven by intrinsic as opposed to extrinsic factors compared to their counterparts in private sector companies (Borzaga and Tortia 2006). However, the view that money is the primary motivator in relation to work performance is a very powerful one. Many organizations believe that PRP, including many business people who sit on the boards of Third Sector organizations, is the most effective way of motivating employees. However, the research evidence does not, generally, support the enthusiasm for PRP. Thompson (1993) found that employees do not believe that PRP motivates them and that it can be demotivating for some staff. Marsden and French (1998) found particular problems with using PRP in relation to public services. Kohn (1993, 1998) expresses a more fundamental objection to PRP, which is particularly relevant in the Third Sector, arguing that extrinsic rewards, at best, only secure temporary compliance, but actually undermine the intrinsic motivators that lead to long-term performance. The fundamental assumption that you should work harder because you will get a reward undermines the whole basis of the Third Sector, which assumes a fundamental commitment to work hard to improve the lives of our fellow citizens. With PRP systems, this intrinsic commitment can be 'crowded out' (Theuvsen 2004). This argument is supported by a study (Deckop and Cirka 2000) of the implementation of a PRP scheme in a Third Sector organization, which resulted in a reduction in the intrinsic motivation of the staff, who were previously highly motivated. Behaviour can shift as a result of PRP schemes, but often towards the measurable aspects of the job and away from some other important, but less measurable, aspects. The sense of injustice when the scheme is perceived to be applied unfairly also reduces the staff's intrinsic motivation.

It may be that PRP is effective in certain very defined situations, such as cold selling, where:

- the objectives to be achieved are clear and measurable;
- the tasks to achieve the objectives are not fulfilling in themselves;
- that the objectives are achievable;
- that everyone has a fair chance of achieving the objectives;
- employees believe that extra effort will result in improved performance;
- that good performance will be recognized and rewarded fairly, without favouritism;
- that the reward on offer is sufficient to justify the extra effort.

Brown and Yoshioka (2003) argue that attachment to the specific mission of an organization is important in attracting individuals to work for a Third Sector organization, but that pay is important in being able to retain the member of staff.

STRATEGIC PLANNING AND PARTICIPATION

The early theories of strategic planning in the design and planning schools tended to emphasize the importance of a top-down traditional command and control management approach and in particular the role of the CEO in the planning process (see Chapter 3). As planning processes became more sophisticated, the increasing tendency in companies became to employ expert planners to forecast the future and lead the process of setting strategy.

Mintzberg (1994), however, is particularly scathing about the detachment of planners from the operations of the company. He argues that it is precisely the 'soft' information that comes from a day-to-day hands-on involvement in the operational aspects of a company that is crucial to making strategic decisions. Mintzberg's emphasis on learning and visionary approaches to creating strategy requires the active involvement of managers who are crucial 'nerve centres' of information. He argues that managers must take active charge of the strategy making process. In doing so, they must make use of their tacit knowledge; their intuitive processes must be allowed liberal rein; and they must have intimate contact (not detachment from) the organization's operations.

Bass (1970), in a series of experiments, showed that people were more productive and more satisfied when they operated their own plans instead of other people's. He suggested various reasons for this:

- productivity and satisfaction are lower when planning for others because the sense of accomplishment is less when executing someone else's plan;
- there is less tendency to try to confirm the validity of another's plan by executing it successfully – less confidence that it can be done;
- there is less commitment to see that the plan works well;
- there is less flexibility and less room for modification and initiative to make improvements in an assigned plan;
- there is less understanding of an assigned plan;
- human resources are not so well utilized;
- there are more communication problems and consequent errors and distortions in following instructions;
- there are competitive feelings aroused between planners and doers to such an extent that it appears that if the former 'win' the latter 'lose'.

Basinger and Peterson (2008) have demonstrated, in a case study, the development of entirely different attitudes to change of the in-group and out-group, depending on the extent that the stakeholders were allowed to participate in the decisions about a key strategic change (a merger in this case).

For all these reasons, many of the recent texts on strategic planning and strategic management emphasize the value of wide participation in the processes of strategic analysis, formation and choice, in order to both improve the quality of the strategic decisions and improve the likelihood that plans will be implemented effectively.

This emphasis on wide participation, providing clear goals which clarify the positive impact that the work has on people, and on regular feedback, is particularly evident in the literature on planning and management in the Third Sector and emphasizes the need to establish strategic management processes that actively involve the board, managers, staff, volunteers and other stakeholders, if they are to be committed to making any plan into a reality.

Grewe *et al.* (1989) promote a participative approach to planning, which they argue has benefits for the participants which are as important as the contents of the plan, because it promotes a common vision of the future and its implications for the organization, including any necessary changes, more effective group problem solving skills and recognition that continuous planning is a management necessity. Hudson (1995) argues that participation and communication mechanisms are particularly important in Third Sector organizations, because those who believe in a cause usually want to take part in decision-making and also want to know what other parts of the organization are doing.

The human relations movement has played an important role in the development of particular methodologies for engaging large numbers of people together in order to engage whole systems in creating rapid change (Bunker and Alban 1997). Some of these – Search Conference (Emery and Purser 1996) and Future Search (Weisbrod and Janoff 1995) – have been used frequently as community planning and development tools as well as for organizational development. The ICA Strategic Planning Process, in particular, has been used extensively in the USA and Canada as a community development technique to involve large numbers of people in the community in a change process. It involves six key steps (Spencer 1989):

1. focus on the key issue, question or problem;
2. map out a clear practical vision;
3. analyse the obstacles to achieving the vision;
4. set the strategic directions (brainstorm for overcoming obstacles);
5. design the systematic actions/strategies to achieve the vision;
6. draw up an agreed-upon time line for implementation.

Letts *et al.* (1998) in *High Performance Nonprofit Organisations: Managing Upstream for Greater Impact* argue that investing in the development of the internal capacity of Third Sector organizations and not just in specific programmes is crucial to their success. In particular, they argue that investing strategically in human resource management is particularly important.

Participation in decision-making can also have other significant consequences. Webster and Wylie (1988) and Courtney (2005), from their research on the use of strategic planning techniques in the Third Sector, suggest that widening the level of consultation can also have another kind of impact. In particular they show that the wider the level of participation the less likely it is that there will be a 'major change outcome', as the process is likely to produce a compromise solution which is acceptable to all the participants.

RESOURCE–BASED THEORIES OF STRATEGY

There is, however, an even more fundamental perspective on the role of human (and other) resources in relation to strategy. Resource-based theories of strategy start from the perspective that the resources of an organization are the principal source of competitive advantage (Wernerfelt 1984; Dierickx and Cool 1989; Peteraf 1993; Kay 1994). Strategy should therefore start with a consideration of the distinctive resources of the organization, rather than the conventional view that resources should only be considered in assessing the organization's ability to implement the desired strategy.

The resource-based view distinguishes between those resources which are readily available to all organizations and those that are distinct or unique to the particular organization, which therefore should be carefully analysed and nurtured. Various criteria have been suggested for determining that a particular resource provides competitive advantage:

- it already exists in the organization;
- it provides innovative capability;
- it proves a real advantage over other organizations;
- it is difficult to substitute for or imitate;
- the advantage will accrue to the organization;
- the resource has durability.

John Kay (1994) suggests that distinctive capabilities relate particularly to three resource areas:

- innovation capability;
- reputation, particularly for quality;
- architecture: internal within the organization, externally with suppliers and/or clients/customers, and in the sense of networks between organizations.

Hamel and Prahalad (1994) argue that three areas distinguish what they call core competencies:

- they must make a real impact on how the customer perceives the organization and its services (or products);
- they must be unique or at least really special;
- they need to be able to be extended to new services (or products).

More recently, the importance of knowledge to organizations has come to the fore as critical to the success of an organization. This knowledge may be in a patent, licence or the particular practices of an organization, but it also may reside in the people in the organization. This is likely to be true in many Third Sector organizations where much of the knowledge is not routinized but resides in the heads of the trustees, staff and/or volunteers. This is also a danger, as the individuals with the knowledge in their heads may leave and take it with them. The organization needs to ensure that the distinctive knowledge that exists is retained and nurtured.

The significance of the resource-based approach for the strategic management of organizations, particularly Third Sector organizations, is that the human resource requirements don't necessarily simply follow the determination of organizational strategy (Chandler's 'structure follows strategy'), but that the people and their distinctive competencies within the organization are a vital asset to the organization, which should provide important clues to where it is likely to be most effective in future and therefore its strategic direction.

MOTIVATING VOLUNTEERS

Much of the research and theoretical models discussed above apply equally to the Third Sector as to other sectors. One of the distinctive aspects of the Third Sector, however, is the involvement of volunteers where there is no material reward for the work contribution to the organization: it is gift-work.

Mitchell and Yates (1996) suggest that volunteers are motivated by five factors: intrinsic values; personal recognition and realization; social interaction; sense of debt or obligation; and altruism. Clary *et al.* (1996) suggested six categories of motivations or psychological functions that may be met by volunteering; and a study in the US confirmed these categories and suggested the following order of importance:

- values function: people may volunteer to express or act on values important to self (e.g. altruism);
- enhancing function: volunteering may allow people to engage in psychological development and enhance their self-esteem;
- understanding function: people may volunteer as they see it as an opportunity to increase their knowledge of the world and develop and practise particular skills;
- social function: volunteering may help people 'fit in' and get along with social groups they value;
- career function: people may volunteer to gain experiences that will benefit their careers;
- protective function: volunteering may help people to cope with inner anxieties and conflicts.

An Australian study (ABS 1996) found the following reasons for individuals deciding to become a volunteer (in order of frequency):

- help others/community;
- personal/family involvement;
- personal satisfaction;
- to do something worthwhile;
- social contact;
- felt obliged/just happened;

- use skills/experience;
- to be active;
- religious beliefs;
- other;
- to learn new skills/gain work experience/reference.

In the UK, the reasons that people give as to why they volunteer (Cabinet Office 2007) include the following (in order of frequency):

- I want to make things better: help people;
- the cause was important to me;
- I had time to spare;
- I wanted to meet people, make friends;
- connected to family/friends' interests;
- there was a need in the community;
- use existing skills;
- part of my philosophy of life;
- friends/family do it;
- learn new skills;
- part of my religious belief;
- no one else to do it;
- help get on in my career;
- had received voluntary help myself;
- get a recognized qualification;
- already involved with the organization;
- connected with my interests/hobbies;
- give something back.

These reasons fall into a number of different overlapping categories:

- personal altruistic philosophy (values function): part of my philosophy of life, part of my religious belief, I want to make things better (help people), there was a need in the community;
- personal development (career and understanding functions): learn new skills, help get on in my career, get a recognized qualification, use existing skills;
- link to the cause/interests/organization: the cause was important to me, connected to family/friends' interests, already involved with the organization, connected with my interests/hobbies;
- reciprocity: had received voluntary help myself, give something back;
- social connection (social function): I wanted to meet people, make friends;
- influenced by others volunteering: friends/family do it;
- other: I had time to spare, no one else to do it.

It may be that in such a survey some people may be unwilling to acknowledge some aspects of their motivations which are seen as selfish, e.g. protective, understanding, career and social functions.

The UK research also cross-referenced the motivations to volunteer with both the type of volunteering role and the type of volunteer, which showed that different kinds of people volunteer for different reasons and that engaging in a particular type of volunteering role (e.g. joining a committee vs becoming a youth football coach) may be for very different reasons and may occur at different ages.

Crutchfield and Grant (2008) in their study of successful US Third Sector Organizations (including Habitat for Humanity – see case study in Part VI) argue that successful organizations are particularly good at motivating people to volunteer, especially motivating outsiders to become evangelists for the organization. They suggest there are four rules of engagement:

- *Communicate your mission, vision and values*: start by communicating your values, building a strong culture and creating emotional 'hooks' to engage and inspire others around the values.

- *Create meaningful experiences*: give volunteers meaningful experiences that align with the mission of the organization. Involve them in more than just volunteering or giving a donation. Have them experience your work in person.

- *Cultivate evangelists*: convert volunteers into evangelists who will spread the word amongst their own networks. Cultivate high-powered super-evangelists whose values and interests align with the organization's and who can help to create organizational momentum.

- *Build a beloved community*: once you have built a larger community, cultivate it over time by providing ways for members to connect through conferences, communication tools, technology and special member programmes.

In a study of volunteers who stopped volunteering for a centre which helped victims of sexual assault and domestic violence, it was found that they didn't just drop out because their motivation waned. It was found that they dropped out to preserve their own positive self-feeling, when there was a gap between the actual volunteer experience and the experience they thought they would have, resulting in feelings of anger and disappointment.

Instead of looking at the reasons for volunteering amongst current or recent volunteers, a US study (Sundeen *et al.* 2007) explored the barriers to volunteering amongst non-volunteers. They identified three common barriers:

- lack of time;
- lack of interest;
- ill health.

SUMMARY

This chapter has explored organizations and strategy from a human relations perspective, which coincides with the culture of many Third Sector organizations. This perspective emphasizes the positive role of people in an organization. Research which demonstrates the positive effect of participation and consultation on job performance and satisfaction has been highlighted, suggesting that more participative approaches to strategic management are also likely to be effective. The resource-based view of strategy has also been discussed which suggests that the distinctive or core competences in an organization, many of which reside in the heads and hearts of the trustees, staff and volunteers, are crucially important in determining the most appropriate future strategy of an organization.

QUESTIONS

1. What do you think are the most important factors in getting people to work hard?
2. What are the key factors that motivate staff in Third Sector organizations? Is it different from other sectors?
3. Do comparatively poor salaries and working conditions matter in the Third Sector? Why?
4. To what extent does work motivation change the longer you are in a job?
5. Should there be performance-related pay in Third Sector organizations? Why?
6. In what way do theories of human motivation affect thinking about strategic management processes?
7. What non-financial rewards might an organization consider in order to motivate staff?
8. Are there limitations, or potentially negative consequences to, the involvement of staff and volunteers in the strategic management of Third Sector organizations?
9. List the distinctive or core competencies/capabilities/resources of a Third Sector organization you know.

DISCUSSION TOPIC

Are the motivations of volunteers different from that of paid staff in Third Sector organizations?

SUGGESTED READING

Sheila Hayward (1996) *Applying Psychology to Organizations*, Hodder & Stoughton.

Lisa Matthewman, Amanda Rose and Angela Hetherington (2009) *Work Psychology*, Oxford University Press.

Edgar Schein (1988) *Organizational Psychology*, 3rd edn, Prentice-Hall.

Peter Warr (ed.) (1996) *Psychology at Work*, Penguin.

15 LEAD OR MANAGE?

OVERVIEW

In the previous chapter, different approaches to understanding the motivation of staff and volunteers ('followers' in leadership jargon), which is critical in actually implementing an organization's strategy, were explored. The other side of the coin is the leadership and management in Third Sector organizations and its ability to motivate staff. In this chapter, therefore, the focus will be on the leadership and management required to drive strategic development and change in an organization.

LEARNING OBJECTIVES

After studying this chapter, you should be able to:

- describe the roles of a manager;
- articulate the suggested differences between management and leadership;
- identify different types of leadership;
- describe a contingency-based approach to leadership and management;
- understand the need for a toolbox of management and leadership skills.

The literature on leadership and management is huge. It is easy for practising managers to get swamped and thoroughly confused by the number of competing theories available.

MANAGEMENT

The verb 'manage' comes from the Italian *maneggiare* (to handle, especially tools), which in turn derives from the Latin *manus* (hand). The French word *mesnagement* (later *ménagement*) influenced the development in meaning of the English word 'management' in the seventeenth and eighteenth centuries.

Chapter 3 concerned the development of strategic management and the early work on the concept of a scientific approach to the study of organizations in general and the role of the manager in particular. In the early part of the twentieth century, Fayol (1916) articulated five functions of management:

- planning;

- organizing;
- command;
- coordination;
- control.

Forecasting was later added to this list.

In contrast, Mary Parker Follett (1868–1933), who wrote on the topic in the early twentieth century, defined management as 'the art of getting things done through people'. She described management as a philosophy.

The traditional command and control approaches developed in the late nineteenth and early twentieth century have had an enduring influence on how management has been perceived throughout the following century and are still particularly relevant to industries with a high level of standardization, such as international fast food companies.

The MBA (Master of Business Administration) was invented by Harvard University in 1921 and since then has developed as an important discipline in nearly all universities across the globe.

In 1973, Peter Drucker defined the work of a manager as:

- planning;
- organizing;
- integrating;
- measuring.

He was also ahead of his time in identifying the importance of 'social impacts and social responsibilities' for managers. He also unusually included four chapters addressing management in 'public-service' institutions.

Henry Mintzberg (1973), probably the world's leading writer on both management and strategy, researched the actual nature of managerial work, observing and analysing the activities of the CEOs of five private and semi-public organizations. He identified ten separate managerial roles, defined as 'an organized collection of behaviours belonging to an identifiable function or position', in three subcategories:

Interpersonal contact:

- figurehead: the manager performs ceremonial and symbolic duties as head of the organization;
- leader: fosters a proper work atmosphere and motivates and develops subordinates;
- liaison: develops and maintains a network of external contacts to gather information.

Information processing:

- monitor: gathers internal and external information relevant to the organization;
- disseminator: transmits factual and value based information to subordinates;
- spokesperson: communicates to the outside world on performance and policies.

Decision-making:

- entrepreneur: designs and initiates change in the organization;

- disturbance handler: deals with unexpected events and operational breakdowns;
- resource allocator: controls and authorizes the use of organizational resources;
- negotiator: participates in negotiation activities with other organizations and individuals.

Mintzberg analysed individual manager's involvement in these ten roles and identified four clusters of independent variables: external, function related, individual and situational. He concluded that eight role combinations were 'natural' configurations of the job:

- contact manager: figurehead and liaison;
- political manager: spokesperson and negotiator;
- entrepreneur: entrepreneur and negotiator;
- insider: resource allocator;
- real-time manager: disturbance handler;
- team manager: leader;
- expert manager: monitor and spokesperson;
- new manager: liaison and monitor.

Mintzberg's study exposed various managerial myths, particularly the view that managers spend most of their time in high level strategic and analytical tasks, such as scanning the external environment, planning their organization's strategic direction and making major policy decisions, rather than the true picture of fallible human beings who are continuously interrupted to sort out operational issues and staff problems. Indeed, half of the formal managerial activities studied lasted less than nine minutes. Mintzberg also found that, although individual capabilities did influence the implementation of a role, it was the organization that determined the need for a particular role, addressing the common belief that it was predominantly a manager's skill set that determines success. Effective managers develop ways of working, given their job description and personal preference, and match these with the situation at hand.

MANAGEMENT CHARTER INITIATIVE

In the UK, with concern about the quality of management in British companies and other organizations in the 1980s, an attempt was made to improve management by articulating more clearly the roles and competencies required of managers at different levels in an organization and then basing accreditation on these national standards. The Management Charter Initiative (MCI) suggested that, up to and including middle management, the key work roles of managers were:

- managing people;
- managing finance;
- managing operations (which later became activities);

- managing information.

These key work roles were further broken down into units for managers at different levels. The middle management units were as follows (* indicates unit is identical for first line managers):

- Managing people: recruit and select personnel; develop teams, individuals and self to enhance performance*; plan, allocate and evaluate work carried out by the teams, individuals and self*; create, maintain and enhance effective working relationships*.

- Managing finance: monitor and control the use of resources; secure effective resource allocation for activities and projects.

- Managing operations (which later became activities): initiate and implement change and improvement in services, products and systems; monitor, maintain and improve service and product delivery.

- Managing information: seek, evaluate and organize information for action*; exchange information to solve problems and make decisions.

Each unit was further broken down into individual elements.

MCI also later developed competency standards for senior managers, which reflected the more strategic responsibilities of senior managers explored in this book, including:

- Understanding and influencing the environment: external trends, internal strengths and weaknesses; stakeholders.

- Setting the strategy and gaining commitment.

- Planning, implementing and monitoring: programmes, projects and plans; delegation and action; culture; monitoring.

- Evaluating and improving performance.

Understanding of management roles continuously develops. The National Management Standards were revised in 2004 and again in 2008 and are now known as the Management and Leadership National Occupation Standards. They are now structured under the following six headings:

- managing self and personal skills;

- providing direction;

- facilitating change;

- working with people;

- using resources;

- achieving results.

The 2008 revised standards place greater emphasis on leadership (discussed later in this chapter) and other aspects of work which have gained significance in recent years, for example in the areas of:

- customer service;

- knowledge management;

- procurement;

■ managing redundancy.

All the 2008 Management and Leadership Standards, shown in Box 15.1, do not apply to all management roles. In various cases, e.g. B5, B6, B7, there are choices to be made depending on the particular role. Each detailed unit (e.g. A2) provides:

■ A description of the skills required.

■ The outcomes of effective performance (what a person must be able to do to achieve the standard).

■ Behaviours which underpin effective performance.

■ Knowledge and understanding: general knowledge and understanding; industry/sector specific knowledge and understanding; context specific knowledge and understanding.

BOX 15.1   MANAGEMENT AND LEADERSHIP NATIONAL OCCUPATIONAL STANDARDS (2008)

A – Managing Self and Personal Skills
    A1 Manage your own resources
    A2 Manage your own resources and professional development
    A3 Develop your personal networks
B – Providing Direction
    B1 Develop and implement operational plans for your area of responsibility
    B2 Map the environment in which your organization operates
    B3 Develop a strategic business plan for your organization
    B4 Put the strategic business plan into action
    B5 Provide leadership for your team
    B6 Provide leadership in your area of responsibility
    B7 Provide leadership for your organization
    B8 Ensure compliance with legal, regulatory, ethical and social requirements
    B9 Develop the culture of your organization
    B10 Manage risk
    B11 Promote equality of opportunity and diversity in your area of responsibility
    B12 Promote equality of opportunity and diversity in your organization
C – Facilitate Change
    C1 Encourage innovation in your team
    C2 Encourage innovation in your area of responsibility
    C3 Encourage innovation in your organization
    C4 Lead change
    C5 Plan change
    C6 Implement change
D – Working with People
    D1 Develop productive working relationships with colleagues
    D2 Develop productive working relationships with colleagues and stakeholders
    D3 Recruit, select and keep colleagues
    D4 Plan the workforce
    D5 Allocate and check work in your team

▶

D6 Allocate and monitor the progress and quality of work in your area of responsibility
D7 Provide learning opportunities for colleagues
D8 Help team members address problems affecting their performance
D9 Build and manage teams
D10 Reduce and manage conflict in your team
D11 Lead meetings
D12 Participate in meetings
E – Using Resources
E1 Manage a budget
E2 Manage finance for your area of responsibility
E3 Obtain additional finance for the organization
E4 Promote the use of technology within your organization
E5 Identify, assess and control health and safety risks
E6 Ensure health and safety requirements are met in your area of responsibility
E7 Ensure an effective organizational approach to health and safety
E8 Manage physical resources
E9 Manage the environmental impact of your work
E10 Take effective decisions
E11 Communicate information and knowledge
F – Achieving Results
F1 Manage a project
F2 Manage programme of complementary projects
F3 Manage business processes
F4 Develop and implement marketing plans for your area of responsibility
F5 Resolve customer service problems
F6 Monitor and resolve customer service problems
F7 Support customer service improvements
F8 Work with others to improve customer service
F9 Build your organization's understanding of its market and customers
F10 Develop a customer focused organization
F11 Manage the achievement of customer satisfaction
F12 Improve organizational performance
(Management Standards Centre (MSC) available for download from www.management-standards.org/standards/full-list-2008-national-occupational-standards)

Minor amendments have also been made to a significant number of units to take account of the various issues that have become increasingly important since 2004 due to changes in government legislation, cultural and environmental development, and technological advances:

■ ageism;

■ cultural awareness;

■ diversity and inclusion;

■ EU impact and regulations;

■ globalization;

■ international benchmarking;

- managing diverse teams;
- managing growth;
- managing remote teams;
- managing without power;
- managing your boss;
- matrix management;
- sustainability.

Mintzberg (2009), in his follow-up to his seminal 1974 research, has expressed disappointment at the lack of recent proper empirical research into management and what managers actually do.

In 2009, Owen argued that management has got harder and more ambiguous and now requires three kinds of skill sets:

- intelligence quotient: rational management, of the kind that has been discussed in this chapter so far;
- emotional quotient: emotional management;
- political quotient: political management.

Each of these, according to Owen, requires specific skills:

IQ – rational management:

- starting at the end: focusing on outcomes;
- achieving results;
- making decisions;
- solving problems;
- strategic thinking;
- financial skills, including managing costs;
- setting and managing budgets.

EQ – emotional management:

- motivating people: creating willing followers;
- influencing people;
- coaching;
- delegating;
- handling conflict;
- giving informal feedback;
- managing yourself;
- using time effectively;
- surviving the management marathon;
- learning the right behaviours (people focus, positive outlook, professional behaviour).

PQ – political management:

- Building a power base on the basis of the seven key power sources: money; information; skills; clients/customers; access – gate-keeping; permissions – the power to approve or say 'no'; scarce resources.
- Acquiring power: at the heart of the empire through building relationships, information and networks; at the outposts of the empire, where there may be more scope for initiative.
- Taking control: telling stories (vision: where we are going, how we are going to get there, and how you can help) and setting your agenda.
- The art of 'unreasonable' management: the ability to be firm, even ruthless, if required, without being unpleasant.
- Building power networks: becoming indispensable.
- Managing people and change.
- Political games: balance morality and survival.

Mintzberg (2009) would endorse the inclusion of the soft skills (e.g. Owen's EQ and PQ) as being clearly part of the discipline of management. Other writers (Zaleznik 1993; Kotter 1990), however, make a clear distinction between management and leadership.

MANAGEMENT VS LEADERSHIP

According to this view, management is concerned primarily with planning, organizing and controlling the use of organizational resources to achieve the agreed goals. Management promotes stability, efficiency and effectiveness. It ensures the organization runs smoothly and reduces risk and solves problems. It includes all Owen's rational management skills.

Table 15.1 Suggested differences between management and leadership

Management	Leadership
Promotes stability	Promotes change
Reduces risk	Takes calculated risks
Thinks short and medium term	Thinks long term
Solves problems to achieve goals	Promotes an inspiring vision and motivates people to buy into it
Manages existing services efficiently	Inspires excellence and continuous improvement in service provision and identifies new opportunities
Sets objectives for staff and provides supervision	Inspires and motivates staff to see the bigger picture and a greater commitment
Ensuring compliance	Creating passion and commitment
Keeps external stakeholders informed	Motivates and inspires trust and confidence in external stakeholders so they become champions
Promotes the organization	Influences others to champion the cause

On the other hand, leadership is often considered to provide passion, integrity, vision, determination, inspiration, innovation and calculated risk-taking. It requires political nous (Owen's PQ). It creates long-term opportunities. It motivates people and the organization to greatness (Jim Collins's (2006) level 5 leadership). It provides a role model that lifts everyone's vision of what is possible.

According to this view, in short, management is from the head, leadership from the heart. Table 15.1 highlights some of the suggested differences between management and leadership.

LEADERSHIP

Although there is no common agreed definition of leadership, there is probably agreement (Northouse 2001) that leadership involves several key themes:

- leadership is a process;
- it involves influencing others;
- it takes place within a group context;
- it involves achieving, or aiming to achieve, goals.

Leadership can be defined as the ability to use interpersonal influence, rather than formal authority, for the purposes of achieving organizational goals. 'True leadership only exists if people follow when they have the freedom not to' (Collins 2006: 13).

Kotter (1988: 25) defines leadership as 'a process of creating a vision for others and having the power to translate this vision into a reality and then to sustain it'. More recent thinking about leadership emphasizes the roles of followers as well as that of leaders. On this basis, Rollinson (2002: 351) defines leadership as 'a process in which a leader and followers interact in a way that enables the leader to influence the actions of followers in a non-coercive way towards the achievement of certain aims or objectives'.

Leadership is often described as something that is only exercised by people at the top of an organization. However, in the last 20 years, writers and researchers have become conscious of the fact that leadership can be either formal (position of authority) and/or informal (skills and/or experience). In this perspective, everyone can develop and use leadership skills regardless of their role.

LEADERSHIP THEORY

Early thinking on leadership emphasized the distinctive characteristics of great leaders (the 'trait theory' of leadership, also known as the 'great man' approach), such as Alexander the Great, Julius Ceasar, Abraham Lincoln and Winston Churchill. Early philosophical writings such as Plato's *Republic* and Plutarch's *Lives* explored the question: What qualities distinguish an individual as a leader? Underlying this search was the early recognition of the importance of leadership and the assumption that it is rooted in the characteristics that certain individuals possess.

In the nineteenth century, Carlyle (1841) in *Heroes and Hero Worship* tried to identify the talents, skills and physical characteristics of men who rose to power. Francis Galton (1869) in his *Hereditary Genius* examined leadership qualities in the families of powerful men. After showing that the numbers of eminent relatives dropped off the more distant the relative, genetically speaking, he concluded that leadership was inherited, i.e. leaders are born, not made. Both of these works lent great initial support to the notion that leadership is rooted in characteristics of the leader. For decades, this trait-based perspective dominated empirical and theoretical work in leadership. Using early research techniques, researchers conducted over a hundred studies proposing a number of characteristics that distinguished leaders from non-leaders, including intelligence, dominance, adaptability, persistence, integrity, socioeconomic status and self-confidence.

In trait theory there are 'charismatic' approaches which examine charismatic leaders 'who by force of their personalities are capable of having a profound and extraordinary effect on followers' (House and Baetz 1979; Conger and Kanungo 1988).

Charisma has also been defined as 'the ability to exercise diffuse and intensive influence over the normative or ideological orientations of others' (Etzioni 1961: 203). Lewis (2003) suggests that there is a preponderance of dominant charismatic leaders in the Third Sector, where they serve as role models. House and Baetz (1979) identified charismatic leaders by their effect on their followers such that the followers of charismatic leaders:

- have a high degree of loyalty, commitment and devotion to the leader;
- identify with the leader and the mission of the leader;
- emulate his or her values, goals and behaviour;
- see the leader as a source of inspiration;
- derive a sense of high self-esteem from their relationship with the leader and his or her mission;
- have an exceptionally high degree of trust in the leader and the correctness of his or her beliefs.

Jay Conger and Rabindra Kanungo (1988) developed a four-stage charismatic leadership theory, in which effective leaders:

1. develop a vision;
2. communicate the vision and motivate followers to go beyond the status quo;
3. build trust by exhibiting qualities of expertise, success, risk-taking and unconventional actions;
4. demonstrate ways of achieving the vision by empowerment, behaviour modelling, etc.

Khatri *et al.* (1999) researched managers and the staff in ten companies in Asia. They argue that part of the problem with previous research in charismatic leadership is treating vision as part of charisma (House 1977; Bass 1985; Conger and Kanungo 1987; Conger 1989). They argued that the two concepts are independent of each other. One (charisma) is concerned more with the heart and the other (vision) more with the head. They suggest that charisma has two factors: social sensitivity and persuasive personality traits;

whereas the two key factors for vision are expertise and analytical skills, and futuristic vision. In their research on the relation between these factors and the two variables of performance and follower commitment, they found the following relationships:

- Charismatic factors: social sensitivity (improves follower commitment and performance); persuasive personality traits (improves follower commitment).
- Visionary factors: expertise and analytical skills (improves performance); futuristic vision (improves performance).

Only social sensitivity increases both follower commitment and performance. The researchers also suggested that, while there may be some innate qualities, both charismatic and visionary factors can be learnt.

CRITIQUES OF TRAIT THEORIES

One of the criticisms of the trait theory of leadership is that it ignores the dark side of leadership. In 1996, Marcia Whicker coined the term, 'toxic leaders' for leaders who are 'maladjusted, malcontent, and often malevolent, even malicious' (Goldman 2010). Many of the proposed leadership traits, highlighted above, could apply equally to some of the world's most evil and destructive leaders (e.g. Hitler, Pol Pot, Stalin or the Reverend Jim Jones) as well as to those that are seen as having made a positive contribution to humankind (e.g. Gandhi, Martin Luther King or Nelson Mandela). Hogan *et al.* (1990) also found that charisma has a dark side. They argue that these failed charismatic leaders fall into three groups:

- the High Likeability Floater, who rises effortlessly in an organization because he or she never makes any enemies;
- the Homme de Ressentiment, who seethes below the surface and plots against his or her enemies;
- the Narcissist, whose energy and self-confidence and charm lead him or her up the corporate ladder.

They suggest narcissistic people often land leadership jobs, such as CEOs, because they are bold, assertive, attractive and powerful, but fail as leaders in, for example, building a company because they never admit mistakes. They suggest that it is a myth that great leaders are simply charismatic. They found that they also tend to be humble. This was also a finding of Jim Collins in his study of 'good to great' companies.

Trait theories have also been criticized for being based mainly on studies of white males, reinforcing a masculine style of leadership (see p.298).

The strongest critiques of trait theories have come from research which suggests that the kind of leadership that is required in one situation (managing a law firm) is not necessarily what is required in a different situation (commanding an army). People who are effective leaders in one context are not necessarily effective leaders in another context. In the middle of the twentieth century, reviews of leadership research studies (e.g. Stodgill 1948; Mann 1959) found that while some traits were common across a number of studies (intelligence, dominance, self-confidence, high level of energy and task-related knowledge), the overall evidence suggested that persons who are leaders in one situation may not necessarily be leaders in other situations. Churchill, for example, is thought of as a great war leader, but as a much less successful peacetime one. Subsequently, leadership may be less characterized as an enduring individual trait, and more as one subject to the requirements of the situation. This contingency approach dominated much of the leadership theory and research for the following few decades. Hosmer (1982), however, pointed out that contingency theories of leadership do not account for the success of one organization within one industry/subsector over others. Later leadership researchers (Kenny and Zaccaro 1983; Lord *et al.* 1986; Smith and Foti 1998; Tagger *et al.* 1999; Kickul and Neuman 2000; Northouse 2001; Judge *et al.* 2002; Arvey *et al.* 2006; Foti and Hauenstein 2007), however, using more sophisticated research tools, were able to show that individuals can and do emerge as leaders across a variety of situations and tasks. They also found that significant relationships do exist between leadership and such individual traits as:

- intelligence;
- adjustment;
- extraversion;
- conscientiousness;
- openness to experience;
- determination;
- general self-efficacy.

Zaccaro (2007) criticized these later trait studies for focusing on only a small set of individual attributes, such as the 'big five' personality traits, to the neglect of: cognitive abilities, motives, values, social skills, expertise and problem-solving skills; failing to consider patterns or integrations of multiple attributes; not effectively distinguishing between those leader attributes that are generally not malleable over time and those that are shaped by, and bound to, situational influences; and not considering how stable leader attributes account for the behavioural diversity necessary for effective leadership.

BEHAVIOURAL/STYLE THEORY

Behavioural theories of leadership are greatly influenced by the human relations theories of motivation (following on from Lewin *et al.* 1939), discussed in the previous chapter. They focus on what leaders do, rather than leadership traits.

Influenced by early studies in Ohio (Fleishman 1953; Fleishman *et al.* 1953) and Michigan (Shackleton and Wale, cited in Chmiel 2000), the two-factor theory of leadership was developed by Blake and Mouton (1964) to correlate the extent that a leader focuses on the people or on the task(s) (see Table 15.2).

Tannenbaum and Schmidt (1958) put the two orientations (task and people) at either end of a continuum, so that a leader can be allocated to a point on the continuum. This two-factor theory, like trait theory, still suggests there is an ideal form of leadership which combines a focus of the task and the people, i.e. team management,

Table 15.2 Blake and Mouton's Leadership Grid

High person orientation	Cosy club management		Team manage-ment
Medium person orientation		Middle-of-the-road management	
Low person orientation	Impoverished management		Task management: low staff morale
	Low task orientation	Medium task orientation	High task orientation

Source: Adapted from Blake and Mouton (1964).'

Table 15.3 Schmid's four-cell model

		Task Focus	People Focus
	Internal		
Focus			
	External		

Source: Adapted from Schmid (2006).

regardless of the situation. Schmid (2006) suggests a four-cell model (see Table 15.3). One axis reflects Blake and Mouton's orientation towards either people or the task. The other reflects the extent to which the leader's focus is internal or external. He suggests that there is no ideal leadership orientation, but that it needs to change with the context, particularly the stage in the organizational life cycle.

Likert (1967) developed a classification, breaking down leadership styles into four main types of system:

System 1: primitive authoritarian

System 2: benevolent authoritarian

System 3: consultative

System 4: participative

He argued that most companies are around 2½ on this scale, and that the research evidence supports the hypothesis that organizations using System 4 or moving closer to it are obtaining better results in terms of productivity, quality and labour relations.

Odiorne (1987) argued that management is most effective when employees are integrated into the organization, i.e. their needs are being met while fulfilling organizational goals. He views the primary goal of management, therefore, to be the creating of conditions whereby individuals can control their own work behaviours. Arguably,

Third Sector organizations, particularly those which are focused on mutual aid and membership, are more likely to operate somewhere between Systems 3 and 4.

Lewin *et al.* (1939), in a classic experiment comparing the impact of autocratic, democratic and laissez-faire leadership styles in boys' clubs, found that the democratic leadership style was preferred and produced a more positive group climate. Maier (1967) found that effective leaders are concerned with both the task to be performed and the group process and enlist the involvement of the group in the management of both.

Leadership styles, along a continuum, might be described in more detail as:

- primitive authoritarian: autocratic, coercive, telling, rewards and punishment;
- manipulative authoritarian: which appears benevolent but only to manipulate people to carry out the wishes of the leader;
- benevolent authoritarian: leader decides in the best interests of the organization and explains/sells the decision;
- consultative: consults staff for their views, but leader decides;
- participative: followers actively participate in the decision-making process;
- democratic: majority decision, chaired by the leader;
- delegate: the decision is delegated to followers;
- laissez-faire: abdicating responsibility for making decisions.

There is research evidence, highlighted in the previous chapter, that staff and volunteers are likely to be more motivated, and therefore require a more participative, democratic or delegatory style of management, if:

- they are involved setting organization, team and job goals;
- the organization's goals are perceived to be worthwhile;
- the job involves completing definable pieces of work that clearly contribute to achieving organizational goals;
- they are given the autonomy to determine how the job goals are to be achieved;
- the work gives them the chance to use and develop a range of skills;
- they get feedback on achieving the job goals.

SERVANT LEADERSHIP

At one end of the continuum can be found what has been described as 'servant leadership' and which was developed by Robert K. Greenleaf in 1970 and is attractive to many in the Third Sector, especially from a faith perspective. The servant leader serves the people he or she leads, which implies that employees are a valued end in themselves, rather than a means to an organizational purpose or bottom line.

Greenleaf did not provide a definition of 'servant leadership'. Larry C. Spears (2004), however, who has served as President and CEO of the Robert K. Greenleaf

Center for Servant Leadership since 1990, has extracted a set of ten characteristics that he considers are central to the development of a servant leader:

- *Listening*: a servant leader has the motivation to listen actively to others in the organization, including the non-verbal.

- *Empathy*: a servant leader attempts to understand and empathize with others. Workers may be considered not only as employees, but also as people who need respect and appreciation for their personal development.

- *Healing*: a claimed strength of a servant leader is the ability to heal oneself and others. A servant leader tries to help people solving their problems and conflicts in relationships. This, it is claimed, leads to the formation of an organizational culture, in which the working environment is characterized as dynamic, fun and with no fear of failure.

- *Awareness*: a servant leader should cultivate general awareness and especially self-awareness, and should have the ability to view situations from a more integrated, holistic and value-based position.

- *Persuasion*: a servant leader does not take advantage of his or her power and status by coercing compliance; but rather tries to convince others.

- *Conceptualization*: a servant leader thinks beyond day-to-day organizational realities. He or she constructs a personal vision by reflecting on the meaning of life, and derives specific goals and implementation strategies.

- *Foresight*: it is important for a servant leader to: foresee the likely outcome of a situation; learn from the past; achieve a better understanding about the current reality; and identify consequences for the future.

- *Stewardship*: CEOs, staff, volunteers and trustees have the task to hold their institution in trust for the greater good of society. Servant leadership is seen as an obligation to help and serve others. Openness and persuasion are more important than control.

- *Commitment to the growth of people*: a servant leader believes that people have an intrinsic value beyond their contributions as employees or volunteers and will, therefore, nurture their personal, professional and spiritual growth.

- *Building community*: a servant leader identifies the means to build a strong community both within his or her organization and more widely.

Spears (2004) suggests that these ten characteristics are by no mean exhaustive, nor should they be applied rigidly, but should be a guide to personal development. In short, servant leaders are supposed to devote themselves to:

- serving the needs of organization members;
- focusing on meeting the needs of those they lead;
- developing employees and volunteers to bring out the best in them;
- coaching/mentoring staff and volunteers and encouraging their self-expression;
- facilitating personal growth of all who work with them;

■ listen well to build a sense of community and joint ownership.

It is argued that servant leaders are effective because the needs of followers are so looked after that they reach their full potential, hence perform at their best (recall the research findings on social sensitivity above, which showed that it increased the commitment and performance of followers). A strength of this way of looking at leadership is that it encourages leaders to think harder about how to respect, value and motivate people reporting to them.

Mitch McCrimmond (2010) argues, however, that servant leadership has paternalistic overtones as it suggests leaders doing things for staff and volunteers rather than helping them to think for themselves. Serving people's needs, he suggests, creates the image of being slavish or subservient. In addition, leaders are also likely to be responsible for serving the needs of clients/customers and other stakeholders ahead of those of employees. Leaders also need to be tough to deal with underperformance or inappropriate behaviour, otherwise they will collude in the development of an inappropriate and ineffective organizational culture. In difficult financial times, leaders may need to have to make people redundant. He suggests that treating employees as partners is more respectful and valuing, and that it makes more sense to say simply that leaders should consider the needs of employees, and not be a servant to them. Shifting metaphors from leaders-as-autocrats to leaders-as-servants is going from one extreme to the other. Neither end of the spectrum, he suggests, is very revealing about how real organizations function in practice.

The value in the servant leadership approach may be in promoting some values that are important in getting the best out of staff and volunteers, and which are often espoused by Third Sector organizations:

■ selflessness, e.g. being willing to make sacrifices for the organization and staff and volunteers in the organization and giving other people credit;

■ appreciating the distinctive contribution that people make to the organization;

■ showing genuine concern for the lives of staff and volunteers;

■ listening to the needs and aspirations of others and responding appropriately;

■ coaching and mentoring staff and volunteers to enable them to develop;

■ role modelling positive values that you want to be reflected consistently in the culture of the organization, e.g. trust, honesty and integrity;

■ emphasizing the learning from situations rather than blame.

RESEARCH EVIDENCE

There is some research evidence that, in certain situations, an autocratic leadership style can increase productivity, but which leads to poor internal relationships. Autocratic leadership can be particularly effective in increasing productivity in situations which are highly stressful to employees. There is also some research, however, which shows that more democratic leadership can improve both productivity and internal relationships, and other research which does not find it improves task accomplishment.

ADAIR'S THREE-FACTOR MODEL

Adair (1979) suggests a model with three key leadership functions:

- concern for the task;
- concern for the individuals;
- concern for the team.

He argues that managers need to be equally concerned about all three tasks if they are to be successful.

FUNCTIONAL LEADERSHIP

Functional leadership theory, developed particularly by Hackman and his colleagues (see Hackman and Wageman 2005; Hackman and Walton 1986) and Zaccaro *et al.* (2001), is useful in addressing the specific leader behaviours expected to contribute to team or organizational effectiveness. This theory argues that the leader's main job is to ensure that whatever is necessary for a group to achieve its task(s) is done. Leaders can, therefore, be said to have done their job well when they have contributed to group effectiveness and cohesion (Hackman and Walton, 1986; Fleishman *et al.* 1991; Hackman and Wageman 2005). While functional leadership theory has most often been applied to leadership of a team (Zaccaro *et al.* 2001), it has also been effectively applied to broader organizational leadership as well (Zaccaro 2001). Research on functional leadership (Hackman and Walton 1986; Kozlowski *et al.* 1996; Zaccaro *et al.* 2001; Hackman and Wageman 2005; Morgeson 2005; Klein *et al.* 2006) has identified five broad functions a leader performs when promoting a team or organization's effectiveness. These functions include:

- environmental monitoring;
- organizing subordinate activities;
- teaching and coaching subordinates;
- motivating others;
- intervening actively in the group's work.

TRANSACTIONAL VS TRANSFORMATIONAL LEADERSHIP

Bryman (1996) has suggested that many of the traditional models of leadership are only appropriate in relatively stable periods for an organization. Various new paradigm models have been suggested to deal with handling substantial change in fast-moving turbulent environments. Burns (1978), discussing political leadership, proposed the following distinction:

- Transactional leadership: performance for reward.

■ Transformational leadership: empowering followers and making them partners in the change process. This involves inspiring people to move away from self-interest and to develop an increasing awareness of the interests of others and the overall purpose. It transforms followers to perform beyond their expectations (Bass 1985). This kind of leadership requires individualized consideration, intellectual stimulation, inspirational motivation and idealized influence – all of which engender trust and respect.

In a study of German choir conductor leadership, Rowold and Rohmann (2009) found that positive emotions are more associated with transformational leadership and negative emotions more associated with transactional leadership. Transformational leadership is associated with greater singer satisfaction, effort and effectiveness.

CONTINGENCY APPROACH

The contingency approach to leadership theory has continued to be influential. In this approach different styles of leadership are required in different situations. Therefore effective leaders need to develop a toolbox of different styles they can use in different situations. All staff (and volunteers) are different and require different approaches to motivate them, according to Fiedler (1967) and Hersey and Blanchard (1982), depending on:

■ the perceived legitimacy (power and authority) of the leader amongst followers;
■ the perceived ability of the leader amongst followers;
■ the clarity of the task;
■ the perceived legitimacy of, and commitment to, the goals/task;
■ the nature of the task and the situation;
■ the culture of decision-making in the organization;
■ the ability and experience of the followers (e.g. do they need to be told?);
■ the personalities of the followers (e.g. some people like being given clear direction, other people resent it).

It has also been argued that the readiness of followers (Hersey and Blanchard 1982) is also critical to the appropriate leadership style on two dimensions: directive behaviour and supportive behaviour. Different levels of follower readiness require one of the following four leadership approaches:

■ delegatory (low directive and low supportive leadership behaviour in situations of high follower readiness);
■ supporting/participatory (low directive and high supportive leadership behaviour in situations of moderate to high readiness);
■ coaching/selling (high directive and high supportive leadership behaviour in situations of moderate follower readiness);

- directive, i.e. telling (high directive and low supportive leadership behaviour in situations of low follower readiness).

Some Third Sector leaders/managers struggle with situations where they are required to make tough unpopular decisions for the good of the organization, because of the desire to be liked and to be seen to be supportive.

If leaders find that their leadership style is not achieving the required results in a situation, according to Fiedler, they have several choices:

- they can change their style;
- they can change the situation (e.g. they may have the power to dismiss staff who are uncooperative);
- they can leave the leadership situation.

They may also be able to access other sources of legitimate authority (e.g. the board).

PATH–GOAL THEORY

Using a contingency approach, Robert House and his colleagues (1974, 1979) argue that leadership is about the leader adjusting his or her actions to complement the situation, to compensate for what is lacking. Drawing on the Expectation Theory of Motivation, where the followers believe that their efforts will result in improved performance (expectancy) and will be rewarded (instrumentality), and they value the outcome of the work they do (valence), little leadership is required. In other situations (work context and followers), however, leaders need to adopt some combination of four leadership behaviours, i.e. paths to achieving the work goal and achieve satisfaction:

- directive;
- supportive;
- achievement-orientated;
- participative.

Kerr and Jermier (1992) developed the concept of substitutes for leadership, i.e. situations that make leadership unnecessary or neutralize it:

- Neutralizes both supportive and task-orientated leadership: low leader power or authority; leader physically separated; indifference towards organizational rewards.
- Substitutes for both supportive and task-orientated leadership: professional orientation; cohesive work group.
- Substitutes for supportive leadership: job intrinsically satisfying.
- Substitutes for task-orientated leadership: experience and ability of staff; highly structured routine tasks.

GOOD TO GREAT: LEVEL 5 LEADERSHIP

Jim Collins (2001), in his *Good to Great* study of successful American companies, outlined five levels of leadership. He found that sustainably great companies tended to have, what he calls, level 5 leadership. In his follow-up monograph (2006), applying the principles to social sector organizations, he argues that the same paradigm applies:

Level 5: Builds enduring greatness, by getting things done within a diffuse power structure, through a mixture of personal humility and professional determination.

Level 4: Effective leader: engenders a commitment to organizational vision and goals and stimulates a high standard of performance.

Level 3: Competent manager: organizes people and resources towards effective and efficient pursuit of agreed objectives.

Level 2: Contributing team member: uses capabilities to help achieve group objectives. Works effectively in a group setting.

Level 1: Highly capable individual: makes a productive contribution through knowledge, skills, talent and good work habits.

ISSUES ABOUT GENDER AND CULTURAL DIFFERENCES

Care needs to be taken when making pronouncements about appropriate leadership styles, based usually on research on certain types of workers in the USA. An understanding of cultural differences can have a profound impact on views of leadership roles, particularly around power distance and gender egalitarianism. The research evidence suggests that women managers tend to be more democratic and participative in their leadership styles (Eagly and Johnson 1990) and more team orientated (Ferrario 1994) – the Third Sector has a majority of female employees and a larger proportion of women managers than in other sectors. Bass *et al.* (1996) highlighted various studies that suggested that women tended to use clusters of behaviour associated with transformation, rather than transactional leadership. Making sweeping generalizations can, of course, be dangerous.

Hofstede (1980) suggests that different cultures have five dimensions that are very relevant to leadership styles and behaviours:

- power distance: the extent that equality/inequality of power is expected;
- individualism/collectivism: the extent that the importance is given to individuals or to cohesive groups;
- masculinity/femininity: the extent of emphasis on assertiveness and the rational or on relationships and the needs of staff;
- uncertainty/avoidance: the extent that people can be ambiguous;
- long-term orientation: as opposed to short-term orientation.

This suggests that leadership styles and behaviours will be different in different countries, even within countries, although there is some evidence that cultural differences are narrowing.

RESEARCH ON THIRD SECTOR LEADERSHIP

There is limited research on leadership and management in Third Sector organizations and the similarities and differences in leadership and management between the sectors. Taliento and Silverman (2005) interviewed leaders who led both private sector and Third Sector organizations and identified five factors which mean that Third Sector leaders would need to adapt the practices used in private sector contexts:

- smaller scope of authority in the Third Sector;
- a wider range of stakeholders who expect consensus;
- the need for innovative metrics to monitor performance;
- the requirement that Third Sector CEOs pay more attention to communications;
- the challenge of building an effective organization with limited resources and training.

Peterson and Van Fleet (2008) compared private sector and Third Sector leaders and, having found that 11 of the 15 leadership behaviours were common between the sectors, identified two managerial leader behaviours particularly valued by Third Sector employees, both in situations of stability and crisis: role clarification and compelling direction. Private sector employees only valued them in a crisis. Structuring rewards and autonomy/delegation, which were important in the private sector, were not considered to be important at all in the Third Sector.

Myers (2004) in a study of 20 Third Sector CEOs found that both practical and social managerial wisdom shaped through informal experience, rather than formal training, were particularly important in managerial performance. There is also significant research (Gulati and Westphal 1999; Maitlis 2004) on the importance of developing and maintaining productive relationships with governing bodies in the Third Sector.

SUMMARY

This chapter has explored various models of management and leadership and the relationship between the two concepts. It has examined traditional perspectives on management and the creation of management standards. It has outlined the various trait theories of leadership and their shortcomings. It has also described behaviour/style models of leadership and highlighted other approaches, including transformational, servant and functional leadership. The importance of the context in which leadership is exercised and the readiness of followers have been explored. The relevance of the various approaches for strategic management in the Third Sector has been discussed.

QUESTIONS

1. What are some of the characteristics of a great leader that have been proposed?
2. What different leadership styles are there? In what situations might each be appropriate?
3. Does leadership and management in the Third Sector need to be different from other sectors? How? Why?
4. What are the shortcomings of trait theories?
5. Are leadership and management different?
6. What are the roles of a manager?
7. Is leadership theory biased against women?
8. What situations reduce the need for leadership?

DISCUSSION TOPIC

Are leadership and management in the Third Sector different from the private sector?

SUGGESTED READING

Lisa Matthewman, Amanda Rose and Angela Hetherington (2009) *Work Psychology*, Oxford University Press.

Jo Owen (2009) *How to Lead*, 2nd edn, Pearson/Prentice-Hall.

Derek Rollinson (2002) *Organisational Behaviour and Analysis*, Prentice-Hall.

Paul. E Spector (2006) *Industrial and Organizational Psychology: Research and Practice*, John Wiley & Sons.

Gary A. Yukl (2005) *Leadership in Organizations*, Prentice-Hall.

16 MANAGING CHANGE

OVERVIEW

Many well developed strategies and initiatives have died a death because of the challenges presented in trying to manage change. Organizational change happens through individuals, and the truth is that most people find change difficult and painful. There is a sense of loss in giving up well-established ways of working, which can lead to apparently irrational denial, anger, diversionary activities and/or withdrawal. There need to be convincing and objective reasons why the current way of working is not satisfactory, a clear picture of what the new situation will look like, what the benefits will be, and what the steps from the current situation to the future one will be. This chapter explores the issue of change management and some of the tools and models available to help understand and deal with the processes.

LEARNING OBJECTIVES

After studying this chapter, you should be able to:

- describe some of the tools and models used to understand change and change management;
- outline suggested stages of managing and responding to change;
- describe some of the key issues that an organization needs to address in managing change, using the McKinsey 7-S model.

RESISTANCE TO CHANGE

Sometimes senior managers and trustees find it difficult to understand resistance to change, even change that seems, to them, very positive. Different people react in different ways to change. Ross and Segal (2002) have identified five types of people (5 Cs), in the way that they respond to change:

- Champions: who stick their neck out and help to drive change;
- Chasers: who need convincing about the value of the change, or will simply run with the pack;
- Converts: who need strong evidence for, and value of, the need for the change;

- Challengers: who will constantly ask difficult questions. They operate from a 'if it ain't broke, don't fix it' mode.

- Changephobics: who are immovable and cause dissent. They don't like any change and will derail or slow down the desired change.

It is useful to be aware of some of the generic drivers of resistance to change. The following are some of the likely drivers (Nadler 1983; Cherrington 1989):

- Habit: people do not like their familiar work routines disrupted. New habits have to be learnt, which requires time and energy.

- Security: will the changes reduce the security of my position?

- Loss of skills: will the changes require different skills from mine?

- Fear of the unknown: many people have a considerable fear of uncertainty which can result in dysfunctional behaviour in the face of change.

- Economic considerations: will the changes result in job cuts, or reductions in salary, or other terms and conditions?

- Loss of power: will the changes reduce my influence in the organization?

- Social considerations: the need to conform to group norms amongst colleagues against management, or appearing to accept changes, so as not to be seen as disruptive, but subtly undermining the changes.

- Lack of awareness: not having a real understanding of the changes and the reasons for, or benefits of, them.

- Distrust of management: from previous experiences.

PLANNED VS UNPLANNED CHANGE

Strategy is all about change and the previous chapters all describe rational processes for planning the future of the organization and how it can respond to the increasing requirements of its beneficiaries and other stakeholders and a changing external environment. This chapter deals with the response of individuals to organizational changes and the way organizations can manage a change process. It is important to also be conscious that not all change takes place because it is planned using some of the approaches highlighted above. Often organizations have to respond to unexpected internal or external changes, due to unexpected changes in the external environment. Some of the models and techniques that can be used to think about managing change, both planned and unplanned, are highlighted below.

CHANGE QUADRANTS

Kotter (1990) has suggested a model which helps to assess the extent to which the motivation to change in an organization is 'warm' or 'cold'. There are two dimensions to this. One concerns the organization in general, i.e. a cold organization is one dominated by rules and procedures to ensure effective control and coordination; a warm organization is one with shared norms and values, with an enthusiasm to improve

Table 16.1   Kotter's warm or cold model

Warmth of the change situation		Organizational warmth	
		Cold	**Warm**
	Cold	Intervene	Transform
	Warm	Implement	Innovate/renew

Source: Based on Kotter (1990).

performance. The other dimension concerns the particular motivation to change in the particular circumstances, i.e. a cold motivation for change is an objective response to a situation (obligated); a warm motivation is one which is driven by personal and professional ambitions (willing) (see Table 16.1).

The four strategies an organization can adopt, depending on the quadrant, are:

- Intervene: top-down design and implementation of change. Limited participation.
- Transform: extensive participation to gain ideas on achieving clear final goals.
- Implement: top-down mobilizing of the organization through middle managers.
- Innovate/renew: utilize energy and ambition to create and realize a long-term vision. Motivate to build something together.

FORCE FIELD ANALYSIS

A useful and simple technique that can be adapted to a number of different situations is Force Field Analysis, which was developed by Kurt Lewin (1957). His insight was that the current situation is the result of the equilibrium between opposing forces. This technique is used to determine the strength of those factors which support change against those which inhibit or oppose it. In considering the external environment it can be useful to look at the organization's mission or particular aims or objectives and to suggest those factors which will support their achievement and those which might prevent or inhibit them. The size of the arrows can be used to indicate the strength of the forces (see Figure 16.1).

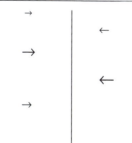

Fig 16.1   Lewin's Force Field Model

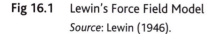

Source: Lewin (1946).

THREE-STEP CHANGE MODEL

To help conceptualize how organizations might think about a change management process, Lewin (1957) also developed a simple three-step change management model:

Unfreeze – Move – Freeze

Unfreezing involves unlearning something which may be deeply embedded in the person, and creating the motivation to change. This usually involves the following three mechanisms:

- Inducing discomfort about the current arrangements, behaviours or attitudes, so they are disconfirmed.
- Setting up sufficient guilt or anxiety to motivate change. There may still be denial or avoidance if the guilt or anxiety is at a low level.
- Creating psychological safety, so the person feels safe to give up the old way of operating, through reassurance that the change is possible.

Once the motivation is there, *moving* is the development of new behaviours and attitudes on the basis of new information and understanding. This normally involves two key mechanisms:

- identification with a role model, mentor, friend or some other person, to see things from the other's point of view, particularly when the behaviours and attitudes are role-modelled by the other person;
- obtaining information from a range of sources, relevant to the particular change issue, that supports the change.

Refreezing is about stabilizing the changes, rather than drifting back to the old comfortable attitudes and behaviours. Two key mechanisms are relevant here:

- institutionalizing the changes through new structures, job descriptions, policies and procedures, and mechanisms for showing that new procedures are being followed consistently;
- reinforcing and rewarding the changed behaviour and attitudes and providing quick wins.

A case study of change in a community-based organization (Medley and Akan 2008) highlighted the continuing relevance of the Lewin three-stage model.

MANAGING TRANSITIONS

William Bridges (1991) developed a similar three-stage model of managing transitions, which introduced several new insights:

Ending – Neutral zone – New beginning

Some of the value of Bridges's model are in:

- Highlighting the sense of loss and mourning that some staff may experience in change processes (Kubler-Ross 1973) and this needs to be acknowledged. The experience of loss may result in denial, anger, resistance and negotiation, before, hopefully, achieving the stages of acceptance and commitment. Rituals may be important to honour what is passing.

- Recognizing when you are in the neutral zone or period of uncertainty and the anxiety that this can create.

- Supporting the creation of the new beginning, which needs to enable people to see the purpose behind the change, picture how this new organization will look and feel, have a step-by-step plan of how to get there, and play a part in the outcome.

BECKHARD AND HARRIS'S CHANGE FORMULA

Beckhard and Harris (1987) developed a Change Formula which builds on some of the insights above and is often represented as $(A \times B \times D) > X$, where A is the level of dissatisfaction with the status quo; B is the perceived desirability of the proposed change or end state; D is the practicality of the change (minimal risk and disruption); and X is the perceived cost (in human and emotional terms as well as more practical costs) of changing.

The model suggests that change will occur when A, B and D together are greater than the perceived cost of changing. A change management strategy, therefore, needs to address one or more of the following challenges:

- increase the level of dissatisfaction with the status quo;

- increase the perceived desirability of the proposed change or end state;

- increase the practicality of the change and reduce the risk and disruption;

- reduce the perceived cost (in human and emotional terms as well as more practical costs) of changing.

KOTTER'S EIGHT-STEP MODEL OF CHANGE

Kotter (1996) suggests that effectively bringing about organizational change usually requires eight key steps:

1. establish a sense of urgency;
2. form a powerful guiding coalition;
3. create a clear positive vision of what the outcome of the change will look like;
4. communicate the vision;
5. empower others to act on the vision;
6. plan for and create short-term wins;
7. consolidate improvements and produce still more change;
8. institutionalize new approaches.

Dees *et al.* (2002) suggest adding the following three tasks to Kotter's key steps from the work of Rosabeth Moss Kanter (1983):

1. tune into the environment (listen to staff) to assess what is working and what is not;
2. learn to persevere;
3. make everyone a hero: reward and celebrate the implementation of the vision.

Menzies Lyth (1988) in a groundbreaking study of nursing in London focuses on the psychology of change and the need for staff to be able to deal with anxiety by being 'held' by their organization (what she calls 'containment'), so they can 'safely acknowledge and manage their difficult feelings, can free up their minds to think, and can engage with the primary task of change' (Barrett 2012: 6). Barrett (2012) suggests some actions to create this containment as follows:

- modelling steady stewardship of your organization;
- fostering a supportive culture which is mindful of difficult feelings;
- arranging ongoing structured psychological support for staff whose work is routinely stressful;
- ensuring role clarity and appropriate role authority;
- providing as much structure and consistency as possible during periods of change;
- facilitating and enabling powerful team discussions;
- ensuring organizational clarity through rigorous analysis of your strategy;
- managing upwards.

7–S MODEL

Consultants McKinsey (Pascale and Athos 1981; Pascale 1990) developed the 7-S model of organizational subsystems that need to be addressed by major organizational change processes. The seven Ss are as follows:

- *Staff*: making sure there are the right people in the right roles, who know what is expected of them, to deliver the new situation. Collins (2001) argues that in all sectors having the 'right people on the bus' is key to an organization moving from good to great. Helping staff to feel they have an important and clear role in the new situation is important.
- *Skills*: How best to value and use the current skills of the staff and volunteers, while at the same time to analyse what training and development support to provide for staff and volunteers in the new skills and knowledge that are required?
- *Systems*: what new systems and procedures need to be put in place to embed the new situation so it does not slide backwards?
- *Style*: what is the appropriate management style and culture to role model for all staff and volunteers in the new situation?
- *Shared values*: making the values/principles that should underpin all the activities of the organization, especially in the new situation, very clear.

- *Strategy*: are there clear plans, objectives and timetables to bring about the changed situation and achieve the agreed aims and objectives?
- *Structure*: what is the right organizational structure to ensure effectiveness in the new situation?

These seven Ss can be shown in a matrix in order to assess the change requirements from each of the combinations.

SUMMARY

The insights from the various change management models and frameworks highlighted in this chapter would suggest the following key principles:

- Most people find change difficult and painful.
- There is a sense of loss in giving up well-established ways of working, which can lead to apparent irrational denial, anger and withdrawal. Staff need to be supported and listened to through change.
- There need to be convincing and objective reasons why the current way of working is not satisfactory. There is a need to build this case from a range of sources.
- There needs to be a clear picture of what the new situation will look like, what the benefits will be, and what the steps from the current situation to the future one will be.
- Resistance to change will be in reverse proportion to the sense of ownership or involvement people have in the change. Involve, consult and inform.
- People's biggest anxiety is about their role in the new arrangements: will they have one? Will they be able to cope? Will they lose status? They will need reassurance.
- Organizational change happens through individuals. It is important to build and support a powerful coalition of respected individuals throughout the organization who will champion the change.
- The sooner people perceive the actual benefits of the change the better, so aim for some quick wins.
- Leaders need to role model and champion the new arrangements, behaviours and attitudes, and praise, support and reward staff leading the change.
- Create a sense of urgency and minimize the time spent in the period of the unknown.
- Institutionalize the new arrangements (the seven Ss) to ensure behaviour and attitudes do not slip back to the earlier comfort zone.

QUESTIONS

1. Why do some people resist change?
2. Describe at least three models of change management.

3. What are the factors that make some change management situations more challenging than others?

4. What steps might an organization take to improve the management of a change situation?

5. In what ways might managing change be different in a Third Sector organization than in other sectors?

6. What are the four most common drivers of change in the Third Sector?

7. Consider a change situation in an organization you know. What are the drivers for, and the barriers against, the change?

8. Consider a change situation that you have been in and were unhappy about. Describe the feelings you had.

DISCUSSION TOPIC

Are staff and volunteers in Third Sector organizations likely to be more or less resistant to change than in other sectors?

SUGGESTED READING

Richard Beckhard and Reuben T. Harris (1987) *Organizational Transitions: Managing Complex Change*, Addison-Wesley.

William Bridges (1991) *Managing Transitions*, Perseus.

Esther Cameron and Mike Green (2004) *Making Sense of Change Management*, Kogan Page.

Nigel Gann (1996) *Managing Change in Voluntary Organisations: A Guide to Practice*, Open University Press.

John P. Kotter (1995) 'Leading edge: why transformation efforts fail', *Harvard Business Review*, 73(2), 59–67.

Kurt Lewin (1957) *Field Theory in Social Science*, Harpur.

Abraham, Maslow (1954) *Motivation and Personality*, Harper.

Edgar, Schein (1988) *Organizational Psychology*, 3rd edn, Prentice-Hall.

PART VI
CASE STUDIES

INTRODUCTION

Most of the following case studies are drawn from publicly available information, mainly annual reports and websites, supplemented, where necessary, with information from key players within the organization. All the studies are designed to illustrate issues highlighted in the main text of the book. At the end of each study there is a series of questions for discussion or individual work.

LEARNING OBJECTIVES

While the learning from each case study will be different, taken as a whole the case studies should enable the reader, who has tried to answer the questions given at the end of each study, to understand:

- the different kinds of strategies that Third Sector organizations adopt, consciously or unconsciously;
- the difference between planned and emergent strategies;
- the potential implications of some kinds of strategy;
- the impact of a changing external environment;
- different phases of organizational development;
- the significance of the founder, both positively and negatively;
- the impact of the lobbying by Third Sector organizations in changing legislation and policy at national and international level;
- some of the difficulties of organizational change.

THE BIG ISSUE

The Big Issue was launched in 1991 by Gordon Roddick, co-founder of the Body Shop, and A. John Bird in response to the growing number of rough sleepers on the streets of London. Roddick was inspired by a newspaper called *Street News*, sold on the streets of New York. Upon his return from America he enlisted the help of Bird, who had experience in the print trade and who himself had slept rough. The two believed that the key to solving the problem of homelessness lay in helping people to help themselves. They were therefore determined to offer a legitimate alternative to begging. All vendors received training, signed a code of conduct and could be identified by badges which included their photo and vendor number.

The Big Issue was first sold by ten vendors on the streets of London in September 1991, initially as a monthly publication. In June 1993 the title went weekly, and regional editions soon followed. In addition to the original, which covers London, the South East, East Anglia, The Midlands and the South West, there are four other editions of the magazine which collectively cover the whole of the UK: *Big Issue Scotland, Big Issue Wales, Big Issue in the North* and *Big Issue South West*. There are 2,600 vendors around the UK. Total income in 2008/09 was £1,114,279 against expenditure of £1,005,541. Similar magazines are also now produced and sold in Australia, the Republic of Ireland, South Korea, South Africa, Japan, Namibia, Kenya, Malawi and Taiwan.

In November 1995, The Big Issue Foundation (a company limited by guarantee and a registered charity) was created with the aim of tackling the underlying issues which cause homelessness and of supporting vendors in their journey away from the streets. Since its creation the Foundation has provided services and referrals to address issues around housing, health, finances, education and employment. It also exists to support vendors in fulfilling their personal aspirations in a model they call service brokerage, whereby service brokers, who have a high level of knowledge of the services available, work alongside the vendor to access the appropriate services on the journey towards independence. The Big Issue Foundation builds around the unique trust which homeless people establish with service brokers, while selling the magazine, to connect vendors with the vital support and solutions that will help them continue to rebuild their lives and journey away from homelessness. The Foundation, as well as running its own services, also works in partnership with other service providers to ensure the provision of appropriate services, including in the Foundation's offices.

The Big Issue Foundation supports vendors as they address the issues which have led to them experiencing a life on the streets, as well as helping tackle the harsh reality of that life. Hundreds of vendors, for example, are not registered with a GP. One-third of vendors are mugged for their takings. Half of the vendors have considered suicide.

The Foundation operates a vendor savings scheme, a vendor support fund, a big awards scheme and a savings top-up scheme, all designed to promote and support self-help. The vision of the Big Issue Foundation is to extend the support provided to vendors throughout the UK and in doing so to create a brighter future in which vendors are happier, healthier and safer. There is also now a Big Issue in the North Trust and the Big Issue Foundation in Scotland.

MEASURES OF SUCCESS

The Foundation measures and reports on the following performance indicators:

- the number of vendors who have achieved their personal sales goals;
- the number of vendors who opened a bank/credit union account;
- the number of vendors rehoused in temporary accommodation;
- the number of vendors rehoused in permanent accommodation;
- the number of vendors who accessed the health service;
- the number of vendors who started substance misuse treatment;
- the number of vendors who accessed addiction treatment;
- the number of vendors who achieved their personal aspirations.

The Big Issue and its co-founder John Bird, have received various awards for their work including:

- October 2008: the Ernst & Young Social Entrepreneur of the Year award;
- October 2004: winner of United Nations Habitat Scroll of Honour Award;
- May 1996: shortlisted for United Nations 'Best Practice' Award;
- November 2004: John Bird named BBC London Legend.

The Big Issue has been the centre of much controversy among publishers of street newspapers, mainly because of its business model. Publishers of some other street newspapers, especially in the United States, have criticized it for being overly 'commercial' and having a flashy design and populist content. According to these critics, street newspapers ought to focus on covering political and social issues that affect the homeless, rather than on emulating mainstream newspapers to generate a profit. Publishers of some smaller papers, such as *Making Change* in Santa Monica, California, said they felt threatened when *The Big Issue* began to publish in their area. Other papers have also criticized *The Big Issue* for its professional production and limited participation by homeless individuals in writing and producing the newspaper. Others, however, have stated that *The Big Issue* uses a successful business model to generate a profit to benefit the homeless, and its founder John Bird has said that it is 'possible to be both profitable and ethically correct'.

The world economic crisis and cuts in public expenditure in the UK has caused concern in the Foundation in relation to a new generation of people who are homeless and requiring support.

QUESTIONS

1. How many strategies can you identify in the history of the *Big Issue*?
2. Create a logic model for The Big Issue Foundation.
3. Using a PESTLE analysis, outline the key external factors that are likely to influence *The Big Issue*'s future development.
4. What are the arguments for and against *The Big Issue* magazine covering more social, economic and political issues?

DISCUSSION TOPIC

Should resources of the Big Issue Foundation not be concentrated on preventing someone becoming homeless, rather than on the provision of support afterwards?

SOURCES

Tessa Swithinbank (2001) *Coming Up from the Streets: The Story of The Big Issue*, Earthscan.

The Big Issue Foundation Trustees Report and Audited Accounts for the year ended 31 March 2009.

The Big Issue websites: www.bigissue.com and bigissue.org.uk.

BLACK SASH

In 1955, when six South African women aroused the support of thousands of other, mainly white, women to march in protest against the Senate Bill and the Separate Representation of Voters Bill (which would finally disenfranchise 'coloured' voters) they could have had little idea of what was to follow. Calling themselves the Women's Defence of the Constitution League, they were united in opposition to the violation of the entrenched clause in the South African Constitution of 1910. Their determination came as a sharp challenge to a government intent on securing its hold on power and entrenching apartheid. The women's challenge failed, however, and public outrage gradually seemed to fade, at least among the majority of the white population. But the women of the League were determined not to put away their black sashes, worn in mourning at the death of constitutional rights; instead, they formally took on the name of the Black Sash and embarked on new campaigns.

The first year of the existence of the Black Sash had paralleled a different struggle, as black women were increasingly feeling the might of the 'pass laws', which had already been vigorously applied against black men, depriving them of the freedom to choose where to live and work. The founding generation of the Black Sash had become more and more aware of the extent of the erosion of the rule of law, the 'legal' racial segregation and the damage to society inflicted by the policy of migrant labour. They were determined to oppose unjust laws, but also to try to assist those who suffered as a result. In 1958 a Bail Fund was started to assist people, mainly women, who were arrested as a result of the pass laws.

Soon afterwards, the first Black Sash advice office was opened in Cape Town, offering a free paralegal service of information and support. Over the following five years, advice offices were opened in five other centres, where there were regional structures of the Black Sash. These were staffed mainly by volunteers supported by men and women from the townships who acted as interpreters.

The following 20 years were bitter ones for those who opposed apartheid and believed in a united society free of discrimination and injustice. The political movements that represented the majority of black South Africans were driven underground or into exile. Many voices of opposition were silenced. Membership dwindled and some of its regions were forced to close in the face of severe intimidation and hopes faded for peaceful change through a political process. Each day, however, its advice offices were still filled with people whose daily lives demonstrated the inhumanity of a system that broke up families, neighbourhoods and communities.

The constant quest to create real change drove the Black Sash to carry out research, study the laws, follow parliamentary debates through Hansard, read Government Gazettes, write articles, pamphlets and letters to the press, hold public meetings, and always to protest: standing silently outside Parliament and at other public sites carrying placards – and when that was forbidden, finding other ways and other places for public demonstrations.

In the second half of the 1970s, there came a new groundswell of change in South Africa, demonstrated in various different ways: in the rise of Black Consciousness as a powerful influence (followed by the brutal killing of Steve Biko in 1977); in the student protests of 1976 and the aftermath; in the increasing strength of the African National Congress in exile, as well as secretly among its adherents inside the country; and in the growing inability of the state to enforce some of its policies, demonstrated most visibly by the great numbers of people who simply defied the pass laws and settled around the cities in spite of the bulldozers.

Resistance inevitably brought greater repression. The work of the Black Sash expanded to monitor and record the protests, rallies and marches that were being met with ever-stronger police reaction. Lists were kept as people were banned and banished, died in detention, disappeared into lengthy periods of imprisonment without trial, or were tear-gassed, arrested and wounded. Black Sash members themselves were arrested, taken into detention, kept under surveillance and harassed.

The establishment of the United Democratic Front in 1983 brought together a number of organizations in a concerted push to exert pressure for change. In 1985 and then 1986, the beleaguered state introduced a State of Emergency. Once again many voices were silenced. Black Sash members, the majority of whom had a measure of protection as white, middle-class women, felt the responsibility of still having a degree of political freedom to speak out. They added to the wedge of pressure forcing the pace of change, and gradually preparations began for the new society.

Monitoring the pass law courts further deepened the Black Sash's understanding of the terrible price that black people were paying for white supremacy. Black Sash members were active in monitoring, analysing and reporting on the growing conflict across the country, taking statements and observing events such as meetings, rallies and funerals. The monitoring of legislation, and of government policy and action, formed a major part of the work, and in the 1990s – even as the organization shifted its focus – a LegiWatch group was formed, which continued to monitor legislation and the workings of Parliament. A national advocacy monitor was appointed, and today this has grown into a team that continues to be a central element of Black Sash work. Every comment, every statistic, every statement issued by the Black Sash was underpinned by the daily experience in the advice offices, in rural fieldwork and in personal witness. This strong foundation of first-hand knowledge earned the respect of many who came to rely on its information, and it remains an important factor today.

In 1990, when political parties were unbanned and political prisoners released, amid terrible ongoing violence, Nelson Mandela walked free after 27 years. In his first public speech he said: 'the Black Sash was the conscience of white South Africa'. During this time, the organization took part in the work on the new constitution, in debates about the nature of the transition and the shape of the new society, and extensive voter education in preparation for the first all-inclusive election for a national government.

The year 1994 heralded a further major turning point in the history of South Africa. The achievement of constitutional democracy and the subsequent adoption of the Constitution of the Republic of South Africa in 1996 – 'one law for one nation' – were the outcome of a process of negotiation that had often seemed far out of reach.

As the very foundations of the society began to change, the Black Sash, too, had to consider what its role should be and embark on developing a new focus and new structure. It began to change itself, and gradually – often painfully – it moved away from being an organization that was member-driven, mainly volunteer, and almost entirely made up of white women. It evolved into the new structure of an NGO, led by a national director accountable to a board of trustees, with a special focus on the socioeconomic rights of the poorest and most vulnerable sector of society.

The advice offices, through 40 years of fighting apartheid and ten years of building democracy, had a proven track record of effective delivery. The queues of those navigating bureaucratic corridors and seeking clarity on their rights had shortened, but Black Sash's experience in this sphere remained invaluable. Contributing to the building of the paralegal movement in order to enhance access to justice was considered to be a worthwhile quest. Engaging the courts to test the rights of citizens within the new Constitution and its Bill of Rights was one Black Sash felt was of immense benefit to the democratic framework.

Increasingly Black Sash worked in collaboration with other civil society organizations and government to tackle the twin scourges of poverty and HIV/Aids as an essential commitment to realizing their dreams of a more egalitarian society.

A small, effective national advocacy unit prepares informed commentary on draft legislation for politicians who, unlike in the past, generally welcome civil society's contribution. This advocacy is done in partnership with those at the coalface in the advice offices. Maintaining the balance between advocacy and advice-giving is an achievement of which they are particularly proud.

Black Sash's vision was as follows: 'our vision is for a transformed organisation working in and for a transformed society. Ten years of working for democracy has shown us that transformation is a complex, challenging process that takes time'. It has now been shortened to 'Making human rights real' (Black Sash 2011 annual report).

The current trustees of the Black Sash are women from different parts of South Africa, each with special skills and interests in the work of the organization. The values and principles that underpinned the movement through the first 40 years of its existence have been enshrined in its new role and form. The Sash is today an organization of diverse South Africans who share an appreciation of being a young democracy and how policy, legislation and administration impact on people's lives. They have a vision for the unfolding of just laws and a competent and reliable administration that will benefit the particular needs of the poorest and most vulnerable in our society.

QUESTIONS

1. How many different strategies has Black Sash engaged in since it was established?
2. What have some of the distinctive competencies/capabilities of the Black Sash been that made it successful?
3. Where is the evidence that Black Sash changed or adjusted its strategy in light of the changing external environment?

DISCUSSION TOPIC

What are the arguments for and against being involved in providing direct advice to individuals as well as public advocacy and campaigning?

SOURCE

Black Sash website: www.blacksash.org.za.

Black Sash 2011 Annual Report www.blacksash.org.za/docs/blacksash_2011_annualreport.pdf.

BRYSON CHARITABLE GROUP

Bryson Charitable Group is a registered charity and social enterprise, in operation since 1906. In 1921, just after the First World War, the Belfast Charity Organisation Society expanded to become the Belfast Council of Social Welfare (BCSW). It was at this time, in fact, that the idea of a Social Service Centre was first mooted but, unfortunately, this scheme had to wait for over 20 years before it could be implemented because of the chronic social conditions of the interwar period. The BCSW changed its name to the Belfast Voluntary Welfare Society (BVWS) in 1974. In the late 1980s the organization became known as Bryson House, after the historic building it occupied in Belfast city centre, which had been the host to a large number of fledgling Third Sector organizations and initiatives, under its entrepreneurial chief executive, Peter McLachlan, who constantly identified innovations that could be beneficial to Belfast. On the death of Peter McLachlan, the leadership of the organization was split, with one senior director taking responsibility for care services and the other for environmental services.

In 2006, due to an increased number of services that the charity provided in recycling, training, energy awareness, multicultural activities, water sports training and increased care services throughout the province, a decision was made to change the name of the charity from Bryson House to Bryson Charitable Group, based on a social enterprise model. The structure of the organization reverted to one with a single chief executive.

By 2010, the turnover of the Bryson Charitable Group had increased to over £24 million, a 22 per cent increase on the previous year (92 per cent of which came from public sector contracts). Two-thirds of the turnover of the group was on environmental recycling and energy efficiency services.

In terms of governance, each of the Group's business units are responsible for the delivery of its own services, with HR, ICT, premises and finance provided as a shared service across the group. Each business unit has its own board, the chair of which sits on the board of the Bryson Charitable Group. The Group employs 642 staff working across Northern Ireland. In 2009/10 it achieved a Mark of Excellence against the EFQM Excellence Model in the Northern Ireland quality awards, in addition to various awards for individual business units and services.

MISSION, VISION AND VALUES

Vision: 'Bryson's vision is to be a leader in creating a just and sustainable society'.

Mission: 'We are committed to identifying and developing sustainable responses to existing and emerging social need'.

Values: Bryson's Mission and Vision statements are underpinned by their value base. To service users and stakeholders they are:

- non-judgemental, approachable and treat everyone equally as an individual;
- committed to making a positive impact on people's lives;
- developing individual potential and creating hope for the future.

Bryson Charitable Group services are:

- delivered to high standards of quality to achieve client satisfaction;
- reliable, professional and efficient;
- accessible and inclusive, offering support, empowerment and choice;

The organization:

- is built on commitment to hard work through teamwork and strong leadership;
- promotes a learning culture and sustainable approach to continuously improving how they do things;
- encourages its people to treat one another with respect and to value everyone's contribution;
- works inclusively in partnership with other services, organizations and communities;
- has been changing lives for a century.

The Bryson Charitable Group uses the Balanced Scorecard approach (see Chapter 9). The performance measures include:

- the percentage of contracts due for renewal that were successfully renewed;
- the percentage of new contracts bid for that were secured;
- the ratio of grants to grant applications (target of 15:85);
- the percentage of stakeholders reporting overall satisfaction with services (annual survey);
- the percentage of stakeholders that said the Bryson Charitable Group were effective and creative in using their resources;
- the percentage of stakeholders that felt the Bryson Charitable Group improved the quality of life of service-users.

SERVICES

The Bryson Charitable Group has a wide diversity of programmes and services, including in the social services field, the environment, training and employability, watersports and cultural diversity.

Social services:

- independent advocacy service for adults with learning disabilities in the greater Belfast area;

- family support service offering practical help and emotional support to families experiencing difficulties or under stress;
- 'Home From Hospital' providing a short-term service to people who have been in hospital and who require additional support/assistance to rehabilitate at home;
- domiciliary care providing care and support to older people and people with a physical disability living in their own homes in the west of the province;
- 'Neighbourly Care Scheme' providing support to people who are vulnerable and living within the community;
- laundry service providing a weekly service of fresh bed linen to people managing incontinence;
- 'Golden Years Service' in the Western Health & Social Care Trust area;
- family support service in County Donegal;
- student unit/practice learning centre providing social work/care practice learning opportunities in the wider voluntary sector.

Environmental services:

- Bryson recycling processes waste material to ISO 90001 and 14001 standards. It has four depots around Northern Ireland, a kerbside box service and a materials recovery facility.
- Bryson electrical recycles white goods: a commercial service.
- Bryson Energy: The National Energy Advice Service is operated by Bryson Energy and the Energy Saving Trust, offering free advice and support on how to save energy in the home, low carbon transport, renewable technologies, water and waste, with offices in Belfast, Enniskillen and Derry/Londonderry.

Training and employability – North City Training:

- Steps to Work programme for long-term unemployed adults;
- the Step Ahead programme providing placements in voluntary and community organizations;
- Training for Success and Apprenticeship Programmes;
- Young Person's Employment Initiative;
- European programmes (Local Employment Intermediary Service and European Social Fund) football apprenticeships for young people.

Watersports:

- Lagan watersports centre offers canoeing, kayaking, rowing, sailing and power-boating to community, youth and school groups, businesses and individuals, and is staffed by nationally qualified instructors.

Cultural Diversity Multi-Cultural Resource Centre:

- intercultural support, advice and research to minority ethnic groups and asylum-seekers, combating the causes of racism;

- One Stop Service contracted by the Refugee Council (UK) to provide advice and support to destitute asylum seekers while they apply for assistance through the National Asylum Support Service provisions;
- Refugee Integration and Employment service;
- newcomer families and children support.

Other:

- Volunteering: providing a variety of opportunities for people interested in volunteering, including befriending, practical help, the arts and environmental projects. Young people are also sent to volunteer in other European countries.

The chief executive of the Bryson Charitable Group sees several key challenges in the current environment:

- how to create greater awareness of social enterprise and how it can work to scale;
- how to balance giving people space to develop in areas they specialize in and create a sense of purpose across the diverse organization;
- how to overcome the protectionism of some public bodies who are keen to bring services in-house.

QUESTIONS

1. Is 'Charitable' in the name of the group in conflict with its social enterprise model?
2. What are the advantages and disadvantages in having such a diverse portfolio of services?
3. From the case study, create a SWOT analysis of the Bryson Charitable Group.
4. What are the external environmental trends that have driven the expansion of the Bryson Charitable Group?
5. Are there disadvantages in being focused on obtaining and delivering public sector contracts?

DISCUSSION TOPIC

Do Third Sector organizations bring anything distinctive to the delivery of public sector contracts?

SOURCES

Bryson Charitable Group Annual Review 2009–2010.

The Bryson Charitable Group (2011) 'Cover story', *Agenda NI*, issue 47, June/July, www.brysongroup.org.

COIN STREET COMMUNITY BUILDERS

Coin Street Community Builders (CSCB) is a development trust and social enterprise based on the South Bank of the River Thames between Waterloo Bridge and Blackfriars Bridge in London. Since its creation in 1984, CSCB has been involved in the redevelopment of the OXO Tower, Gabriel's Wharf market and the setting up of four housing cooperatives (Mulberry, Palm, Redwood and Iroko) in new buildings commissioned by CSCB.

Thirty years ago the South Bank area of London was bleak and unattractive. It had a dying residential community, few shops and restaurants and a weak local economy. In response to the state of the area, local people drew up a planning strategy to reverse the destruction of their community through the building of new homes and community facilities. Central to this strategy was the development of eight, largely derelict, Coin Street sites.

In 1977, after a developer announced plans to build Europe's tallest hotel and over 1 million square feet of office space on the sites, the Coin Street Action Group was set up. It drew up alternative plans for local housing, a new riverside park and walkway, and managed workshops, shops and leisure facilities. Seven years of campaigning, including two year-long public inquiries, followed.

A number of office developers competed for the site and then joined forces. After the second inquiry, planning permission was granted for both the office development and the community schemes. Half of the area was owned by the office developers and half by the Greater London Council (GLC). The GLC had originally supported the office developers but, after 1981, it decided to support the community scheme. In 1984 the office developers eventually sold their land to the GLC which, in turn, sold the whole 13 acre (5.5 hectare) site to CSCB, which had been set up to make the area a better one in which to live, to work and to visit, for £1 million. The purchase was financed through loans from the Greater London Enterprise Board and the GLC, based on a business plan showing loans being serviced from temporary uses of the land, such as car parking. The purchase price reflected restrictive covenants and the fact that much of the area had been derelict for over 30 years. As the company improved the neighbourhood and established commercial activity, property values increased, thus allowing the company to repay the loans and borrow more for future investment from banks and the Nationwide Building Society, which are repaid out of commercial income, including commercial tenancies, venue hire and fees.

Along much of the Thames, exclusive offices, hotels and private housing developments had 'cut off' existing communities from the river. CSCB wanted to open up the river for everyone to enjoy, and so, between 1984 and 1988, it organized the demolition of derelict buildings, the completion of the South Bank riverside walkway and the laying out of a new riverside park, called Bernie Spain Gardens, after Bernadette Spain, one of the original Coin Street Action Group campaigners. This opened up spectacular views of the Thames, St Paul's Cathedral and the City. Both Bernie Spain Gardens and the Thames Path (between the National Theatre and Sea Containers House) are owned, managed and maintained by CSCB. This stretch of the riverside now attracts visitors from all over the world, as well as being a resource enjoyed by those who live or work in the area. In 2007, CSCB moved into new offices in The Coin Street neighbourhood centre. As well as offices, the building includes a day nursery and crèche, conference and meeting facilities and a neighbourhood cafe.

The CSCB company is limited by guarantee, which means that it can carry out commercial activity but profits must be ploughed back into public service objectives rather than distributed to shareholders. All members of the company are required to live locally and so understand the needs and opportunities of the area. It employs a staff team to develop, manage and maintain the site and oversee its community and enterprise support programmes. Associated charities also support education, arts and community activities. CSCB works closely with neighbouring businesses and arts organizations through another not-for-profit company, the South Bank Employers' Group, and with other stakeholders through the South Bank Partnership. Members have also set up a registered housing association, Coin Street Secondary Housing Co-operative and, for each residential development, a tenant-owned 'primary' co-op.

In 1993 the boards of CSCB, Coin Street Secondary Housing Co-operative and Coin Street Centre Trust agreed a shared set of aims and objectives to guide their activities:

General:

- to ensure that in all of its initiatives the group recognizes the multicultural character of London and seeks to implement the group's equal opportunities policies;
- to encourage the involvement of local residents and tenants in planning and implementing specific initiatives and to ensure that in all of its activities the Coin Street Group is sensitive to their needs and aspirations;
- to promote, support and encourage the establishment of housing cooperatives, community development trusts and other innovative ways of meeting housing and community needs;
- to work with others to create a healthy and balanced London economy which supports its residential communities effectively and provides a wide range of employment opportunities for London residents.

The South Bank:

- to work with others to promote and improve the South Bank as an area in which to live, to work, and as an area to visit;
- to work with others to improve the management and amenity of public areas in and around the South Bank;
- to oppose developments which are likely to have an adverse effect on the environment or the economy of the South Bank;

- to improve health care services and facilities in and around the South Bank;
- to extend the range of leisure and recreational facilities in and around the South Bank;
- to extend the range of shopping facilities in and around the South Bank;
- to improve educational and childcare provision in and around the South Bank.

The Thames:

- to protect and enhance the River Thames as an amenity for those living in, working in or visiting London and to promote its use for recreation and water-borne transport.

The Coin Street Site:

- to develop the Coin Street area in accordance with CSCB's covenants and the objectives of the Coin Street Group;
- to assist Coin Street Secondary Housing Co-operative in developing affordable housing;
- to ensure that developments in the Coin Street area are carried out to a high standard utilizing the skills of contemporary designers and artists;
- to ensure that in the design, specification and management of its properties the Coin Street Group uses materials and practices which recognize the need to sustain the Earth's resources;
- to ensure that in the design, specification and management of its properties the Coin Street Group is sensitive to the needs of those with disabilities;
- to ensure that property owned by the Coin Street Group is managed effectively and creatively in a manner which is sensitive to tenants' needs and the objectives of the Coin Street Group;
- to assist Coin Street Secondary Housing Co-operative in establishing effective and viable management services which offer good value for money and are sensitive to the needs of primary cooperatives.

Information and training:

- to publicize the objectives and activities of the Coin Street Group and to support and assist organizations with similar objectives;
- to assist Coin Street Secondary Housing Co-operative in the provision of information and training to tenants and prospective tenants, to housing associations and statutory bodies, to the general public, and to other organizations and individuals;
- to assist in the provision of employment and enterprise training.

Because of the huge interest in the success of the CSCB, a consultancy arm was developed providing visits, masterclasses and more intensive consultancy support, based on the model in Figure CS.1:

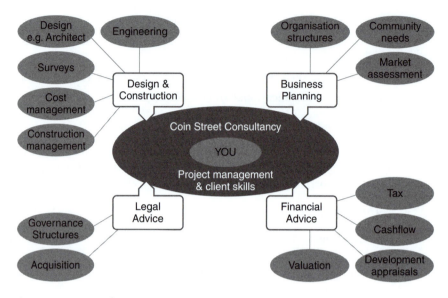

Fig CS.1   Intensive support consultancy
Source: www.coinstreet.org.

QUESTIONS

1. What are the distinctive competencies/capabilities that have led to the success of Coin Street Community Builders?
2. Describe Coin Street Community Builders' asset development strategy.
3. Create a logic model for Coin Street Community Builders.
4. How important was the campaigning strategy, to influence the external stakeholders, for the initial success of the initiative?
5. Which external factors might be different now from what they were ten or twenty years ago?
6. How might the management of the company be different now than in 1984?

DISCUSSION TOPIC

To what extent is the Coin Street model replicable in other geographical areas in a more challenging economic climate?

SOURCE

The Coin Street Community Builders website: www.coinstreet.org.

Intensive support consultancy model accessed 23 October 2012 from www.coinstreet.org/coin-street.org/index.php?option=com_content&view=article&id=186&Itemid=1072

COMIC RELIEF

Comic Relief is a charity which was founded as Charity Projects in the UK in 1985 by the comedy scriptwriter Richard Curtis and Alexander Mendis, in response to famine in Ethiopia. The main public face of Comic Relief's appeal is Red Nose Day, a biennial telethon held in March, alternating with sister project Sport Relief. Comic Relief is one of the two high profile telethon events held in the UK, the other being Children in Need. Comic Relief was launched on BBC1, on Christmas Day 1985, from a refugee camp in Sudan.

The idea for Comic Relief (the trading name of Charity Projects) came from the noted charity worker Jane Tewson, who had dyslexia and left school without qualifications, but later attended lectures at Oxford while working as a cleaner in the city. In 1981, at age 23, she founded Charity Projects in London, with funding from Lord (Tim) Bell and numerous other donations. Its initial focus was tackling homelessness in Soho, London.

Tewson is also the originator of several other innovative Third Sector organizations and ideas for community strengthening, notably in the UK and Australia, including Pilotlight. She believes in making charity 'active, emotional, involving and fun', by building connections between people of different backgrounds, cultures, wealth and social positions. Her approach 'embraces human connection as a vital part of social change'.

Comic Relief/Charity Projects is a company limited by guarantee with charitable status. It states that its mission is to 'drive positive change through the power of entertainment' (Comic Relief website). It has a three-year strategic plan and also sets annual priorities.

From the beginning, one of the fundamental principles behind Comic Relief was the 'Golden Pound Principle' where every single donated pound (£) is spent on charitable projects. All operating costs, such as staff salaries, are covered by corporate sponsors and interest earned on money waiting to be distributed.

In 2002, Comic Relief and BBC Sport teamed up to create Sport Relief, a new initiative aiming to unite the sporting community, culminating in a night of sport, entertainment and fund raising on BBC One television. Sport Relief is a biennial charity event, and the campaign deliberately alternates years with Red Nose Day, Comic Relief's flagship event.

In 2009 Comic Relief decided on three long-term priorities in terms of social change: malaria, Education for All (Millennium Development Goal 2) and mental health in the UK. The same year it also launched a website calling for a financial transaction tax, the 'Robin Hood' tax, which would be charged on each major transaction in the financial markets, to be used to alleviate global poverty.

Since the charity was started in 1985, Comic Relief has raised over £650 million. In 2009/10 it received £72.2 million, compared to £97.2 million in the previous year.

It gave out 297 grants in 2009/10, totalling £59.2 million. It has inspired similar independent initiatives in the USA, Australia, Germany and Finland.

There has been some concern in certain sections of the press about the lack of gender equality in the causes supported by Comic Relief, with much funding going to more politicized women's charities or charities focusing on females. Writing in *The Spectator* Ross Clark raised the question: 'why do all these women's charities ... feel the need to disguise their fundraising in the pratfest that is Comic Relief rather than appealing directly to the public?'. He added: 'are they worried that if the British public realized where their money was going they would be less inclined to be so generous?' (Clark 2007). However, the need for a gender bias has been supported by most world development organizations which recognize the disadvantaged position of women and the key role played by women in most societies in tackling poverty and inequality.

In 1999 Jane Tewson received a CBE for her foundational work with Charity Projects and other projects. In March 2000, she was named by *The Times* newspaper as one of the top ten innovators of the 1990s in the UK. In 2007 she was named Social Entrepreneur of the Year in the Victoria Tasmania awards and in 2010 she received a Philanthropy Advocate Award from UK Beacon Awards Winners.

QUESTIONS

1. Why do you think Comic Relief has been so successful? What are its distinctive competencies/capabilities?
2. What are the advantages and disadvantages in focusing on only three priorities for grant-giving (i.e. malaria, education for all and mental health in the UK)?
3. Is it justified to favour projects run by women?
4. What are the advantages and disadvantages in the founder remaining involved with the organization he or she created (Jane Tewson now lives in Australia)?

DISCUSSION TOPIC

How should Comic Relief measure its effectiveness?

SOURCES

Charity Projects Audited Accounts for 2009/10.

Clark, R. (2007) *Read the small print before you donate*, The Spectator online 21 March 2007, accessed 23 October 2012 www.?S=red+the+small+print+before+you+donate.

Comic Relief Vision & Principles for UK grant-making, www.comicrelief.com/about-us.

www.ignitingchange.org.au.

www.pilotlight.org.uk.

COMMUNITY ACTION NETWORK

Founded in 1998, Community Action Network (CAN) was the vision of three innovators of social change: Lord Andrew Mawson, Adele Blakebrough and Helen Taylor Thompson.

The Bromley by Bow Centre, founded by Lord Mawson, created the first integrated health facility in the UK, known as a Healthy Living Centre. He established one of the first integrated nurseries in the UK and pioneered one of the first Communiversities in Britain.

The Kaleidoscope project, founded by Adele Blakebrough, pioneered a unique community response to drug treatment, as one of the first drugs projects in Britain to offer a needle/syringe exchange scheme. It took an enabling, holistic approach to clients and reaches around 700 clients per year.

Mildmay Mission Hospital, founded by Helen Taylor Thompson, established the first mothers' and children's hospice in Europe. It pioneered physiotherapy and rehabilitation services for AIDS survivors and runs initiatives to share best practice with carers in Africa. She also founded Thare Machi, the Starfish Initiative, a charity taking mobile IT-based education to women and girls in the developing world.

In 1995, Mawson, Blakebrough and Taylor joined forces to run The Great Banquet in London, bringing together more than 30,000 people from across the capital. Following its success and with financial support from the business community, they founded CAN in 1998 to:

- promote social entrepreneurship and spread understanding of the term;
- identify and promote social entrepreneurs around the UK;
- create an online network for peer support, advice and promote the grassroots activity of social entrepreneurs.

Today CAN is now recognized as one of the UK's leading organizations for the development, promotion and support of social entrepreneurs and social enterprises. It also runs its own social enterprise – CAN Mezzanines, which provides shared office spaces for Third Sector organizations. CAN has supported the creation of:

- replication of the CAN Mezzanine 'concept' with partners;
- the launch of *Social Enterprise* magazine;
- UnLtd, a £100m foundation for social entrepreneurs;

- high impact programmes to support social enterprise growth and replication, including the Beanstalk social franchising project;
- business support projects for refugees and asylum seekers, BME and faith groups.

Since CAN's foundation, the terms 'social entrepreneur' and 'social enterprise' have also become much better recognized. The Department of Business, Enterprise and Regulatory Reform estimates there are in excess of 55,000 social enterprises in Britain today, contributing over £8 billion to the economy. They are a vibrant and vital part of our enterprise culture, generating innovative business solutions to some of the most pressing and intractable needs in society. CAN's mission is to help more achieve the real and public recognition they deserve.

CAN investment deploys a range of business supports into social enterprises, including the pioneering Breakthrough programme, which works with the corporate and finance sectors to leverage capital funds and strategic growth support into leading social enterprises.

In CAN's view, social enterprise has come of age. Social enterprises aren't solely an alternative to public service delivery or innovative business solutions to social problems. CAN believes that social enterprise holds a new space in civil society and can:

- create greater community cohesion;
- build a sense of local pride and ownership;
- encourage a belief in positive action in the communities they seek to serve;
- often reach the most vulnerable people in our society and they do this in imaginative and entrepreneurial ways;
- give a voice to the voiceless and a hand to the vulnerable;
- influence government legislation, consumer behaviour and the way we behave in civil society;
- respond to social need, from the grassroots up, often changing lives, communities and futures along the way.

CAN is a registered charity working as a social enterprise. Its vision is of a social economy buoyed by a thriving social enterprise market. Its mission is to help social entrepreneurs achieve it.

QUESTIONS

1. What are the characteristics of a social entrepreneur?
2. What kinds of support might social entrepreneurs require?
3. What defines an initiative as being a social enterprise?
4. To what extent do social enterprises need to adopt the kind of competitive strategies of the private sector?

DISCUSSION TOPIC

Famously, 80 per cent of new private sector companies close within two years. As they operate in the public marketplace, is the same percentage of social enterprises likely to fail?

SOURCE

The CAN website: www.can-online.org.uk.

THE CO-OPERATIVE GROUP

> A co-operative is an autonomous association of persons united voluntarily to meet their common economic, social and cultural needs and aspirations through a jointly-owned and democratically controlled enterprise.
>
> (The International Co-operative Alliance Statement on the Co-operative Identity, Manchester, 1995)

The Co-operative Group, which began in Rochdale in 1844, is now the UK's largest mutual business, owned not by private shareholders but by almost six million consumers. It is the UK's fifth biggest food retailer, the leading convenience store operator, a major financial services provider, the UK's largest funeral services provider and the largest farming operation. The Group operates over 5,000 retail trading outlets, employs more than 110,000 people and has an annual turnover of £13.7 billion. As well as having clear financial and operational objectives, the Group has also set out its social and sustainability goals in an Ethical Plan, which specifies almost 50 commitments.

Like any business, the Co-operative Group aims for commercial success. However, even more important is the way they do business and how they use their profits. The Group believes that it should offer its customers both value and values, making them different from other large retailers.

The Group's members are its owners: as a consumer cooperative, the business is run for the benefit of the members. That means that members are involved in democratic decision-making and share in the profits. Members also set a social and campaigning agenda that the Group supports. They have become pioneers in areas such as Fairtrade and combating climate change.

The Group has more than eight businesses and includes:

- Co-operative Food has over 3,000 food stores and supermarkets around the UK. Its own-brand food range combines quality with ethically sourced products. They are the only retailer to sell food grown on their own farms and are the biggest supporter of Fairtrade with over 200 lines.

- Co-operative Travel is the UK's largest independent travel agency, with over three million passengers every year, operating over 360 high street travel agencies, plus call centres, online booking and a specialist cruise operation.

- Co-operative Pharmacy is the third largest pharmacy chain in the UK, with nearly 800 branches and dispensing over 53 million prescriptions a year. Its aim is to be recognized as the leading ethically and socially responsible pharmacy.

- Co-operative Funeralcare is the UK's leading funeral director, running more than 800 funeral homes across the country.

- Co-operative Bank has over 250 high street branches (including Britannia) offering a range of banking products from mortgages and loans to current accounts, credit cards, saving and investments. They have an ethical policy based on the views of customers, which sets out the businesses they will and will not provide banking services and investment of funds to.

- Smile Internet Bank is a full-service internet bank offering online services including current accounts, investment, savings and ISAs, funds, credit cards, loans and mortgages.

- Co-operative Insurance offers insurance products, including car, home, life and health, building and contents, travel and commercial insurance. They have a customer-led Ethical Engagement Policy reflecting customer views on a range of ethical issues, and in 2006 became the UK's first insurer to launch an Eco-Motor Insurance policy.

- Co-operative Legal Services provides legal advice over the phone. Services cover will writing, managing probate, moving home, legal assistance with personal injury and employment claims.

PURPOSE, VISION, AIMS

Regarding its purpose, vision and aims, the Co-operative Group states (Co-operative Group website):

Our purpose:

- to serve our members by carrying on business as a co-operative in accordance with co-operative values and principles.

Our vision:

- to build a better society by excelling in everything we do.

Our aims:

- to be a commercially successful business;
- to meet the needs of our customers and the communities we serve;
- to respond to our members and share our profits;
- to be an ethical leader;
- to be an exemplary employer;
- to inspire others through co-operation.

VALUES

Regarding the underlying values which influence Co-operative membership and the way it runs all of its businesses, the Group states (Co-operative Group website):

Our co-operative values:

- self-help: we help people to help themselves;
- self-responsibility: we take responsibility for, and answer to, our actions;
- democracy: we give our members a say in the way we run our businesses;
- equality: no matter how much money a member invests in their share account, they still have one vote;
- equity: we carry out our business in a way that is fair and unbiased;
- solidarity: we share interests and common purposes with our members and other co-operatives.

Our ethical values:

- openness: nobody's perfect, and we won't hide it when we're not;
- honesty: we are honest about what we do and the way we do it;
- social responsibility: we encourage people to take responsibility for their own community, and work together to improve it;
- caring for others: we regularly fund charities and local community groups from the profits of our businesses.

The Group has an ethical operating plan, *Leading the Way (2011–2013)* which outlines 50 social responsibility commitments from supporting cooperatives and ethical finance to animal welfare, protecting the environment and inspiring young people.

MEMBER PARTICIPATION

Members participate in decision-making democratically through a network of member representatives and a pyramid of area, regional and group committees/boards.

QUESTIONS

1. The Co-operative Group distributes its profits to its owners. Should it not be considered to be part of the private sector?
2. What are the commercial costs and benefits of operating ethically?
3. Is there any synergy between the Co-operative Group's different businesses?

DISCUSSION TOPIC

What are the advantages and disadvantages of a co-operative model for a business like the Co-operative Group?

SOURCES

The Co-operative Group website: www.co-operative.coop.

Our vision and Aims http://www.co-operative.coop/corporate/aboutus/ourvisionandaims/*Leading the Way – a revolutionary approach to social responsibility – Ethical Operating Plan (2011– 2013)*, www.co-operative.coop/join-the-revolution/our-plan.

THE EDEN PROJECT

The Eden Project is a visitor attraction in a reclaimed 160-year-old exhausted china clay quarry near St Austell, in Cornwall, England. It was established as one of the Landmark Millennium Projects to mark the year 2000 in the UK. It includes the world's largest greenhouse. The complex is dominated by two gigantic enclosures consisting of adjoining domes that house plant species from around the world. Each enclosure emulates a natural biome. The domes consist of hundreds of hexagonal and pentagonal, inflated, plastic cells supported by steel frames. The first dome emulates a tropical environment, and the second a Mediterranean environment.

While restoring the Lost Gardens of Heligan in the early 1990s, the Eden founder, Tim Smit, became fascinated with stories that connected plants to people and brought them alive. He enlisted the help of Philip McMillan Browse (Horticultural Director of the Lost Gardens of Heligan and former Director of RHS Wisley) and Peter Thoday (former President of the Institute of Horticulture) to put together a team of expert horticulturalists to create the Eden Project.

Building the attraction had many challenges. The capital cost of establishing the centre was £86 million, of which only half came from the Millennium Commission. In the first two months of construction it rained every day; 43 million gallons of rainwater drained into the pit. This prompted the engineers to come up with a subterranean drainage system that now collects all the water coming on to the site, which is used to irrigate the plants and flush the toilets, while the rainwater that falls on the biomes is used to maintain the humidity inside the Rainforest Biome. Today almost half of the water needs are provided from water harvested on site.

The main heating source for both biomes is the sun. The back wall acts as a heat bank, releasing warmth at night. The two layers of air in the triple-glazed windows provide insulation. The complex also uses 'green tariff electricity' – the energy comes from one of the many wind turbines in Cornwall, which were among the first in Europe. In December 2010 the Eden Project received permission to build a geothermal electricity plant which will generate approximately 4 megawatts, enough to supply Eden and about 5,000 homes.

There are around 1 million plants, including some 4,000 species and cultivars. Most are not rare, except for the few that tell stories of the need for conservation, and have not been taken from the wild. Many were grown from seed in the Eden Project nursery; others came from botanic gardens, research stations and supporters, mostly in Europe and the UK. Some of the plants are insect-pollinated, others wind-pollinated.

In 2005, the Eden Project launched 'A Time of Gifts' for the winter months, November to February. This features an ice rink covering the lake, with a small cafe/

bar attached, as well as a Christmas market. Cornish choirs regularly perform in the biomes.

'The Core', which opened in September 2005, provides the Eden Project with an education facility, incorporating classrooms and exhibition spaces designed to help communicate Eden's central message about the relationship between people and plants. Accordingly, the building has taken its inspiration from plants, most noticeable in the form of the soaring timber roof, which gives the building its distinctive shape.

Controversially, one of the companies the Eden Project currently partners with is the British mining company Rio Tinto Group. Rio Tinto is set to begin mining in Madagascar for titanium dioxide. Critics say that this will involve the removal of a large section of coastal forest, and may cause extensive damage to the unique biodiversity of the Malagasy flora and fauna.

The Eden Trust is a registered charity. In 2009/10 the Eden Project had a turnover of £30 million. Over 10 million people have visited the Project, which has also had a major positive impact on the local economy in Cornwall. Visitors provide 71 per cent of the Project's income in terms of entrance fees and merchandizing.

Roger Jones has argued that the Eden Project is a classic example of entrepreneurial strategizing, in three key phases:

- The pioneering and early adoption phase: entrepreneurs with innovative and creative ideas linked to personal determination and perseverance of the driving founders, and the challenges to bring those ideas to fruition – but without a clear strategic fit or direction, and with no accessible resources or money!

- The strategic change and transition phase: entrepreneurs recognizing that determination and perseverance are not enough to convert ideas and innovation into tangible strategic business outcomes.

- The reluctant acceptance phase: entrepreneurs 'reluctantly accepting' the necessity of organizational structure, governance paradigms and strategic clarity imposed by major stakeholders, enabling the venture to proceed to launch.

QUESTIONS

1. What business is the Eden Project in: a tourism visitor attraction, a local economic regeneration initiative, an educational project, a botanical centre, an environmental campaigning organization, a charity helping those in need?

2. Who are the Eden Project's competitors?

3. What makes for a great social entrepreneur?

4. How might a social entrepreneur have to adapt if he or she is to stay with an expanding project after the early entrepreneurial phase is over?

5. From what you know of the Eden Project carry out a PESTLE analysis of the external factors which may affect its future development.

DISCUSSION TOPIC

What criteria should a Third Sector organization, like the Eden Project, use to decide whether a private sector company, like Rio Tinto, is a suitable partner or sponsor?

SOURCES

The Eden Project website: www.edenproject.com.

Eden Team (ed.) (2008) *Eden Project: The Guide 2008/9*, Eden Project Books.

Roger Jones (2005) *Eden Project Case Teaching Notes*, Pearson Education.

Richard Mabey (2005) *Fencing Paradise: Exploring the Gardens of Eden*, Eden Project Books.

Hugh Pearman and Andrew Whalley (2003) *The Architecture of Eden*, Eden Project Books.

Tim Smit (2001) *Eden*, Bantam Press.

THE EMMAUS COMMUNITY

The first Emmaus Community was founded in Paris in 1949 by Father Henri-Antoine Groues, better known as the Abbé Pierre, a Catholic priest, MP and former member of the French Resistance during the Second World War. As an MP, he fought to provide homes for those who lived on the streets of Paris.

One night, a man called Georges, who had been released after 20 years in prison, only to become homeless and attempt suicide because his family was unable to cope with his reappearance, was brought to Abbé Pierre. The Abbé did not just offer him a place to sleep. He asked for his help. He told Georges about homeless mothers and their children who came to him looking for help and told Georges he could not cope with the problem on his own. Could Georges join him in his mission to help them? Georges became the first Emmaus Companion, living with Abbé Pierre and helping him to build temporary homes for those in need, first in the priest's own garden, then wherever land could be bought or scrounged. He later said: 'whatever else he might have given me – money, home, somewhere to work – I'd have still tried to kill myself again. What I was missing, and what he offered, was something to live for'.

In 1951, Abbé Pierre resigned as an MP to devote himself to fighting homelessness and poverty. He had relied on his salary to pay for Georges and the 18 men who now formed the first Community and were still building homes for those who desperately needed them. So the former MP and resistance hero toured the smart restaurants of Paris asking for donations. The Companions were outraged. They told Abbé Pierre firmly that begging compromised their – and his – self-respect. Instead, to raise the money they needed, they became 'rag pickers', collecting things that people no longer wanted and selling them on. So the concept of Companions running self-supporting businesses, with the profits going to those in greater need, was born.

Emmaus Communities spread across France as the Abbé brought the horrors faced by the poor to the world's attention. One day in January 1954 he learnt that the baby of a homeless couple had frozen to death overnight. Some days later he heard that an old woman had died of hypothermia on the streets, having been evicted from her home. Angered by these needless deaths, Abbé Pierre sent an open letter to newspapers and made a radio appeal to the nation. It soon turned Emmaus into a major international charity. The French public responded generously and gifts and support flooded in. Emmaus Communities opened across France. Abbé Pierre became an international figure and travelled the world spreading the word about Emmaus, causing Emmaus Communities to be established in mainland Europe, French West Africa, the Far East and South America. Each one retains the ideals of the first Communities – giving people the chance to support themselves and help others.

In the UK, each Emmaus Community and Group (apart from in the very early stages) is an independent charity, governed by a local board of trustees. This enables them to retain their own character and adapt to local circumstances. They also benefit from being part of a national federation, including coordination, mutual support and the chance to learn from one another. The UK national federation, Emmaus UK, a charity registered in England and Wales and a company limited by guarantee number, is managed by a board of trustees, elected by Communities. The majority of Federation Board members are also involved with their local Community or Group. The Board is also responsible for the Federation Office, based in Cambridge, which provides support to local projects and coordination on a national level.

Each Emmaus Community aims to become financially self-supporting through its trading activity, primarily the resale of furniture and household goods donated by the public. Any surplus is used to help others in need. Newer Communities rely on donations and grants to cover their costs while the business develops, but all projects aim to become financially self-sustaining within three years of opening. Emmaus Groups rely on fundraising to acquire a site, build/convert accommodation and set up the business. The Federation Office is also funded by donations and grants, both to provide its support services and also to help any Communities or Groups that urgently need funds. Independent research indicated that an Emmaus Community saves the taxpayer £800,000 per year in services forgone.

QUESTIONS

1. How would you demonstrate the social return on investment of an Emmaus Community?
2. What are Emmaus's distinctive competencies/capabilities?
3. How would you describe Emmaus's expansion in strategy terms?
4. Describe Emmaus's strategy as a logic model.
5. What external environmental factors are likely to influence the further development of Emmaus?

DISCUSSION TOPIC

Should housing and support for homeless people not be provided by the state, rather than charities like Emmaus?

SOURCE

Emmaus Community UK website: www.emmaus.org.uk.

THE FAIRTRADE FOUNDATION

The Fairtrade Foundation is the independent non-profit organization that licenses use of the Fairtrade Mark on products in the UK in accordance with internationally agreed Fairtrade standards. The Foundation was established in 1992 by CAFOD, Christian Aid, Oxfam, Traidcraft, the World Development Movement and the National Federation of Women's Institutes. The first Fairtrade certified product, Green & Black's Maya Gold Chocolate made with cocoa from Belize, was launched in 1994, shortly followed by Cafédirect coffee and Clipper tea.

In 1996, the first in a range of Percol single origin and organic Fairtrade coffees was launched. In January the following year, Fairtrade coffee became widely available to the catering trade and a campaign was launched to target restaurants and institutions. MPs Glenda Jackson, Simon Hughes and Peter Bottomley tabled an Early Day Motion in support of the Palace of Westminster serving Fairtrade refreshments, which attracted support from over 100 MPs and the House of Commons switched to Fairtrade Tiki Caffé in all of its refreshment outlets.

In 1998, the first honey to carry the Fairtrade Mark was launched by Equal Exchange. Divine Chocolate launched the first farmer-owned Fairtrade chocolate company, teaming up with the Kuapa Kokoo cooperative in Ghana and funded by a Department for International Development loan. Bristol, Nottingham, Bath and Norwich City councils became the first local authorities to convert to Fairtrade coffee and tea. Following an initiative led by the Co-operative Bank and Clare Short MP, top UK businesses, including Alliance & Leicester, Lucas Varity, Jarvis and the Woolwich, started offering Fairtrade coffee to their staff. The following year, insurance giant CGU (now AVIVA) was the latest large company to offer staff coffee, tea and hot chocolate with the Fairtrade Mark, through its vending machines.

In 2000, the first Fairtrade bananas were launched in over 1,000 Co-op stores. Other supermarkets swiftly followed suit. Co-op Fairtrade milk chocolate bars, the first supermarket own-label Fairtrade Mark product, jointly branded with pioneering Divine chocolate, were launched. The Co-operative Bank launched a Fairtrade Pledge to encourage their customers to switch to Fairtrade. Coffee and tea carrying the Fairtrade mark become available in the first national coffee shop chains to offer Fairtrade. Churches were targeted with action packs for Fairtrade Fortnight.

Fairtrade Foundation staff with members of the Women's Institute visited banana farmers in the Windward Islands and produced a film to link women farmers to women consumers. Fairtrade chocolate bar Dubble in aid of Comic Relief was launched, with an award winning education pack taking Fairtrade into 15,000 UK schools. The first Fairtrade composite product, Traidcraft Apricot Geobar, was launched.

By 2001, the retail value of annual Fairtrade sales had reached £30 million – equivalent to £1 being spent every second. Fruit Passion, the first range of fruit juices to carry the Fairtrade Mark, was introduced into supermarkets. Garstang in Lancashire declared itself 'the world's first Fairtrade Town'. The Transport and General Worker's Union, with nearly 1 million members, voted to promote Fairtrade tea and coffee.

In 2002, the new international Fairtrade Mark was launched. Colombian coffee was the first of a range of Sainsbury's own brand Fairtrade Mark products and was soon selling around 1 million Fairtrade bananas a week and offering own-label Fairtrade coffee, tea and chocolate. Starbucks began offering Fairtrade coffee as an option and Pret A Manger began offering only Fairtrade filter coffee. The *Spilling the Beans* report on the poverty of large numbers of people involved in the coffee trade was revised and in this year.

The Fairtrade Chocolate Chip Cake was launched by the Co-op, which won Multiple Retailer of the Year at the Retail Industry Awards 2002, in part due to its commitment to Fairtrade, including launching the first supermarket own-label Fairtrade instant coffee granules in 1,000 stores, switching all of its own-label chocolate to Fairtrade and selling Fairtrade pineapples. The annual retail value of Fairtrade Mark sales in the UK reached £45 million, i.e. almost £1.50 every second, with roast and ground coffee taking 14 per cent of the UK market.

In 2003, a poll showed recognition of the Fairtrade mark at 25 per cent and understanding of what the Mark means at 33 per cent. The number of Fairtrade Towns reached 19 and the Greater London Authority announced its intention to work towards Fairtrade City status. The number of Fairtrade retail products increased to over 130.

In 2004, as the Fairtrade Mark celebrated its tenth birthday in the UK, the Fairtrade Foundation won the UK Charity of the Year award. AMT Coffee became the first coffee chain to switch to 100 per cent Fairtrade. Marks & Spencer switched all the coffee sold in its 198 in-store Café Revives to Fairtrade. The number of Fairtrade retail products reached 350, including roses, footballs and wines. Tesco unveiled its own-label range of Fairtrade products. Organizations including the BMA, the Salvation Army and the Youth Hostel Association switched to Fairtrade certified products.

In 2005, Manchester and Salford became the joint one hundredth Fairtrade Towns. The one thousandth church achieved 'Fairtrade church' status from the Foundation. There were, by then, over 700 Fairtrade retail and catering products available in the UK. The world's first Fairtrade coconuts become available at Sainsbury's. The first Fairtrade certified cotton was launched at a press launch themed 'Cotton on to Fairtrade' in London. The first Fairtrade certified rice from the Himalayan foothills in North India was launched.

In 2006, retail sales of Fairtrade products were estimated at £290 million, up 46 per cent from 2005, with growth across all product areas. Over 1,500 Fairtrade retail and catering products were available in the UK. The first Fairtrade ice cream made with Fairtrade certified sugar was launched with Ben & Jerry's Fairtrade Vanilla. An international conference on Fairtrade Towns was held in London bringing together delegates from 17 different countries across Europe and North America.

In 2007, Loose Fairtrade certified bananas were launched by Sainsbury's and Waitrose. A public survey revealed that awareness of the Fairtrade Mark had risen to

57 per cent of the adult population. Sales of Fairtrade certified products topped £500 million. The following year, the Co-op switched all of its own-label hot beverages to Fairtrade. Tate & Lyle announced their commitment to convert 100 per cent of its retail branded sugar to Fairtrade. The Fairtrade Foundation launched *Tipping the Balance*, a vision to double the impact of UK Fairtrade by 2012.

In 2009, Cadbury Dairy Milk committed to going Fairtrade. Starbucks rolled out their 2008 announcement to go 100 per cent Fairtrade for all espresso-based coffees in the UK and Ireland. The first Muslim action guide to Fairtrade was launched with support from Muslim Aid and Islamic Relief. The Fairtrade Foundation hosted a conference on the effect of the food crisis for small producers.

South Africa became the first African Fairtrade market initiative, with support from the Fairtrade Foundation. Sainsbury's completed conversion of all their own-label roast and ground coffee to Fairtrade.

In addition to the founders, Foundation member organizations now also included Banana Link, Methodist Relief and Development Fund, Nicaragua Solidarity Campaign, People & Planet, SCIAF, Shared Interest Foundation, Soroptimist International, Tearfund and the United Reformed Church. The Foundation is the UK member of Fairtrade Labelling Organizations International, which unites 21 labelling initiatives across Europe, Japan, North America, Mexico and Australia/New Zealand as well as networks of producer organizations from Asia, Africa, Latin America and the Caribbean.

The Fairtrade Foundation is a registered charity. It is also a company limited by guarantee, registered in England and Wales. The Foundation works to the definition of Fair Trade agreed by FINE, a working group of the four international Fair Trade networks (Fairtrade Labelling Organizations International, International Fair Trade Association, Network of European World Shops and the European Fair Trade Association):

> Fair trade is a trading partnership, based on dialogue, transparency and respect that seeks greater equity in international trade. It contributes to sustainable development by offering better trading conditions to, and securing the rights of, marginalized producers and workers – especially in the South. Fairtrade Foundation website

The current vision of the Fairtrade Foundation is:

> Our vision is of a world in which justice and sustainable development are at the heart of trade structures and practices so that everyone, through their work, can maintain a decent and dignified livelihood and develop their full potential. Fairtrade Foundation website

To achieve this vision, the Fairtrade Foundation seeks to:

> transform trading structures and practices in favour of the poor and disadvantaged. By facilitating trading partnerships based on equity and transparency, Fairtrade contributes to sustainable development for marginalized producers, workers and their communities. Through demonstration of alternatives to conventional trade and other forms of advocacy, the Fairtrade movement empowers citizens to

campaign for an international trade system based on justice and fairness. Fairtrade Foundation website

The mission of the Fairtrade Foundation is:

The Foundation's mission is to work with businesses, community groups and individuals to improve the trading position of producer organizations in the South and to deliver sustainable livelihoods for farmers, workers and their communities by:

- being a passionate and ambitious development organization committed to tackling poverty and injustice through trade;
- using certification and product labelling, through the Fairtrade mark, as a tool for our development goals;
- bringing together producers and consumers in a citizens' movement for change;
- being recognized as the UK's leading authority on Fairtrade. Fairtrade Foundation website

The four key areas of activity of the Fairtrade Foundation are:

- providing an independent certification of the trade chain, licensing use of the Fairtrade Mark as a consumer guarantee on products;
- facilitating the market to grow demand for Fairtrade and enable producers to sell to traders and retailers;
- working with partners to support producer organizations and their networks;
- raising public awareness of the need for Fairtrade and the importance of the Fairtrade Mark.

The Fairtrade Foundation's staff work in six distinct teams:

- *Certification*: the Fairtrade Mark is a registered certification mark which the Foundation licenses to companies to use on products which comply with international Fairtrade standards and contractual requirements. The Certification Department ensures such compliance by setting up a licence agreement with each company specifying the product(s) which may carry the Mark, approving every separate use of the Mark and text referring to Fairtrade, and auditing each licensee's Fairtrade activities.
- *Commercial relations*: covering both food and non-food products, the Commercial Relations department is responsible for building business engagement. They are responsible for working with commercial operators to grow their sales of Fairtrade certified products, with integrity, through deepening commitment to existing product categories, greater product visibility and through the introduction of new product areas.
- *Policy and communications*: the Policy and Communications department at the Fairtrade Foundation aims to build public awareness and consumer demand for Fairtrade. Its programmes and campaigns include local campaigning development (including Fairtrade campaigns in towns, universities, schools and faith networks), media relations, PR and publications.

- *Marketing*: the team aims to make Fairtrade the first choice for consumers and businesses. Areas of focus include online marketing, supporter services and campaigns such as Fairtrade Fortnight.
- *Producer partnerships*: the team provides a focal point in the Foundation for the development of existing and new standards, communications with and support for producer organizations, facilitating the sourcing of products that underpin the growth of the UK Fairtrade market, and research and policy development to improve continually understanding and delivery of work in support of poverty reduction through trade.
- *Finance and resources*: the team provides central support to the four operational teams in the Foundation and looks after finance, information technology, human resources, fundraising and office management for the organization. The team is also responsible for the running of the governance function of the Foundation through the annual general meeting and meetings of the board of trustees.

CRITICISMS

Along with its success the Fairtrade movement has faced some criticism. Colleen Haight (2011) argues that:

- the high price of coffee, generally, and the global demand for better quality coffee means that many Fairtrade growers can now get better prices on the open market;
- the premiums paid by consumers are not necessarily going directly to farmers for improvements in social conditions, education, etc.;
- obtaining and maintaining a Fairtrade label requires significant bureaucracy, which has implications for illiterate small coffee growers;
- the quality of Fairtrade coffee is uneven;
- the benefits of Fairtrade do not go to poor migrant labourers;
- the model is technologically outdated.

QUESTIONS

1. What are the external environmental factors that are likely to influence the future success or otherwise of the Fairtrade Foundation?
2. What strategies has the Fairtrade Foundation adopted over its history, and why?
3. How should the Fairtrade Foundation measure success?
4. Who are the Fairtrade Foundation's competitors? How should it respond to them?

DISCUSSION TOPIC

Does the Fairtrade movement influence world poverty?

SOURCES

The Fairtrade Foundation website: www.fairtrade.org.uk.

www.fairtradefoundation/what_is-fairtrade/fairtrade_foundation.aspx.

The Fairtrade Foundation's strategy for 2008 to 2012: Tipping the Balance: The Fairtrade Foundation's Vision for Transforming Trade 2008–2012, http://www.fairtrade.org.uk/includes/documents/cm_docs/2008/F/Final.pdf.

A. Nicholls and C. Opal (2004) *Fair Trade: Market-Driven Ethical Consumption*, Sage Publications.

Fairtrade Foundation (2002) *Spilling the Beans on the Coffee Trade*, 2nd edn.

Colleen Haight (2011) *The Problem with Fair Trade Coffee*, Stanford Social Innovation Review Summer 2011.

FIVE LAMPS

Five Lamps is a social enterprise that aims to 'transform lives, raise aspirations, remove barriers and offer choice to families, business and communities'. It supports the community by reinvesting any profit back into the business. It is a company limited by guarantee, registered charity and community development finance institution. Five Lamps has four integrated areas of business:

- *Youth services*: in response to a need identified by the local community, Five Lamps established its own youth service. Its purpose-built youth facility 'The Youthy' was opened in 2000 and provides a range of services and activities for young people aged 7 to 18 years.

- *Financial inclusion*: Five lamps has a dedicated Financial Inclusion Team which offers affordable personal loans with payments that suit the finances of its customers. It also provides first-stage debt advice.

- *Enterprise*: Five Lamps supports people who are thinking about starting their own business, along with current businesses who may need support with a business loan and a range of support services including one to one advice, business planning, coaching workshops and training.

- *Employability*: Five Lamps supports people who are looking for work, training and volunteering opportunities. It also has an Employer Engagement service which matches people to employers' needs.

Five Lamps is based at Thornaby in Teesside and has offices across the North East. Its youth, enterprise and employability services are mostly delivered in Teesside; however, it is planning to replicate its successful model of delivery across the North East. Its financial inclusion service is delivered to specific areas of identified need across the North East. It worked with 20,000 people in 2009/10, generating an income of over £2.5 million, including a surplus of over £400,000.

Five Lamps has implemented a social audit framework. The social accounting includes surveys of various stakeholders, such as an assessment of how well the organization lives up to its values as well as measuring outcomes and primary and secondary impact in relation to its objective of growing each of its five business areas of:

- financial inclusion/personal lending: it issued 9,752 Growth Fund loans during 2010 (overachieving its target by 12 per cent);

- Communities Fund employability contract: Five Lamps accounts for 73 per cent of the total job outcomes within the whole contract;

- hard-to-reach unemployed customers, numbering 9,998;

- Neighbourhood Enterprise Gateways: 300 new businesses supported and 900 receiving enterprise coaching;
- youth services: 91 young people supported through the Foundation Learning Tier, 36 young people positively progressing from this tier and 6,472 young people accessing youth activities at the Youthy.

In 2010 Five Lamps also piloted the use of the 'Rickter scale' to measure progress of each client on soft outcomes within their employability service.

QUESTIONS

1. Describe the strategic choices made by Five Lamps from the evidence in the case study.
2. List the main stakeholders of Five Lamps. What might they hope for from Five Lamps?
3. Using PEST, what are the external environmental factors that will affect the future development of Five Lamps?
4. Draw up a vision statement for Five Lamps.
5. What are the advantages and disadvantages of Five Lamps being a charitable company limited by guarantee?

DISCUSSION TOPIC

Could the Five Lamp services be provided equally well by a private company?

SOURCES

The Five Lamps Organisation Directors/Trustees report and audited accounts 2009/10:
Five Lamps Social Accounts: Measuring our Impact 2010.
The Five Lamps website: www.fivelamps.org.uk.

HABITAT FOR HUMANITY

Habitat for Humanity International was founded in 1976 by Millard and Linda Fuller. The concept was born at Koinonia Farm, a small, interracial, Christian community outside of Americus, Georgia, founded in 1942 by farmer and biblical scholar Clarence Jordan. Koinonia Farm became a community where all people are treated equally, resources are shared and great responsibility is placed on being wise stewards of land and natural resources. It supports its work and community by selling what it produces: eggs, chickens, milk and hogs. In 1950 the Jordan family and other Koinonians were excommunicated from Rehoboth Southern Baptist Church for their views on racial equality and in 1956 the local business community began boycotting Koinonia products.

The Fullers first visited Koinonia in 1965, having recently left an affluent lifestyle and successful business in Montgomery, Alabama, to begin a new life of Christian service. At Koinonia, Jordan and Fuller developed the concept of 'partnership housing', where those in need of adequate shelter worked side by side with volunteers to build simple, decent houses. The houses would be built at no profit and interest would not be charged on the loans. Building costs would be financed by a revolving fund called The Fund for Humanity. The fund's money would come from the new homeowners' house payments, no-interest loans provided by supporters and money earned by fund raising activities. The monies in the Fund would be used to build more houses.

In 1968, Koinonia laid out 42 half-acre house sites with four acres reserved as a community park and recreational area. Capital was donated from around the country to start the work. Homes were built and sold to families in need at no profit and no interest. The basic model of Habitat for Humanity was begun. In 1973, the Fullers decided to apply the Fund for Humanity concept in developing countries. The Fuller family moved to Mbandaka, Zaire (now the Democratic Republic of Congo) to offer affordable yet adequate shelter to 2,000 people. After three years of hard work to launch a successful house building programme, the Fullers returned to the United States.

In September 1976, Millard and Linda Fuller called together a group of supporters to discuss the future of their dream. Habitat for Humanity International (HFHI) as an organization was born at this meeting. Construction began on the first house in San Antonio, Texas, Habitat's first affiliate. In 1979, the first Habitat house in Americus was built and Guatemala became the first Habitat affiliate in Latin America.

In 1984, former US President Jimmy Carter took part in their first Habitat work project, the Jimmy Carter Work Project, in New York City. Their personal involvement in Habitat's ministry brought the organization national visibility and sparked interest in its work across the nation. A tithe programme was written into Habitat's US affiliate covenant. HFHI experienced a dramatic increase in the number of new affiliates around the country. In 1986 the first Habitat affiliate in Canada was approved. The following year, Habitat was established in Australia. In 1988 Habitat's Global Village short-term mission programme, which offered vacation builds around the world, was established. In 1990, Abilene, Texas, became the five hundredth US affiliate; one of the original residents, Bob and Emma Johnson, paid off their mortgage on the first Koinonia Partnership home; and the first international Campus Chapter began at the University of Technology in Lae, Papua New Guinea.

By 1991, Habitat's ten thousandth house was built. The first Habitat ReStore, selling quality used and surplus building materials donated from outside companies and organizations, was opened in Winnipeg, Canada. Proceeds from ReStores helped local affiliates fund the construction of Habitat houses. The following year, the first Native American affiliate was approved to address the need for decent housing in Indian reservations. The Sumter County Initiative began with the goal to eliminate poverty housing in Americus and Sumter County, Georgia, by the year 2000. US President Bill Clinton and Vice President Al Gore worked on a Habitat for Humanity house in Atlanta, Georgia. The first Habitat ReStore in the United States opened in Austin, Texas.

In 1993, Habitat completed its twenty thousandth house worldwide during a 20-house blitz build in Americus, Georgia. HFHI's board of directors established a Department of Environment within the organization that later became the Construction and Environmental Resources Department to educate Habitat affiliates on how to build the best quality houses at the lowest possible cost. The Entebbe Initiative was approved, putting more responsibility for Habitat building outside the United States into the hands of national partners. By 1994, Habitat was the seventeenth largest homebuilder in the United States.

In 1996, Habitat dedicated its fifty thousandth house worldwide in Pensacola, Florida. The fifty thousand and first house was also celebrated in Mexico City (the six thousand five hundredth Habitat house built in Mexico). Building projects began in Romania and Hungary. India's first affiliate, HFH Khammam, celebrated its twelfth anniversary and dedicates its one thousandth house. The following year, Habitat's sixty thousandth house was dedicated in Dallas, Texas. Leaders of the United States Congress kicked off National Homeownership Week by beginning work with Habitat on 'The Houses that Congress Built'. The next year, Habitat's seventy thousandth house was dedicated in Canton, Ohio.

Habitat's eighty thousandth house was dedicated, in 1999, in Mexico City. The Women Build Department's first formal initiative, First Ladies Build, brought together women governors and first ladies in each of the 50 states to build houses with families in need. The Jimmy Carter Work Project in the Philippines was the largest ever, with 14,000 volunteers from 32 countries building 293 houses. A new programme, the 21st Century Challenge, encouraged communities to set a date by which they would eliminate poverty housing in their areas. Habitat relocated its Latin America Caribbean office from Americus, Georgia, to San José, Costa Rica, to move services closer to the field.

In 2000, Habitat's one hundred thousandth house was dedicated in September in New York City. Victory was declared over substandard housing in Americus and throughout Sumter County, Georgia. Decentralization continued as the Asia Pacific office moved to Bangkok, Thailand, and the Africa Middle East office moved to Pretoria, South Africa. The following year, Millard and Linda Fuller travelled to Africa to celebrate the twenty thousandth house built on the continent of Africa and celebrated its 25th anniversary.

In 2003, Habitat's one hundred and fifty thousandth house was built, in Romania. The fifty thousandth US and Latin America house milestone was also reached. 'Building on the Dream' was introduced as an annual event in honour of Dr Martin Luther King's legacy. The following year, HFHI reached its 100-country goal. HFHI and the UN Human Settlements Program partnered to address urban poverty and disaster relief issues in developing countries. In 2005, in Knoxville, Tennessee, Habitat celebrated the construction of its two hundred thousandth house, providing decent shelter for 1 million people since its founding in 1976.

By 2011 Habitat had built more than 400,000 houses, sheltering more than 2 million people worldwide, with national partners in nearly 90 countries. There are special programmes for various different kinds of volunteers, such as youth, college students and women. There are partnerships with churches, corporate organizations and special programmes. Disaster response has become an integral part of Habitat's work as well.

QUESTIONS

1. How would you describe Habitat for Humanity's strategy?
2. Create a logic model for Habitat for Humanity.
3. How should Habitat for Humanity measure success?
4. What are Habitat for Humanity's distinctive capabilities/competencies that have led to its success?
5. What external factors might impact on the future development of the organization?

DISCUSSION TOPIC

What role should faith-based organizations play in the provision of services for disadvantaged people?

SOURCE

Habitat for Humanity International website: www.habitat.org.

MENCAP

In 1946, Judy Fryd, a mother of a child with a learning disability, formed The National Association of Parents of Backward Children. She wrote to *Nursery World* magazine inviting other parents to contact her. Many wrote back to Judy expressing their anger and sorrow at the lack of services for their children.

In 1955, the association changed its name to The National Society for Mentally Handicapped Children and opened its first project, the Orchard Dene short-stay residential home. In 1958, the National Society launched a ground-breaking action research project called the Brooklands Experiment. This compared the progress of children with a learning disability who lived in hospital with a group of children who were moved to a small family environment and cared for using educational activities modelled on those in 'ordinary' nurseries. After two years, the children in the home-like environment showed marked improvements in social, emotional and verbal skills. The success of the experiment was published around the world.

In 1963, the Society opened their new hostel and training workshop in Slough, Buckinghamshire – the first training centre of its kind for adults with a learning disability.

In 1966, the 'Gateway Clubs' were started, offering sports and leisure opportunities for people with a learning disability. In 1969, the society shortened its name to Mencap.

In 1975, Mencap's influence and campaigning work saw people with a learning disability included in the Further and Higher Education Act. Mencap set up the first homes and community-based accommodation for people with a learning disability in the UK. In 1985, Mencap's services for people with profound and multiple learning disabilities were founded and its 'Pathway' employment service began. A new national survey of disabled people was conducted which now included people with a learning disability.

In the 1990s, people with a learning disability were elected as Mencap national assembly members and became fully involved in decisions about how the organization was run. In 1995 the Disability Discrimination Act, which aimed to end the discrimination faced by many disabled people and to guarantee their civil rights, was passed. In 1998 Golden Lane Housing for people with a learning disability was established.

In 2004, Mencap launched its new five-year corporate strategy called 'Equal Chances', which focused on securing equal chances in life for all people with a learning disability.

The following year, the government published a report called *Improving the Life Chances of Disabled People* and set out plans to improve the quality of life of disabled adults and children by 2025. In 2008, Mencap rebranded as part of plans to make it a more modern and dynamic organization. In 2009 the Department of Health published *Valuing People Now* – a three-year plan for learning disability services in England. In the same year, the UK finally ratified the United Nations Convention on the Rights of Persons with Disabilities. It reaffirmed that disabled people have the same human rights as non-disabled people.

MENCAP'S VISION, MISSION AND VALUES

The following is taken from Mencap's 2011–2016 strategic plan, *Shaping our Future*.

Mencap is the leading voice of learning disability. Everything we do is about valuing and supporting people with a learning disability, and their families and carers.

What Mencap wants (our vision): a world where people with a learning disability are valued equally, listened to and included. We want everyone to have the opportunity to achieve the things they want out of life.

How Mencap will achieve this (our mission): we will

- listen to people with a learning disability;
- fight for the changes that people with a learning disability, and their families and supporters, want and need;
- support all people living with a learning disability in all parts of their lives;
- give excellent information and advice;
- work with people and groups that want the same things we do.

Mencap believes in (our values):

- being people centred;
- empowering, including and respecting all people;
- challenging wrong ways of thinking about learning disability;
- transforming lives;
- being brave and developing new ideas.

QUESTIONS

1. How many different strategies can be identified from the case study?
2. Will Mencap be able to live up to the commitment in its mission to 'support all people living with a learning disability in all parts of their lives'?
3. Express the Mencap mission in only one sentence.
4. How should Mencap measure its success?
5. What external environmental factors are likely to influence the development of the organization in future?

DISCUSSION TOPIC

Is the language that is used to describe learning disability and people with a learning disability important? Should Mencap keep its current name?

SOURCES

Mencap website: www.mencap.org.uk.

Shaping our Future 2011–2016 Strategic Plan Mencap downloaded from www.mencap.org.uk/about-us/shapingourfuture.

MITCHAM CRICKET GREEN

Mitcham Cricket Green is one of the oldest cricket grounds in the world; cricket has been played there for 300 years. Close to the Cricket Green are several other greens, all equally old, and once part of the historic London commons. Together they form the Mitcham Cricket Green Conservation Area.

Mitcham Cricket Green Community and Heritage (MCGCH) is a local organization with about 90 members. It aims to protect the Conservation Area from encroaching development and to ensure that use of the area as a recreational space grows. MCGCH had a wealth of ambitious ideas for the area and, with so many schemes floating about, they came to the Building Community Consortium (part of Locality) for help to organize their thinking and start the process of making practical plans.

Tony Burton is a member of MCGCH. He said: 'We're a group of people who care passionately about our local area, but we recognize we'd benefit from being a stronger organisation ... We didn't have a specific goal in mind – it was more a question of recognising our strengths and weaknesses. We're able to generate a wide range of ideas, but we need to curtail our enthusiasm and be disciplined about prioritising.'

Jeremy Fennell and Andy Perkin, development officers at Locality and experts in organizational development, worked with Tony Burton and the rest of the group to help them prioritize their ideas and also to focus their identity and aims as an organization. Jeremy said: 'Mitcham Cricket Green Community and Heritage Group came to us wanting a vision for the area and a vision for themselves as an organisation. They have loads of ideas and are very quick to see the potential in even the smallest things. The challenge is to ground those ideas and make them achievable.'

Andy started the process by taking a few of the group on a simple walk around the neighbourhood. He said: 'We did a walking tour around the greens to look at the area's key features and environment. Then I asked them to identify the most important buildings and spaces. They knew it all already of course, but it was just a question of getting it down on paper.'

From that starting point, Jeremy, Andy and MCGCH worked out the group's four most important strategic tasks: caring for the local environment and historic buildings; raising their profile; working in partnership with other groups; and celebrating the area with the local community.

The next stage of the Building Community Consortium's work is to help MCGCH prioritize which projects they want to take forward. Tony said: 'We've created a fairly daunting list of projects – developing a bid to the Heritage Lottery Fund to engage people in the local area; identifying local assets and registering them under the Community Right to Bid; restoring the memorial stone on the cricket ground and launching an audio trail to explore the area.'

Jeremy said: 'It's about harnessing all their experience and expertise in a plan and working towards a common aim. With the right project they can demonstrate a track record with the local community, funders and the local authority to match the strength they have already on planning issues.'

They are campaigning on a wide range of issues:

- The future of the Vestry Hall and old fire station, in collaboration with Merton Council and other voluntary groups.
- Floodlit sports pitches: they have strongly resisted a proposal from Merton Council for a floodlit sports pitch next to the bowling green which would destroy a large area of valuable woodland.
- Canons house and grounds: they are working with Merton Council to restore this eighteenth-century gem and open it up to community use. They are also keen to enhance the open space around Canons Leisure Centre and restore the historic running track.
- Tramlink: there are proposals to extend the Tramlink into Mitcham town centre. The tram is a very important asset to the area but they are concerned that plans are already being drawn up which will put the route across Cranmer Green Nature Reserve when alternatives are available.

Other current activities include:

- walks, talks and open days which celebrate and explore the local area;
- monitoring planning applications and influencing planning and conservation policies;
- mounting campaigns to raise awareness;
- ensuring the long-term future of cricket on the ground where it has been played continuously longer than anywhere else in the world;
- working with other local groups, including Mitcham Cricket Club, voluntary organizations and local churches;
- participating in official working groups and other networks;
- raising funds and increasing membership.

QUESTIONS

1. Write a mission statement and a vision statement for MCGCH.
2. What values would you say underpin the group's work?
3. Who are MCGCH's stakeholders?
4. What strategic choices has the group made?
5. Is a resource-based approach to strategy particularly relevant to MCGCH? What are its distinctive resources/assets?

DISCUSSION TOPIC

How should MCGCH measure its progress?

SOURCE

Further information available from www.mitchamcricketgreen.org.uk www.locality.org.uk/wp-content/uploads/Mitcham-Cricket-Green.pdf.

PATHS

In 2007 a range of voluntary and statutory agencies were brought together in the Lurgan/Brownlow area of County Armagh to identify the needs and desired outcomes for children and young people in the area. A large-scale survey was undertaken of children in the local schools. The results of this survey were compared with the available evidence for children in Northern Ireland, the UK and Europe. This comparison identified a particular problem for local children in relation to social and emotional learning. It was therefore agreed to focus on this issue as the desired outcome, with schools as the most appropriate location to deliver a suitable programme.

A search of the international 'what works' evidence, particularly Blueprints, identified PATHS, developed by staff at Penn State University, USA, as the most appropriate proven programme to achieve the desired change for children aged six to ten.

With funding from Atlantic Philanthropies, a new organization was established, Together4All, which began negotiating with the developer of the programme to adapt it for use in Northern Ireland. It was also agreed to undertake an RCT evaluation of the programme, involving 12 schools, randomly allocated into the intervention and control groups. The control group schools were to receive PATHS only after a delay of two years. Coaches were appointed to help adapt the programme and support schools in its delivery. The evaluation was guided by an expert advisory committee, including international experts.

In total, it took around two years to adapt fully the PATHS programme for Northern Ireland, involving extensive and prolonged negotiation with both the developer of the programme, who was concerned with ensuring the fidelity of the content, and the distributor of the programme materials, who was concerned with their design, both of whom received fees according to the number of classes delivering PATHS in school. Issues of adaptation included spelling (from American English), names of characters, sporting references, cultural identities and visual representations.

The evaluation has supported the efficacy of the programme and the original organization has merged to become part of national children's charity, Barnardo's. Sales of the adapted materials in the UK (and even the US) have demonstrated the potential of the adapted programme to be delivered extensively in the UK through a social franchise model.

QUESTIONS

1. What are some of the strengths and weaknesses of the social franchise model?

2. What are the potential advantages and disadvantages of the merger of a community-based organization with a larger national voluntary organization?
3. What are the strategic advantages of the merger from the point of view of Barnardo's as a UK-wide charity?
4. What are the advantages of an RCT evaluation?
5. Are there situations where an RCT evaluation is not possible or not appropriate?
6. What changes in the external environment might increase the take up of PATHS?

DISCUSSION TOPIC

In what ways is the culture of a large third sector organization likely to be different from a small one? In what ways would the culture be different if PATHS was being promoted by a private sector organization?

SOURCE

www.barnardos.org.uk.

DŴR CYMRU/WELSH WATER

Dŵr Cymru/Welsh Water is a company which supplies drinking water and wastewater services to most of Wales and parts of western England. Since 2001 it has been owned by Glas Cymru, a non-profit company limited by guarantee. Any profits are reinvested in the company. It has 3,000 employees.

Welsh Water originated in 1974 from the privatization of the Welsh Water Authority which itself had its origins in the Welsh National Water Development Authority that was created by the 1973 restructuring of the water industry in England and Wales. It took over various local public-sector water boards and river authorities. It also took over the water undertaking responsibilities of 11 Welsh Local authorities.

The Welsh Water Authority was privatized by stock market flotation in 1989, along with the other nine regional water authorities, which provided the company with a substantial surplus for some years, which it used to diversify into a range of sectors including leisure (hotels, fishing, etc.). It renamed itself Hyder in 1996 after taking over a local electricity company (SWALEC) and becoming a water and electricity multi-utility.

However, in 1999/2000, following the windfall tax on utility profits and the 1999 Ofwat price review, Hyder got into financial difficulties which led to its breakup following a takeover battle. Western Power Distribution purchased Hyder on 15 September 2000, with a view to acquiring its electricity distribution business, and rapidly sold off Hyder's other assets. Following a 'people's bid', Welsh Water was sold in 2001 by WPD to Glas Cymru for £1, along with £1.85 billion of Hyder debt. Under its licence Glas Cymru may not operate in sectors other than water.

Under Glas Cymru's ownership, Welsh Water's assets and capital investment are financed by bonds and retained financial surpluses. The Glas Cymru business model aims to reduce Welsh Water's asset financing cost, the water industry's single biggest cost.

Financing efficiency savings to date have largely been used to build up reserves to insulate Welsh Water and its customers from any unexpected costs and also to improve credit quality so that Welsh Water's cost finance can be kept as low as possible in the years ahead.

In 2012 Welsh Water announced a £1 billion investment programme over three years.

QUESTIONS

1. What are the advantages and disadvantages in Dŵr Cymru/Welsh Water being operated as a non-profit company?

2. Write a mission statement for Dŵr Cymru/Welsh Water.

3. What external factors might influence the success or otherwise of Dŵr Cymru/ Welsh Water?

4. What strategies should Dŵr Cymru/Welsh Water consider for the future?

DISCUSSION TOPIC

Should other essential utilities and services be run as non-profit enterprises?

SOURCES

Welsh Water website: www.dwrcymru.com.

www.guardian.co.uk/business/2012/june/13/welsh-water-dwr-cymru-investment.

REFERENCES

Acar, W. (1987) 'Organizational processes and strategic postures: cross-classification or continuous', *Proceedings of the General Systems Society*, J70–J84.

Accountability 1000 standard (2000) www.accountability.org.uk.

Adair, J. (1979) *Action-centred Leadership*, Gower.

Adair, J. (2006) *Effective Leadership*, CIPD.

Adams, J. S. (1965) *Inequity in Social Exchange*, Academic Press.

Adizes, Ichak (1999) *Managing Corporate Lifecycles: how and why corporations grow and die and what to do about it*, rev. edn, Prentice-Hall.

Alderfer, C. P. (1972) *Existence, Relatedness and Growth: human needs in organizational settings*, Free Press.

Allison, M. and Kaye, J. (2005) *Strategic Planning for Nonprofit Organizations*, Wiley.

Ambrosini, V. (2007) 'Economic perspectives', in M. Jenkins, V. Ambrosini and N. Collier (eds), *Advanced Strategic Management*, Palgrave Macmillan.

Anderson, T. J. (2000) 'Strategic planning, autonomous actions and corporate performance', *Long Range Planning*, 33(2), 184–200.

Andrews, K. R. (1980) *The Concept of Corporate Strategy*, 2nd edn, Irwin.

Andrews, G., Peters, L. and Teesson, M. (1994) *The Measurement of Consumer Outcome in Mental Health: A Report to the National Mental Health Information Strategy Committee*, Clinical Research Unit for Anxiety Disorders.

Andrews, K. R. (1971) *The Concept of Corporate Strategy*, 2nd edn 1987 Richard D. Irwin.

Anheier, H. K. (2000) 'Managing nonprofit organisations: towards a new approach', Civil Society working paper 1, Centre for Civil Society, London School of Economics and Political Studies.

Anheier, H. K. (2005) *Nonprofit Organisation: Theory, Management, Policy*, Routledge.

Anheier, H. K. and Salamon, L. M. (2006) 'The nonprofit sector in comparative perspective', in W. E. Powell and R. Steinberg (eds), *The Non-profit Sector: A Research Handbook*, 2nd edn, Yale University Press.

Ansoff, H. I. (1965) *Corporate Strategy*, Pelican.

Ansoff, I., Avner, J., Brandenberg, R. C., Partner, F. E. and Radosevich, R. (1970) 'Does Planning Pay?', *Long Range Planning*, 3(2).

Ansoff, I. and McDonnell, E. (1990) *Implanting Strategic Management*, Prentice-Hall.

Anthony, R. N. and Young, W. (1984) *Management Control in Nonprofit Organizations*, 4th edn 2008, Irwin.

Ardrey, R. (1970) *The Social Contract: a personal inquiry into the evolutionary sources of order and disorder*, Atheneum.

Argenti, J. (1965) *Corporate Planning*, Allen & Unwin.

Argenti, J. (1989) *What's SWOT in strategic analysis*, Human Resource Exceutive hr-www. exec.com.

Argyris, C. (1952) *An Introduction to Field Theory and Interaction Theory*, Labor and Management Center.

Argyris, C. (1964) *Integrating the Individual and the Organization*, Wiley.

Argyris, C. and Schon, D. A. (1974) *Theory in Practice: increasing professional effectiveness*, Jossey-Bass.

Argyris, C. and Schon, D. A. (1978) *Organizational Learning: atheory of action perspective*, Addison-Wesley.

Argyris, C. and Schon, D. A. (1996) *Organizational learning II: theory, method and practice*, Addison-Wesley.

Arvey, R. D., Rotundo, M., Johnson, W., Zhang, Z. and McGue, M. (2006) 'The determinants of leadership role occupancy: genetic and personality factors', *The Leadership Quarterly*, 17, 1–20.

Arvidson, M. (2009) 'Impact and evaluation in the UK Third Sector: reviewing literature and exploring ideas', TSRC working paper series.

Arvidson, M., Lyon, F., McKay, S. and Moro, D. (2010) 'The ambitions and challenges of SROI', Third Sector Research Centre working paper 49, December.

Au, C.-F. (1996) 'Rethinking Organizational Effectiveness: Theoretical and Methodological Issues in the Study of Organizational Effectiveness for Social Welfare Organizations', *Administration in Social Work*, 20(4), 1–17.

Australian Bureau of Statistics (ABS) (1996) *Voluntary Work – Australia* June 1995, Cat No. 4441.0 Canberra: agps, 1996.

Ayal, I. (1986) 'Planning for a professional Association', *Long Range Planning*, 19(3), 51–8.

Baden-Fuller, C. and Stopford, J. M. (1992) *Rejuvenating the Mature Business: the competitive challenge*, Harvard Business School Press.

Balduck, A.-L. and Buelens, M. (2008) 'A two-level competing values approach to measure nonprofit organisational effectiveness', working paper, Universiteit Gent.

Ball, M. (1989) *Multiple Funding in the Voluntary Sector*, Voluntary Services Unit, Home Office.

Barman, E. (2007) 'What is the Bottom Line for Nonprofit Organizations? A History of Measurement in the British Voluntary Sector', *Voluntas: International Journal of Voluntary and Nonprofit Organizations*, 18(2), 101–15.

Barnard, C. (1938) *The Functions of the Executive*, Harvard University Press.

Barnard, H. and Walker, P. (1994) *Strategies for Success*, NCVO.

Barney, J. B. (1991) 'Firm Resources and Sustained Competitive Advantage', *Journal of Management*, 17(1), 99–120.

Barr, A., Hashhagen, S. and Purcell, R. (1996) *The Monitoring and Evaluation of Community Development*, Scottish Community Development Centre/VAU.

Barrett, J. (2012) *Containment – finding the psychological space for change*, Cass Business School.

Barry, B. W. (1986) *Strategic Planning for Non-Profit*, Amherst Weider Foundation.

Barry, D. and Elmes, M. (1997) 'Strategy retold: toward a narrative view of strategic discourse', *Academy of Management Review*, 22, 429–52.

Bart, C. K. and Tabone, J. C. (1998) 'Mission statement rationales and organisational alignment in the not-for-profit health care sector', *Health Care Management Review,* 23(4), 54–69.

Bartlett, C. A. and Ghoshal, S. (1989) *Managing across Borders,* Harvard Business School Press.

Bartlett, C. A. and Ghoshal, S. (1998) 'Beyond strategic planning to organizational learning: lifeblood of the individual corporation', *Strategy and Leadership,* Jan/Feb, 34–9.

Basinger, N. W. and Peterson, J. R. (2008) 'Where you stand depends on where you sit: participation and reactions to change', *Nonprofit Management and Leadership,* 19(2).

Bass, B. M. (1970) 'When planning for others', *Journal of Applied Behavioural Science,* VI, 2, 1551–71.

Bass, B. M. (1985) *Leadership and Performance beyond Expectations,* Free Press.

Bass, B. M. (1990) *Bass and Stodgill's Handbook of Leadership : theory, research and application,* 3rd edn, Free Press.

Bass, B. M. (1998) *Transformational Leadership: industrial, military and educational impact,* Erlbaum.

Bass, B. M., Avolio, B. J. and Atwater, L. (1996) 'The transformational and transactional leadership of men and women', *International Review of Applied Psychology,* 45, 5–34.

Batsleer, J. (1995) 'Management and organisation', in J. Davis Smith, C. Rochester and R. Hedley (eds), *An Introduction to the Voluntary Sector,* Routledge.

Beck, T., Lengnick-Hall, C. and Lengnick-Hall, M. L. (2008) 'Solutions out of context: examining the transfer of business concepts to nonprofit organizations', *Nonprofit Management and Leadership,* 19(2).

Beckhard, R. F. and Harris, R. T. (1987) *Organizational Transitions: managing complex change,* Addison-Wesley.

Behrens, T. and Kelly, T. (2008) 'Paying the piper: foundation evaluation capacity calls the tune.', *New Directions for Evaluation,* 119, 37–50.

Bennis, W. G. (1966) *Changing Organizations,* McGraw-Hill.

Bennis, W. and Nanus, B. (1985) *Leaders: the strategies for taking charge,* Harper & Row.

Benz, M. (2005) 'Not for the profit, but for the satisfaction? Evidence on worker well-being in non-profit firms', *Kyklos,* 58(2), 155–76.

Berger, P. and Luckman, T. (1967) *The Social Construction of Reality,* Doubleday.

Beveridge, W. (1948) *Voluntary Action,* Allen & Unwin.

Bigelow, B., Stone, M. M. and Arndt, M. (1996) 'Corporate political strategy: a framework for understanding nonprofit strategy', *Nonprofit Management and Leadership,* 7(1).

Billis, D. (1984) 'The missing link: some challenges for research and practice in voluntary sector management', in B. Knight (ed.), *Management in Voluntary Organisations,* ARVAC.

Billis, D. (1993) *Organising Public and Voluntary Agencies,* Routledge.

Billis, D. and Harris, M (1996) (eds) *Voluntary Agencies: challenges of organisation and management,* Macmillan.

Blake, R. R. and Mouton, J. S. (1964) *The Managerial Grid,* Gulf Publishing.

Blake, R. R. and Mouton, J. S. (1978) *The New Managerial Grid,* TX.

Blau, P. M. and Scott, W. R. (1962) *Formal Organisations,* Routledge & Kegan Paul.

Block, S. R. and Rosenberg, S. (2003) 'Toward an understanding of founder's syndrome: an assessment of power and privilege among founders of nonprofit organizations', *Nonprofit Management and Leadership,* 12(4), 353–68.

Bluedorn, A. C. (1980) 'Cutting the Gordian knot: a critique of the effectiveness tradition in organisational research', *Sociology and Social Research*, 64, 447–96.

Blumberg, P. (1968) *Industrial Democracy: the sociology of participation*, Schoken.

Boboc, I. (2005) *Self-management Strategies for the Romanian Non-governmental Organisations*, www.megabyte.ulm.ro/arhiva/decebrie2008/document12.pdf.

Bodley-Scott, S. (2010) 'Rethinking your Strategy', *Strategy Magazine*, (1–24), June.

Bolman, L. G. and Deal, T. E. (1991) *Reframing Organizations*, Jossey-Bass.

Bolton, M. (2003) *Voluntary Sector Added Value: a discussion paper*, NCVO.

Bontis, N. (1999) 'Managing organisational knowledge by diagnosing intellectual capital: framing and advancing the state of the field', *International Journal of Technology Management*, 18(5–8), 433–62.

Bontis, N., Dragonetti, N., Jacobsen, K. and Roos, G. (1999) 'The knowledge toolbox', *European Management Journal*, 17(4), 391–402.

Boris, E. T. and Streuerle, C. E. (2006) 'Scope and dimensions of the nonprofit sector', in W. E. Powell and R. Steinberg (eds), *The Non-profit Sector: A Research Handbook* 2nd edn, Yale University.

Borzaga, C. and Tortia, E. (2006) 'Worker Motivations, Job Satisfaction, and Loyalty in Public and Nonprofit Social Services', *Nonprofit and Voluntary Sector Quarterly*, 35, 225–248.

Boschken, H. L. (1988) *Strategic Design and Organizational Change*, University of Alabama Press.

Bovaird, T. (2004) 'Public–private partnerships: from contested concepts to prevalent practice', *International Review of Administrative Science*, 70(2), 199–215.

Bovaird, T. and McKenna D. (2011) *Co-producing the Goods: how can Swansea's strategic partnerships improve the way they work with the public?*, Governance International.

Bovaird, T. and Rubienska, A. (1996) 'Marketing in the voluntary sector,' in S. P. Osborne (ed.), *Managing in the Voluntary Sector*, International Thomson Business Press.

Bowman, C. and Asch, D. (1987) *Strategic Management*, Macmillan.

Boyd, B. K. (1991) 'Strategic planning and financial performance', *Journal of Management Studies*, 28, 353–74.

Bozzo, S. (2000) 'Evaluation resources for nonprofit organizations: usefulness and applicability', *Nonprofit Management and Leadership*, 10(4), 463–72.

Bradach, J. (2003) 'Going to scale: the challenge of replicating social programmes', *Stanford Social Innovation Review*, Spring, 19–25.

Bradshaw, P., Murray, V. V. and Wolpin, J. (1992) 'Do nonprofit boards make a difference? An exploration of the relationships among board structure, process and effectiveness', *Nonprofit and Voluntary Sector Quarterly*, 21(3).

Brenton, M. (1985) *The Voluntary Sector in British Social Services*, Longman.

Bresser, R. K. and Bishop, R. C. (1983) *Dysfunctional Effects of Formal Planning*, Academy of Management.

Bridge, S., Mutagh, B. and O'Neill, K. (2008) *Understanding the Social Economy and the Third Sector*, Palgrave Macmillan.

Bridges, W. (1991) *Managing Transitions*, Perseus.

Brodie, E., Anstey, G., Vanson, T. and Piper, R. (2012) *Quality Assurance in the Voluntary and Community Sector: a scoping paper*, NCVO.

Brown, L. D. and Covey, J. (1987) 'Organizing and managing private development agencies', PONPO working paper 129, Yale University.

Brown, M. G. (1996) *Keeping Score: Using the Right Metrics to Drive World-Class Performance*, Quality Resources.

Brown, W. A. and Yoshioka, C. F. (2003) 'Mission attachment and satisfaction as factors in employee retention', *Nonprofit Management and Leadership*, 14(1).

Brudney, J. L. and Golec, R. R. (1997) 'Organisational benchmarks, impact, and effectiveness assessments: closing the measurement circle', in 'The changing social contract', *Independent Sector Spring Research Forum*, 36–46.

Bryman, A. (1996) 'Leadership in organizations', in S. R. Clegg, C. Hardy and W. R. Nords (eds), *Handbook of Organisational Studies*, 276–92.

Bryson, J. M. (1988) *Strategic Planning for Public and Non-Profit Organizations: a guide to strengthening and sustaining organizational achievement*, Jossey-Bass.

Bryson, J. M. (1994) 'Strategic Planning and Action Planning for Nonprofit Organizations', in R. D. Herman & Associates, *The Jossey-Bass Handbook of Nonprofit Leadership and Management*.

Bryson, J. M. (1995) *Strategic Planning for Public and Non-Profit Organizations*, Jossey-Bass.

Bunker, B. B. and Alban, B. T. (1997) *Large Group Interventions: engaging the whole system for rapid change*, Jossey-Bass.

Burgelman, R. A. (1980) 'Managing innovating systems: a study of the process of internal corporate venturing', PhD dissertation, Columbia University.

Burgelman, R. A. (1988) 'Strategy making as social learning process: the case of internal corporate venturing', *Interfaces*, May/June, 18(3), 74–85.

Burgoyne, J., Pedlar, M. and Boydell, T. (1994) *Towards the Learning Company*, McGraw-Hill.

Burkhart, P. J. and Reuss, S. (1993) *Successful Strategic Planning: a guide for nonprofit agencies and organizations*, Sage.

Burns, J. (1978) *Leadership*, Harper & Row.

Burns, T. and Stalker, G. M. (1961) *The Management of Innovation*, Oxford.

Butler, R. J. and Wilson, D. C. (1990) *Managing Voluntary and Non-profit Organisations*, Routledge.

Byington, D., Martin, P. Y., diNitto, D. M. and Maxwell, M. S. (1991) 'Organizational affiliation and effectiveness: the case of rape crisis centers', *Administration in Social Work*, 15, 83–103.

Cabinet Office (2007) *Helping Out: a national survey of volunteering and charitable giving*, Office of the Third Sector.

Cadbury, A. (1992) *Report of the Committee on the Financial Aspects of Corporate Governance*, Gee Publishing.

Cairns, B. Harris, M. and Young, P. (2005) 'Building the capacity of the Third Sector: challenges of theory and practice', *International Journal of Public Administration*, 28, 869–85.

Callaghan, K. (2009) 'Evaluation Ladder (drugs and housing) Evaluation Support Scotland', www.evaluationsupportscotland.org.uk.

Campbell, D. (2003) 'Outcomes assessment and the paradox of nonprofit accountability', *Nonprofit Management and Leadership*, 12(3).

Cameron, K. (1982) 'The relationship between faculty unionism and organization effectiveness', *Academy of Management Journal*, 25, 6–24.

Carlyle (1841) *Heroes and Hero Worship,* Chapman & Hall.

Carman, J. G. (2010) 'The accountability movement: what is wrong with this theory of change?', *Nonprofit and Voluntary Sector Quarterly,* 39(4), 383–403.

Carman, J. G. and Fredericks, K. A. (2008) 'Nonprofits and evaluation – empirical evidence from the field', *New Directions for Evaluation* 119, 51–71.

Carnegie UK Trust (2007) *Scenarios for Civil Society,* Carnegie UK Trust.

Carr, C. (1996) *Choice, Chance and Organizational Change,* AMACOM.

Carr, W. and Kemmis, S. (1986) *Becoming Critical,* Falmer.

Caudrey (1995) *Survey of Strategic Planning Tools,* Whitehill Clarke/ACENVO.

CENI (Community Evaluation Northern Ireland) (2010) *Measuring Up – a review of evaluation practice in the voluntary and community sector,* CENI.

Centre for Civil Society (2006) *Report on Activities July 2005–August 2006,* Centre for Civil Society.

Centre for Business Performance (2010) *The Impact of Investors in People on Firm Performance,* Cranfield University School of Management.

Champy, J. and Hammer, M. (1993) *Reengineering the Corporation,* HarperBusiness.

Chandler, A. D. Jr (1962) *Strategy and Structure,* MIT Press.

Chandler, D. G. (2002) *The Military Maxims of Napoleon: introduction and commentary,* Greenhill Books.

Chanan, G. (1991) *Taken for Granted,* Community Development Foundation.

Chauhan, Y. (1998) 'A planned journey into the unknown', Centre for voluntary organisations working paper 20, London School of Economics.

Cherrington, J. D. (1989) *Organizational Behavior: the management of individual and organizational performance,* Allyn & Bacon.

Child, J. (1984) 'New technology and developments in management organization', *Omega,* 12(3), 211–23.

Chmiel, N. (2000) *Work and Organisational Psychology: A European Perspective,* Blackwell.

Clark, J. (2007) *Voluntary Sector Skills Survey 2007 England,* UK Workforce Hub/Skills for Health/NCVO.

Clark, J. and Newman, J. (1997) *The Managerial State,* Sage.

Clary, E. G. and Snyder, M. (1991) 'A functional analysis of altruism and prosocial behavior: the case of volunteerism', in Margaret S. Clark (ed.), *Prosocial Behavior,* Sage.

Clary, E. G., Snyder, M. and Stukas, A. A. (1996) 'Volunteers' motivations: findings from a national survey', *Nonprofit and Voluntary Sector Quarterly,* Dec, 25(4), 485–505.

Clausewitz, K. von (1984) *On War,* Princeton University Press.

Clutterbuck, D. and Dearlove, D. (1996) *The Charity as Business: managing in the voluntary sector, learning from the private sector,* Directory of Social Change.

Coghlan, D. (1987) 'Corporate strategy in Catholic Religious orders', *Long Range Planning,* 20(1), 44–51.

Cole, G. D. H. (1945) 'A retrospect of the history of voluntary social service', in A. F. C. Bourdillon (ed.), *Voluntary Social Services: their place in the modern state,* Methuen.

Collins, J. (2001) *Good to Great,* Random House Business.

Collins, J. (2006) *Good to Great and the Social Sectors,* Random House Business.

Collins, J. C. and Porras, J. I. (1994) *Built to Last,* Random House Business.

Collins, J. C. and Porras, J. I (1997) *Built to Last – successful habits if visionary companies,* Random House Business.

Committee on the Financial Aspects of Corporate Governance (1992) *Report of the Committee on the Financial Aspects of Corporate Governance,* Gee Publishing.

Conger, J. A. (1989) *The Charismatic Leader: behind the mystique of exceptional leadership,* Jossey-Bass.

Conger, J. A. and Kanungo, R. N. (1987) 'Toward a behavioural theory of charismatic leadership in organizational settings', *Academy of Management Review,* 12, 637–47.

Conger, J. A. and Kanungo, R. N. (1988) *Charismatic Leadership: the elusive factor in organizational effectiveness,* Jossey-Bass.

Connoly, T., Conlon, E. and Deutsch, S. (1980) 'Organizational effectiveness: a multiple constituency approach', *Academy of Management Review,* 5, 211–17.

Connolly, P. and York, P. (2003) *Building the Capacity of Capacity Builders,* The Conservation Company.

Cooke, R. A. and Rousseau, D. M. (1988) 'Behavioral norms and expectations: a quantitative approach to the assessment of organizational culture', *Group and Organization Studies,* 13, 245–73.

Cooperrider, D. L. and Whitney, D. (1999) *Collaborating for Change: appreciative enquiry,* Berret-Koehler.

Coopey, J. (1995) 'The learning organization, power, politics and ideology', *Management Learning,* 26(2).

Cornforth, C. (ed) (2003) *The Governance of Public and Non-profit Organizations: what do boards do?,* Routledge.

Cornforth, C. and Edwards, C. (1998) *Good Governance: developing effective board-management relations in public and voluntary organisations,* CIMA.

Courtney, R. B. (1992) *Making a Difference: the story of the Simon Community,* Simon Community Northern Ireland.

Courtney, R. B. (1995) *Planning a Fundraising Strategy,* 2nd edn, NICVA.

Courtney, R. B. (1996) *Managing Voluntary Organizations: New Approaches,* ICSA.

Courtney, R. B. (2005) 'An examination of the strategic management of nonprofit organisations with particular reference to housing associations', unpublished PhD thesis, Queen's University Belfast.

Craig, J. C. and Grant, R. M. (1993) *Strategic Management,* Kogan Page.

Crainer, S. (2000) *The Ultimate Business Library,* 2nd edn, Capstone.

Crittenden, J. C. (2000) 'Spinning straw into gold: the tenuous strategy, funding and financial performance linkage', *Nonprofit and Voluntary Sector Quarterly,* 29(1), Supplement.

Crittenden, W. F., Crittenden, V. L. and Hunt, T. G. (1988) Planning and stakeholder satisfaction in religious organizations', *Journal of Voluntary Action Research,* 17, 60–73.

Crutchfield, L. R. and Grant, H. M. (2008) *Forces for Good: the six practices of high-impact nonprofits,* Jossey-Bass.

Cummings, S. (1993) 'The first strategists', in B. de Wit and R. Meyer (eds), *Strategy Process, Concepts, Context, Cases,* Prentice-Hall.

Cutt, J. (1998) 'Performance measurement in non-profit organisations: a note on integration and focus within comprehensiveness', in G. Dinsdale, J. Cutt and V. Murray (eds), *Performance and Accountability in Non-profit Organisations,* University of Victoria School of Public Administration Papers in Public Policy No. 4.

Cutt, J. and Murray, V. (2000) *Accountability and Effectiveness Evaluation in Non-Profit Organisations,* Routledge.

Cyert, R. M. (1975) *The Management of Nonprofit Organizations,* D. C. Heath.

Cyert, R. M. and Marsh, J. G. (1963) *A Behavioral Theory of the Firm,* Prentice-Hall.

Daft, R. L. (2010) *Understanding the Theory and Design of Organizations,* International Edition, South Western.

Dart, R. (2004) 'The legitimacy of social enterprise', *Nonprofit Management and Leadership,* 14(4), 411–24.

D'Aunno, T. (1992) 'The effectiveness of human service organizations: acomparison of models', in Y. Hasenfield (ed.), *Human Services as Complex Organizations,* Sage.

D'Aunno, T. A., Sutton, R. I., and Price, R. H. (1991) 'Isomorphism and external support in conflicting institutional environments: the case of drug abuse treatment units', *Academy of Management Journal,* 34(3), 636–78.

Davis, R. C. (1928) *The Principles of Factory Organization and Management,* Harper & Row.

Davis, R. C. (1951) *The Fundamentals of Top Management,* Harper & Row.

Davis Smith, J. (1991) *Voluntary Activity: a survey of public attitudes,* Voluntary Action Centre.

Davis Smith, J. (1992) 'An uneasy alliance', in R. Hedley and J. Davis Smith (eds), *Volunteering and Society: principles and practice,* Bedford Square Press.

Davis Smith, J. (1995) 'The voluntary tradition: philanthropy and self-help in Britain 1500–1945', in J. Davis Smith, C. Rochester and R. Hedley (eds), *An Introduction to the Voluntary Sector,* Routledge.

Deakin, N. (1995) 'The perils of partnership', in J. Davis Smith, C. Rochester and R. Hedley (eds), *An Introduction to the Voluntary Sector,* Routledge.

Deakin, N. (1996) *Report on the Future of the Voluntary Sector,* NCVO.

Deckop, J. and Cirka, C. C. (2000) 'The risk and reward of a double-edged sword: effects of a merit pay program on intrinsic motivation', *Nonprofit and Voluntary Sector Quarterly* 29(3), 400–18.

Dees, J. G., Anderson, B. B. and Wei-Skillern, J. (2002) 'Pathways to social impact: strategies for scaling out successful social innovations', Centre for the Advancement of Social Entrepreneurship, CASE working paper series 3.

Dees, J. G., Emerson, J. and Economy, P. (2001) *Enterprising Nonprofits,* Wiley.

Dees, J. G., Emerson, J. and Economy, P. (2002) *Strategic Tools for Social Entrepreneurs,* Wiley.

Department of Social Development (DSD) (2006) *Toolkit to Measure the Added Value of Voluntary and Community Based Activity,* DSDNI.

Department of Trade and Industry (2002) *Social Enterprise: a strategy for Success,* DTI www.dti.gov.uk/socialenterprise.

De Vogel, S. H., Sullivan, R., McLean, G. H. and Rothwell, W. J. (1995) 'Ethics in OD', in W. J. Rothwell, R. Sullivan and G. N. McLean (eds), *Practicing Organizational Development,* Pfeiffer.

Devaro, J. and Brookshire, D. (2007) 'Promotions and incentives in non-profit and for-profit organisations', *Industrial and Labour Relations Review,* 60(3), 311–39.

Dierickx, I. And Cool, K. (1989) 'Asset stock accumulation and the sustainability of competitive advantage', *Management Science*, 34(12).

Dierkes, M. and Bauer, R. A. (eds) (1973) *Corporate Social Accounting*, Praeger.

DiMaggio, P. J. and Anheier, H. K. (1990) 'The sociology of nonprofit organizations and sectors', *Annual Review of Sociology*, 16, 137–59.

Doane, D. (2001) *Corporate Spin: the troubled teenager years of social reporting*, Central Books.

Doherty, B., Foster, G., Mason, C., Meehan, J., Meehan, K., Rotheroe, N. and Royce, M. (2009) *Management for Social Enterprise*, Sage.

Donnelly-Cox, G. and O'Regan, A. (1999) 'Resourcing organisational growth and development: a typology of Third Sector service delivery organisations', paper presented to IRSPSM Aston.

Drucker, P. F. (1954) *The Practice of Management*, Harper & Row.

Drucker, P. F. (1964) *Managing for Results*, Harper & Row.

Drucker, P. F. (1965) *Managing for Results*, Harper & Row.

Drucker, P. F. (1966) *The Effective Executive*, Harper & Row.

Drucker, P. F. (1973) *Management: tasks, responsibilities, practices*, Harper Business.

Drucker, P. F. (1980) *Managing in Turbulent Times*, Pan.

Drucker, P. F. (1985) *Innovation and Entrepreneurship*, Harper & Row.

Drucker, P. F. (1990) *Managing the Nonprofit Organization – principles and practices*, HarperBusiness.

Dunnette, M. D., Campbell, J. P. and Hakel, M. D. (1967) 'Factors contributing to job satisfaction and dissatisfaction and in six occupational groups', *Organisational Behaviour and Human Performance*, 2, 143–74.

Duque-Zuluaga, L. C. and Schneider, U. (2008) 'Market orientation and organizational performance in the nonprofit context: exploring both concepts and the relationship between them', *Journal of Nonprofit & Public Sector Marketing*, 19(2).

Eagly, A. H. (2007) 'Female leadership advantage and disadvantage: resolving the contradictions', *Psychology of Women Quarterly*, 31(1), 1–12.

Eagly, A. H. and Johnson B. T. (1990) 'Gender and leadership style: a meta-analysis' *Psychological Bulletin*, 108(2), 233–56.

Eccles, R. and Nohria, N. (1992) *Beyond the Hype: rediscovering the essence of management*, Harvard Business School Press.

Eccles, R. and Nohria, N. (1997) 'Strategy as a language game', in S. Segal-Horn (ed.), *The Strategy Reader*, Blackwell.

Edwards, M. (2004) *Civil Society*, Polity.

Edwards, M. and Sen, G. (2000) 'NGOs, social change and the transformation of human relationships: a 21st century civic agenda', *Third World Quarterly*, 21(4), 605–16.

Edwards, R. L. and Eadie, M. S. (1994) 'Meeting the change challenge: managing growth in the nonprofit and public human services sectors', *Administration in Social Work*, 18(2), 107–23.

Edwards, R. L.,Yankey, J. A. and Altpeter, M. A. (eds) (1998) *Skills for Effective Management of Nonprofit Organisations*, NASW Press.

Eliot, J. and Pottinger, J. (2008) *From Here to There: managing change in third sector organisations*, Performance Hub/NVCO.

Elkington, J. (1998) *Cannibals with Forks: the Triple Bottom Line of 21st Century Business,* Capstone

Elmore, R. F. (1978) 'Organizational models of social program implementation', *Public Policy,* 26, 185–228.

Emery, M. and Purser, R. E. (1996) *The Search Conference: theory and practice,* Jossey-Bass.

Erez, M. and Arad, R. (1986) 'Participative goal-setting: social, motivational and cognitive factors', *Journal of Applied Psychology,* 71, 591–7.

Erez, M. and Zidon, I. (1984) 'Effect of goal acceptance on the relationship of goal difficulty to performance', *Journal of Applied Psychology,* 69, 69–78.

Etzioni, A. (1961) *A Comparative Analysis of Complex Organizations,* Free Press.

Etzioni, A. (1964) *Modern Organizations,* Prentice-Hall.

Evans, E. and Garvey, B. (eds.) (2006) *Mission Impossible?,* nfpSynergy.

Evans, E. and Saxton, J. (2004) *Innovation Rules!,* nfpSynergy.

Fahy, J. and Smithee, A. (1999) 'Strategic marketing and the resource-based view of the firm', *Academy of Marketing Science Review,* 10, 1–20.

Falshaw, J. R., Glaister, K. W. and Tatoglu, E. (2006) 'Evidence on formal strategic planning and company performance', *Management Decision,* 44(1), 9–30.

Fayol, H. (1949 [1916]) *General and Industrial Management,* tr. Constance Storrs, Pitman.

Feinstein, K. W. (1985) 'Innovative management in turbulent times: large-scale agency change', *Administration in Social Work,* 9(3), 35–46.

Ferrario, (1994) 'Women as managerial leaders', in M. J. Davidson and R. J Burke (eds), *Women in Management: current research issues,* Paul Chapman.

Fiedler, F. E. (1967) *A Theory of Leadership Effectiveness,* McGraw-Hill.

Fiedler, F. E. and Garcia, J. E. (1987) *New Approaches to Effective Leadership,* John Wiley & Sons.

Firstenberg, P. B. (1979) 'Profit minded management in the nonprofit world', *Management Review,* 68, 8–13.

Fleishman, E. A. (1953) 'The measurement of leadership attitudes in industry', *Journal of Applied Psychology,* 38(1), 153–8.

Fleishman, E. and Harris, E. F. (1962) 'Patterns of leadership behavior related to employee grievances and turnover', *Personnel Psychology,* 15, 43–56.

Fleishman, E., Harris, E. F. and Burtt, H. E. (1953) *Leadership and Supervision in Industry,* Bureau of Educational Research, Ohio State University.

Fleishman, E., Mumford, M. D., Zaccaro, S. J., Levin, K. Y., Korotkin, A. L. and Hein, M. B. (1991) 'Taxonomic efforts in the description of leadership behavior: a systems and functional interpretation', *The Leadership Quarterly,* 4, 245–87.

Flynn, N. and Talbot, C. (1996) 'Strategy and strategists in UK local government', *Journal of Management Development,* 1(15), 24–37.

Follett, M. P. (1941) *Dynamic Administration,* Harper & Row.

Forbes, D. P. (1998) 'Measuring the unmeasurable: empirical studies of non-profit organization effectiveness', *Non-profit and Voluntary Sector Quarterly,* 27(2), 159–82.

Ford, J. D. and Ford, L. W. (1990) 'Designing organizations for growth', unpublished working paper, Ohio State University.

Foti, R. J. and Hauenstein, N. M. A. (2007) 'Pattern and variable approaches in leadership emergence and effectiveness', *Journal of Applied Psychology*, 92, 347–55.

Fox, E. M. and Urwick, L. F. (1973) *Dynamic Administration: the collected papers of Mary Parker Follett,* 2nd edn, Pitman.

Fredrickson, J. W. (1984) 'The comprehensiveness of strategic decision processes: extension, observations and future directions', *Academy of Management Journal*, 27, 445–66.

Fredrickson, J. W. and Acquinto, A. L. (1989) 'Intention and creeping rationality in strategic decision processes', *Academy of Management Journal*, 32, 516–42.

Fredrickson, J. W. and Mitchell, T. (1984) 'Strategic decision processes: comprehensiveness and performance in an industry with an unstable environment', *Academy of Management Journal*, 27, 399–423.

Freeman, R. E. (1984) *Strategic Management: a stakeholder approach,* Pitman.

Friedman, M. (2002) *Using Results and Performance Accountability to Improve the Wellbeing of Children and Families,* Fiscal Policy Studies Institute.

Frumkin, P. and Andre-Clark, A. (2000) 'When missions, markets and politics collide: values and strategy in the nonprofit human services', *Nonprofit and Voluntary Sector Quarterly*, 29(1), Supplement, 141–63.

Galton, F. (1869) *Hereditary Genius,* Macmillan.

Gann, N. (1996) *Managing Change in Voluntary Organisations: a guide to practice,* Open University Press.

Garrick, J. and Rhodes, C. (1998) 'Deconstructing organizational learning: the possibilities for a post-modern epistemology of practice', *Studies in the Education of Adults,* 30(2).

Gasper, D. (1999) *Evaluating the 'Logical Framework Approach': towards learning oriented development evaluation,* Institute of Social Studies.

Georgopoulos, B. S. and Tannenbaum, A. S. (1971) 'A study of organizational effectiveness', in J. Ghorpade (ed.), *Assessment of Organizational Effectiveness: issues, analysis and readings,* Goodyear.

Gerard, D. (1983) *Charities in Britain: conservatism or change?,* Bedford Square Press.

Gerstner, L. V. (2002) *Who Says Elephants Can't Dance? Inside IBM's historic turnaround,* Collins.

Geus, A. de (1988) 'Planning as learning', *Harvard Business Review*, March/April, 70–4.

Gherardi, S. (1999) 'Learning in the face of mystery', *Organization Studies*, 20(1).

Ghobadian, A. and Woo, H. S. (1994) 'Characteristics, benefits and shortcomings of our major quality awards', *International Journal of Quality and Reliability Management*, 13(2), 10–44.

Gifford, J. (2010) *History Lessons: what business and management can learn from the great leaders of history,* Marshall Cavendish.

Gilbert, X. and Strebel, P. (1988) 'Developing competitive advantage', in J. B. Quinn, H. Mintzberg and R. M. James (eds), *The Strategy Process*, Prentice-Hall.

Gimbert, X., Bisbe, J. and Mendoza, X. (2010) 'The role of performance measurement systems in strategy formulation processes', *Long Range Planning*, 43, 477–97.

Glisson, C. and Martin, P. (1980) 'Productivity and efficiency in human service organizations as related to structure, size and age', *Academy of Management Journal*, 23, 21–37.

Glueck, W. F., *et al.,* (1982) 'Four faces in strategic management', *Journal of Business Strategy*, Winter.

Goldman, A. (2010) How to treat toxic shock *Strategy Magazine*, June 24.

Gomes, R. C. and Liddle, J. (2009) 'The balanced scorecard as a performance management tool for third sector organizations: the case of the Arthur Barnardes Foundation', *Brazilian Administration Review,* 6(4), 354–66.

Gonella, C., Pilling, A. and Zadek, S. (1998) *Making Values Count: Contemporary experience in social and ethical accounting, auditing and reporting,* ACCA.

Goodsell, C. T. (2006) 'A new vision for public administration', *Public Administration Review,* 66, 623–35.

Goold, M. (1997) 'Institutional advantage: a way into strategic management in not-for-profit organisations', *Long Range Planning,* 30(2), 291–3.

Gouldner, A. W. (1971) 'Organizational analysis', in J. Ghorpade (ed.), *Assessment of Organizational Effectiveness: issues, analysis and readings,* Goodyear.

Grant, H. M. and Crutchfield, L. R. (2007) 'Creating high impact nonprofits', *Stanford Social Innovation Review*, Fall, 32–41.

Grant, H. M. and Crutchfield, L. R. (2007) *Forces for Good: the six practices of high impact nonprofits,* Jossey-Bass.

Grant, R. (1997) 'The resource-based theory of competitive advantage: implications for strategy formulation', in S. Segal-Horn (ed.), *The Strategy Reader*, Blackwell.

Grant, R. M. (2003) 'Strategic planning in a turbulent environment: evidence from the oil majors', *Strategic Management Journal,* 24 (6), 491–517.

Green, J. and Griesinger, D. (1996) 'Board performance and organizational effectiveness in non-profit social services organizations', *Nonprofit Management and Leadership,* 6, 381–402.

Greenberg, E. (1982) 'Nonprofit agencies: competing for scarce resources', *Journal of Business Strategy,* 2(3).

Greenleaf, R. K. (1977) *Servant Leadership: a journey into the nature of legitimate power and greatness,* Paulist Press.

Greenley, G. E. (1986) 'Does strategic planning improve performance?, *Long Range Planning,* 19(2).

Greiner, L. E. (1972) 'Evolution and Revolution as Organizations Grow', *Harvard Business Review,* 76(3) 55–68.

Greenley, G. E. (1989) *Strategic Management,* Prentice-Hall.

Greiner, L. E. (1998) 'Evolution and revolution as organizations grow', *Harvard Business Review,* 76(3), May/June, 55–68.

Grewe, T., Marshall, J. and O'Toole, D. (1989) 'Participative planning for a public service', *Long Range Planning,* 22(1), 110–17.

Grossman, A. and Rangman, V. K. (2001) 'Managing multi-site nonprofits', *Nonprofit Management and Leadership,* 11(3), 321–37.

Gruber, R. E. and Mohr, M. (1982) 'Strategic management for multiprogramme nonprofit organizations', *California Management Review,* 24(3), 15–22.

Guild, M. and Saxton, J. (2011) *Look nfpSynergy have done my PEST analysis,* nfpSynergy.

Gulati, R. and Westphal, J. D. (1999) 'Cooperative or controlling? The effects of CEO-board relations and the content of interlocks on the formation of joint ventures', *Administrative Science Quarterly,* 44, 473–506.

Gupta, R., Choudhry, D. G. and Gupta, S. N. P. (2011) 'Where are current performance measurement frameworks leading companies to: from academic and practitioner perspectives', *International Journal of Research in Computer Application and Management,* 1(5), July.

Gutch, R. (1992) *Contracting Lessons from the US,* NCVO.

Gutch, R., Kunz, C. and Spencer, K. (1990) *Partners or Agents,* NCVO.

Haberberg, A. (2000) 'Swotting SWOT', *Strategy,* September.

Haberberg, A. and Rieple, A. (2008) *Strategic Management: theory and application,* Oxford University Press.

Hackman, J. R. and Lawler, E. E. (1971) 'Employee reactions to job characteristics', *Journal of Applied Psychology,* 55, 259–86.

Hackman, J. R. and Oldham, G. R. (1975) 'Development of the job diagnostic survey', *Journal of Applied Psychology,* 60, 159–70.

Hackman, J. R. and Oldham, G. R. (1979) *Work Redesign,* Addison-Wesley.

Hackman, J. R. and Wageman, R. (2005) 'A theory of team coaching', *Academy of Management Review,* April, 30(2), 269–87.

Hackman, J. R. and Walton, R. E. (1986) 'Leading groups in organizations', in P. S. Goodman (ed.), *Designing Effective Work Groups,* Jossey-Bass.

Hailey, J. (1999) Strategic indicators of NGO values, paper presented to the European conference on the challenges of managing the Third Sector, University of Edinburgh, June.

Hailey, J. and Sorgenfrei, M. (2003) 'Measuring success: issues in performance management', keynote paper at the INTRAC 5th International Evaluation Conference, Netherlands.

Hall, P. D. (1994) 'Historical perspectives on nonprofit organizations', in R. D. Herman et al. (eds), *The Jossey-Bass Handbook of Nonprofit Leadership and Management,* Jossey-Bass.

Hall, S. (1989) *The Voluntary Sector under Attack...?,* Islington Voluntary Action Council.

Hamel, G. (2000) *Leading the Revolution,* Harvard Business School Press.

Hamel, G. and Prahalad, C. K. (1994) *Competing for the Future,* HBS Press.

Hamel, G. and Prahalad, C. K. (1997) 'Strategy as stretch and leverage', in S. Segal-Horn (ed.), *The Strategy Reader,* Blackwell.

Hammer, W. C. (1974) *Reinforcement Theory and Contingency Management in Organizational Settings,* St Clair Press.

Hammer, M. and Champy, J. (1993) *Reengineering the Corporation – a manifesto for business revolution,* Harper Business.

Handy, C. (1981) *Improving the Effectiveness of the Voluntary Sector,* NCVO.

Handy, C. (1988) *Understanding Voluntary Organizations,* Penguin.

Hannan, M. T. and Freeman, J. (1977) 'Obstacles to comparative studies', in P. S. Goodman and J. M. Pennings (eds), *New Perspectives on Organizational Effectiveness,* Jossey-Bass.

Harris, M. (1993) 'The power and authority of governing bodies: three models of practice in service providing agencies', working paper, Centre for Voluntary Organisations, London School of Economics.

Harris, M. (1997) *Voluntary Associations: five organisational challenges,* London School of Economics.

Harris, M. and Billis, D. (1986) *Organising Voluntary Agencies,* NCVO.

Harris, M. and Hutchison, R. (2002) '*Success factors in non-profit mergers: lessons from HIV/ AIDS agencies',* in the UK paper to 2001 ARNOVA conference.

Harvey Jones, J. (1987) 'Introduction', in I. Ansoff (ed.), *Corporate Strategy,* Penguin.

Hasenfield, Y. and Gidron, B. (1993) 'Self-help groups and human service organisations: an interorganisational perspective', *Social Services Review*, June, 217–36.

Hatch, S. (1980) *Outside the State,* Croom Helm.

Hatten, M. L. (1982) 'Strategic management in not-for profit organizations', *Strategic Management Journal*, 3, 89–104.

Hayes, T. (1996) *Management Control and Accountability in Non-profit/voluntary Organisations*, Ashgate.

Hayward, S. (1996) *Applying Psychology to Organizations,* Hodder & Stoughton.

Heffron, F. (1989) *Organization Theory and Public Organizations: the political connection,* Prentice-Hall.

Heijden, K. van der (1996) *Scenarios: the art of strategic conversation,* Wiley.

Heimovitics, R. D., Herman, R. D. and Jurkiewicz, C. L. (1993) 'Executive leadership and resource dependence in nonprofit organizations: a frame analysis', *Public Administration Review*, 53(5), 419–27.

Heimovitics, R. D., Herman, R. D. and Jurkiewicz, C. L. (1995) 'The political dimension of effective nonprofit leadership', *Nonprofit Management and Leadership*, 5(3), 233–48.

Henderson, B. (1979) *Henderson on Corporate Strategy,* Abt Books.

Henderson, B. (1970) *The Product Portfolio,* Boston Consulting Group.

Henderson, B. D. (1984) *The Logic of Business Strategy*, Ballinger.

Henriques, A and Richardson, J. (2004) *The Triple Bottom Line: does it all add up?*, Earthscan.

Herdan, B. (2006) *The Customer Voice in Transforming Public Services: independent report from the review of the Charter mark scheme and measurement of customer satisfaction with public services,* Cabinet Office.

Herman, R. D. (1994) 'Conclusion: preparing for the future of nonprofit management', in R. D. Herman *et al.* (eds), *The Jossey-Bass Handbook of Nonprofit Leadership and Management,* Jossey-Bass.

Herman, R. D. and Heimovics, R. D. (1994) 'A cross-national study of a method for researching non-profit organizational effectiveness', *Voluntas,* 5(1), 86–100.

Herman, R. and Renz, D. (1996) 'Thesis on nonprofit organizational effectiveness', *Nonprofit and Voluntary Sector Quarterly*, 28(2).

Herman, R. and Renz, D. (1998) 'Nonprofit organizational effectiveness: contrasts between especially effective and less effective organizations', *Nonprofit Management and Leadership*, 9, 23–38.

Herman, R. and Renz, D. (1999) 'Multiple constituencies and the social construction of nonprofit organizational effectiveness', *Nonprofit and Voluntary Sector Quarterly,* 19, 293–306.

Herman, R. D. and Renz, D. O. (2008) 'Advancing nonprofit organizational effectiveness research and theory', *Nonprofit Management and Leadership*, 18(4) 399–415, Summer.

Herman, R. and Tulipana, F. (1985) 'Board-staff relations and perceived effectiveness in non-profit organizations', *Journal of Voluntary Action Research*, 14, 48–59.

Hernandez, C. M. and Leslie, D. L. (2001) 'The difficulties of succeeding a charismatic leader', *Nonprofit Management and Leadership,* Summer, 11(4), 493–97.

Herold, D. M. (1972) 'Long range planning and organizational performance', *Academy of Management Journal.*

Hersey, P. and Blanchard, K H. (1982) 'Leadership style: attitudes and behaviours', *Training and Development Journal*, 36(5), 50–2.

Hersey, P. and Blanchard, K H. (1988) *Management of Organizational Behaviour*, Prentice-Hall.

Hertzberg, F. (1968) 'One more time: how do you motivate employees', Harvard Business Review, 52–62.

Hill, T. and Westbrook, R. (1997) 'SWOT analysis: it's time for a product recall', *Long Range Planning*, 30(1), 46–52.

Hind, A. (1996) *The Governance and Management of Charities*, Voluntary Sector Press.

HM Government (2012) *Growing the Social Investment Market: progress update.*

HM Treasury (2002) *Cross Cutting Review*, TSO, September.

HM Treasury (2007) *The Future Role of the Third Sector in Social and Economic Regeneration: Final Report*, TSO, July.

HM Treasury and Cabinet Office (2007) *The Future Role of the Third Sector in Social and Economic Regeneration: Final Report*, Stationery Office.

Hofer, C. W. (1976) 'Research on strategic planning: asurvey of past studies and suggestions for future efforts', *Journal of Economic Business* 28(3).

Hofer, C. W. and Schendel, D. (1978) *Strategic Formulation: analytical concepts*, West Publishing Company.

Hofstede, G. (1967) 'The game of budget control: how to live with budgetary standards and yet be motivated by them', *Operational Research Society*, 20(3), 388–90.

Hofstede, G. (1980) *Culture's Consequences: international differences in work-related values*, Sage.

Hofstede, G. (1981) 'Management control of public and not-for-profit activities', *Accounting Organizations and Society*, 6(3), 193–211.

Hogan, R., Raskin, R. and Fazzini, D. (1990) 'The dark side of charisma', in K. Clark and M. Clark (eds), *Measures of Leadership*, Leadership Library of America, 343–54.

Home Office (1990) *Efficiency Scrutiny of Government Funding of the Voluntary Sector*, HMSO.

Home Office (2004) *ChangeUp: Capacity building and infrastructure framework for the voluntary and community sector*, TSO.

Home Office (2005) Developing Capacity: next steps for ChangeUp, TSO, March.

Hosmer, L. T. (1982) 'The importance of strategic leadership', *Journal of Business Strategy*, 3(2), 47–57.

House, R. J. and Mitchell, T. R. (1974) 'Path-goal theory of leadership', *Journal of Contemporary Business*, 3, 81–98.

House, R. J. (1977) 'A theory of charismatic leadership', in J. G. Hunt and L. L. Larson (eds), *Leadership: the cutting edge*, Illinois University Press, 189–207.

House, R. J. and Baetz, M. L. (1979) 'Leadership: some empirical generalizations and new research directions', *Research in Organizational Behavior*, I.

House, R. J. and Mitchell, T. R. (1977) 'Path-goal theory of leadership', *Journal of Contemporary Business*, Autumn, 81–97.

Howard, R. J. (1982) *Three Faces of Hermeneutics*, University of California Press.

Hudson, M. (1995) *Managing Without Profit*, Penguin.

Hudson, M. (2005) *Managing at the Leading Edge,* Jossey-Bass.

Inter-departmental Group on Voluntary Activities and Community Development (1996) *Guidance on the Commissioning and Conduct of Evaluations of Voluntary Organisations in Northern Ireland,* VAU.

International Co-operative Alliance (1995) *Statement of Co-operative Identity,* ICA.

Ip, Y. K. and Koo, L. C. (2004) 'BSC strategic formulation framework: a hybrid of balanced scorecard, SWOT analysis and quality function deployment', *Managerial Auditing Journal,* 19(4), 533–43.

Isham, J., Kolodinsky, J. and Kimberley, J. (2006) 'The effects of volunteering for nonprofit organizations on social capital formation: evidence from a state-wide survey', *Nonprofit and Voluntary Sector Quarterly,* 35(3), 367–83.

Jackson, A. and Irwin, D. (2007) *Tools for Strategic Planning: what works best,* Performance Hub.

James, B. G. (1985) 'Reality and the fight for market position', *Journal of General Management,* Spring, 45–57.

Janis, I. L. (1972) *Victims of Groupthink,* Houghton Mifflin.

Janis, I. L. (1982) *Groupthink: psychological studies of policy decisions and fiascos,* Houghton Mifflin.

Jansson, B. S. and Taylor, S. H. (1978) 'The planning contradiction in social agencies: great expectations versus satisfaction with limited performance', *Administration in Social Work,* 2(2).

Jay, A. (1987) *Management and Machiavelli,* Business Books.

Jeavons, T. H. (1992) 'When the management is the message: relating values to management practice in nonprofit organizations', *Nonprofit Management and Leadership,* 2(4), 403–17.

Jenkins, J. C. (1977) 'Radical transformation of organizational goals', *Administrative Science Quarterly,* 22(4), 568–86.

Jenster, P. V. and Overstreet, G. A. (1990) 'Planning for a non-profit service', *LongRange Planning,* 23(2), 103–11.

Jobson, J. and Schneck, R. (1982) 'Constituent views or organizational effectiveness: evidence from police organizations', *Academy of Management Review,* 25, 25–46.

Jochum, V. and Pratten, B. (2006) *Values into Action,* NCVO.

Johnson, G. (2001) 'Mapping and re-mapping organizational culture', in G. Johnson and K. Scholes (eds), *Exploring Public Sector Strategy,* Prentice-Hall.

Johnson, G. and Greenwood, R. (2007) 'Institutional theory perspective', in M. Jenkins, V. Ambrosini and N. Collier (eds), *Advanced Strategic Management,* 2nd edn, Palgrave Macmillan.

Johnson, G. and Scholes, K. (1993) *Explaining Corporate Strategy,* Prentice-Hall.

Johnson, G., Scholes, K. and Whittington, R. (2008) *Exploring Corporate Strategy,* 8th edn, Prentice-Hall.

Johnson, N. (1981) *Voluntary Social Services,* Martin Robertson.

Johnson, T., Richardson, K. and Turnbull, G. (2007) *Expanding Values: a guide to social franchising in the social enterprise sector,* SIPS Transnational Partnership, Sustainable Business Concepts for the Social Economy.

Jones, I. W. and Pollitt, M. G. (1998) *The Role of Business Ethics in Economic Performance,* Macmillan.

Joyce, P. (1999) *Strategic Management for the Public Services,* Open University Press.

Joyce, P. and Woods, A. (1996) *Essential Strategic Management,* Butterworth-Heinemann.

Judge, T. A., Bono, J. E., Ilies, R. and Gerhardt, M. W. (2002) 'Personality and leadership: a qualitative and quantitative review', *Journal of Applied Psychology,* 87, 765–80.

Kanter, R. M. (1983) *The Change Masters,* Simon & Schuster.

Kanter, R. M. (1989) *When Giants Learn to Dance: mastering the challenges of strategy, management and careers in the 1990s,* Simon & Schuster.

Kanter, R. M. (2009) *Supercorp: how vangard companies create innovation, profits, growth and social good,* Profile Books.

Kanter, R. M. and Brinkerhoff, D. (1981) 'Organizational performance: recent developments in measurement', in R. H. Turner and J. F. Short, Jr (eds), *Annual Review of Sociology 1981,* 321–49.

Kanter, R. M. and Summers, D. V. (1987) 'Doing well while doing good', in W. W. Powell (ed.), *The Nonprofit Sector: A Research hHandbook,* Yale University Press.

Kaplan, R. S. (2001) 'Strategic performance measurement and management in nonprofit organizations', *Nonprofit Management and Leadership,* 11(3), Spring, 353–70.

Kaplan, R. S. and Norton, D. P. (1992) 'The balanced scorecard-measures that drive performance', *Harvard Business Review.*

Kaplan, R. S. and Norton, D. P. (1996) *The Balanced Scorecard,* Harvard Business School Press.

Kaplan, R. S. and Norton, D. P. (2004) *Strategy Maps: converting intangible assets into tangible outcomes,* Harvard Business Press.

Kare-Silver, M. de (1997) *Strategy in Crisis,* Macmillan.

Karger, D. W. and Malik, Z. A. (1975) 'Long range planning and organizational performance', *Long Range Planning,* Nov/Dec, 6, 60–4.

Katsioloudes, M. L. and Butler, L. M. (1996) 'The importance of strategic planning activities in nonprofit organizations', unpublished paper presented to the 1986 ARNOVA annual conference New York.

Katz, D. and Kahn, R. L. (1966) *The Social Psychology of Organizations,* Wiley.

Katz, R. (1978) 'Job longevity as a situational factor in job satisfaction', *Administration Science Quarterly,* 23, 204–23.

Katzell, R. A. and Yankelovich, D. (1975) *Work, Productivity and Job Satisfaction: an evaluation of policy related research,* Psychological Corp.

Kaufman, R. (1991) *Strategic Planning Plus,* Scott Foresman.

Kay, J. (1994) *Foundations of Corporate Success,* Oxford University Press.

Kearns, K. P. (1996) *Managing for Accountability: preserving the public trust in public and nonprofit organizations,* Jossey-Bass.

Kearns, K. P. (2000) *Private Sector Strategies for Social Sector Success,* Jossey-Bass.

Kearns, K. P. and Scarpino, G. (1996) 'Strategic planning research – knowledge and gaps', *Nonprofit Management and Leadership,* 6(4).

Keating, B. P. (1979) 'Prescriptions for efficiency in nonprofit firms', *Applied Economics,* 11, 321–32.

Kendall, J. (2003) *The Voluntary Sector,* Routledge.

Kendall, J. and 6P (1994) 'Government and the voluntary sector', in S. Saxon-Harold and J. Kendall (ed.), *Researching the Voluntary Sector*, vol. 2, Charities Aid Foundation.

Kendall, J. and Knapp, M. (1995) 'A loose and baggy monster: boundaries, definitions and typologies', in J. Davis Smith, C. Rochester and R. Hedley (eds), *An Introduction to the Voluntary Sector*, Routledge.

Kendall, J. and Knapp, M. (1996) *The Voluntary Sector in the UK*, Manchester University Press.

Kendall, J. and Knapp, M. (1998) 'Evaluation and the voluntary nonprofit sector: emerging issues', in D. Lewis (ed.), *International Perspectives on Voluntary Action: reshaping the third sector*, Earthscan.

Kendall, J. and Knapp, M. (1999) *Measuring the Outcomes of Voluntary Activity*, VAU.

Kendall, J. and Knapp, M. (2000) 'Measuring the performance of voluntary organisations', *Public Management*, 2(1).

Kennedy, C. (1996) *Managing with the Gurus*, Century Business Books.

Kennerley, M. and Neely, A. (2001) 'Performance measurement frameworks – a review', in A.D. Neely (ed.), *Business Performance Measurement: theory and practice*, Cambridge University Press.

Kenny, D. A. and Zaccaro, S. J. (1983) 'An estimate of variance due to traits in leadership', *Journal of Applied Psychology*, 68, 678–85.

Kerr, S. and Jermier, J. M. (1992) 'Substitutes for leadership: their meaning and measurement', *Organizational Behavior and Human Performance*, 22, 375–403.

Khatri, N., Ng, H. A. and Lee, T. (1999) 'The distinction between charisma and vision', *Asia Pacific Journal of Management*, 18(3), 373–93.

Kickul, J. and Neuman, G. (2000) 'Emergence leadership behaviors: the function of personality and cognitive ability in determining teamwork performance and KSAs', *Journal of Business and Psychology*, 15, 27–51.

Klausen, K. K. (1995) 'On the malfunction of the generic approach in small voluntary associations', *Nonprofit Leadership and Management*, 5(3), 275–90.

Klein, K. J., Zeigert, J., Knight, A. P. and Xiao, P. (2006) 'Dynamic delegation: shared hierarchical and deindividualized leadership in extreme action teams', *Administrative Science Quarterly*, 51, 590–621.

Knapp, M. R. J. (1984) *The Economics of Social Care*, Macmillan.

Knauft, B., Berger, R. A. and Gray, S. T. (1991) *Profiles of Excellence: achieving success in the profit sector*, Jossey-Bass.

Knight, B. (1993) *Voluntary Action*, HMSO.

Kohjasten, M. (1993) 'Motivating private versus public sector managers', *Public Personnel Management*, 22(3), 391–401.

Kohl, J. P. (1984) 'Strategies for growth: intervention in a church', *Long Range Planning*, 17(6), 76–81.

Kohn, A (1993) 'Why incentive plans cannot work', *Harvard Business Review*, 71(5), 54–63.

Kohn, A. (1998) 'Challenging behaviourist dogma: myths about money and motivation', *Compensation and Benefits Review*, 30, 27–37.

Kong, E. (2008) 'The development of strategic management in the non-profit context: intellectual capital in social service non-profit organizations', *International Journal of Management Review*, 10(3), 281–99.

Koteen, J. (1989) *Strategic Management in Public and Nonprofit Organizations,* Praeger.

Kotter, J. P. (1988) *The Leadership Factor,* Free Press.

Kotter, J. (1990) *A Force for Change: how leadership differs from management,* Freel Press.

Kotter, J. P. (1995) 'Leading edge: why transformation efforts fail', *Harvard Business Review,* 73(2), 59–67.

Kotter, J. P. (1996) *Leading Change,* Harvard Business School Press.

Kozlowski, S. W. J., Gully, S. M., McHugh, P. P., Salas, E., and Cannon-Bowers, J. A. (1996) 'A dynamic theory of leadership and team effectiveness: developmental and task contingent leader roles', in G. R. Ferris (1996) 'Team Leadership and Development: theory, principles, and guidelines for training leaders and teams', *Research in Personnel and Human Resource Management,* 14, 253–305.

Kramer, R. M. (1981) *Voluntary agencies in the Welfare State,* University of California Press.

Kramer, R. (1992) 'Voluntary organizations: contracting and the welfare state', in J. Batsleer, C. Cornforth and R. Paton (eds), *Issues in Voluntary and Nonprofit Management,* Addison-Wesley.

Kramer, R. M. (2004) 'Alternative paradigms for the mixed economy: will sector matter?', in A. Evers and J.-L. Laville (eds), *The Third Sector in Europe,* Edward Elgar, 219–36.

Krug, K. and Weinberg, C. B. (2004) 'Mission, money and merit: strategic decision-making but nonprofit managers', *Nonprofit Management and Leadership,* 14(3), Spring.

Kubler-Ross, E. (1973) *On Death and Dying,* Routledge.

Kushner, R. and Poole, P. (1996) 'Exploring structure effectiveness relationships in nonprofit arts organizations', *Nonprofit Management and Leadership,* 7, 119–36.

Lan, Z. and Rosenbloom, D. H. (1992) 'Editorial', *Public Administration Review,* 52(6).

La Piana, D. (2005) *Play to Win: the nonprofit guide to competitive strategy,* Jossey-Bass.

Lawler, E. E. III (1986) *High-involvement Management,* Jossey-Bass.

Lawler, E. and Rhode, J. (1976) *Information and Control in Organizations,* Goodyear.

Lawrie, A. (1994) *The Complete Guide to Business and Strategic Planning for Voluntary Organisations,* Directory of Social Change.

Leadbeater, C. (2007) *Social Enterprise and Social Innovation: strategies for the next Ten Years,* Cabinet Office of the Third Sector.

Learned, E. P., Christensen, C. R., Andrews, K. R. and Guth, W. D. (1965) *Business Policy: text and cases,* Irwin.

Leat, D. (1993) *Managing across Sectors: similarities and differences between forprofit and nonprofit organisations,* Volprof City University Business School.

Leat, D. (1995) *Challenging Management,* Volprof City University Business School.

Leavitt, H. J. (1963) *The Social Science of Organizations,* Prentice-Hall.

Letts, C. W., Ryan, W. P. and Grossman, A. S. (1998) *High Performance Nonprofit Organizations: managing upstream for greater impact,* Wiley.

Levitt, T. (1960) 'Marketing myopia', *Harvard Business Review.*

Lewin, K. (1946) 'Action research and minority problems', *Journal of Social Issues,* 2(4), 34–46.

Lewin, K. (1957) *Field Theory in Social Science,* Harper.

Lewin, K., Lippit, R. and White, R. (1939) 'Patterns of aggressive behaviour in experimentally created "social climates"', *Journal of Social Psychology,* 10, 271–99.

Lewis, D. (2003) 'Theorizing the organization and management of non-governmental development organizations', *Public Management Review*, 5(3), 325–44.

Lewis, J. (1996) 'What does contracting do to voluntary agencies? in D. Billis and M. Harris (eds), *Voluntary Agencies: Organisation and Management in Theory and Practice*, Macmillan.

Light, P. C. (2002) *Pathways to Nonprofit Excellence*, Brookings Institution Press.

Likert, R. (1967) *The Human Organization*, McGraw-Hill.

Lillis, C. and Shaffer, P. (1977) 'Economic output as an organizational effectiveness measure for universities', *Academy of Management Journal*, 20, 476–82.

Lindblom, C. E. (1959) 'The science of muddling through', *Public Administration Review*, 19(2).

Lindenberg, M. (2001) 'Are we at the cutting edge or the blunt edge? Improving NGO organizational performance with private and public sector strategic management frameworks', *Nonprofit Management and Leadership*, 11(3), Spring.

Lippitt, R., Watson, J. and Westlet, B. (1958) *Dynamics of Planned Change*, Jossey-Bass.

Locke, E. A. (1968) 'Towards a theory of task motivation and incentives', *Organizational Behavior and Human Performance*, 3, 157–89.

Locke, E. A., Shaw, K. N., Saari, L. M. and Latham, G. P. (1981) 'Goal setting and task performance: 1969–1980', *Psychological Bulletin*, 90, 125–52.

Lord, R. G., De Vader, C. L. and Alliger, G. M. (1986) 'A meta-analysis of the relation between personality traits and leader perceptions: an application of validity generalization procedures', *Journal of Applied Psychology*, 71, 402–10.

Lubelska, A. (1996) *Strategic Management Challenges: 'Researching the Voluntary Sector,'* conference paper at Manor House Birmingham University Aston University Business School.

Lyon, F. and Arvidson, M. (2011) *Social Impact Measurement as an Entrepreneur Process*, TSRC briefing paper 66, November.

Lyon, F. and Fernandez, H. (2012) 'Scaling up social enterprises: strategies taken from early years providers', TSRC working paper 79, April.

Lyons, M. (1996) 'On a clear day … strategic management for VNPOs', in S. P. Osborne (ed.), *Managing in the Voluntary Sector*, International Thomson Business Press.

Machiavelli, N. (1950) *The Prince and Discourses*, Modern Library.

MacMillan, I. C. (1983) 'Competitive strategies for not-for-profit organizations', *Advances in Strategic Management*, Vol. 1.

Maier, N. R. F. (1967) *Psychology in Industrial Organizations*, Houghton Mifflin.

Maier, N. R. F. (1973) *Psychology in Industrial Organzsations*, rev. edn, Houghton Mifflin.

Maitlis, S. (2004) 'Taking it from the top: how CEOs influence (and fail to influence) their boards', *Organization Studies*, 25, 1275–311.

Maloney, W., Smith, G. and Stoker, G. (2000) 'Social capital and associational life', in S. Baron, J. Field and T. Schuller (eds), *Social Capital: critical perspectives*, Oxford University Press.

Management Standards Centre (2008) *Management and Leadership: National Occupational Standards*, MSC.

Mann, R. D. (1959) 'A review of the relationships between personality and performance in small groups', *Psychological Bulletin*, 64, 241–70.

March, J. G. and Simon, H. A. (1959) *Organizations*, Wiley.

Marshall, T. F. (1996) 'Can we define the voluntary sector?', in D. Billis and M. Harris (eds), *Voluntary Agencies: challenges of organisation and management*, Macmillan.

Marsden, D. and French, S. (1998) *What a Performance: performance-ralated pay in the public services,* Centre for Economic Performance London School of Economics and Political Science.

Martin, A. O. and Peterson, M. (1987) 'Two-tier wage structures: implications for equity theory', *Academy of Management Journal*, 30(2).

Maslow, A.H. (1943) 'A theory of human motivation', *Psychological Review*, 50(4), 370–96.

Maslow, A. (1954) *Motivation and Personality,* rev. edn 1937, Harper.

Mason, D. (1984) *Third Sector Enterprise Management,* Plenum.

Mastrofski, S., Ritti, R. and Snipes, J. (1994) 'Expectancy theory and police productivity', *Law Society Review*, 28(1), 113–48.

Matthews, D. (1996) 'Can public life be regenerated?', paper presented at Independent Sector conference on 'Measuring the impact of the not-for-profit sector on society' 5–6 September 1996, Washington.

Mayo, E. (1945) *The Social Problems of and Industrial Civilization,* Harvard University Press.

McCarthy, G., Greatbanks, R. and Yang, J. B. (2002) 'Guidelines for assessing organizational performance against the EFQM model of excellence using the Radar Logic Manchester School of management', https://phps.portals.mbs.ac.uk/portals/49/docs/jyang.

McClelland, D. C. (1961) *The Achieving Society,* Van Nostrand.

McConkey, D. D. (1975) *MBO for Nonprofit Organizations,* AMACOM.

McCrimmond, Mitch (created 16 August 2010) www.leadersdirect.com.

McGahan, A. M. and Porter, M. (1997) 'How much does industry matter really?', *Strategic Management Journal*, Summer Special Issue 15–30.

McGrath, J. E. (1984) *Group Interaction and Performance,* Prentice-Hall.

McGregor, D. M. (1960) *The Human Side of Enterprise,* McGraw-Hill.

McKinsey & Co (2001) *Effective Capacity Building in Nonprofit Organizations,* VPP.

McLaughlin, C. (1986) *The Management of Non-profit Organizations,* John Wiley.

McNeece, C. and Thyer, B. (2004) 'Evidence-based practice', *Journal of Evidence-based Practice*, 1(1), 7–25.

Medley, B. C. and Akan, O. H. (2008) 'Creating positive change in community organizations: a case for discovering Lewin', *Nonprofit Management and Leadership*, 18(4), 485–96, Summer.

Menzies Lyth, I. (1988) *Containing Anxiety in Institutions,* vol. 1, Free Association Books.

Meyer, J. W. and Rowan, B. (1977) 'Institutionalized organizations: formal structure as myth and ceremony', *American Journal of Sociology*, 83, 340–63.

Meyer, M. W. and Gupta, V. (1994) 'The performance paradox', *Research in Organizational Behavior,* 16, 309–69.

Meyer, J. and Rowan, B. (1991) 'Institutionalized organizations: formal structure as myth and ceremony', in W. Powell and P. diMaggio (eds), *The New Institutionalism in Organizational Analysis,* University of Chicago Press.

Meyer, M. and Zucker, L. (1989) *Permanently Failing Organizations,* Sage.

Mguni, N. and Bacon, N. (2010) *Taking the Temperature of Local Communities – The Wellbeing and Resilience Measure (WARM),* The Young Foundation Local Wellbeing Project.

Micklethwait, J. and Wooldridge, A. (1996) *The Witch Doctors,* Heinemann.

Miles, R. E. and Snow, C. C. (1978) *Organizational Strategy: structure and process,* McGraw-Hill.

Miller, C. C. and Cardinal, L. B. (1994) 'Strategic planning and firm performance: a synthesis of more than two decades of research', *Academy of Management Journal,* 37, 1649–65.

Miller, D. (1976) 'Strategy making in context: ten empirical archetypes', PhD thesis, McGill University Montreal.

Miller, D. (1979) 'Strategy, structure and environment', *Journal of Management Studies,* 16, 294–316.

Miller, D. (1992) 'The generic strategy trap', *Journal of Business Strategy,* 13(1).

Miller, D. (1997) 'Configurations of strategy and structure: towards a synthesis', in S. Segal-Horn (ed.), *The Strategy Reader,* Blackwell.

Milward, H. (1994) 'Nonprofit contracting and the hollow state', *Public Administration Review,* 54(1).

Miner, J. B. (1984) 'The unpaved road over the mountain: from theory to applications', *The Industrial/Organizational Psychologist,* 21, 9–20.

Minnesota Council of Nonprofits (2010) *Principles and Practices for Nonprofit Excellence,* MCN.

Mintzberg, H. (1973) *The Nature of Managerial Work,* Harper & Row.

Mintzberg, H. (1979) *The Structure of Organizations: a synthesis of research,* Prentice-Hall.

Mintzberg, H. (1987) 'Crafting strategy', *Harvard Business Review,* 66–75.

Mintzberg, H. (1994) *The Rise and Fall of Strategic Planning,* Prentice-Hall.

Mintzberg, H. (2009) *Managing,* Prentice-Hall.

Mintzberg, H., Ahlstand, B. and Lampel, J. (1998) *Strategy Safari: a guided tour through the wilds of strategic management,* Prentice-Hall.

Mintzberg, H. and Quinn, J. B. (1996) *The Strategy Process: Concepts, Contexts, Cases,* 3rd edn, Prentice-Hall.

Mintzberg, H. and Waters, J. (1997) 'Of strategies, deliberate and emergent', in S. Segal-Horn (ed.), *The Strategy Reader,* Blackwell.

Mintzberg. H. and Westley, F. (1992) 'Cycles of organizational change', *Strategic Management Journal,* 13, 39–59.

Mirvis, P. (1992) 'The quality of employment in the nonprofit sector: an update on employee attitudes', *Nonprofit Management and Leadership,* 3, 23–41.

Mitchell, J. C. (1983) 'Case and situational analysis', *Sociological Review,* 31, 187–211.

Mitchell, M. and Yates, D. (1996) 'How to attract the best volunteers', *Nonprofit World,* 14(4), 47–8.

Moore, J. I. (1992) *Writers on Strategy and Strategic Management,* Penguin.

Moore, M. H. (2000) 'Managing for value: organizational strategy in for-profit, non-profit and government organizations', *Non-Profit and Voluntary Sector Quarterly,* March, 29 supplement 1, 183–208.

Moore, M. H. (2003) 'The public value scorecard: a rejoinder and an alternative to "strategic performance/measurement and management in non-profit organizations" by Robert Kaplan', The Hauser Center for Nonprofit Organizations, The Kennedy School of Government, Harvard University working paper 18.

Morales Jr, H. R. (1997) 'Earning income through trade and exchange', in L. M. Fox and S. B. Schearer (eds), *Sustaining Civil Society: strategies for resource mobilization,* Civicus.

Morgan, G. (1983) *Beyond Method,* Sage.

Morgan, G. (1986) *Images of Organizations,* Sage.

Morgeson, F. P. (2005) 'The external leadership of self-managing teams', *Journal of Applied Psychology,* 90(3), 497–508.

Morrissey, M., Harbison, J., Healy, K., McDonnell, B. and Kelly, J. (2005) *Mapping Social Capital,* CFNI/CENI.

Morrissey, M., Healy, K. and McDonnell, B. (2008) *Social Assets Research – a new approach to understanding work in communities,* CFNI/CENI.

Moss Kanter, R. (1983) *The Change Masters – innovation for productivity in the American Corporation,* Simon & Schuster.

Moxham, C. (2009) 'Performance measurement: examining the applicability of the existing body of knowledge to nonprofit organizations', *International Journal of Operations and production Management,* 29(7), 740–63.

Murray, V. (2001) 'The state of evaluation tools and systems for nonprofit organizations', *Accountability: A Challenge for Charities and Fundraisers (New Directions for Philanthropic Fundraising),* 31, 39–50.

Murray, V. and Balfour, K. (1999) *Evaluating Performance Improvement in the Non-profit Sector: challenges and opportunities,* Altruvest.

Murray, V., Bradshaw, P. and Wolpin, J. (1992) 'Power in and around non-profit boards: a neglected dimension of governance', *Nonprofit Management and Leadership,* 3(2), 165–82.

Murray, V. and Tassie, B. (1994) 'Evaluating the effectiveness of nonprofit organizations', in R. D. Herman *et al.* (eds), *The Jossey-Bass Handbook of Nonprofit Leadership and Management,* Jossey-Bass.

Myers, J. (2004) 'Developing managers: a view from the nonprofits Sector', *Journal of European Industrial Training,* 28, 639–56.

Nadler, D. A. (1983) *Concepts for the Management of Organizational Change,* Delta Consulting Group.

Nathan, Lord (1990) *Effectiveness and the Voluntary Sector,* NCVO.

Neely, A. D. (2002) *Business Performance Measurement: theory and practice,* Cambridge University Press.

Neely, A., Adams, C., and Kennerley, M. (2002) *The Performance Prism: The Scorecard for Measuring and Managing Business Success* (Harlow: Financial Times/ Prentice-Hall).

Nelson, R. and Winter, S. (1982) *An Evaluation Theory of Economic Change,* Harvard University Press.

New Economics Foundation (2008) *Measuring Value: A Guide to Social Return on Investment (SROI),* NEF.

Newman, W. (1975) *Constructive Control: design and use of control systems,* Prentice-Hall

Newman, W. H. and Wallender III, H. N. (1978) 'Managing nonprofit enterprises', *Academy of Management Review,* 3, 24–31.

nfpSynergy (2010) *It's competition but not as we know it,* nfpSynergy.

Nicholls, A. (2006) 'Introduction', in A. Nicholls (ed.), *Social Entrepreneurship: new models of sustainable social change,* Oxford University Press.

Nicholls, A. (2009) 'We do good things don't we? Blended value accounting in social entrepreneurship', *Accounting, Organizations and Society,* 34(6–7), 755–69.

Nicholls, J., Lawlor, E., Neitzert, E. and Goodspeed, T. (2009) *A Guide to Social Return on Investment*, London Office of the Third Sector, The Cabinet Office.

Niven, P. R. (2003) *Balanced Scorecard Step-by-Step for Government and Nonprofit Agencies*, 2nd edn 2008, Wiley.

Nonaka, I. (1991) 'Toward middle-up-down management', *Sloan Management Review*, 29(3).

Northouse, P. (2001) *Leadership: theory and practice*, 2nd edn, Sage.

Nutt, P. C. and Backoff, R. W. (1992) *Strategic Management of Public and Third Sector Organizations*, Jossey-Bass.

O'Clery, C. (2007) 'The billionaire who wasn't', *Public Affairs*.

Odom, R. Y. and Boxx, W. R. (1988) 'Environmental, planning processes and organisational performance of churches', *Strategic Management Journal*, 9, 197–205.

Odiorne, G. S. (1987) *The Human Side of Management*, Lexington Books.

Ohmae, K. (1982) *The Mind of the Strategist*, McGraw-Hill.

Osborne, D. and Graebler, T. (1992) *Reinventing Government*, Addison-Wesley.

Osborne, S. P. (1996) *Managing in the Voluntary Sector*, International Thomson Business Press.

Osborne, S. P. (1998) *Voluntary Organizations and Innovation in Public Services*, Routledge.

Osborne, S. P. and Tricker, M. (1995) 'Researching non-profit effectiveness', *Voluntas*, 6(1), 93–100.

Osborne, S. P., Chew, C. and McLaughlin, K. (2008) 'The once and future pioneers? The innovative capacity of voluntary organizations and the provision of public services: a longitudinal appraisal', *Public Management Review*, 10(1), 51–70.

Oster, S. M. (1995) *Strategic Management for Nonprofit Organizations: theory and cases*, Oxford University Press.

O'Toole, J. (1986) 'Why good companies get into trouble', *New Management*, Summer, 60–4.

Owen, D. (1964) *English Philanthropy: 1660–1960*, Harvard University Press.

Owen, J. (2009) *How to Manage*, 2nd edn, Pearson Prentice-Hall Business.

Packard, T. (2010) 'Staff perceptions of variables affecting performance in human service organizations', *Nonprofit and Voluntary Sector Quarterly*, December, 39(6), 971–90.

Pascale, R. and Athos, A. (1981) *The Art of Japanese Management*, Penguin.

Pascale, R. T. (1990) *Managing on the Edge*, Viking Penguin.

Paton, R. (1991) 'The social economy: value-based organizations in the wider society', in J. Batsleer, C. Cornforth and R. Paton (eds), *Issues in Voluntary and Nonprofit Management*, Addison-Wesley.

Paton, R. (2003) *Managing and Measuring Social Enterpises*, Sage.

Paton, R. and Cornforth, C. (1992) 'What's different about managing in voluntary and nonprofit organizations?', in J. Batsleer, C. Cornforth and R. Paton (eds), *Issues in Voluntary and Nonprofit management*, Addison-Wesley.

Patton, M. Q. (2008) *Utilization-focussed Evaluation*, 4th edn, Sage.

Patrickson, M and Bamber, C. (1995) 'Introduction', in M. Patrickson, V. Bamber and G. J. Bamber (eds), *Organizational Change Strategies, case studies of human resource and industrial relations issues*, Longman.

Payne, R. L. (1996) 'The characteristics of organisations', in P. B. Warr (ed.), *Psychology at Work*, 4th edn, Penguin.

Pearce, J. A. and David, F. (1987) 'Corporate mission statements: the bottom line, 'Academy of Management Executive, 1(2), 109–16.

Pearce, J. A., Robbins, K. and Robinson, R. B. (1987) 'The impact of grand strategy and planning formability on financial performance', Strategy Management Journal, 8(2).

Pekar, P. Jr. and Abraham, S. (1995) ' Is strategic management living up to its promise?', Long Range Planning, 28(5), 32–44.

Perlmutter, F. D. and Gummer, B. (1994) 'Managing organizational transformations', in R. D. Herman et al. (eds), The Jossey-Bass Handbook of Nonprofit Leadership and Management, Jossey-Bass.

Perry, L. (1993) 'Effects of inequity on job satisfaction and self-evaluation in a national sample of African-American workers', Journal of Social Psychology, 133(4).

Perry, L T., Stott, R. G. and Smallwood, W. N. (1993) Real-time Strategy, John Wiley.

Peteraf, M. (1993) 'The cornerstones of competitive advantage: a resource-based view', Strategic Management Journal, 14, 179–91.

Peters, T. J. (1987) Thriving on Chaos, Knopf.

Peters, T. and Austin, N. (1985) A Passion for Excellence, Collins.

Peters, T. and Waterman, R. H. Jr (1982) In Search of Excellence: lessons from America's best run companies, Harper & Row.

Peterson, T. O. and Van Fleet, D. D. (2008) 'A tale of two situations: an empirical study of behavior by not-for-profit managerial leaders', Public Performance and Management Review, 31, 503–16.

Pettigrew, A. and Whipp, R. (1993) 'Managing the twin processes of competition and change: the role of intangible assets', in P. Lorange, Chakravarthy, B. S., J. Roos and A. Van de Ven (eds), Implementing Strategic Processes: change learning and co-operation, Blackwell.

Pfeffer, J. (1981) Power in Organizations, Pitman.

Pfeffer, J. (1982) Organizations and Organization Theory, Pitman.

Pfeffer, J. and Salancik, G. R. (1978) The External Control of Organizations: a resource dependence perspective, Harper & Row.

Philips, T. R. (1940) Roots of Strategy, Military Service.

Philips, T. R. (1989) Roots of Strategy, rev. edn, Military Service.

Phills, J. A. Jr (2005) Integrating Mission and Strategy for Nonprofit Organisations, Oxford University Press.

Phipps, K. A. and Burbach, M. E. (2010) Strategic Leadership in the Nonprofit Sector: opportunities for research, Institute of Behavioral and Applied Management.

Piercy, N. F. (2002) Market-led Strategic Change, Butterworth-Heinemann.

Pinchot, G. III (1985) Intrapreneuring, Harper & Row.

PLAN 2005 Social Audit Report www.socialaudit.co/2005/process2005/process2005-whatissa.html.

Pollitt, C. (1990) Managerialism and the Public Services: the Anglo-American experience, Blackwell.

Poole, D. L., Nelson, J., Carnahan, N. G., Tubiak, C. (2000) 'Evaluating performance measurement systems in nonprofit agencies: the program accountability quality scale (PAQS)', American Journal of Evaluation, 21(1), 15–26.

Porter, M. E. (1980) Competitive Strategy, The Free Press.

Porter, M. E. (1985) *Competitive Advantage: creating and sustaining superior performance,* The Free Press.

Porter, M. E. (1997) 'What is strategy', in S. Segal-Horn (ed.), *The Strategy Reader,* Blackwell.

Powell, C. T. (1992) 'Strategic planning as competitive advantage', *Strategic Management Journal,* 13, 551–8.

Powell , P. J. and DiMaggio,W. W. (1983) 'The iron cage revisited: institutional isomorphism and collective rationality in organizational fields', *American Sociological Review,* 48, 147–60.

Prashar, U. (1991) 'Introduction', in *The Voluntary Agencies Directory,* Bedford Square Press.

Pruzen, P. and Thyssen, O. (1990) 'Conflict and consensus: ethics as a shared value horizon for strategic planning', *Human Systems Development,* 9, 134–52.

Purcell, M. E. and Hawtin, M. (2010) 'Piloting external peer review as a model for performance improvement in third-sector organizations', *Nonprofit Management and Leadership,* 20(3), Spring.

Purvis, A., Lowrey, J. and Law, R. (2009) *Exploring a Distance Travelled Approach to WORKSTEP Development Planning,* Department of Work and Pensions.

QSTG (Quality Standards task Group) (2000a) *Excellence in View: a guide to the EFQM Excellence Model for the voluntary sector,* NCVO.

QSTG (Quality Standards task Group) (2000b) *Self-assessment Workbook: measuring success,* NCVO.

Quarter, J., Mook, L. and Richmond, B. J. (2003) *What Counts: social accounting for nonprofits and cooperatives,* Prentice-Hall.

Quinn, J. B. (1980) *Strategic Change: logical incrementalism,* Richard D. Irwin.

Quinn, J. B. (1988) 'Strategies for Change', in H. Mintzberg and J. B. Quinn (eds), *The Strategy Process: concepts, context, cases,* Prentice-Hall.

Quinn, R. and Rohrbaugh, J. (1983) 'A spacial model of effectiveness criteria: towards a competing values approach to organizational analysis', *Management Science,* 29, 363–77.

Rapp, C. and Poertner, J. (1992) *Social Administration: a client centred approach,* Longman.

Rathgeb Smith, S. and Gronbjerg, K. A. (2006) 'Scope and theory of government-nonprofit relations', in W. E. Powell and R. Steinberg (eds), *The Non-profit Sector: a Research handbook,* 2nd edn.

Rauschenberger, J., Schmitt, J. and Hunter, J. E. (1980) 'A test of the need hierarchy concept by a Markov model of change in need strength', *Administrative Science Quarterly,* 25, 654–70.

Raynard, P. and Murphy, S. (2000) *Charitable Trust? Social auditing with voluntary organisations,* NEF/ACEVO.

Reed, J., Jones, D. and Irvine, J. (2005) 'Appreciating impact: evaluating small voluntary organisations in the United Kingdom', *Voluntas,* 16(2), 123–41.

Rees, J., Mullins, D. and Bovaird, T. (2011) 'Third sector partnerships for service delivery: an evidence review and research project', TSRC briefing paper 60, June.

Reid, K. and Griffith, J. (2006) 'Social enterprise mythology: critiquing some assumptions', *Social Enterprise Journal,* 2(1), 1–10.

Reimann, B. C. (1975) 'Organizational effectiveness and management's public values: a canonical analysis', *Academy of Management Journal,* 18(2), 224–41.

Rice, J. J. (1997) 'Strategic vision in non-profit organisations: providing a clear direction for the future', *Journal of Volunteer Administration*, 15(4), 30–9.

Richardson, A. and Goodman, M. (1983) *Self-help and Social Care: mutual aid organisations in practice*, Policies Studies Institute.

Ring, P. S. and Perry, J. L. (1985) 'Strategic management in public and private organizations: implications of distinctive contexts and constraints', *Academy of Management Review*, 10, 276–86.

Robbins, K. C. (2006) 'The nonprofit sector in historical perspective: traditions of philanthropy in the West', in W. E. Powell and R. Steinberg (eds), *The Non-profit Sector: a research handbook*, 2nd edn, Prentice-Hall.

Robbins, S. P. (1990) *Organization Theory: structure, design and applications*, 3rd edn, Prentice-Hall.

Rochester, C. (1995) 'Voluntary agencies and accountability', in J. Davis Smith, C. Rochester and R. Hedley (eds), *An Introduction to the Voluntary Sector*, Routledge.

Roller, R. H. (1996) 'Strategy formulation in nonprofit social services organizations: a proposed framework', *Nonprofit Management and Leadership*, 7(2), 137–53.

Rollinson, D. (2002) *Organizational Behaviour and Analysis*, 2nd edn, Financial Times/ Prentice-Hall.

Ross, B. and Segal, C. (2002) *Breakthrough Thinking for Nonprofit Organizations: creative strategies for extraordinary result*, Jossey-Bass.

Rouse, P. (2003) 'An integral framework for performance measurement', *Management Decision*, 41(8), 791–805.

Rowold, J. and Rohmann, A. (2009) 'Relationships between leadership styles and followers' emotional experience and effectiveness in the voluntary sector', *Nonprofit and Voluntary Sector Quarterly*, 38(2), 270–86.

Rubin, M. S. (1988) 'Sagas, ventures, quests and parlays: a typography of strategies in the public sector', in J. M. Bryson and R. C. Einsweiler (eds), *Strategic planning – threats and opportunities for planners*, Planners Press.

Rumelt, R. P. (1991) 'How much does industry matter?', *Strategic Management Journal*, 12(3).

Rumelt, R. P. (2011) *Good Strategy/Bad Strategy – the difference and why it matters*, Profile Books.

Salamon, L. M. (1987) 'Partners in public service: the scope and theory of government–nonprofit relations' in W.W. Powell (ed.), *The Nonprofit Sector: a research handbook*, Yale University Press.

Salamon, L. M. (2010) *Nonprofits, Innovation and Performance Measurement*, The Johns Hopkins Listening Post Project, Nonprofit Innovation and Performance Measurement, Johns Hopkins University.

Salamon, L. M. and Anheier, H. K. (1993) 'A comparative study of the non-profit sector: purposes, methodology, definition and classification', in S . Saxon-Harrold and J. Kendall (eds) *Researching the Voluntary Sector*, Vol. 2 Charities Aid Foundation.

Salamon, L. M. and Anheier, H. K. (1994) *The Emerging Sector – an overview*, Johns Hopkins University.

Salamon, L. M. and Anheier, H. K. (1996) *The International Classification of Nonprofit Organizations, ICNPO Revision 1 1996*, Johns Hopkins University.

Salancik, G. R. and Pfeffer, J. (1977) 'An examination of need-satisfaction models of job attitude', *Administrative Science Quarterly*, 22, 427–56.

Salipante, P. F. and Golden-Biddle, K. (1995) 'Managing traditionality and strategic change in nonprofit organizations', *Nonprofit Management and Leadership,* 6(1), 3–20.

Sargeant, A. (2009) *Marketing Management for Nonprofit Organizations,* 3rd edn, Oxford University Press.

Savas, E. S. (1977) 'Organizational strategy, performance and management technology', *Administration in Social Work,* 1(2), 149–60.

Savitz, A. W. and Weber, K. (2006) *The Triple Bottom Line: how today's best-run companies are achieving economic, social and environmental success,* Wiley.

Sayles, L. (1972) 'The many dimensions of control', *Organizational Dynamics,* 21–31.

Schein, E. H. (1988) *Organizational Psychology,* 3rd edn, Prentice-Hall.

Schein, E. H. (1992) 'Organizational culture and leadership', in S. Saxon-Harold and J. Kendall (eds), *Researching the Voluntary Sector,* vol 1, CAF.

Schepers, C., de Gieter, S., Pepermans, R., Du Bois, C., Caers, R. and Jegers, M. (2005) 'How are Employees in the Nonprofit Sector Motivated?', *Nonprofit management and Leadership,* 16(2), 191–208,

Schmid, H. (2006) 'Leadership styles and leadership change in human and community service', *Nonprofit Management and Leadership,* 17(2), Winter.

Schneider, J. A. (2007) 'Connections and disconnections between civic engagement and social capital in community-based nonprofits', *Nonprofit and Voluntary Sector Quarterly,* 36(4), 572–97.

Schneider, A. and Locke E. A. (1971) 'A critique of Herzberg's classification system and a suggested revision', *Organizational Behavior and Human Performance,*12 (6), 441–56.

Schofield, J. (1996) 'Business Planning for Voluntary and Nonprofit Organizations' in S. P. Osborne (ed.) *Managing in the Voluntary Sector,* International Thomson Business Press.

Schumaker, P. (1980) 'The effectiveness of militant tactics in contemporary urban protest', *Nonprofit and Voluntary Sector Quarterly,* 9, 131–48.

Schwartz, P. (1991) *The Art of the Long View,* Doubleday.

Scott, D. and Russell, L. (2001) 'The experience of service delivery agencies', in M. Harris and C. Rochester (eds), *Voluntary Organisations and Social Policy in Britain: perspectives on change and choice,* Palgrave Macmillan.

Scott, W. R. (1977) 'Effectiveness of organizational effectiveness studies', in P. S. Goodman and J. M. Pennings (eds), *New Perspectives on Organizational Effectiveness,* Jossey-Bass.

Scott, W. R. (1992) *Organizations: rational, natural and open systems,* 3rd edn, Prentice-Hall.

Seanor, P. and Meaton, J (2007) 'Making Sense of Social Enterprise', *Social Enterprise Journal,* 3, (1) 90–100.

Seashore, S. E. and Yuchtman, E. (1968) 'Factorial analysis of organisational performance', *Administrative Science Quarterly,* 12, 377–95.

Seashore, W. R. (1983) 'A framework for an integrated model of organizational effectiveness', in K. S. Cameron and D. A. Whetten (eds), *Organisational Effectiveness: a comparison of multiple models,* Academic Press.

Seeger, J. A. (1991) 'Reversing the images of BCG's growth/share matrix', in H. Mintzberg and J. B. Quinn (eds), *The Strategy Process: concepts, contexts and cases,* Prentice-Hall.

Selby, C. C. (1978) 'Better performance from nonprofits', *Harvard Business Review,* Sept/Oct, 92–8.

Selznick, P. (1957) *Leadership in Administration: asociological interpretation,* Row, Peterson.

Senge, P. (1990) *The Fifth Discipline: the art and practice of the learning organization*, Doubleday.

Senge, P. M. (1990) *The Fifth Discipline*, Doubleday.

Senge, P. M. (2000) 'Give me a level long enough ... and single-handedly I will change the world', in P. M. Senge, *The Jossey-Bass Reader on Educational Leadership*, Jossey-Bass.

Setterberg, F. and Schulman, K. (1985) *Beyond Profit – the complete guide to managing the nonprofit organization,*) Harper & Row.

Sharp, C., Bitel, M., Gross, T. and Jones, J. (2007) *Successful strategies: real learning from real experiences,* Performance Hub.

Sheehan, R. M. Jr (1996) 'Mission accomplishment as philanthropic organization effectiveness: key findings from the Excellence in Philanthropy project', *Nonprofit and Voluntary Sector Quarterly*, 25, 110–23.

Sheehan, R. M. (2010) *Mission Impact: breakthrough strategies for nonprofits*, John Wiley.

Siciliano, J. I. (1997) 'The relationship between formal planning and performance in nonprofit organizations', *Nonprofit Management and Leadership*, 7(4), 387–403.

Siciliano, J. I. and Floyd, S. W. (1993) 'Nonprofit boards, strategic management, and organizational performance: an empirical study of YMCA organizations', PONPO working paper 183, Yale University.

Simmons, R. (2003) *The New Leisure Trusts*, Institute of Leisure and Amenity Management.

Simmons, R. (2004) 'A trend to trust? The rise of new leisure trusts in the UK', *Managing Leisure: an International Journal*, 9(3), 159–77.

Simon, H. A. (1947) *Administrative Behaviour: a study of decision-making processes in administrative organisations*, Macmillan.

Singh, K. K. (1996) 'The impact of strategic planning process variation on mission performance in nonprofit mental health service organizations', paper presented at ARNOVA conference, 7–9 November 1996, New York.

Skinner, B. F. (1938) *Science and Human Behaviour*, Macmillan.

Slatter, S. (1994) *Corporate Recovery: successful turnaround strategies and their implementation*, Harvard University Press.

Smircich, L. (1983) 'Concepts of culture and organizational analysis', *Administration Science Quarterly*, 28, 339–58.

Smith, A. (1979) *An Enquiry into the Nature and Causes of the Wealth of Nations*, ed. R. H. Campbell and A. S. Skinner, Oxford University Press.

Smith, Bucklin & Associates (1994) *The Complete Guide to Nonprofit Management*, Wiley.

Smith, D. and Shen, C. (1996) 'Factors characterizing the most effective nonprofits managed by volunteers', *Nonprofit Management and Leadership*, 6, 271–89.

Smith, D. H. (1991) 'Four sectors or five – retaining the member-benefit sector', *Nonprofit and Voluntary Sector Quarterly*, 20(2), 137–50.

Smith, J. A. and Foti, R. J. (1998) 'A pattern approach to the study of leader emergence', *The Leadership Quarterly*, 9, 147–60.

Smith, S. R. (1992) 'Nonprofit organisations in the age of contracting', working paper presented at NCVO conference, 7–8 September 1992, London.

Smith, S. R. and Gronbjerg, K. A. (2006) 'Scope and theory of government nonprofit relations', in W. E. Powell and R. Steinberg (eds), *The Nonprofit Sector: A Research Handbook,* 2nd edn, Yale University Press.

Smith, S. R. and Lipsky, M. (1993) *Nonprofits for Hire the welfare state in the age of contracting,* Harvard University Press.

Smith, R. J. (1994) *Strategic Management and Planning in the Public Sector,* Longman.

Smith, T. (1992) *Accounting for Growth,* Century.

Sowa, J. E., Selden, S. C. and Sandfort, J. R. (2004) 'No longer unmeasurable? A multidimensional integrated model of nonprofit organizational effectiveness', *Nonprofit and Voluntary Sector Quarterly,* 33(4), 711–28.

Spears, L. (2004) 'Practicing Servant Leadership', *Leader to Leader,* 34, Fall.

Spencer, L. J. (1989) *Winning through Participation,* Kendall/Hunt.

Stacey, R. D. (1993) *Strategic Management and Organizational Dynamics,* Pitman.

Standley, A. P. (2001) 'Reinventing a large nonprofit: lessons from four voluntary health associations', *Nonprofit Management and Leadership,* 11(3), Spring.

Steers, R. M. and Porter, L. W. (1983) *Motivation and Work Behaviour,* McGraw-Hill.

Steinberg, R. (2006) 'Economic theories of nonprofit organizations', in W. E. Powell and R. Steinberg (eds), *The Non-profit Sector: a research handbook,* 2nd edn.

Steiner, G. (1979) *Strategic Planning: what every manager should know,* Free Press.

Steiner, J. R., Gross, G. M., Ruffolo, M. C. and Murray, J. J. (1994) 'Strategic planning in nonprofits: profit from it', *Administration in Social Work,* 18(2), 87–106.

Stodgill, R. M. (1948) 'Personal factors associated with leadership: a survey of the literature', *Journal of Psychology,* 25, 35–71.

Stodgill, R. M. (1974) *Handbook of Leadership: a survey of theory and research,* Free Press.

Stone, M. M. (1989) 'Planning as strategy in nonprofit organizations: an exploratory study', *Nonprofit and Voluntary Sector Quarterly,* 18(4).

Stone, M. and Crittenden, W. (1993) 'A guide to journal articles on strategic management in non-profit organizations, 1977 to 1992', *Nonprofit Management and Leadership,* 4(2).

Stone, M. M., Bigelow, B. and Crittenden, W. (1999) 'Research on strategic management in nonprofit organizations: synthesis, analysis, and future directions', *Administration and Society,* 31(3).

Summers, H. G. jr. (1981) *On Strategy: the Vietnam war in context GPO,* Strategic Studies Institute US Army War College.

Sundeen, R. A., Raskoff, S. A. and Garcia, M. C. (2007) 'Differences in perceived barriers to volunteering to formal organizations: lack of time versus lack of interest', *Nonprofit Management and Leadership,* 17(3), 279–300, Spring.

Sussman, Carl (2003) 'Making change: the role of adaptive capacity in organizational effectiveness', *Nonprofit Quarterly, 21 December.*

Szabat, K. and Simmons, K. (1996) 'Nonprofit organizations and their strategic planning practices', paper presented at ARNOVA conference New York, 7–9 November 1996.

Szabat, K., Smither, J., Simmons, K. Seltzer, J. (1996) 'The relation between strategic planning practices and effectiveness in nonprofit organizations', paper presented at ARNOVA conference New York 7–9 November 1996.

Tagger, S., Hackett, R. and Saha, S. (1999) 'Leadership emergence in autonomous work teams: antecedents and outcomes', *Personnel Psychology,* 52, 899–926.

Taliento, L. and Silverman, L. (2005) 'A corporate executive's short guide to leading', *nonprofits', Strategy and Leadership,* 33 (2), 5–10.

Tannenbaum, R. and Schmidt, W. H. (1958) 'How to choose a leadership pattern', *Harvard Business Review*, Mar/April, 95–102.

Taylor, F. W. (1911) *The Principles of Scientific Management*, Harper & Row.

Taylor, B. (1997) 'The return of strategic planning – once more with feeling', *Long Range Planning*, 30(3), June, 334–44.

Taylor, S. J. and Bogdan, R. (1984) *Introduction to Qualitative Research Methods*, John Wiley.

Taylor, M. and Warburton, D. (2003) 'Legitimacy and the role of UK third sector organisations in the policy process', *Voluntas*, 14(3), 321–38.

Teasdale, S. (2010) 'Explaining the multifaceted nature of social enterprise: impression management as (social) entrepreneurial behaviour', *Voluntary Sector Review*, 1(3), 271–92.

Theuvsen, L. (2004) 'Doing better while doing good: motivational aspects of pay for performance effectiveness in non-profit organisations', *Voluntas*, 15(2), 117–36.

Thompson, M. (1993) *Pay and Performance: the employee experience*, IMS Report 218 Institute of Manpower Studies.

Thompson, P. and McHugh, D. (2002) *Work Organisations: a critical introduction*, Palgrave Macmillan.

Thune, S. S. and House R. J. (1970) *Where Long Range Planning Pays Off*, Business Hemsons.

Tinkelman, D. and Donabedian, B. (2007) 'Street lamps, alleys, ratio analysis, and nonprofit organizations', *Nonprofit Management and Leadership*, 18(1), 5–18.

Tober, J. (1991) 'Strategic planning in organizations and environments', PONPO working paper 165, Yale University.

Treacy, M. and Wiersema, F. (1995) *The Discipline of Market Leaders*, HarperCollins.

Tsui, A. S. (1990) 'A multiple constituency model of effectiveness: an empirical examination at the human resource subunit level', *Administrative Science Quarterly*, 35, 458–83.

Tzu, S. (1963) *The Art of War*, tr. S. B. Griffith, Oxford University Press.

United Way of America (1996) 'Measuring program outcomes: a practical approach', *www.unitedway.org/outcomes*.

Unterman, I. and Davies, R. H. (1982) 'The strategy gap is not for profits', *Harvard Business Review*, May–June, 30–40.

Unterman, I. and Davies, R. H. (1984) *Strategic Management for Not-for-profit Organizations: from survival to success*, Praeger.

Uphoff, N. (1995) 'Why NGOs are not a third sector: a sectoral analysis with some thoughts on accountability, sustainability and evaluation', in M. Edwards and D. Hulme (eds), *Non-governmental Organisations – performance and accountability: beyond the magic bullet*, Earthscan.

Uphoff, N. (1996) 'Understanding social capital: learning from the analysis and experience of participation', *Institutional Analysis*, 215–49.

Urban Institute (2006) *Building a Common Outcome Framework to Measure Nonprofit Performance*, Urban Institute.

Urwick, L. (1943) *The Elements of Administration*, Pitman.

Urwick, L. (1956) *The Golden Book of Management*, Newman Neame.

Urwick, L. and Brech, E. F. L. (1956) *The Making of Scientific Management*, vol. 1, Management Publications Trust.

Vaill, P. B. (1990) *Management as a Performance Art,* Jossey-Bass.

Valentin, E. K. (2001) 'SWOT analysis from a resource-based view', *Journal of Marketing Theory and Practice,* 9(2), 54–69.

Van de Ven, A. H. (1980) 'Problem solving, planning and innovation', *Human Relations,* 33(10), 711–40.

Van Eerde, W. and Thierry, H. (1996) 'Vroom's expectancy models and work-related criteria: a meta-analysis', *Journal of Applied Psychology,* 81, 575–86.

Van Wijck, P. (1994) 'Evaluating income distributions', *Journal of Economic Psychology,* 15(1).

Von Clausewitz, K. (1976) *On War,* tr. M. Howard and P. Poret, Princeton University Press.

Vroom, V. H. (1964) *Work and Motivation,* Wiley.

Waalewijn, P. and Segaar, P. (1993) 'Strategic management: the key to profitability in small companies', *Long Range Planning,* 26(2), 24–30.

Waddock, S. (2004) 'Parallel universes: companies, academics and the progress of corporate citizenship', *Business and Society Review,* 109(4), 5–42.

Walker, J. M. (1983) 'Limits of strategic management in voluntary organizations', *Journal of Voluntary Action Research,* 12(3).

Warr, P. (ed.) (1996) *Psychology at Work,* Penguin.

Wasdell, D. (1980) 'Long range planning and the church', *Long Range Planning,* 13.

Watson, T. Jr (1963) *A Business and its Beliefs,* McGraw-Hill.

Web, S. (1990) *Planning Strategy for Voluntary Organisations,* The Industrial Society.

Webster, S. A. and Wylie, M. L. (1988) 'Strategic Planning in Human Services', *Journal of Sociology Welfare,* 12(3), 25–43.

Weihrich, H. (1982) 'The TOWS matrix: a tool for situational analysis', *Long Range Planning,* 15(2), 54–66.

Weisbrod, B. (1987) *Nonprofit Organizations: A Dictionary of Economic Theory and Doctrine,* Macmillan.

Weisbrod, M. R. and Janoff, S. (1995) *Future Search,* Berret-Koehler.

Weiss, C. H. (1998) *Evaluation,* 2nd edn, Prentice-Hall.

Wernerfelt, B. (1984) 'A resource-based view of the firm', *Strategic Management Journal,* April-June, 171–80.

Westall, A. (2009) 'Value and the Third Sector', working paper on ideas for future research, Third Sector Research Centre Briefing Paper 25.

Whittington, R. (1993) *What is Strategy – and does it matter?,* Routledge.

Wilcox, P. J. (2006) *Exposing the Elephants creating exceptional nonprofits,* Wiley.

Wilkinson, A. and Wilmott, H. (1995) *Making Quality Critical,* Routledge.

Willard, R (2002) *The Sustainability Advantage: seven business case benefits of a triple bottom line,* New Society.

Wolch, J. (1990) *The Shadow State: government and voluntary sector in transition,* The Foundation Centre.

Wood, D. (2009) 'Tough questions', *Caritas Magazine,* September, www.charitiesdirect.com.

Wortman, M. S. (1979) 'Current concepts and theories of strategic management in not-for-profit organizations in the 1980s', paper presented at the American Institute for Decision Sciences, November.

Wortman, M. (1981) 'A radical shift from bureaucracy to strategic management in voluntary organisations', *Journal of Voluntary Action Research*, 10, 62–81.

Wright, P. M., McMahon, G. C. and McWilliams, A. (1994) 'Human resources and sustained competitive advantage: a resource-based view', *International Journal of Human Resource Management*, 5(2), 301–26.

Young, D. R. (1985) 'What business can learn from nonprofits', in D. Hyman, K. Parkum and V. Parkum (ed.), *Models of Health and Human Service in the Nonprofit Sector*, University Park Association of Voluntary Action Scholars, 14th Annual Meeting 1–4 October 1986, Pennsylvania State University Harrisburg.

Young, D. R. and Sleeper, S. S. (1988) *National Associations and Strategic Planning*, Working Paper 138, Yale Program on Non-Profit Organizations.

Young, D. (1989) 'Beyond tax exemption: a focus on organizational performance versus legal status', in V. Hodgkinson, R. W. Lyman et al. (eds), *The Future of the Nonprofit Sector*, Jossey-Bass.

Yuchtman, E. and Seashore, S. E. (1967) 'A system resource approach to organizational effectiveness', *American Sociological Review*, 32, 891–903.

Yukl, G. (2005) *Leadership in Organizations*, Prentice-Hall.

Zaccaro, S. J. (2001) *The Nature of Executive Leadership: a conspetual and empirical analysis of success*, APA Books.

Zaccaro, S. J. (2007) 'Trait-based perspectives of leadership', *American Psychologist*, 62, 6–16.

Zaccaro, S. J., Rittman, A. L. and Marks, M. A. (2001) 'Team leadership', *The Leadership Quarterly*, 12, 451–83.

Zack, M. H. (2005) 'The strategic advantage of knowledge and learning', *International Journal of Learning and Intellectual Capital*, 2(1).

Zaleznik, A. (1993) 'Managers and leaders: are they different?', in W. E. Rosenback and R. L Taylor (eds), *Contemporary Issues in Leadership*, Westview Press.

Zammuto, R. F. (1984) 'A comparison of multiple constituency models of organisational effectiveness', *Academy of Management Review*, 9, 606–16.

Zerubavel, E. (1991) *The Fine Line*, University of Chicago Press.

Zuluaga, L. C. and Schneider, U. (2006) 'Market orientation and organisational performance in the non-profit context – exploring both concepts and relationship between them', Working Paper 01/2006, University of Vienna.

INDEX

Printed and bound in Great Britain by
CPI Antony Rowe, Chippenham and Eastbourne